MY QUEER WAR

MY QUEER WAR

James Lord

Farrar, Straus and Giroux   New York

Farrar, Straus and Giroux
18 West 18th Street, New York 10011

Distributed in Canada by D&M Publishers, Inc.
Printed in the United States of America
First edition, 2010

Library of Congress Cataloging-in-Publication Data
Lord, James.
    My queer war / James Lord.
        p.   cm.
    ISBN: 978-0-374-21748-8 (hardcover)
    1. World War, 1939–1945—Personal narratives, American.   2. Gays in the
military—United States—Biography.   3. Gay men—United States—Biography.
4. Soldiers—United States—Biography.   5. Lord, James.   I. Title.

D811.L643A3 2010
940.54'4973092—dc22
[B]

                                                            2009029500

Designed by Jonathan D. Lippincott

www.fsgbooks.com

1   3   5   7   9   10   8   6   4   2

Part I

IN THE UNITED STATES

One

NOVEMBER 1942

It all began beside the war-torn sea. In Atlantic City. Truly a queer setting—out of place for an epic adventure, let alone a good venue for making a young man ready to perform the daredevil feats of wartime avaiators. Yet this second-rate, overbuilt resort had been dreamed up like the locus of a psychedelic fantasy by the U.S. Army Air Force for the basic training of would-be fliers into the wild blue yonder. All the Xanadu pleasure domes left vacant by wartime retrenchment were thought well suited for billeting transient thousands of glassy-eyed rookies. Of the derelict hotels having survived the Great Depression, not to mention the Panic of '93, the flakiest was the Chelsea, a dilapidated pile of enthralling ugliness set at the seedy end of the celebrated boardwalk.

Along those damp and treacherous planks that dreary November afternoon slouched a sullen troop of soldiers. I was one of them: a college dropout, single, aged nineteen, and white, number 12183139, brown of hair and eye, with a straight nose, sensuous mouth, slightly protuberant chin, average of height, weight, build, unremarkable, in short, in every outward aspect.

Which was wholly to the good. Being unremarkable in that ragtag rabble of GIs, all attired exactly alike, I ran no risk of betraying my lurid, shaming, guilty secret. Never mind that by a blatant lie I'd already betrayed civic decency by putting on the U.S. Army's uniform. But I could chalk that up to poetic license. Writing was already my good excuse for almost anything that needed excusing. Much did.

How it happened that I had become a private in Flight B of the 989th TSS was a poor joke, a joke, indeed, so furiously unfunny that it dwelt by itself as an existential black hole. Anyway, I marched laboriously against the icy winds beneath the oncoming dusk toward our billet in the Hotel Chelsea. Only eleven days in uniform then, I'd dropped out of college just three weeks before under the flimsiest of pretenses. Pretense, indeed, promised to be permanent military apparel, within which I could feast upon discontent, a disguise, moreover, expected to fool everyone but which, of course, made me misfortune's fool.

The lobby of the Chelsea smelled of old age, sewage, and soldiers' sweat. A slovenly sergeant materialized from the staircase and ordered us to get our asses into a room, any room on the floors above and double up snap on the spot with anybody willing, two rooks to a room, two cots, two footlockers, and no shit.

Such an unprecedented option offered a hint of potential companionship on the spur of the moment. The army experience, after all, advertised its facility for creating buddies, the happenstance of warfare famous for forging bonds between men, having, in fact, made heroes of soldiers embracing each other in foxholes while the gentle rain of shrapnel burst above them in the vivid air.

Across the smelly crowd in the hotel lobby I'd already spotted a good-looking GI lost in the middle distance, and I thought, Why not? He was wonderfully fair, features almost too fine, a Botticelli of angelic allure, tall and slender. He was apparently unaccompanied as yet by any makeshift pals, so I kept close behind on the cramped upstairs climb. When he lurched under the ungainly duffel bag into a room on the malodorous third floor, I was at his heels before a rival could crowd in.

Hopping aside from the thudding fall of his duffel bag, he flung himself across the cot beside the window. I took the place by the door and waited, companionably leaving to him the prerogative of greetings. My wait while I waited extended ever so slowly beyond titillating anticipation as he lay like a heap of oblivion, absent eyes fixed on nothing. I breathed in and breathed out for what it was worth, and evidently it wasn't worth much, because the roommate of my optimistic expectation soon seemed, in reality, as much like thin air as thin air itself.

Eventually, however, he hawked and spit out, "This dump eats shit."

An observation, if you like, well taken, and in accent native to the outlying reaches of New York City. Thus angelic Botticelli immediately matured into a Caravaggio boy of the streets. No overture to conversation, of course. But there I was, and I *was* there and had to say so. Timidly standing, tentatively taking steps in the direction of camaraderie, I held down my hand and said, "Hi. Name's Jim Lord. Guess we'd better get acquainted."

He squinted, shifted, scowled, steely about the gray eyes, ignoring the presumptuous hand, then at last, however, snarled, "Teves. Joe Teves."

"Okay," I said, swallowing the shame of hostility.

So he must have known. Known without knowledge, without understanding, yet with the sly menace of the male of the species. God knows beasts can be beautiful. And beauty can bedevil the best of precautions. Still, how, but *how*, could I have betrayed the lonely and loathsome self of that ghastly thunderclap of awareness in the grim dusk of October adolescence? The streak of pain vibrated also in the stagnant confine of that catastrophic hotel, the very vibration being surely what I'd come there for. For which, indeed, I'd volunteered to forsake Kierkegaard and Kafka, offering to the future an aptitude for matters of guilt.

My roommate, needless to say, never became my friend, much less a buddy, barely an acquaintance. Good looks went bad in a hurry. Botticelli, Caravaggio all mutated almost overnight into Hieronymus Bosch. As we became ensnared in reciprocal contempt, such words as were spitefully breathed back and forth had only to do with mops, washrags, and the danger of dirt. He promptly found a flock of pals with whom to chew the fat, numbers like himself from the wrong side of the Harlem River, none of whom even offered me a cigarette. Anyway, I didn't smoke. How gladly, however, I'd have nursed a clandestine bottle of Four Roses.

At my hateful college I used to carry a pint around the campus in a paper bag. This earned a scolding from the dean and worsened the sniffiness of classmates whose scrutiny I'd hoped to divert from inner affliction and focus upon the outer distinction of one who dared to live with a difference. This was no good, and rather worse than that, so I consequently hated the college and everyone in it with a passion almost equal to the loathing I'd felt for myself ever since that terrible twilight. Walking back to the prep school dorm after my piano lesson, with Beethoven's Rondo resonant still, along the cement sidewalk strewn with dead leaves, I suddenly saw like an appalling sunburst, fatal and final, that what I really wanted to do with the good-looking boys whose best pal I longed to be was not just horsing around in the locker room but doing freely with them in bed after lights out everything I had always till then been compelled to do in solitude with myself. In short, the creature I'd suddenly seen was that abnormal, that abominable thing called a homosexual, a loathsome mistake of nature, a cultural criminal whom any feeling person would naturally put in prison. So I vowed I'd never, *ever* succumb to the vile desires roused by those football-playing jocks and their curly-haired cheerleaders.

You might think that to wake up gay is no big deal. If you're straight, you certainly would. But be the spoiled son of a creationist family, whether in Memphis, Montevideo, or Madras, and your wake-up dream is a nightmare of hopeless craving to get into the pants of a pretty sailor, and you're doomed to a lifetime of disgusting torment. Mind you, I'm talking about a Massachusetts prep school in '38. Nowadays everything's supposed to be okay; congressmen and ambassadors boast of boyfriends. And yet . . . parents in Dallas, Dijon, or Dar es Salaam hardly hope that their kids will grow up to live in sin with same-sex partners and maybe—even day after tomorrow—would disown them if they did.

It was all very well to hate college and despise those alluring fraternity brothers in their varsity sweaters. But how the hell was I going to get out of there? The fix—and its suppositious remedy—were of a character to confound the authors of *Either/Or*, *The Castle*, and then some. I sat down at my university desk in the windy, irrational recklessness of that October 1942 and wrote to my parents a letter that I thought both purposeful and tricky, leaving at the same time, I felt, no loophole for the trick to be turned on me, suggesting, intimating that maybe—*maybe!*—it might be worthwhile to ponder the possibility that I *might* volunteer for the army, in the uncertain interim leave college so as to peacefully think things over. And wasn't I already a writer, after all, my senior thesis at prep school having, indeed, been a biography of Beethoven? Oh, yes, I *was* already a writer, needing to learn how words can make fools of those who set out to toy with them. Meaning's not meant to be the plaything of understanding. The trick was promptly and fatefully turned, while I'd thought myself an ingenuous young fellow out of some story by Thomas Mann, a Tonio Kröger-to-be.

Mom and Dad wrote by return mail, approving and praising my manly decision and idealistic self-sacrifice at this time of peril for our homeland. So I had unwittingly made ready for a future that would turn out to be the lunatic destination of my dearest dreams.

That overcast morning, Thursday, November 5, 1942, I plodded alongside my proud father to the United States Army recruitment center on Lexington Avenue in New York City, prepared to go through with the military make-believe no matter what it cost. Nor did the nitwit eventuality of risking one's life in defense of the nation provide an instant's pause. So I went inside to sacrifice my liberty, not to mention the pursuit of happiness, in order to combat infamy and evil throughout the world.

The fitness inspection for this noble purpose took place amid a joshing and jostling crowd of stark-naked rookies-to-be. The lavish vision of so many penises might have been exciting to a homo. It wasn't. Disturbing, rather, and alarming. Malaise begotten by ice-cold fear of excitement's danger. After the hypodermics and the rude, crude medics, the rectal plus the genital intrusions, show your teeth, fingernails, metatarsal arches, blink your fucking eyes, take a deep breath, and you're face-to-face with the ultimate question mark of manliness: a blasé, believe-it-or-not lieutenant psychiatrist says, "Do you like girls?" Or prefer confinement in a federal penitentiary for the remainder of your unnatural life, sexual leprosy not wanted, queers unfit to honor the flag of their forebears. And I, to tell the truth, had known a couple of likable girls, so I said, "Yes. Yes, sir."

As a volunteer I was privileged to choose among the army's prestigious outfits the one in which I'd be most honored to serve. I said, "The air force." A sergeant callously recorded my choice on a piece of paper, as if no daring defiance of gravity were called for, and that was how I set out upon everyman's career in space. Anyway, I'd never been up in an airplane. So I was made ready for basic training as a wearer of wings. This was basic, in point of fact, to survival. Not entirely physical but very psychic. You were about to be manufactured as a numbered machine wearing a uniform, marching up and down, back and forth, around and around, here and there, fast and slow according to instructions for the futility of the function and not meant to be a state of being, snap to it or you're dead on your feet. Teves's ilk loved it. I was at its mercy, of which there was none.

My nemesis was a beer-bellied gorilla named Sullivan, slave driver of the parade ground, a regular army master sergeant. This ape was called Bathwater Sullivan because a marcher's slightest misstep brought forth jungle roaring: "Keep in step, you clumsy motherfucker, or it'll be your bathwater." Personal hygiene being odorously negligible for the simian sergeant, one wondered. Had this demented primate been traumatized by an overdose of H_2O or was he merely a bestial Bible Belter obsessed by John the Baptist's bathtub? The unwashed sarge, in any case, was a certifiable shit with a savage aptitude for bullying, fortified by the flair of a born-again sadist for spotting *the* rookie most vulnerable to vicious ferocity. That from day one was me, and smelly Sully fell into the implacable habit of marching immediately beside me, bellowing his ape-man orders into my ear. TotheleftMAACH. TotherearMAACH. TotherightMAACH. RightleftrearMAACHand-MAACHandMAACH. And onthedoubleMAACH till your flat feet burn on the griddle of last year's pancakes, and every footfall falls into the furnace of fatigue, while Sullivan shouts, "Lift your lousy legs, Lord, you piss-poor fuckhead."

Out of every hour of torment, however, ten minutes' blur of rest were allowed on the perimeter of nothingness. Virgil granting Dante an instant of surcease. No good to me, however, as I crouched apart from my platoon on the freezing slough of despond, often failing to stifle my malaise, stop the swell of tears, while such craven lack of backbone got laughed at by virile trainees glad to sneer at the absence of grit. And in the quagmire of self-pity stood nobody to turn to to console the feckless stumbler. Worse still was the fear that my lamentable lapse of restraint might betray to sturdier men-at-arms the guilty presence of a pansy weakling in their midst. So I had to be careful. This called for a devious bent, which I cultivated.

Marching was not the only initiation to the rudiments of hell on earth, though thanks to Bathwater, it became the most personal. There was plenty to make physical abjection pass for fun. From black dawn to blacker dusk. Starting with socket-wrenching calisthenics before you woke up. Prone on your belly under acres of barbed wire, you wriggled beneath make-believe bullets whizzing in the machine-gun breeze six inches above your butt, sergeants screaming, "Eat that dirt, you stinking cocksuckers." And you choked on it. Then climbing the walls of splintered planks prepared to rip raw your fingernails, sprawling on the far side onto frozen mud before you could dream of hoisting your carcass hand over hand up aching ropes into some kind of nonexistence. After the firing range your shoulder was bruised black and blue, eardrums drumming to deafen the afternoon. And none of that lunatic drill had the least fucking thing to do with flying. You were enslaved by the unfeeling earth and the cruel inhumanity of the watching ocean.

Worse was the gnawing solitude. In the midst of backslapping soldiery, in the mess hall, the toilets, shower room, out-of-doors and in, no one spoke to me, met my eye, agreed with my glance, or pretended I was anything like everybody else. Maybe that was the rightful consequence of my knowing I never would be. Still, one might have expected even as a desperate gesture of mutable fellow feeling that Teves would sometime speak of something more companionable than the sheen of dust beneath my cot. He never did.

The fool's gold of poetic license wasn't the only palliative for self-pity. There was music too, melody, harmony, the metronome of solace. In one of the raddled ground-floor rooms of the Hotel Chelsea stood a decrepit upright piano, a moldering Mason and Hamlin, with its battered stool, a downcast survivor of prosperity's shipwreck. Still, it wasn't too disastrously out of tune to play, only two keys, both black, missing. I delighted in this dishonored instrument, resorting to it with a soulful sense of deliverance whenever at liberty and alone, which was seldom. The piece I was happiest to return to even in the wretched setting of the Chelsea was the easy, early one by Beethoven, the Rondo in C Major, the very same I'd been practicing that fatal afternoon when I saw beyond the dead leaves on the sidewalk the hideous homosexual leering at me. But even that sickening awareness of Beethoven—himself a soul beset by suffering—brought the clement idea of salvation. Alone at the keyboard though I may have been, the jangling didn't go unheard by other inhabitants of the hotel, who sometimes peeked in to snicker and sneer. Soon enough, indeed, they would be inspired to make a mockery of both Beethoven and his incompetent interpreter.

A mimeographed order on the Chelsea bulletin board directed Flight B to show up in toto two days later at 10:00 a.m. in the huge convention hall.

When I was there, seated up front, it looked like every last GI in Atlantic City must have been present, a couple of thousand talking heads at least. The poop was that we were in for a lecture about the thrills of combat from some bombardier having recently loosed tons of TNT onto enemy submarine pens. He was late. The cloying emptiness of the stage was aggravated by the pitch-black presence of a concert grand piano. So an NCO got up in front of the microphone and said we'd have to wait, advice received with groans, but by way of placating restive troops he ordered some soldier, anyone able would do, to get his ass up there and play that piano.

"Come on," he barked, "gotta be some kid out there knows how to tickle the ivories."

Nobody spoke. Silence devoured the hall. Standard operating procedure in the army: do nothing, say nothing, see nothing, hear nothing, and, above all, volunteer for nothing. I slithered in my seat.

The NCO insisted.

Then my compassionate companions from the Chelsea started clamoring, pointing me out, shouting, "Here's the one, here's the one, Lord, Lord, Lord."

"Okay, kid," cried the NCO, "get your friggin' ass up here. Let's hear ya play."

Sick, stumbling, stage frightened instantly out of my boots, I got to the stage and to the piano, the Black Death, a Steinway, a beauty, and sat down while the fighting man audience clapped like a single pair of diabolical paws preparing for the kill.

And what magic deus ex machina could mere music in extremis provide? The Rondo, its melody reviving the ghastly afternoon of the dead leaves? But nobody out there would know. And the multitudinous squirm of impatience had already begun to stretch its sinews.

Beethoven then, the man whose music had made musicians con-
querors. C major. I put my fingers to it, very, very pianissimo and a
little more largo than necessary, but the instrument—no matter how
I did—the instrument was a genius. And anyway, I *could* have done
worse.

The first snarl from the jungle public came quickly, the deadly
growl in the huge throat rousing to a roar of ridicule, angered expectations furiously slavering for the finish.

The NCO beast came from behind, dragging me back by the arm-
pits, snarling, "That's no music."

Instant hatred knocked the stuffing out of me, stumbling backward off the stage, every soldier under that odious roof jeering, the
entire hall in a turmoil of mockery.

I fled to the exit, burst onto the boardwalk, the wounding ocean
wind in my face, and ran for all I was worth to hide my humiliation in
the Hotel Chelsea.

Teves sauntered in in time for chow, drawling with derision born in
the far Bronx, "Some piss-poor excuse you are for a horse's ass."

Punishment was forthcoming. By running away without leave from
the scene of disgrace, I'd technically been AWOL. The posted penalty:
KP duty continuous for an eight-day week. Police, kitchen or no, was
a putrid euphemism, meaning solitary confinement in the hotel's cellar oubliette, condemned to peel a hillock of ice-cold potatoes never
to be diminished by sloppy slicing with a dull knife, supply replenished
by night. A foulmouthed PFC brought down tepid slop on a tin tray.
And to keep the convict at hard labor, a corporal occasionally came
along at the end of a nauseating cigar and observed that I sure was
meant for better things, and the MPs'd be glad to tickle my gonads
with a pair o' pliers, what the hell!, and he'd spit on the floor.

My only companions in the potato penitentiary were the cock-
roaches that darted in an endearing ballet around the monticule of
peelings built by my incompetent handiwork. 'Twas meager allevia-
tion, to be sure, of imprisonment's misery, frozen tubers freezing my
fingers, dullness of the knife nicking chapped and reddened hands,
flecks of blood on the dead vegetables. Oh, I deserved nothing better!

All in all, I doubtless did deserve to be punished, because Beethoven
could only have been booed by such a benighted audience. The deaf

composer of course would not have heard the roaring of the rabble, though even on his deathbed he raged against indignity and shook his fist toward the coming of the night.

So I took out my notebook and set down a dozen lines of very free verse entitled "Beethoven's Hands." To be sure, the glorious composer had not failed, only the guilty upstart. And there I was supposing I'd already been introduced to the entire reductio ad absurdum of the military condition. At all events, two and a half quite queer years would have to be put behind the wounded and the dead before chance sat me once again before a piano, and then I played it unwisely and unlawfully so as to trifle with the enemy.

Presently, time having freed me from potato purgatory, the preposterous promise of Thanksgiving loomed. I had none to give, especially to myself, but welcomed with dogged stiffness of lip my parents, come to Atlantic City to celebrate the twentieth anniversary of my birth. How they privately appraised the evolution of my sham resolve to serve my homeland as a common soldier I couldn't tell. It seemed only decent to offer sham enthusiasm as ministration to their peace of mind. Consciously devious, I did. And the parental birthday gift served handsomely to ease filial inner conflict. Mindful that a private's pay could not provide amenities previously taken for granted by the self-sacrificing and patriotic student, they volunteered to send monthly checks that would allow for large easement of constraints. I was fittingly appreciative. We all smiled, I kissed my mother, shook hands with Dad, and they drove away after dinner.

The personality-ravaging regimen of basic training proceeded apace. No time out. No time in. No end of trammels contrived to exhaust endurance. No sparing mental stress. The bullets above the barbed wire grew riskier, climbing walls higher, obstacles crueler in brute pursuit of standard operating procedures. And the bathwater gorilla bellowing in my ear like an enraged silverback in the mountain thickets of the Belgian Congo. Recruits, not yet certified dogfaces, ceaselessly bitched. Even Teves whined in his sleep. I economized complaint for poems, and indeed, I was in luck, for nobody ever sniffed out those jingles of discontent secreted in the coffin of my footlocker.

Then Jesus' birthday beckoned across the freezing slush, its tinsel proximity signaled by wreaths of celluloid holly, phony snow, Santa's moth-eaten reindeer, and "White Christmas," a counterfeit carol crooned across the frigid airwaves by Bing Crosby, a major culprit in the yuletide scam. The Savior's big party, however, turned out to bestow a real-life cause for celebration.

A mystic gift would be offered to every fledgling airman by the end of the year, allowing the new one perchance to be happy: termination at last of the U.S. Army Air Forces' ordeal of basic training. All personnel would be loosed anon to soar beyond planetary limitations, hearkening to the siren song of the wild blue yonder, winging through the mysteries of the universe. And why not? Tomorrow and tomorrow and tomorrow seemed likely to drive a decent bargain of self-sacrifice on behalf of the homeland. As for myself, alone with the fateful wager for which I had volunteered, having consequently sworn to stand by all eventualities, not to mention their cost . . . my heart said Happy New Year to the prospect of leaving forever that hateful resort beside the Atlantic Ocean.

Farewell too to the Chelsea, stinking of terminal rot, and to the malodorous respiration of its inhabitants, to none of whom I said goodbye, nor did a single one whisper adios to me on the dust-encrusted stairway as we trudged downward for the last time. Teves, vivid with empty malice, stared the other way. Not a glance of acknowledgment from any who had slurped their rations, bitten their fingernails, and pissed and shit by my side. Never mind the extremities of stamina labored through together.

But what of the myth of military camaraderie? Consider the Sacred Band of ancient Greece, those 150 couples of soldier lovers, incorruptible hoplites, faithful to one another till death, homosexuality winning pride of place in the heartland of civilization. Unthinkable now amid the bitching, lurching troops in our rackety truck riding to the railroad station en route to destinations determined by madmen. Those Theban youths of yore would be remanded to prison by God's courts-martial today.

Even as we waited on the icy platform to board an oncoming train, terra incognita yawned ahead with boredom and terror toward the battlefields of World War II.

Two

JANUARY 1943

The train was a veteran of the railway war's Lackawanna action, in which, unfortunately, its injuries had not been fatal. Shuddering westward over backbreaking roadbeds, the dingy coaches conveyed a riotous cacophony of griping GIs, even a gold bar looie contributing authority to the hubbub. Escape from our seaside purgatory was beginning badly: C rations, no Coke, no ketchup, no french fries. Cigar and cigarette smog semisuffocating, while by nightfall the stench of overflowing toilets was nauseating. So several soldiers threw up, everything exacerbating the midnight jimjams, catch sleep if you can, lucky not to wake up with your ass in a puddle of puke.

Thus, as the afternoon of the following day dwindled, wrathful gusts nipping in from the frostbitten lake, our joyless troop arrived in the Windy City. My unarmed companions wagged about Dillinger and Capone. I brooded about the great Seurat I'd miss seeing in the Art Institute. Chicago, however, was not to be our destination, was a mere stopping place for further travel across the continent, requiring a change of stations and of trains caused by some quirk of railroad business. This occasioned a miracle.

Aligned along a platform so immaculate as to be almost beauteous stood a gleaming procession of forest green Pullman sleeping cars, luxurious glitter emanating from their comfortable windows. All for the wild-eyed, whistling troops, Flight B was allotted an entire car, impeccable as if sanitized by year-round spring cleaning. And so a world-weary master sergeant came along to explain about upper and lower berths: two men to a berth, and keep hands off your neighbor's you know what.

It was like a movieland romance, the elegant train promising a happy destination. Dumping my gear in a hurry by a lower, I had hardly had time to catch up with my senses when a lanky fellow came along the aisle and said, "Mind if I bunk with you?"

"Sure," I said quickly. He looked about fifteen years old, blond, eyes true blue, a cute kid, not the Teves type, and God knew I was all too ready to take another chance.

It was he who held out his shy hand, said, "The name's Edwards. Billy. Billy Edwards. Good to know you." A dulcet resonance of the South when he spoke, that, too, attractive.

"Jim Lord," I said. His palm roughened by calluses.

The train with almost immobile grace glided away from Chicago while we ate our evening rations together, Billy Edwards and I. He once or twice uttered a murmur of satisfaction. Not a talkative boy. Preparing our berth for the night, he helped awkwardly, unfamiliar with this job but no more so than our neighbors laughing and swearing.

There's nothing nicer than the army for demonstrating how all men—zoologically at least—are created equal, thus doing away with the last laughable wisps of modesty. GIs sleep in their underwear, often without. If Billy looked fifteen in uniform, he gained a well-developed decade when he took it off. He kept on his undies, though. So did I.

A Pullman car berth accommodating one person slides serenely into prodigies of imagination. For two it conveys each passenger onto ticklish confines of corporeal (could it become carnal?) contingency. That was the frightening part.

I got in first, against the window, and Billy climbed under the covers beside me. "Good night now," he said, turning onto his left side, away from me, facing the privacy of the heavy green curtains enclosing every berth.

I drew my breath, not knowing what I was doing, but caught it back in my throat before "sweet dreams" escaped me. Then the wait for sleep kept risk in abeyance while I held myself away from the body beside me. Billy's breathing soon confided that he slept. My own oblivion played hide-and-seek while the physical presence of the boy sent fear shivering down my veins as the unthinking rule of nature's innocence excited desire. And yet I'd long since vowed never, ever to succumb to the vile lust of the day of the dead leaves.

What faultless freedom in the morning, Billy and I gazing out the window, allowing our reflections to make friends with each other.

He had been introduced to daylight in the Ozark highlands, where daddy tended to the windy orchards, a thousand winesaps in bloom in the spring, and sometimes brown bears came down out of Taum Sauk Mountain and frightened the mules. It was a dream, he said, that country, and so was he. Never before been farther from home than the recruitment office at Fort Leonard Wood, only slightly acquainted with ABCs and two times two, though no matter, listening with alert eyes while I rambled on about elm trees and sweet-water lakes in New England. We were undisturbed by soldiers riding almost in our laps, joshing about the indoor sport of sleeping together man to man.

Space swelled across the magnitude of the plains, as if some cosmic whisk broom had swept the country clear, leaving land free to fructify in its vastness. I was seized by an embrace of emotion at the grandeur of this nation, toward which, indeed, till that moment I'd felt no appropriate proportion of awe. My homeland: its gift of liberty as precious as life itself. Those sovereign states united in the pursuit of happiness. They were mine, and to their principles, in a trance of feeling, I dedicated the destination of my journey.

In my breast pocket I carried a blue notebook, responsively slipped it out, and started writing. For after all, I *was* a writer, already a dutiful worker with words. They spilled out of my pencil, one page careering to another, licensed freedom of verse, phrases hurried with twenty-year-old sentiment, never mind the naive warp of undisciplined feeling.

When Billy asked what I was doing, I said, "Got to be quiet to write." He couldn't guess.

It was all about America. Vistas, fields and floods, deserts, glaciers, geysers, canyons, dormant volcanoes. Great rivers. The Golden Gate Bridge, the Pennsylvania Turnpike, Lewis and Clark, Washington, Sam Houston and Custer, Stephen A. Douglas. New York and Boston, Baton Rouge, Little Rock, Frisco, Seattle, and Portland. The coast of Maine, Mexican Gulf. A world within the world.

Stanzaic profusions of jejune emotion, semi-Sandburgian overflow of patriotic puffery and ever so sincere, presciently entitled "To My Homeland." Presciently? Oh, yes. Qua poetry this was dross. My war would tell me why again and again. But prescience in the matter of a homeland: that edification indeed would be the Promethean gift of warfare, the nightmares thereof, for which, of course, the wait of a lifetime would not be too long.

We laid over a day in Denver. The city was powdered with snow, and we stamped about along the white sidewalks, Billy and I. He was a miraculous child, tossing snowballs across the thin air. I'd have loved to hug him. But then. Any fool would see that I was queer, crazy about this pink-cheeked kid. And I'd be rendered to shackles of guilt.

After dark our magic train started chugging into the mountains at about 20 mph. So we lay once more beneath our blanket to sleep together on the assumption of magnanimous innocence. And when I woke, his arm lay across my belly, as it would have, I supposed, lain across his dog asleep in the apple green highlands of Missouri.

Oh, California, that lodestone luring dreamers and desperadoes. The golden destination that overnight made millionaires of paupers, cattle barons of cowboys, Hollywood stars of elevator boys, prostitutes of prima donnas, day laborers of playboys, sexual predators of priests, all for the fun of proving this land of sumptuous agriculture, overflowing oil wells, and catastrophic earthquakes to be, indeed, El Dorado. Which it would be, all right, for me. The vital, decisive, immanent turning point of lifetime's adventure was to take place in California.

"Gosh," said Billy. "The folks back home'll never get over my getting a look at the Pacific Ocean."

The wheels screamed while we slid down the final slopes toward the orange groves and optimistic vineyards. That was the last night Billy and I slept together in the Pullman berth. No train trip would ever convey such lovely insouciance. The tick of time had taken us gently into A.D. 1943.

From the respite of the train Flight B got loaded into rattletrap trucks for a ride through citrus groves to a holding camp near the nonstrategic town of Merced. Tents only, chilly wintry mists notwithstanding. No PX. No USO. I ran into Billy twice in the chow line, said hi, and we were accidental GIs once more in the wasteland of faces. I knew I'd never see him after that and thought—I can't tell you why—he was such a rarity that it would be reasonable, and right, for him to be killed somewhere far from home, never to come back and grow old in the Ozarks.

Wouldn't you know the U.S. Army would deem a racetrack an appropriate accommodation for a crowd of soldiers, men anyway addicted to gambling, unmindful while the dice rolled that the actual odds at stake were their own chances of survival? It was called Tanforan, an eyesore in the tacky township of San Bruno, itself an afterbirth of nearby Frisco. It was here that I was transferred from Merced with a dozen others in a three-ton truck that January afternoon.

The racetrack was a sodden mess, its infield a desolation of withered ragweed, the bleachers decrepit tiers of rusting benches. We were lodged in makeshift barracks hurriedly thrown together to accommodate job lots of recruits at the mercy of waiting lists for some assignment. Nobody knew what the fuck we were waiting for. Nobody asked. Nobody cared.

Flight B had flown away into a domesticated, dingy yonder. Fog on filthy feline feet padded inland from the Pacific through mornings of boredom unrelieved by wrenching calisthenics. Having saluted a dozen disgruntled lieutenants, I had nothing to do but board the corroded bus to San Francisco, ride babyland cable cars, and gaze across the bay at Alcatraz. I trudged up and down the lonely hills, longingly eyeing the flaxen-haired Adonis in a uniform like my own or a snappy sailor in tight trousers, fearful at the same time of criminal consequences, disgrace, and shame.

Writing, however, and its doings offered some promise. I'd spotted a bookstore opposite Union Square. A soldier in uniform received the clerk's quick smile and an invitation to browse. Inhaling the sweet scent of newborn books, I idled, scanning titles till one of them stopped me still: *Ulysses*. I knew of the legendary hero famed for wisdom and cunning during his adventuresome homeward voyage after the fall of Troy. Of the novel by Joyce, however, I knew only that it was said to reinvent the mythic odyssey as a journey through the whole world of language, an exploration of myth, history, and religion, chronicling the depths of consciousness, and all that to the far reaches of meaning. I said I'd take it.

I swear I had not the slightest inkling that that purchase would change my life and give eventually to the gleam of the future everything I'd ever longed for. Yet this was imminent in the very name of that bookstore, Newbegin's. To begin anew. Yes. The possession of that book would definitely vouchsafe a new beginning.

I found no friendships at the racetrack. My barracks companions were good-natured goof-offs from Kentucky, content to play the guitar, sing homesick ballads, and wolf down candy bars. I stared wistfully at the good-looking ones but spoke to none.

I might, I ought, to have foreseen that the station from which the night bus plied from Frisco back to San Bruno would be no reliable venue for chance encounters with companionable strangers. The place was always crowded with soldiers and sailors who had had more than a few too many, of whom I was often one. But out of the musty drizzle of an evening around eleven came smiling a potato-faced Mexican, mumbling how much he admired American soldiers, brave fighters for the star-spangled banner. Ever averse to flag-waving flattery, I meandered aside. Mex meandered too, mouthing more servile pap. To hear him was to object to him; besides which he looked well over thirty and was no movie star. Still, he kept on insisting he admired so much all you military men in your nifty uniforms, so lucky to do your bit for your country. All that malarkey. Yet I listened.

Couldn't help feeling, though, something had to be wrong with his enthusiasm, a freakish peculiarity, plus tobacco-stained smile and underwater eyes. To show he really meant what he said, he said, to prove how much he cared about being a pal to servicemen, it'd be swell to let him stand me to a shot of tequila. Just around the corner. His place. A couple minutes' walk, clutching my arm to lead me through the crowd. And I let myself go, needing no shot of tequila, too far gone already on Four Roses, stumbling alongside him into the rain under acrid streetlights, led by the lure that any surrender of sanity can lead to: the fascination of weakness and fear.

"Call me Pancho," he said. "Your name is?"

"Jim." I feebly succumbed.

His place, a worn-out remnant of a building, something left over from the disaster of 1906, in fact, wasn't far. Stairway stinking of cat's piss, rotting refuse, abandon, three flights straight up in the oily murk, Mex's place the last door top floor, a closet with one blind window, dying lightbulb on a wire, a sombrero on a hook, grimy sheets on the shambles of a bed. No chair. Slumping away from the closed door, I wondered what the hell.

Mex hopped onto the bed, fondling the filthy bedclothes, told me to sit down, have a swig, holding over the bottle. Hell, so I had a swig.

Scalding all the way down, my innards on fire, while Pancho lurched onto me, pawing my crotch, fetid gasping in my face. Christ! Fear, fury, I shoved him back across the depraved bed. Out the door headlong down the staircase. Pancho behind me, squealing I'd got to suck his meat, fairy gringo, he'd come in the Yankee mouth. And outside into the scornful rain. A fairy. Yes, I was, a queer schlemiel not worth the time of night.

On the wretched bus back to Tanforan how futile to wonder: What kind of homo would follow the likes of himself into so sordid a snare? Willingly coaxed to the bedside of a man so odious only to run away when his hand closes on your cock? The answer lay across the bay behind prison walls.

Day after day, day after day, I hunkered on my bunk in the oblivious barracks. My moody, melodious companions strummed, hummed, and sang.

> *Weep no more, my lady*
> *Oh, weep no more today*
> *We will sing one song*
> *For the old Kentucky home*
> *For the old Kentucky home far away.*

I never went back to San Francisco. Never again set foot outside the dishonored racetrack. And *Ulysses* lay tantalizingly in my footlocker, a keepsake of the mythical power to turn a lifetime toward its rightful destruction.

Then a sergeant intruded upon my Kentucky home one loony afternoon to cough up orders for 12183139 to be ready to move out the next day at 0800.

Three

FEBRUARY–APRIL 1943

The disaffected steam engine gasped and whined, laboring in spasmodic jerks up the Sierra Nevada away from the wild Pacific. No Billy now. No poetry, either. "To My Homeland" lay wadded up with the dirty underwear in the depths of my duffel bag. And all I could do was entrust the purpose of the journey to the crotchet of its destination.

And it was a pretty queer crotchet, that destination, a place where popular provision was cheaply an offer to all who sought to shrug off vows of everlasting fidelity and to laugh at the idiocy of promises to honor and obey: Reno, Nevada, divorce HQ of the United States. The riverside free-for-all of morality also offered the allure of material loss, should anyone be tempted. Fluorescent gambling hells lined the main drag. And I thought, Fuck all!, never supposing that a bet on the future placed in this tawdry setting might pay profits beyond the wishful thinking of a lifetime. But it would, and did, and if it hadn't, I wouldn't be where I am or what I am or who I am today.

The inevitable trucks awaited alongside the station platform to convey us, nonsensical matériel that we were, a dozen miles outside town across the Nevada uplands to the Reno Army Air Base. In front of a white HQ in neoclassical style, complete with columns, a no-nonsense NCO shouted out lists of names with orders to report to various lesser HQs.

"Lord, Private J. H., 12183139, 856th Chemical Warfare Company, Main Street West."

Chemical warfare? Hadn't I volunteered to serve in the air force? And was this not an air force base? Elephantine hangars lay along a vast black landing field off to the left, and half a dozen pretty planes were poised like glittering dragonflies in the sunshine. I raised my hand and called out that there must be some mistake in my assignment.

The sergeant lazily licked his mouth and in a trove of threatening self-control announced that any error of assignment must be referred to base duty roster at HQ on Friday mornings by appointment as per company commander and in the meantime get the fuck on with it.

Which meant that I was about to become an inorganic element of warfare's chemistry extant in a state of inert uniformity. In a word, nonentity's nonentity.

The base lay sprawled across a tumbleweed plateau of desert sagebrush a couple of thousand feet up in the gemlike air with orange-striped mountain beetling above. Though the month was February, the sun was hot. I perspired, lugging my gear down the slight incline of Main Street past the PX. The barracks were white, doors front and rear, two stories high, laid out in a right-angled grid, neither pillar nor post asymmetrical, the very dust on the breeze well disciplined. The 856th Chemical Warfare Company was almost at the end, a mess hall adjacent, HQ in a small building apart. I dropped my duffel in the sand. Master Sergeant Karlo Stojanac, a stocky bruiser, shiny hair slicked back, midnight eyes, and wine-flushed lips, stood there. He looked me in the eye and said I'd taken my time. I was the last apple on call to fill up the barrel. They'd been waiting on me to bring the company to full strength, and it would stay that way now for the duration. Unless somebody croaked.

The next morning, at nine, the company CO, a captain named Ellis, Phillip W., talked to his men about chemical warfare. Poison gas. First used by the Germans in 1915. Now both Nazis and Allies had stuff more toxic than you had any idea, gas so lethal you'd die in nothing flat unless you put on your mask before you had to. Flamethrowers were toys by comparison. So maybe neither side would be the first to use it. But! Better be prepared. That's why you're here. Be prepared. Make your gas mask your best friend. Eat, sleep, and fuck with your gas mask.

After that introductory oration about the perils of poison gas and seductive necessity of the mask we didn't learn much more from Captain Ellis. But saw plenty of him as he stamped about the area in jet black boots: swarthy and overweight, a shifty, unfriendly slant to the eyes, ordering this man to smarten up his bearing and that one to get busy with polish. In short, we were under the command of an asshole. There was a looie too, lamentably named Hogg, Elmer I., freckled, irritable, and embarrassed by his name. Nor did the troops offer much by way of camaraderie. Nor was I on the lookout for buddies in the Chemical Warfare Service.

CWS basic training, as if the bathwater nightmare of the air force variety hadn't already fouled the production number, was a horror movie, featuring interminable forced marches across the desert, wearing suffocating masks that made it impossible to see where the fuck you were setting down your boots in order to avoid waking the rattlers, iguanas, tarantulas, prairie stoats in the sagebrush. Also the obstacle course, rifle range, foxhole ordeals, plus calisthenics to bust your balls, Sergeant Stojanac smoking while we did a hundred jump-ups. And I was the self sanctioning critic provided with lavish findings for complaint.

Not invited, and not condescending, to mingle in the barracks or the mess hall with fellow enemies of chemicals, I quickly learned it was easy to enjoy solitary PX meals of hot dogs, hamburgers, BLTs, grilled cheeses, chocolate chipsters, banana splits, and all such semigarbage. And weekend passes were readily available for kids obedient to the basic rules of toilet training. So I hurriedly studied how to kiss ass even as I ridiculed ass kissers. Stojanac went easy on me, though continued warning that my mouth would be my comeuppance. Empty Saturday afternoons were spent parading my self-pity alongside the Truckee River in downtown Reno. The city was a tawdry setting for the pageant of jaded harridans wearing silver fox furs and zircon rings, tossing back Old-Fashioned cocktails in the bar of the Riverside Hotel while their alimony was being squandered at the craps tables of Harold's Club by musical comedy cowboys sporting turquoise belt buckles and chromium spurs. But at least the Nazi army besieged at Stalingrad had surrendered, and Errol Flynn had been found not guilty of raping an underaged girl.

Thank God for the movies, and I was in movieland luck in Reno that April Fool's Day Saturday, the sort of luck activating remembrance of the wretched prep school where I myself had been the wretch impersonating a preppy as I walked back weeping from the seedy theater where Margaret Sullavan had just died, leaving her three comrades to march off screen together—as always!—into the MGM gloaming.

For it was at a theater equally seedy just down the block from Harold's gambling hell that *Three Comrades* had been resurrected five years after the lachrymose schoolboy first made their acquaintance. The only film ever distinguished by a scenario extorted from F. Scott Fitzgerald during his Babylonian servitude, it is the story, adapted from a potboiler by Erich Maria Remarque, of three veterans of the defeated kaiser's army and of their losing campaign to make incongruent ends meet amid the anarchy, corruption, and cynicism of postwar Germany. Their incompetent endeavors are redeemed from feckless stupidity only by a blood bond of loyalty, self-sacrifice, and soulful devotion—something almost beyond devotion, beyond tenderness, which they feel for one another. This devotion was orchestrated repeatedly throughout the movie by a melody that throbbed to a crescendo of feeling whenever make-believe begot a crisis and was reprised at the finale as a hymn in praise of comradeship sung by a male chorus with ringing fidelity to the words:

> *Give a man a man beside him*
> *Beside him*
> *Always!*
> *And he'll have a friend to guide him*
> *To guide him*
> *Always!*

Which, of course, was more than enough to make me weep at age sixteen, when weeping was my true-blue playmate. And yes, oh, I did long to find a man beside me who would always be a friend to guide me. But that must have been near the time of the cement sidewalk crisis. Thus, how desperately wrong were my longings even as I luxuriated in the wrong and reconfirmed its verdict. Still, the comrades' melody, the song, the words following beside me all grew so set in the musical repertoire of remembrance that they came to haunt the orchestration of my youth. And in the school chapel stood an obsidian Steinway on which I was permitted to practice when the cowlicked kids were not getting spruced up with dime-store virtue and white shirt awe for the Almighty.

So I picked out the comrades' anthem, played it till even the chapel sighed, sang the song, and whistled it in the robin redbreast morning as I ran for breakfast and for desire under the elms. In addition to the Beethoven Rondo and a little threnody by Mendelssohn, another tune I repeatedly played at the time was Haydn's, a martial air commandeered by the Episcopal Church for glorification of Zion, my fingertips happily deaf to any oracular tinkle hinting of the Sophoclean denouement that my pianistic facility might one day bring about in a cherry blossom dreamworld of anguish and horror.

When I came out onto Reno's main drag from my second meeting with Erich, Otto, and Gottfried, rapt in their mesmerizing melody, the tear ducts were sodden. I knew this was ludicrous, as I was, remembering what day it was: cruel April making me its Fool. So I dropped into the Riverside bar and drank Four Roses till twilight said goodbye to the future.

Ulysses, meanwhile, had not been left dallying alongside the seashore in front of Troy, better known as Dublin, before setting out upon his daylong decades of homeland wandering. It behooved me, I knew, to set out myself upon the inward voyage toward consciousness via exploration of the resources of language, to which, after all, I felt I'd already long since been committed. At all events, I took to carrying the bulky volume around with me whenever I had free time, reading as conscientiously as I could page after page in the difficult desert air. And that's how the book became true to its potential, so to speak, though coincidence, really, is a pretty poor password for the strategies of causality.

Naturally in the PX at noontime I looked pensively across the faces of the crowd. Obliquely, though, always edgy, afraid of being spotted staring at the good-looking ones. And I held on tight to *Ulysses*, keeping his adventure close to my body, as if the physical bond of the Homeric hero would actually aid and abet. Trying to be just one of the boys in the GI fuck-you squeeze toward the counter, I politely awaited my turn among the famished mouths ordering burgers and grilled cheeses, piccalilli on that hot dog, milk shakes black and white.

"Damn it," I cried, "watch yourself, will you!" when someone jostled me so brusquely that the book fell into the stampede underfoot.

Bending down to rescue it, I wasn't quite quick enough; the one who'd caused it to fall had it already, standing, facing me, *Ulysses* in his outstretched hand, and he was smirking and said, "Could this be yours?"

"Well, who the hell else's?" I snapped, seizing it from his fingers, of which, I noticed, the nails were none too clean, adding, "It isn't yours anyway."

"Right you are," he easily rejoined with half a laugh.

He was a corporal, his impeccable uniform the crisp attire of authority. He was not bad-looking; his mop of wiry nutmeg hair, eyes abstract and gray, aggressive mouth and chin added up to a fierce expression. He had suffered severe acne as a kid, and the scarred face had left him personally appealing.

He said, "So you're reading Joyce?"

"Apparently," I said.

The corporal offered a conciliatory nod. "Well, it's an unexpected pleasure, running into Stephen Dedalus in a U.S. Army PX in Reno, Nevada."

"Ditto then," I said with a lift of the spirit, "running into Leopold Bloom."

"On the lookout, are you, for something to eat?"

I shrugged.

"Oh, yes. And we could take the chow outside into the sun and talk about the greatest writer of our time."

"That's Thomas Mann, isn't it?"

"Nah. His mountain's not all that magic, blah-blah-blah. And as for the old fag in Venice, what a relief when he snuffs it."

I looked away above the smoky nothingness.

He asked what I wanted to eat, said he'd take care of it, knew the guy doing the sandwiches. I said a western and Pepsi. He came back with a cardboard box, a self-satisfied crinkle around the eyes, and led the way to the front porch of base HQ. We sat on the steps. Captains and majors came and went without glancing askance at a couple of picnicking enlisted men.

"You must be entitled," I observed.

"I work inside," he replied. "So what's your name?"

"Lord."

"Ah. No relation, I trust, to the monarch of humbug up there in the sky."

"Nothing like that," I said, feeling like he'd taken me into his confidence. "What's yours?"

"MacNally. Keith MacNally, another mick from Council Bluffs, undernourished infant of the WPA." He chuckled.

That's how Ulysses, not the book per se but the wanderer, introduced Keith to my life, bringing about eventually such a surprising denouement that at the last I felt for him nearly as much perverse gratitude as I did dark hatred.

Anyway, that first picnic on the base HQ front porch prospered in the luxury of spontaneous confidences shared by strangers. He was warmly inquisitive. I described my prewar self, about whom I understood little, omitting of course the odious revelation that would have been most revealing. He mocked the devious ruse by which I'd contrived to spurn an education that kids less lucky would have bartered their futures for. I apologetically sighed. Yes, I'd made a mistake. Still, can't one consider with compassion the specious heartache adolescence is party to?

Keith would never be prone to squander compassion. His pity was too pure to be spent on pampered schoolboys who believed themselves luckless because three squares a day, Shakespeare, trigonometry, and masturbation were no antidote for mawkish self-indulgence. He saved his resources of charity for the downtrodden, homeless, and hungry, the dispossessed and forgotten, the truly wretched of the earth. He stood for goodness, and to do that with principled effect, you had to stand very, very firm against the beguilements of compromise, weak-kneed lapses of resolve.

The strictures of his idealism were a wonder, which came onto me in a surprising rush of feeling, an emotion of concord and optimism, trust in the sovereignty of his intellect. Even as we were chewing sandwiches and sipping Pepsi in the hot dazzle of noon, the fait accompli of friendship confided everything to the moment, and both of us could taste the confidence. Of this I was certain: of picnics to come, dinners, drinks and high jinks, memories made day after day, talkative well-being in the citrine glimmer of desert twilights. And as a matter of fact, as things fell out, we often ended up listening to the *Moonlight Sonata*. Keith favored Beethoven.

Not having wanted to tilt the equilibrium of nascent friendship too

soon toward the abjection of my soldierly status, I'd put off complaint till one late afternoon when we went strolling alongside the high berm of the rifle range, furious firing on the far side, occasional pop of handguns. Then it all fell out, my loathing of the 856th Chemical Warfare Company, Ellis, Hogg, Stojanac, the other rooks. How I hated them all, the dry rot of the mind.

Keith worked his jaws and pensively observed that it sounded pretty lousy. "Tolstoy would have said, 'What then must we do?' In Russia in his day the answer was, 'There is no answer.' Doesn't mean we can't mobilize something. Maybe. Let that meander in my head."

He worked in an HQ office that had to do with the efficient provision of mechanized matériel for the dissemination of chemical ordnance from low-flying aircraft. His rank signified administrative resourcefulness, and he was clearly not intimidated by officers. A couple of years older than I, he had been in the army since before Pearl Harbor, and that meant something. So, indeed, what then *could* he do? A lot, as things turned out.

We strolled to the right beyond the berm, while up ahead the hangars loomed in front of the mountains like taxidermic pachyderms, and in between stood a high blank-faced fence of dusty planking festooned on top with rusty barbed wire. As we came closer, you could hear yowling on the other side.

"What the hell!" I exclaimed.

Keith snickered, sneered, said it was a little taste of hell. Base stockade. MPs beating on the prisoners for the fun of it.

I couldn't believe it, and said he sounded as though he thought it was funny.

His composure was indignant. Of course. The army's a joke on everyday decency? We're in the murder business, kid. That's dialectical idealism for you. Toe the line, and toe it tight, or one of your buddies'll beat the shit out of you.

But! That's not right. The guys inside can't have done anything bad enough to deserve a beating.

Sure they have. Discipline's the right side of the army street because it's the *only* side. You walk on the wrong side, it's the stockade, you come back to your unit minus a couple of teeth, purple eyes, that sets an example. It's immanent cause.

I was outraged. The United States doesn't do things like that.

That a fact? Ask Ol' Black Joe what he thinks of the army? Tell you what. Some colored rookie leers at the boobs of a white chippie showing off her hardware, and quicker'n you can say Little Black Sambo the MPs'll be lynching his ass.

The yowling hadn't ceased, and even as I shuddered, it seemed to concern me personally, as if there must be something I could do to rectify the wrong. Or was it, perhaps, a monition that the wrong might be inflicted upon me?

Keith slapped me on the back, and I ran up to the road toward the airfield, gulping the faded air.

His office was more spacious, and amiable, than the cramped catchall that the 856th called its HQ. Three rooms, the first large, several windows facing the darkness, two smaller, all with desks and chairs in SOP formation, Rita Hayworth, Betty Grable, and Stalin on the walls. Stalin?

Uncle Joe, hell, yes, Keith said. He's winning the war for us. Not your FDR Calvinist daydream fireside chitchat. Or Churchill please do not disturb my empire. Stalin's at Stalingrad, winning the war. But it's not going to be your new birth of freedom. Government of the people, okay, but the people have to dance to the geopolitical tune. Stalin learned the hard way, from the ground up, in Siberia. Dostoyevsky's not the only one who faced up to really real reality out there on the steppes.

His talk sounded a little seditious. Maybe he was a bit Red underneath. I wouldn't make an issue of it. I'd prefer to talk about the book that brought us together.

About Mr. Joyce—he can't have been what you'd call a lot of fun, by no means a prankster, though given at times to song, even to dance, when drunk. Keith's father had been somewhat the same sort of fellow—minus the multiplication tables of genius—more the type of Joyce's own father, a drunken no-good. He pawned Keith's bed to pay for applejack when the kid was six; Ma MacNally whimpered uselessly after her dowry'd all been spent on the lads in O'Malley's back room. The loss was repaid by marital pummelings, wherefore when Keith was going on ten, Ma went to the Missouri River for keeps in dead of winter. And Father Fitzgerald said sure 'twas a cryin' shame and more's the pity her dear remains will never repose in sacred soil, while the wake was riotous at O'Malley's and the widower sang a ballad in memory of Parnell, fell face forward straight onto the rim of a solid brass spittoon, lapsing into a coma from which the Almighty failed to waken him.

That day was not deemed a lucky one for the orphan. But Keith Francis MacNally kept his own counsel with bitter fortitude, careful to be courteous to those above him, and exercised so stern a determination toward self-improvement that Iowa Western Community College granted him admission gratis. Valedictorian of his class, his graduation address, "The Primacy of Economic Determinism," stupefied the students and faculty alike. But forces indifferent to academic prestige were overrunning the world, and Keith owed a debt of gratitude to civilization.

So he put his diploma into a cardboard valise, went across the river in which his mother had drowned, and presented himself to the U.S. Army recruitment center in Omaha, Nebraska. That was history.

He waved a commanding hand around his office and said he spent many evenings alone here. As a matter of fact, I was his first guest. He didn't go in much for the buddy business.

Neither, to be sure, did I.

We talked about *Ulysses*, the adventure, the adventurer, the author. Keith said Joyce was more to be admired—revered—than any writer since . . . well, since Pindar, for example, because he made great poetry of a fart and compelled language to his bidding on its knees. Like Uncle Joe politically and the clairvoyant recruits of dialectical materialism. I advanced the beauty and value of Thomas Mann: the moral power, the purity, simplicity, and harmony of his works. Keith would hear none of it. What mattered was the death of traditional literature so that writing could be reborn in the world of money and machines.

Speaking of machines, he asked how I got along with them.

I make out with cars, I said, and typewriters. Why?

Because. He said he'd show me.

Of the two smaller rooms in the office, one was situated at an angle apart from the others, and Keith went in there, turned on the light. The space was narrow but long, held a desk, a leather and chrome swivel seat, and against the wall on a high counter a large, intricate stainless steel machine of some sort.

Like this, he said, passing fingertips along the stressed surface. It's a device for disseminating chemical agents from aircraft. Brand-new. Latest technology. Suppose you could make a scale drawing of it?

Jesus! I exclaimed. What for?

So you can fuck off from the 856th Chemical Warfare Company. I can get you a temporary transfer from there if you can turn out halfway decent scale drawings of stuff like this for training courses for the pilots and bombardiers. The guy we had before was a goofball, so I gave him the push.

A goofball already; it was the very last thing I wanted to be, but by an irrational fusion of the ridiculous with the glorious it happened that the hellish prep school had inflicted a compulsory course in mechanical drawing. The rebellious student had done unaccountably well. Well enough, that is, to dare give Keith's proposal a try. I might not be very good, but no matter. What counted was that I not be very bad.

Keith would make arrangements. How he'd get by the Ellis-Hogg-Stojanac obstacles I'd no idea. At all events, the transfer would be temporary, rescindable in case of crisis, and would not entirely disentangle me from the Chemical Warfare Service. I'd only have to shower, shit, and sleep among the snoofers of the 856th and take no orders from its NCO. Three days later it was done.

Karlo Stojanac said that only a layabout like me could have snuck a trick like that. Didn't know how I'd pulled it off, didn't give a shit, but my buddies'd think it was raw, so watch your ass, Jimmy.

The nickname shocked me. I'd not heard it since kindergarten, and the surprise must have shown because Karlo brusquely patted my forearm, then walked away. I was pleased, shaking my head for the strangeness of it as if at the beginning, so to speak, of a changed life.

Keith introduced me to the other men in the office. A midget PFC named Leroy Childs with a poorly repaired harelip, a blond nonentity overweight gold bar looie called Larry Garlington, a connoisseur of the derring-doings of Terry and his piratical playmates, plus the pseudo-officer in command, a silver bar looie in a little office by himself, his name on a brass plaque, Nathan Carswell, a large Dick Tracy tacked above his desk, upon which reposed a leaning tower of *True Detective*. None of them gave me more than a nodding time of day then or later, nor was it ever needed, for Keith was my timekeeper from first to last.

He came with me that introductory morning when I'd set out the india inks and was going to wash my nibs in the men's room down the corridor beyond the Coke machine, and I said, "Keith, I swear, I wouldn't know how to begin to thank you . . . everything you've done . . . makes all the difference."

Of which, of course, at the time even the man in the moon could hardly have guessed the stupefying extent. And moreover, Keith himself, had he the slightest premonition, would have damned his sentimental impulsiveness. As for me, my dreams, then and later, always seemed unreal and unrealizable.

Keith said, "Think nothing of it. My pleasure. You can say *Ulysses* did the trick. Now, who do you think in all the Reno Army Air Base has ever heard of T. S. Eliot, not to mention George?"

He seemed to notice nothing. Other, to be sure, than the enjoyable assurance of good fellowship. And that evening, alone together in the permissive privacy of the office, when he'd brought a couple of Cokes from the corridor, he said, "Let's hear some music."

He kept a portable record player under his desk and a few LPs, his favorite, he said, the *Moonlight Sonata*, especially the second movement, the murmurous allegretto. He played it again and again, while we hesitated in the languor of cumulative confidences, easygoing fellow feeling taken for granted. Of all composers, Keith said, he most admired Beethoven, defiant defender of unbridled genius, not one to be awed by capricious archbishops or whimsical noblemen. Oh, yes, I thought, keeping it to myself, I knew more about the boorish, irascible rebel than Keith did, and the *Moonlight*, moreover, was Beethoven before Beethoven, when Mozart and Haydn were still audible on the far frontier of heroic things to come. Content to slyly contemplate the placid surrender of Keith's face while we were listening together, I felt my heart irresponsibly adrift to the tune of different harmonies, and I knew I was crazy.

Though in the same uniform, I was almost in a changed skin overnight when I began my new life as a draftsman of intricate machinery. For one thing, an essential, the routine of the 856th no longer applied to me. Keith's office worked a civvy schedule, Monday to Friday, nine to five, weekends only occasionally on duty, sometimes Childs, sometimes Lord. MacNally presided, the looies lost forever in the funny papers. Of a morning consequently I got out of bed only after the barracks had emptied of men stamping, swearing, and insulting the cruelties of the clockwork world. They insulted me too. I laughed and told them, when they set out for forced marches in the desert, to give my love to the rattlers. Karlo said I'd better watch my ass or some sweet night I'd find a tarantula in my bed. I never did and had waffles and milk shakes for breakfast at the PX.

The intricacy of stainless steel prototypes made my pen-and-ink work tense and fatiguing, so I took it easy in my drafting room. Keith told me I'd be well advised not to take my ease too far, and he'd watch out for me, but a proportional quota of production had to be the rule.

Anyway, I learned overnight that his office was *his* entirely, arbitrarily and unquestionably, the Childs, Garlington, Carswell complement a coterie apart, too committed to Wrigley's spearmint, Daddy Warbucks, and true tales of felonious foolery to worry about niceties of efficiency in the Nevadan wilderness. Keith took care of everything, though the quantitative thing he took care of was known only to him, and the rest of us were incidental to the furtherance of his ambitions. For it was clear that his quick attention to the telephone, interoffice memos, and hurry-up errands through HQ corridors was expended for future ascents in rank and power, his office being but a temporary cog in the gears that crunched out technical know-how for trainee aviators.

Occasionally alone during a sunshiny luncheon—it seemed never to rain—if Keith was patching up vouchers for a fucked-up looie, I'd saunter down along the rifle range berm and turn right to pass the fence of the base stockade where I could hear the yowling prisoners. It quickened a tingling in the nape of my neck, and I sucked in my gut against the shiver of excitement and dread. I could see the confines of degradation plain as day. But could not foresee how casually these would confine me in the clutch of wartime chaos amid the Vosges Mountains one year later. And later still, aghast at the tragic geometry of hell, I'd try to make symbolic sense of suffering, shame, and guilt, abetted in this, believe it or not, by Dante.

No such risky feelings or excesses seeped into conversations with Keith, though maybe we seemed to have gone to extremes of companionable sentiment. Three or four weeks along it was amazing how I'd come to care for him. Oh, not simply by way of gratitude because my life was the *Ode to Joy* every day so freely that even the hateful machines labored over became friends. It was much more than that.

The heroism of Beethoven, when we repeatedly listened to the slow movement of the *Moonlight* in the basic shadows of the office, became a favorite postulate: free will of uncompromising genius ready, for example, to rap the fingers of an archduke incompetent at the keyboard.

The diversity of Keith's learning was a surprise frequently renewed. Hegel, of whom I knew nothing, was one of his familiars. He knew Nietzsche too, and Darwin, not to mention Ralph Waldo Emerson, liked to talk about Einstein, the theoretical beauties of the universe. But definitely did not go along with my enthusiasm for Picasso despite Blue Period pictures of forlorn and dispossessed wanderers in the world's gloom. You can't have everything, I told myself, blind to the danger I was falling for.

Reno was not a particularly desirable venue for either of us, neither needing the accommodation of divorce. That is, I didn't. As for Keith, I knew dot about his private life, which remained as securely unknowable as his private parts, though my imagination toyed, so to speak, with both, and at times I caught myself crazily glancing at his crotch.

He, however, did not go gingerly about piercing my personal bubbles and once remarked, "I suppose back in your bourgeois hometown you've got some suitable girl sighing for you over a snapshot."

I said, "Not exactly," trying to make out the purpose of discernment behind those gray eyes. Like all the rest of him, however, they held what concerned them secure from guesswork.

One noontime we were walking down by the landing strip when one of those lovely P-38s was taking off into the blue east. Then in a second about a half mile over the desert the plane exploded, a boiling sunburst of charred orange hurtling earthward, and I clasped Keith's arm, sucking in air, crying, Christ, Keith, look at it, the fucking plane's finished, while it dived into the ground, sending up a geyser of flame and a boom like a million jerricans of nitro. But he jerked away from my hand as if it burned, said nothing, and I had to choke back the sensation of clasping his biceps.

Unthinking, another time, when we sat on the HQ front steps eating grilled cheeses with our milk shakes, laughing because Carswell's flatulence was less poetic than Bloom's, I happily grasped his shoulder,

and he instantly lurched aside, snarling, "Hands off! I can't stand getting pawed."

So I looked away, gasping, "Sorry, sorry, I didn't mean . . ." But I
did, of course, I did mean, and I knew it, and I wondered what the
hell things were coming to, and suddenly I couldn't bear it, and my
eyes were on fire.

The alternative raison d'être of Reno, gambling, also existed outside our purview. I was humdrum indifferent to losing my parents'
admittedly unearned money for sake of tawdry tautological thrills, albeit deaf and dumb and blindly imprudent when, if ever, risk lay like
fata morgana upon the emotional horizon. Keith, on the other hand,
was virtually fanatic about the bedrock immanence of money in the
quantifying phenomenon of human life scratching out survival on an
insignificant mite of matter lost in the question mark of space. To him
money as an abstract unit of account meant nothing. In the insolence
of mankind's idiocy the nonentity of money was self-evident. A dollar
bill, he said, is no better than a slap in the face of Cartesian logic. As a
unit of tender it is meaningless and creeps toward value only as a product of labor, which produces property, which produces law, which
produces the interdependence and freedom of both laborers and proprietors interacting to bring about a nation-state in conflict between
rulers and ruled, the latter bound ultimately to prevail, producing a
classless society in which population and state are the same thing. A
synthesis. You follow me?

"Oh," I said. "I'm with you, sure, but I'm not quite ready for the
dialectical workout."

He chuckled without a glimmer of mirth. "You will be." He nodded gravely. "You'll have to be. It's the future. Trust in Marx. Then
you'll see the big picture."

I said, "I'd like to."

But what about *him*? I wondered. Was everything to be entrusted
to Beethoven and moonlight? A friend to guide me. I gazed at his
profile. Oh, Christ, how the fuck had I gotten into this, whatever it
was I was in? When I walked back after midnight to my miserable
bunk in the 856th, humming the anthem of *Three Comrades*, then I
was back in school again . . . were the dead leaves on the sidewalk, after all, really and truly so terrible? Wasn't Keith a man of the world,

enlightened in matters mature, philosophical, psychiatric, ethical, yes, an advocate of classless, tolerant freedom for every man in a better world? The truth was, to tell the truth, I didn't know, and it didn't make any difference.

What had to happen would happen, and it happened in broad daylight. We were walking through the tumbleweed afternoon on our way to the PX, Keith whistling twixt his teeth, and I as calm as you please said, "I'm in love with you."

He jerked stop in mid-stride. "What? What did you say?"

I said, "I said I'm in love with you. I love you. There it is. I had to tell you."

"You crazy or what? You queer?"

"Yes." I sighed. "Yes, I'm queer. And I'm in love with you."

"Don't tell me. Don't even think about telling me. I don't want to hear about it. You're sick. Homos are sick, perverts, ought to see a doctor, do something about it. Christ's sake, can't you control yourself?"

"Do you think I like it?" I cried, suddenly sickened, remembering the repellent Mexican in San Francisco. "Do you think I like it that I disgust you? No place for a homo in your new world, no tolerance for human frailty?"

"Grow up, boy. You were in the Soviet Union this wouldn't go down. Uncle Joe would whip you into shape. No fairies in the Red Army. No gangrene on the body politic. But I'm not a judge and jury, I'm not the morals police. Could turn you in, but I won't. Sissies can't take it in the stockade. I'm not going to give you the push just because you're a pansy. You go your way, I'll go mine—even if we are in the same office. You do your job, and I'll do mine. We won't talk about this. We won't talk at all. When I think. What a mop-up."

"I'm sorry, Keith."

"Shut up!" he exclaimed. "Don't overdo it. Truth is I've known worse than you, and I don't want to hear about it. Just do your work, you hear me, and don't be late. Don't ever be late." Twisting his head, he turned, tall as time against the callous sky, and strode onto the empty flying field. And the leaves on the dead cement were deader than ever. I'd been a fool to feel that it could ever be otherwise. In love with Keith MacNally? Never.

Four

APRIL 1943

In the office we didn't speak. We saw each other but didn't look. He talked on the telephone, made nice noise with Garlington anent the Katzenjammers, and had Childs hand me memos saying speed up your work, the last drawing was blotted. The looies must have noticed, thought something fishy must have happened. But they couldn't have suspected, could they? Not that I pined for the past. I merely hated everything.

I ate all my meals at the PX, sick too of burgers, grilled cheeses, chocolate chips, Pepsi, black and white, food, what rot. Escapism via the book that a Nobel Prize winner had said was a landmark because it destroys our civilization, and I had just passed through—most appropriately, yes—the Lotus Eaters episode and—of course—entered Hades . . . to think *Ulysses* had been more responsible than I for leading me to such an infernal pass. Time telescoped, and there were heartbreaking flowers in bloom out on the desert.

One day, when I'd dragged my ass back from lunch at the PX, where nobody noticed my book, a typewritten memo lay on the drawing board. From Corporal K. F. MacNally to Private Lord.

> *A generalized intelligence test is to be given to a select number of HQ personnel next Tuesday at 1000 hrs. in the HQ briefing hall. Your name is on the list. A good score could be an opportunity for advancement, and you could use an opportunity. Be there!*
> *signed K. F. MacNally, Corporal*

I'd had tests before blundering into the army, wanted no more, and wanted no help from K. F. MacNally. I didn't give a shit about advancement in the army—only *out* of it. However, he had something on me, and we both knew it, something he could use to destroy me, put me in the stockade. Homos were guilty as charged in the U.S. Army in 1943, and don't you forget it. The only opportunity that meant zip was Keith's freewheeling power to compel me to jump through the hoop of his whim. Still, I had something on him too, all that talk about Uncle Joe, Soviet classless society, everybody caring about everybody else, so much bullshit, forget about the kulaks, phony treason trials, *Darkness at Noon*, Uncle Joe's prewar romance with Adolf. But by the way, what would the inspector general think about having a Red in the ranks?

So I showed up in the briefing hall at nine fifty-nine. There were about two dozen testees, half of them wearing fish-eye glasses, I the only private. Keith sat at the head of the competition in the first row, a scowl of preparedness fixed on his face. On the dais a captain behind a metal table announced the test would be a yes-or-no multiple-choice exam, with a time limit of 150 minutes, allowing 1 minute on average for the response to each questionable proposition. Three sullen staff sergeants passed mimeographed sheets with lists of these propositions, each with a yes or no box, divided into eight subdivisions according to topic: physics, mathematics, biology, geography, political history, social history, cultural history, current affairs. And if taking the test seemed a mockery, the questionable propositions mean business:

Vibrating atoms absorb and emit energy only in discrete quanta.
The square root of 2 is an irrational number.
Mitosis is a process by which chromosomes are replicated.
The Orinoco is a tributary of the Amazon.
The Mississippi Scheme was an English colonial plan for development of the river valley.
The Emancipation Proclamation abolishing slavery was issued to celebrate Union victory in the Civil War.
The New York Armory Show of 1913 was an exhibition of new military weaponry.
The German commander who surrendered Nazi forces at Stalingrad was Field Marshal Keitel.

Propositions as questionable as those did indeed mean business, and it was of the kind transacted by monkeys. Do numbers in conflict with reason exist in the yes or no world? Surely the Orinoco is a Venezuelan river; the Amazon, Brazilian. Or is there a tricky contiguous rivulet? Well, at least I knew about the Armory Show, Duchamp's explosion in a shingle factory, and Keith had gloated so effusively over von Paulus's capitulation you'd have thought he was Marshal Rokossovsky. Concerning three-quarters of the cryptic propositions I knew nothing. Moreover, I didn't give a flying fuck about the army's opinion of my intelligence. Anyway, the test was obviously designed not to learn how much you knew but to establish how little. That was doubtless what the infamous MacNally had had in his vengeful mind from the beginning. I read every sentence but didn't need the jowly captain's minute hand in order to X yes or no, skipping from one box to another down the pages with barefaced abandon. It was no test, not even a quiz, and I finished my guesswork while vibrating atoms were still undecided about the quanta of their energy, but waited another half hour so as not to seem impertinently precocious.

When I presented my pages to the captain, each signed with name, rank, serial number, and permanent assignment, he pursed his lips into a smirk and said, "Child prodigy, huh? In a hurry for the sure thing, huh?"

"Yes, sir," I snappily replied, saluted, spun on my foot, and marched down the hall, followed by the piscine stares of testees.

Later, leaving the drawing board to go snack at the PX, I ran against Corporeal MacNally, who sneered in my face and observed that the sure thing I'd get was likely to be a season in hell.

By which he meant the stockade, not Rimbaud, and I attributed his malevolence to heterosexual bigotry.

Five

MAY–JUNE 1943

An army set down in wartime on a faraway desert was the natural habitat—was it not?—of footloose soldiers in fetching uniforms on the lookout for fellow feeling in the eyes of their semblables. Oh, not the fellow feeling I'd naively fancied to find in the shortsighted eyes of Corporal MacNally. That flimsy infatuation had been warning enough of the peril of revealing one's guilty secret. The *Moonlight Sonata* indeed! Through the treacherous detours of the night I could all but hearken to the screaming of the prisoners in the base stockade, feckless souls like myself, who wanted only an instant's remission of their wrongdoings. Why, you might have thought I wanted to be in their place. As yet, however, I was at the very outset of the experiential complication, leaving neither time, nor space, nor notion, only much much later to be swallowed up by the yawn of liability. Mindful he could betray me in a minute to MP brutality, I kept wary of MacNally.

On the careless tide of PX mealtime I avoided the faces of good-looking GIs, crass common sense advising me to study their boots instead. It was a life of western sandwiches awash in ketchup, soggy cookies, turgid milk shakes, suffocating cigarette air, "The Boogie-Woogie Bugle Boy of Company B." Brain death in the world of standard operating procedure.

I simply got knocked down when one excruciating afternoon after lunch on Devil's Island I was plodding back to Captain Dreyfus's drawing board and a door shot open, a soldier burst forth with cannonball velocity full force on top of me, and down I went, a heap of olive drab rubble.

"Jesus!" he shouted. "Where did you come from?"

Winded, I blinked against the dark silhouette that had caused my downfall, making out a face high above in the silvery daytime. He wasn't wearing a cap. I said, "Where's your cap?"

He laughed. He said, "I was in a hurry," shaking the floppy cap in his left hand, extending the other down to me. "Here. Hold tight. Up you come." He lifted me in a jiffy, almost colliding with him, my body seemingly no heavier in his grip than his cap. "Hope I didn't hurt you."

"No, no," I said, "no, didn't hurt me at all." He hadn't yet quite let go of me, so I drew back against the hand, adding, "Only surprised me."

"No wonder. Sorry about that."

"'S nothing," I mumbled, and somehow the accidental moment seemed to have lasted a little too long, so I said, "You were in a hurry then?"

"In the army everybody's in a hurry waiting to do something in a hurry. Yes?"

His face was filled with light, head a crest of unruly wheat, taller than I in the height of the afternoon, handsome, and it was funny this soldier should have been my assailant, so to speak. I said, "Well then?"

"It's the lunch hour," he said.

"I know. Don't let me keep you."

"I've eaten."

"Me too."

"Well then," he said.

I grinned. It *was* funny. I said, "On my way to work. Base HQ. I work there."

"Quartermaster CWS. I type the bills of lading. You know, all those creepy masks the poor bastards wear marching around in the desert."

"I've been one of them," I said. "Eight fifty-sixth Chemical. Temporary transfer to HQ. CWS still has a mask with my name on it in case I fuck up."

"Watch your back," he said.

"And front," I said. "Better get going. Don't dare be late."

"Well then," he said, quizzical, rocking back and forth on his heels. "Don't go away mad because I knocked you down."

I said, "Don't worry." As if he might have. It was all nonsense, I knew, and walked away without a glance.

Coming through the office door, maybe my face bore a hint of change, for MacNally had developed a threatening wild animal stare and leveled it at me while I walked through, and I despised him more every day.

Of course I remembered exactly which door he had hurtled out of: the rear door of a barracks along the row before the airfield. No necessity had led me there in the first place; I'd simply been sauntering on my way to work. Yet I waited a couple of days but didn't pause in passing there again and waited again a day or two before I found him at the same hour after lunch sitting on the steps, his cap on his head this time.

He said, "I saw you out the window the other day. How you doing?"

"Okay," I said. "Yourself?"

"I'm always on the ready."

"By the way, what's your name?"

"Johannes."

"That's it? That's all?"

"Johannes Kessler. Johannes Friedrich Kessler. Sounds German, doesn't it? It is. I'm a Hun. Not the National Socialist variety. Just German. Want my biography?"

"Sure," I said, and to my surprise I did.

His father and mother, both German, came from Mannheim. After the First War, when the French occupied the Rhineland, they immigrated. Hitler was only a bad joke then. They settled in Idaho, Boise. Father an oculist there. Where I was born. End of story. And your bio? he inquired.

Humdrum American. Bourgeois. As in a tale by Thomas Mann. You know him.

"Not personally." Johannes laughed. "But everybody's read *Buddenbrooks*."

I said I'd been thinking of Tonio Kröger, being a bourgeois manqué myself. Jim Lord from New Jersey. Parents play bridge and badminton. I hated school; college was hell. And now this.

His folks spoke German at home. So some of the neighbors looked the other way in the street. Did I by any chance have a car?

I exclaimed, "What on earth would I do with a car?"

"Go for a ride. Round the country. Anywhere. Round the world." His gray eyes went wide when he smiled, and the daylight seemed to shine out of his face, he was that good-looking.

I said, "Oh."

"It's only a Ford. Roadster. Rumble seat. 'Thirty-seven model. Blue as your eyes."

"They're brown," I said.

"Well, I can see that. I'll take you for a ride on Saturday if we get a pass. If you like."

"Naturally," I said.

"That's it then," he said, and went back into the barracks, as if there were not a cloud in the sky.

It happened, however, that everything had happened too quickly to partake of certainty. The adventitious loomed like an obstacle in the path of normal adventure. Were we like lost children in the forest of make-believe on the tricky border of the intimate? Such unrealistic impetuosity might someday be as risky as a house made of sugar candy.

The car was a beauty, and as a matter of fact, I had always longed to have blue eyes. We drove to the mountains, the windows down, wind murmuring in our hair; the afternoon was yellow, and I suddenly realized that it was the month of May. Johannes was humming a song between his teeth, the melody of it quite audible.

He said, "Your folks call you Jim, I spose?"

"Everybody does."

"Mine call me Hanno. You might as well."

"Wasn't Hanno the nickname of the last of the Buddenbrooks in Thomas Mann's novel? That was Hanno, wasn't it?"

"It is, yes. Germany's greatest writer. Yes, it's Hanno. But he's a symbolic character. The opposition between art and life. A weakling, dies of typhoid fever, as I recall. End of novel. End of dynasty. End of rational tradition. End of old Germany. But then . . . what's in a name?" He laughed, wrinkling his face. "I read somewhere that a pope once kept in the Vatican zoo an elephant named Hanno."

"Then you never forget," I said, "do you?"

"Never," he said.

I thought, My God! This was too soon. But here I was. And there he was. He was humming again. Did he know *my* song? The *Three Comrades* melody I'd learned to play at prep school. On the orange mountainside we snaked up slowly around turnings as tortuous, I thought, as the one we were taking together.

There was a sign saying DONNER PASS. That was where the tragic pioneers got trapped in the snow, freezing to death, and the crazed survivors devoured the corpses of their dead comrades. I didn't mention this to Hanno. He turned off before we got there, and I thought, Well, that's something. And then I thought I didn't know what I thought.

We came along above a lake, a huge one, flat sheen of sapphire set in the glitter of pine trees, a vision like the world without war, when peace was all there was. But I kept poetic excess to myself. We sat down on pine needles, and Hanno lit a cigarette, whorls of smoke drifting from his nostrils, and I memorized the perfection of his profile.

After a pause, very conscientiously putting out his cigarette, he exhaled a puff of air and said, "It's because I'm German. The background going back so far. I like things German. Wagner, Goethe. You care for Wagner, Jim?"

"Don't know really. Saw *Tristan* once. Very long but some good moments. When she dies."

"*Parsifal.*" Hanno sighed. "My parents took me to New York that time. We went to the matinee, and at the end—when he touches Amfortas with the lance—afterward I ran out into the street and cried all the way back to the hotel. Couldn't help myself, and that's a fact."

"Well, yes," I said, "I know." The compulsion of tears. And even then despite the perfection of time and place, my windpipe was parched as I said I knew when I didn't.

We were seated by the crest of a steep decline toward the water above outcroppings of shale and underbrush, and nothing stirred the peaceful sheen of the lake, so it was incredible when Hanno abruptly leaped up without a murmur and went plunging headfirst down the decline. I gasped. All I could do was gasp. And his trampling boots raised a diaphanous haze of dust that half obscured his flailing figure like an ungodly apparition above the reflected sky below when he suddenly disappeared entirely, as if he'd set out purposefully to disappear forever. My mouth went dry. Then almost as suddenly he reappeared, a vision of wild gesturing amid the underbrush, and he began to clamber back up the decline. His face was streaked with dust, a few twigs stuck in the curls, and his breathing came hard and hoarse as he sprawled onto the pine needles without a word.

I said nothing.

Hanno gulped, blew out deep breaths, muttered, "Whew. What a tumble down. Almost could have made it to the water except for the bushes."

I said, "Almost could have made it to the infirmary too."

"Oh, no." He sniffed. "Wotan would have watched out for me."

"What's that?"

"God of war"—he grinned—"watches out for his own."

"Looked like you were out to kill yourself."

"Not me," said Hanno, brushing the twigs from his hair. "I'm no young Werther."

"Who's that?"

"Guy in a story by Goethe. Hopelessly in love. He kills himself."

"Looked like you were out to do the same thing," I said, turning my head. "And what if you had? And I'm the witness, an accessory, so the police could say I was responsible, mmm . . . then what?"

"Oh, come on," Hanno exclaimed, "loosen up on me, will you?"

Needless to say, from that appeal there was no turning away. I showed him a preliminary grin, an angular shrug, and said, "I suppose we'd better be getting back."

"I guess we had."

The return ride to Reno along the course of the Truckee turned out to be foolproof—talk, badinage, adrift on the uncomplicated wind—and Hanno stopped at a gas station to wash his face, came back from the men's room as handsome as Adam. We had supper in the Good Luck Café, and I thought nobody knew what that meant. When we got back to the base, parking the car, Hanno said, "See you tomorrow around six-thirty at the PX."

"You bet," I said.

In a way it was like his crazy careening down the decline above Lake Tahoe, the vertiginous simplicity of taking each other for granted. So we didn't have to talk about ourselves, talked instead about state-of-the art gas masks, rubber underwear in case of catastrophe, machinery so intricate Leonardo da Vinci couldn't have drawn it, the battle of Pepsi vs. Coke, death of Rachmaninov, *The Magnificent Ambersons*, Churchill in Washington, and, of course the rout of Marshal Rommel in North Africa.

Hanno wasn't very sorry for the Nazis. Being German, perhaps he despised them more than we did because they were ruining their homeland. But Marshal Rommel he admired with atavistic fervor. He personified the deathless tradition of a chivalrous, mythic Nordic warrior, to whom martial esprit de corps mattered more than biological élan vital, death preferable to dishonor.

And that's why the Germans will fight to the very end, no matter how bitter, Hanno said. Unconditional surrender be damned, not because they're Nazis but because they're soldiers fighting for their homeland. You'll see. While the Americans—all of us—well, we're not made for soldiering, and when the going gets really bad, and it's going to get very bad if ever we set foot on German soil, you watch out for bad soldiering—you'll see—men shooting themselves in the foot, deserters, the works. Oh, the Allies will win, obviously. More troops, more airplanes, tanks, big guns, more trucks and jeeps, more junk. But—but men who fought for glory on the battlefield and were worshiped by their soldiers like Rommel—forget about toadies like Keitel or maniacs like Heydrich—men like Rommel will win no honor in the history books because they'll say he was fighting for Hitler, not for his homeland. And that's not right.

I protested. If you go to war, you can't count on things coming out right, because war is wrong.

"Oh, Jim," Hanno said, "so sensible. Have you no pipe dreams?"

"Sure, sure, I have," I replied. "More than enough." And even as I asked myself what they were, a thrill of fear flashed through my veins.

Hanno's car became the magic conveyance of our comradeship, our unspoken understanding. That is, we might very well go without a word until time seemed to swell deeper and deeper inside itself while our compatibility came to life outside. The complicit silence. Sometimes we would drive down and around the base's roadways, immaculate air fingering our faces, following a corkscrew itinerary down and around the quiescent rifle range. And afterward, when it was dark, some envious soul sitting on the barracks steps smoking a White Owl cigar would say, "Will you look at 'em? Those two ninnies don't know there's a war on."

Saturdays we'd speed from the base across the tumbleweed plateau, seldom lingering longer in Reno than a five-minute fill-up for gas, oil check, windshield wipe, then onto a third-rate highway going east toward Fernley or heading south to Carson City. It was the latter route that one day got us into trouble.

On a straight stretch halfway to Carson, Hanno said, "I'm going to floor it."

I said, "Terrific!"

The car was six years old but had gone only 12,600 and some odd. So it leaped like a leap frog, the motor howled, tires shrieked, and as we shot past a stand of sage, Hanno thumbed the horn, shouting, "It's the ride of the Valkyries. Yowee!"

The Wagnerian orchestration came quickly, closing in behind, siren screaming, the motorcycle cop on our left, yelling, shaking his arm toward the pebbly roadside, Hanno pulled over, stamping on the brake, and the guilty Ford stood down. The cop braked his bike, hefted a dropsical belly over the cowboy belt, waddled to Hanno's window, his badge blinding in the noonday blaze, sizing us up, and popped his lips, "What haaaave we here? Couple a solcher boys out joyridin', yesssiree, thirty mph pas' the limit lesssn I miss me guess, wastin' gas like Uncle Sam got gas to burn and leanin' on the horrrn like the fuckin' fire department. Lessee license n registration, boy."

Hanno produced the papers, squaring his jaw, and passed them over.

"Iaho, Idaho," mouthed the trooper, thumbing the papers. "Kissler. Funny moniker, Kissler."

"I was born with it."

"No skin offa my nose, sonny."

"Okay then."

"Not okay. Bustin' the limit by thirty, n reckless drivin on top o' that. Breakin' the law. But I tell ya what. Was oncet a solcher maself. Never to kill no fuckin' Germans more's the pity. Run afta plenty a gurrrls maself. What you kids a doin', ridin' round real reckless like, leanin' on ya horrrn, lookin' out fo the gurrrls, ain't ya, hot to cut the mustard, ain't it tha trooooth?'

"If you say so," Hanno grumbled.

" 'Tain't tha trooooth, what ya ridin' roun' fo?"

"We are driving around to enjoy ourselves," Hanno said carefully, supercilious, glancing into the air.

"Thasso, thasso?" cried the trooper. "Ya think ya free te injoy ya-selfs? Think that, do ya?"

"Is there any law against? A free country, isn't it?"

"Free to run ya in fa breakin' the law, sonny boy. You two some kind a screwballs not lookin' out fa the gurrrls, soundin' the huntin' horrrn to injoy yaselfs? Sounds mighty peeculiah to me. Yessirree. Pee-culiah. Don't want nothing to do wiff you kids." He flung Hanno's papers through the window. "Ya weren't in uniform I'd run ya in. So git outta my county n injoy yasself someplace else, ya piss-poor solchers." He stepped away and gestured back toward Reno.

Hanno deliberately gathered his papers, placed them inside his wallet, put the wallet into his shirt pocket, turned the key in the igni-tion, started up and steered the Ford slowly around and drove it slowly in the direction we'd come.

"I don't mind saying," he said when the trooper's image had faded from the rearview mirror, "that man's depraved."

"Sure," I said, and didn't want to hear another word about what had happened—and neither did Hanno.

Ulysses meanwhile had fallen out of luck for me. The recondite tribulations of a prestidigitator with language no longer felt quite so relevant. What was wanted now was something more warming to the workaday heart, less chilled by arcana of the intellect. Joyce said that a man of genius changes the world. He does. And I believed with all my being in the life-enhancing grandeur of genius. Individual men had brought about all the momentous advances of civilization. Dante and Newton, Beethoven, Shakespeare, Michelangelo. Only four of that stat-ure were then living—Einstein, Stravinsky, Thomas Mann, and Picasso—and they were all regrettably remote from Reno, Nevada.

As chance would have it, the final page of *Ulysses* was followed by a list of several hundred books available from the same publisher, includ-ing titles by most of the great men of world literature: Homer, Dante,

Shakespeare, Goethe, Tolstoy, Proust, Joyce, and Mann. My choice had been made for me—or, rather, hadn't *I* been made for it!—and Goethe stared me in the face. The name and address of the bookstore where I had found *Ulysses* were advertised in its flyleaf by an oval sticker. So I wrote a letter to Newbegin's, never forgetting how that name had been constructed to prefigure a new beginning, and how, in fact, it had. Enclosing a five-dollar bill, I ordered a copy of *The Sorrows of Young Werther*, and sent off my letter to 358 Post Street, San Francisco.

The days were suffuse, machines increasingly intricate, mocking by their inscrutable complexity my nonchalant incompetence, drawings progressively messier, myself increasingly careless, MacNally more and more cautious.

Often enough, however, lunchtimes and evenings found good fortune in Hanno's twilit eyes. We talked about gold-crazed prospectors stampeding across the heartless badlands en route to riches and ruin. And wondered what FDR and Churchill would be talking about. No doubt hearty discussions of the cruelest means to bring devastation and humiliation to the German homeland. Still, surmise as to the abominations of wartime did not deter the smiles and sparkle of Saturday afternoons in the blue car, and Hanno sometimes allowed me to drive. And with his beautiful lips slightly parted, he hummed the familiar tune.

"What is it?" I asked. "Always the same. That song?"

" 'Oh Burschenherrlichkeit,' " he said.

"Which means?"

It means "oh, glorious fellowship," he said. His father used to sing it. A student song from the good old days. A Heidelberg song. He'd studied there before med school, and that's how he wasn't in the First War, because there was as much demand for doctors as for cannons, and he graduated just before the end. And Heidelberg . . . it must have been glorious then, when nobody dreamed how soon the sky would fall. If only we could have been there. But now? You can only hope it hasn't been bombed out of existence. Mannheim, they say, only fifteen miles down the river, there's next to nothing left of it. But think of Heidelberg. The university one of the greatest, one of the first. All those students in the medieval streets, singing their hearts out. "Gaudeamus Igitur." I'd give anything . . .

But he stopped abruptly and again began humming.

I'd give anything too, I thought.

Weekend passes we came to take for granted. Karlo never said no. He went easier on me, I thought, than my nuisance status deserved. Hanno apparently, and rightly, got whatever he wanted.

"When we go someplace on the weekend," he said, "why come back to the base for that night? For that matter, why come back to the base at all? Except they'd stick us in the stockade if they caught up with us south of the border."

We set out after BLTs and a couple of Dr Peppers at the PX. The day was a blaze of cloudland, velvet shadows on the sagebrush, hawks floating in the blue. No one argued with our speed, which was easygoing. Hanno had a map.

There's a little place up north a ways, he said. Called Lovelock. Stop there maybe. About a hundred miles. Long's there's a place to sleep, have some supper, sit around, and get tight. What do you say?

Lovelock? Well, of course, it *would* be. And then? I said, Sounds okay.

The desert spread round and round, tawny and flickering, a few cacti measuring space below the mountains, the sigh of our headway almost inaudible under the sky. We had been in that car for a time.

And then the world turned upside down. The sun was on the earth. Or was it a shot of blinding flash in my eyes? It was. From a shard of glass or gold by the roadside. A star exploding in my face. And I looked at Hanno. He was he, oh, my God, but someone else, and would be forever. I noticed a tiny cleft at the root of his nose I'd never seen before, and yet I'd seen everything. It existed only for me. He existed for me alone, speeding on the skyward highway. Of course. He was humming—that song—between his teeth.

How can you tell just when the person you like becomes the one you love? Or just why? You may recall where this happened, never forget what the clock said. But your mind spins in the space of the marvelous, the dazing conjecture of the physical and stupefying transformation of survival. Yes. A lifetime in an instant.

I said, "Hanno."

"What?" he said.

Lovelock as a town wasn't much. Accommodations for passersby were a weathered, overgrown shanty boasting of "Rooms." A beaten-up dump of corrugated siding next door was called the Last Chance Saloon; a diner across the street, Tonto's Eatery. The rooming house had a front porch and half a dozen decrepit rocking chairs like the specters of luckless forty-niners. A codger behind the desk gave us a stainless steel grin, said, "Hail to the troops," and punched a bell. Nobody came. "Plenty a rooms, two bucks a night, special for solchers."

"We'll take one," said Hanno.

"Okey-doke," said the codger. "Nice room. Doubledy bed. Pay in advance. No hard feelings."

"Sure," said Hanno. He put two dollars on the desk.

I said, "I owe you a dollar then."

"Forget it," said Hanno.

I had had no say about the doubledy bed, but of course I was willing. In fear and trembling. The precedent of Billy now was the useless innocence of another lifetime, Hanno being Hanno, his sureness of the moment wearing the smile of tomorrow, with which there would never be an argument.

So when he said, "Let's try the saloon, what do you say, pretend it *is* a last chance—God knows for what—shall we?"

I said I couldn't wait.

It looked as though the last chance had been lost long since, three-legged tables, splintered chairs, and a couple of born losers squinting at empty glasses on the bar, the bartender's death rattle query: "What'll it be, pretty boy?"

Hanno said, "Beer."

"Corn," said the bartender.

Hanno shrugged.

We had three each, and they tasted like murder. The losers talked pinochle, the bartender farted, and we looked at the battered poster for buffalo dances at Fort Apache. Getting pissed was a deliverance.

The boy behind the counter of Tonto's Eatery was an Indian, of course, greasy braids on both shoulders. Tamales and warm beer. When we were ready to go to our room, the sun was a drunken circlet in the vermilion smear.

Room 3 had an enfeebled bulb on a wire above the gray bed. A sink in the corner, one towel. A chair and several wire hangers hanging on nails. Spiderweb fissures mapped the walls. A room where fugitives from the facts of life could go blind from facing the future.

Hanno was humming away, took off his boots and tossed them onto the floor, took off his shirt, his T-shirt, splashed water across his torso so it gleamed, and unbuttoned his pants. He said, "I sleep bare ass. Always slept naked at home. All of us did. Nordic nature cult. You don't mind."

"Christ, no, this is the army," I replied, studying my fingernails. It's true plenty of the 856th slept naked and who cared? *But* this was not the army.

And when he was nude, as foolproof with himself as ABC, I gave in to the universal itch of genital curiosity and saw that in the measure most men most appreciate natural selection had been munificent, albeit I pretended to myself I'd not looked.

"Must be the bourgeois background," I said. "I always slept in my undies myself."

Hanno said, "Then turn off the fucking light and hop in bed."

That bed must have been worn out before Custer's Last Stand, its center a gulch so deep gravity drew our bodies together, our flanks touching in the secrecy beneath the sheet. He said nothing; neither did I. No language to turn to. No machinery of easement.

I labored to master my breathing, subdue the muscular shiver, suspend my being in the inertia of fear. My cock was hard as a rock, desire bursting in my blood, and I knew that I toed the verge of the abyss, the catastrophe of a lifetime, the more threatening and unforgivable for being in the person of the very last man in all the world I would want to wrong. What folly, moreover, could expect that *he* might tolerate the slightest interference with his body lying against my hip. No, no. Were I a man, the adolescent vow above the dead leaves must last me now, now that the most wonderful of earthly contingencies lay beside me.

After an eternity of ten or fifteen minutes he turned on his side, slept, and the sweetness of his respiration restored some confidence to the dark. Inhaling his closeness as deeply as I could, forcing the lungs' contents beyond the limit of sensation, I survived as if I could draw in also his skin and bones, his hair, toenails, and marmoreal thighs, his sex and masculinity inside me so that I could contain him utterly; we would become myself, united as a single being. And I knew that that way lay madness. Mine for him. And terror till at last the bruise of dawn discolored the feverish window.

Hanno leaped from the bed, gazellelike in the spring of his limbs. "Oh, Burschenherrlichkeit!" he cried. "Great day in the fucking morning, Jim."

"You can say that again," I said, waiting, exhausted, for my tumescence also to tire.

We went across the road to the eatery for breakfast. Behind the counter a wide-shouldered, prognathous white man stood, hands on hips, ready for anything.

"Flapjacks," said Hanno.

"Porridge," the counterman pithily retorted, going behind a partition with a ringing of spurs.

"Tonto must be out back, feeding oats to the man's horse." Hanno smirked.

We drove back to the base through the unreal morning, I at the wheel, Hanno in the rumble seat, and as we whizzed through the gates, he sang, "Hi-ho, Silver, away!"

More than anything conceivable, I thought, a photo of Hanno that I could hold against my heart might slightly alleviate its longing. His photographic face in my hands to do with as I wished, what unnatural happiness. It so happened I had a camera. As we stood in the sun beside the car, I said, "Go over there and I'll snap your picture."

His face went blank, and he raised a hand. "Not on your life!" he exclaimed. "I never get my picture taken."

"Ah, come on, only a snapshot."

A rush of annoyance shrouded his eyes. "Don't pressure me. Or I'll—I'll . . ." He turned aside, leaving rancor in the menacing air.

I gulped. "Okay, Hanno, okay. I didn't mean to—"

"Forget it," he said. "I don't want to get snapshotted is all. It's nothing."

But nothing, as always, was everything. I surrendered. Yet I wondered. Such adamant unwillingness to part with a portrait of himself: Might it not mean he had something to fear, some secret dread that only the loss of a likeness could stir? As among primitive peoples who feared that their souls lived in images? Heaven knew what. I, I realized, would never know.

Mail call brought a parcel from San Francisco, Newbegin's again living up to its name. *The Sorrows of Young Werther*, having survived in print for more than a century and a half, wasn't a very weighty volume, only about a hundred pages, and easy to read. But what romantic passion rises from its words like the intoxication Goethe describes, having lived for it himself. Like generations of readers, no doubt, I fancied that Werther's sorrows were such as I had known myself. He, to be sure, kills himself. I had merely walked out one Saturday afternoon away from the dead leaves of the detestable prep school and under the concealment of a flowering copse cut a gash down my left biceps with a horn-handled pocketknife, a wound causing curiosity in the locker room and rude questions to which I had no answers.

I took care not to tell Hanno I had read the tragic German story, for it seemed that by doing so I had taken a liberty out of all proportion to the freedom sanctioned by our friendship.

MacNally meanwhile had grown more and more hostile, increasingly critical of my draftsmanship as amateurish and inadequate. Which is what it had been from the beginning. Sometimes in the morning I'd find the word "Rejected" scrawled in red pencil across a drawing almost finished. He sneered at my newfound friendship, said my pansy buddy must be a Nazi too, with a kraut name like that. And one word to the colonel, what's more, and it'd be stockade time for us both. Oh, those MPs love fairies, gang rape 'em for breakfast.

Newbegin's, as it turned out, by sending *The Sorrows of Young Werther* had sent something more pertinent than ever could have been guessed, for the volume, an anthology, also contained *Death in Venice*, the story by Thomas Mann I'd read and reread already, that spellbinding tale describing on its surface the struggle of every artist between sensuous self-discipline and sensual self-indulgence, and below the surface the degrading, lethal corruption of a surrender to the vice of homosexual desire. The story is told of course in prose of classical eloquence befitting its author's almost filial reverence for Goethe, and indeed, the juxtaposition of the two writers in a single volume, both represented, if not quite personified, by accounts of frustrated desire drawn directly from their own experience, may seem not only an illustrious happenstance of German literature but also a cogent illustration of the Germanic temperament. For after all, the two stories are about the same thing, how love's frustration can beget self-destructive passion leading implacably to suicide: by gunfire for Werther, for Aschenbach by deliberate surrender to the plague.

I took care that Hanno should not see *Collected German Stories.*

Overnight it was summertime, the cactus flowers were gone, and sunshine blazed as brilliantly on the desert at 7:00 a.m. as at high noon. Meanwhile, the invading Japanese were defeated with heavy losses and expelled from the American Aleutian island of Attu in the Bering Sea. German cities were increasingly targets of firestorm bombing, Italian maneuvers were a joke, and none of us for an instant imagined we might fail to win a very worthwhile war. Optimism about the decency of one's duty as a soldier on the right side was certainly a boost to morale, though mine just then needed no boosting. Even the menace of the infamous MacNally seemed nugatory now. The mornings, evenings, afternoons were all made incandescent and secure by the presence of Hanno under the sun.

He said, "Too bad we can't go someplace where there's . . ." He shrugged and gazed toward the distance.

"What?" I asked.

"No one else."

"Oh, but we could. Walk so far into the desert we'd be all alone out there."

"Except for the rattlers. I meant someplace where there are—or were—people who're not anyone else. If you know what I mean."

"I don't. But I'd go anywhere."

"Ghosts," he said. "A ghost town. Funny I didn't think of it. Read about it once in a book. Virginia City. Ever heard of it?"

Had I? "A place in the gold rush?"

"Silver. The silver rush. A handful of tents turned overnight into a town of fantastic luxury, mansions sprouting up like mushrooms, and whorehouses, gambling halls, even a goddamned opera house, if you can believe it. But pretty soon the silver ran out. Half a century ago. Everybody left. A ghost town now. Totally abandoned up there on the mountain. What you think? Like to go there?"

"I'd love to," I said.

"Not far, forty, fifty miles maybe. We could drive on the weekend. Roads must be bad. Spend the night somewhere."

"I'll put in for the pass. Karlo never says no."

But the army's disposition to accommodate the good times of glorious fellowship could not, of course, automatically be made to comply with the expectations of undistinguished enlisted men.

Friday afternoon, shortly before the office was due to close, when I was puffing on my latest drawing to dry the ink, MacNally shouted from the other room, "By the way, Lord, you're on duty this weekend."

How could he have known? Coming out of my cell, I said very calmly, "I have a pass for this weekend."

"Rescinded," he said.

But only if he'd somehow found out, too content to thwart what he despised, might he have plotted to betray its hopes. And my resentment was too bitter to live with. I said, "I've made plans. Not subject to change. I won't change them, so I'm taking my pass."

"You'll do nothing of the kind," he snarled, causing Childs and the looies to stare. "You are on duty for the weekend. Saturday all day, Sunday till noon. That's an order."

"And I know why it's an order," I shouted. "For weeks now you've gone out of you way to be disagreeable, criticize, complain, make my life as unpleasant as possible. Now this!"

"Maybe you'd like me to give my reasons, say why I have no consideration for you. As a person or as a member of the armed forces of this country. How would you like that, you filthy little shit? Anyway, your work stinks."

"I don't care," I cried. "I'm taking my pass, and you can go straight to hell, you lousy bastard."

Lieutenant Garlington slapped his desk with a ruler. "Come on, boys," he appealed, "let's not get into personal squabbles in the office, okay?"

MacNally was not to be frustrated. "I'm very sorry, sir," he stated, "but Private Lord has refused to obey a direct order in line of duty. This office cannot function efficiently without discipline. Insubordination is unacceptable. If we were facing the enemy, it would be a matter for court-martial."

Lieutenant Carswell came from his office. "What seems to be the trouble?"

Garlington wiggled his fingers. "No big deal. Lord wants to go on pass for the weekend. Corporal MacNally's ordered him to stay on duty, and he refuses."

MacNally forced the moment to a crisis. "Private Lord is on temporary assignment to this office. He is not only insubordinate but incompetent, and in my judgment should return to duty with the Eight fifty-sixth Chemical Company. His presence here is no longer useful, and I take exception to it. Either he is sent back to his company with a reprimand or I will request reassignment to another administrative position." Pausing for full effect of his threat, he added, "And I'll get one."

That did it. The lieutenants were pinned to their dependence, and no amount of wiggling could save them from it.

Carswell said, "The corporal is in the right. Larry, you can prepare the papers, you arrange it. I'll sign them, and that's that."

"Oh, hell," said Garlington. "Okay, okay. Private Lord, you have any personal property in the office, collect it, and step into the corridor."

And when I had my musette, passing back through the office, Keith said, "This is the army, buster, you don't like it you can always prove you're a coward and claim you're a conscientious objector."

I marched out, Garlington waiting in the corridor. He said, "This is how it is, and I don't want to hear no more about it, Private Lord. You're so crazy to take your pass, you take it. Assignment here is finished as of now. With censure. We'll send the papers to your CO. Dismissed."

I didn't care. What mattered was not what I was leaving behind but everything I would travel toward.

Hanno driving, we were away in the morning in the blue Ford, a box of sandwiches and a few Cokes in the rumble seat. I didn't explain but said only that I'd finished my business at HQ and would be back on duty with the 856th Monday morning.

When Virginia City had been abandoned in the throes of another century, the roads leading to it had also been left to deteriorate. No signs pointed to the site where millions had been wrested from the mountainside. The trails were dirt and shale, potholed and fragmented. We had to go up in first gear. An aged, bearded geezer was coming down on muleback. We asked directions.

Spitting khaki tobacco juice, he said, "Whaddayas want up there anyways? Ain't nobody left up there now. And you're on the wrong road."

Hanno made a grin. "Just want to look," he said.

"Nothin' left to steal," said the geezer. "Devil done took it all afore the last war. Turn round and go back down couple miles, take ya right, left at the fork, and up ahead ya see what's left a the place. Should a seen it when I was a kid back then. Whorehouses still in business, kids like you, get yaselfs some pussy."

"Oh, well," said Hanno, "we can make do with a few ghosts."

"Ghosts aplenty now"—the geezer sighed—"yes, sir, and the pity of 'em, all were bully boys and girls in the silver godsend long ago." He kicked the tragic ribs of his mule and lurched away.

We turned very carefully on the steep track, followed the geezer's directions and found the ghost of Virginia City along a spur of the mountain. Leaving the Ford, we walked up the main street, nameless now.

And here, indeed, here was the specter of the long since forsaken town, yet for all of that a rather grandiose specter. Once gaudily decorated mansions stood in crestfallen decrepitude, windows blinded, fragments of fretwork sagging above destitute verandas, stairways shattered, remnants of ostentation dangling over rotted doorways, chimneys in ruins, the whole place ravaged and crumbling, haunted like a drunken old dame defiant in the tatters of archaic finery. A far-gone melody of obsolete romance was audible still beyond the eerie silence lying over the funerary town. And the memory of mad wealth squandered in an hour for the dying sighs of moribund whorehouses, and the besotted dreams of wealth in worlds beyond this one.

"I knew it would be like this," said Hanno. "Good thing we came here together. All alone you'd feel like a ghost yourself."

"Unless you ran into Billy the Kid coming out of a saloon."

We ventured inside a couple of collapsing mansions over rotten floorboards and gaped at the tarnished auditorium of the tumbledown opera house, crumbs of gilt, shards of glitter, where *The Girl of the Golden West* certainly never was sung. The ruined vestiges were romantic, godforsaken, poverty-stricken proof of money's poor inability to pay for the good life. Then beyond the end of the street the mountains had begun to rise toward the sun. A glow of gilded memory and imagination emanated for a moment from the forgotten decay of El Dorado. So we strolled back to the blue car and drove down the precipitous trail, leaving Virginia City to the mercy of the sunset.

When we reached a sort of town called Hazen, it was suppertime at a nameless eatery: cauterized steak, last year's rhubarb pie. Across the unpaved street stood Comstock Rooms. Hanno went inside to see if any were free, came back in thirty seconds and said, "Okay." Farther along were a couple of saloons. He turned, adding, "Let's have a couple before we pack in."

The Silver Dollar lay under a pall of noxious haze and stank of cigar butts stagnating in the sawdust.

"Bourbon or beer," said the unshaven bartender.

"Beer," said Hanno, "with a bourbon chaser."

So, I thought, he *is* a man of the world. The combination was heady and went to my head. I felt fine. We had more. Three, was it? Four. There was a song coming from . . . a jukebox? Probably "Buffalo gals, won't ya come out tonight, come out tonight, come out tonight? . . . Buffalo gals . . ." I couldn't have been quite sure. Where, that is, or when. The movie house I used to go to in prep school down from the PO by the reservoir? Maybe.

On the way back to Comstock Rooms, Hanno took my arm. I was aware of it, of his grip. Upstairs in the room I sat on the edge of the double bed, yes. I didn't see very well either. I felt fine, though really somewhere else, slumped backward onto the bed.

"You all right?" he asked.

"Oh, yes," I said. "I'm drunk."

Hanno laughed. "Oh, yes. So am I." He was leaning across above my eyes.

"Oh, Christ." I gulped. "I'm afraid I'm going to be sick."

"Don't worry," he said. He put his hand on my forehead. "I'm here. You'll be all right."

"Oh, yeah, oh, yeah," I mumbled. "Oh, God."

And I was far away. Where there were no people. Before I could say a thing. Ghosts. Ruins. Lost in the dark. I couldn't tell. What. What Hanno was doing. His hands on my clothes. The darkness.

My hangover was a raging cyclone inside my eyeballs. The storm tore detritus from the morning and savaged the sunrise. The naked Apollo looked as fresh as springtime, while with this morbid taste in my mouth I said, "Jesus, what a fuckup. God, I was drunk. What happened? Was I sick?"

"Not quite. I tried to get you comfortable before you conked out."

"Jesus, Hanno. What can I say? I'm just that sorry."

Having gotten into his shorts, he turned, looked over his shoulder, and said, "Forget it."

He was a grown man. I was nothing. This became better, though, after buckwheat pancakes and a glass of milk at the eatery and Hanno told me about the first time he'd gotten drunk, at a dance, and fallen down on the dance floor, carrying a plate of scrambled eggs to his girlfriend. His girlfriend? He'd never before mentioned one.

From Hazen we drove on to Sparks, a real town not far from Reno, had lunch in a real restaurant, wandered back and forth, remembering a long-ago ramble in Virginia City, and by midafternoon were back at base.

I said, "What an outing."

"We'll do it again," said Hanno. "That's a promise."

"Good," I said. "Well . . . I'd better get back to my company. Find out what's been dreamed up for me now I'm not in the HQ. I'll see you."

"Naturally."

We turned away at the same time but not, of course, together.

As if what was bad wasn't bad enough, I found a handwritten memo on my bunk.

> *To Private Lord,*
> *Welcome back to the 856th.*
> *Beginning tomorrow morning, Monday, 14 June, at 5 a.m.*
> *you are assigned to KP duty until further notice.*
> *From Karlo Stojanac, Master Sergeant*

Knowing what that meant and guessing this would be worse than "Beethoven's Hands," I half ran, hurried to Hanno's barracks, first time I'd ever gone inside, bursting through the selfsame door he'd burst out of to knock me down, asking the first soldier I saw, "Where's Kessler?"

But it was Hanno himself who stepped out immediately from behind the opposite bunk, taken aback, his face suddenly on fire. He said, "What's wrong with you?"

Taken aback myself, blushing too, what could I say? What was wrong? But—but was that it? Did *he* know? What *was* wrong! I said, "I'm on KP."

One of the watching soldiers laughed.

Hanno made a warped grin, said, "Everybody's on KP. Sooner or later. That all?"

"Yeah, that's all," I limply acknowledged.

"Right," said Hanno. "So. See you around."

"Sure," I said, "okay," backing out the door, the daytime abrupt across the desert, a P-38 streaking straight at the mountains, and I thought how wonderful if it could explode, beautiful fireball in the catastrophic sky. It didn't. Only I could see the calamity.

In the smelly, snoring dark of 5:00 a.m., a tin voice said, "KP, soldier, move your ass."

I assumed I knew already what it was all about, fooling around in the kitchen, dishing out slop to the chow line, opening tins of baked beans, peeling potatoes at worst, but had no notion of the double *P*: pots and pans. This comeuppance was meted out in a stifling basement, where huge aluminum cauldrons, iron skillets the size of trash can lids, four gallon coffeepots, baking tins, kettles encrusted with the sludge of leftover stews all had to be washed in triple-hot suds, scoured clean with steel wool, and brought to an immaculate shine with Dutch Cleanser. This was backbreaking drudgery never finished, let alone on time, so the cooks were constantly yelling down the stairs to get a fucking move on. Mere exhaustion was poetry compared with the prostration of a day lasting till ten o'clock at night, leaving five to six laughable hours of rest before a return to toil made more odious by certainty its purpose was corporal punishment. My companions in misery, moreover, added to it by ceaseless whining. Not that I felt stouthearted, but the strength to keep my dejection to myself was all I had. After a week I was barely able to stand straight, my hands and forearms were scorched, painful to the touch, while my mind was mired in boiling suds, immersed in the eternal filth of pots and pans. Until further notice . . .

But in the bogus lull of one nothing afternoon Sergeant Stojanac came down the cement stairs. To find out how I was doing, say it was Hogg who'd given the order. Not that that made the difference. It was decent of him to have come. After he'd gone, I felt pleased but not surprised.

Hanno, of course, I never expected to see in the Augean oubliette. If my intrusion into his barracks had caused embarrassment, how much more would ensue from his seeming at all concerned by my plight, any such semblance of care, of course, intolerably compromising?

So what, *what* had I done to deserve this excruciating retribution? That was the question. I was the answer. But I didn't see that.

The second Sunday of my servitude, after thirteen days of ordeal, I was by some error of compunction—Karlo's intercession?—allowed a day of rest. A morning of flawless paradise, the windswept desert a scattering of diamonds. Wanting my fill, and much more than that, of freedom, I walked out into the sage. Way overhead on the far mountaintops a few rivulets of snow still lay gleaming in the highest ravines, and I felt summoned onward and onward toward those steeps where lonely whispers of wind spoke to the listening sky. Up there one would become too exhausted ever to find the way back. They say that by freezing one goes very gently into nothingness. And before long I became a walking extremity of weariness.

Relinquishment of memory. Seduction of surcease. Werther. Aschenbach. It must have been forever I stayed seated, then lay fully outstretched on the crumbling desert floor, musing the lovely yawn of oblivion. Only to be brought back abruptly to where I was, not *what*, by the rude, crude, unprecedented sensation of hunger. So I walked back by the thoughtless path I'd pursued toward futility, hoping only I'd reach the base in time for chow, and I did, and the food was marvelous.

And when I came out of the mess hall, a figure as if from another world materialized in the lee of the barracks away from the sun. It was Hanno, standing straight in the shadow, smoking a cigarette.

I said, "What are you doing here?"

"Isn't that obvious?" he asked politely.

I waited for him to answer his question.

"It's Sunday," he said. "I thought maybe you'd get a Sunday off when I found out you were full-time on KP."

"How did you find out?"

"Asked your sergeant."

"Karlo," I said. "Yes. Well." I looked him hard in the gray eyes. "Well, I did get this Sunday off."

"Come on, Jim," he said.

I smiled into his face. "Let's go for a walk."

We strolled up along the landing field, and the mountains had never been so miraculous. Hanno told me how once a couple of years ago by Horseshoe Bend on the river there he'd been dared by a one-time Olympic sidestroke champion to swim the length of an outflow drainage conduit running underground a couple of hundred yards into an irrigation canal, and he'd done it and while he was underwater in the dark he'd thought he'd never make it, his lungs collapsing, and that probably had been the most thrilling instant of his life. And I said, "I see," remembering the plunge down the slope above Lake Tahoe. Taking risks to show that a lifetime lived without a willingness to take risks shows up a life devoid of anything worth risking.

Five days later the unprecedented, unexpected, unpredictable, unimaginable, and unbelievable but blessed and beautiful salvation came straight out of the dawn. Except for pilots, cadets, mechanics, and aircraft maintenance crews, all the personnel of the Reno base were to be transferred pending future reassignment to a camp across the mountains in California, departure taking place company by company, to begin on Monday, July 5. Men able to provide individual transport were advised to apply for detached travel papers, each to later receive per diem reimbursement of expenses.

I found Hanno in the confusion of preparedness, unembarrassed this time, and said, "Couldn't we wangle something to go together in the Ford?"

"You stole my idea," he said. "I already studied the map, and we're headed to some way station of the pony express called Fresno. Two days'd do it. Technically we're allowed to leave anytime we're ready. I've already got my papers. You ask your pal Karlo."

"Oh, sure," Karlo said, "any kid got the gall you got you could take detached travel to the goddamned moon and likely make it and get a medal for the fun of it."

I offered my best smile.

"Get along with you!" he exclaimed. "And mind you stay out of trouble. Keep an eye on your wristwatch too 'cause in three days you're

AWOL." He gave me the thumbs-up of the emperor for a lucky gladiator.

We drove away into the new sunlight two days later, alone on the
road for a long time, wartime shortage of gas thwarting civilian travel.
No trooper this time either.

The straightaway was empty south of Carson City on the way to
Minden when a grasshopper blizzard fell out of a sky suddenly gone all
wiggly black. Flying, impenetrable downpouring of billions of winged
insects crashing down like thunder onto the Ford's metallic skin, windshield wipers powerless to cleave through the glutinous crust of dying
insects, and a noisome, heaving debris of squishy orthoptera six inches
deep under our tires set the car to shuddering left and right onto the
shoulders of the highway, so Hanno went slower and slower, furiously
gripping the wheel, swearing, with headlights little good against the
insect storm. And the stench was sickening as some hoppers got in
the windows before we could close them, flew in our faces, and I tried
to bat them down and squash them, my hands like glue with their
tobacco-colored juice.

"Locusts," said Hanno. "A plague of locusts. Like something out
of the Bible."

No, I thought, not a biblical blight or scourge visited upon us.
Something far older, wonderful, and legendary. Like Alexander the
Great and his beloved Hephaistion cantering through the Bactrian
ravines on their way to conquer the world.

Then just as suddenly the sky became marvelously empty, as if the
otherworldy storm of bugs had been but the imagination of an ancient storyteller.

We got out of the car to try to clean away some of the disgusting grasshopper corpses, but it was hopeless without water, so we
had to drive on thirty, forty miles before reaching a makeshift service
station.

When the fierce-faced woman attendant came from her shack, she
gasped. "Hoppers," she shrieked. "Merciful God, keep 'em away from
here. Can eat an acre to the bone in five minutes."

Hanno said he thought they were headed north, and she sighed,
clasping skeletal hands in prayerful supplication.

Anyway, there was lots of water. We washed the car over and
around, back to front, in and out, more than once till it recovered its

true-blue personality, washed our hands and faces too, bought some gas from the lady, and set out anew, having put the insect blizzard into the lockbox of memory.

The mountains above loomed beautifully in the noonday heaven, the highest snowfields as pristine up there as the world on the first morning, man and woman guiltless still in the Garden. On a flowery downslope we came on a ramshackle eatery, had cheeseburgers there bathed in ketchup, peaches the size of baseballs, jelly doughnuts, and paper cups of springwater from a stoneware jug, and patriotic chitchat from the proprietor, all for a dollar fifty.

"You see," said Hanno, "it pays to be servicemen."

"Oh, well," I said.

We drove on for a time in silence. A time, I felt, rather longer than freedom called for. It was *the* silence I regretted, not *his*. His silence, because it was his, I worshiped, because I worshiped him, beside whom nevertheless I sat in the tenseness of fear he might feel a quiver of reprehensible adoration. The fear was opportune, because I felt my toes might already be damp from the fateful flow of the Rubicon. So, after all, the least I could do was keep silent. What craze possessed me I naturally can't say, for very soon I broke our silence by saying, "Maybe I should drive for a while."

"Well," said Hanno, "I'll be all right with the driving. I know where we're going."

To be driven by him in his direction was all right, of course, as long as he was. Whether or not he knew where we were going, nothing on earth could have made me happier than to go there with him.

Coming down into a wrinkle of greenery called Meadow View, we were welcomed by a barbecue café, went in there, and ate spareribs with our fingers. Still farther down the valley widened with citrus groves on either side, and there was a sign pointing off to the right for Sutter Creek. We didn't go there.

Twilight the color of his eyes had begun gathering cloudscapes in the west. Presently we came to a place evocative of major catastrophe, a very ordinary little town called San Andreas, epicenter presumably of the famous, ominous fault, disequilibrium of the earth's surface causing frequent earthquakes, some of them disasters, as at Frisco in '06.

Hanno said, "You sleep easy in a place that's risky. I like that," and jumped out of the car in front of a B and B, ran inside, came back after

ninety seconds, saying, "Nothing in there for us," and drove straight
out of town.

Place-names in that part of California may have been intended to
provoke the reflections of passersby because the town due south of
San Andreas was called Angels Camp. Hanno laughed out loud. "Not
the camp we're headed for," he puffed, giving the Ford a meaningful
burst of speed, and we were gone almost before we'd been there.

Driving on in the graying dusk, we came to Modesto, and this time
he said, "Right! Modesty's our name, isn't it, Jim?"

What—who?—was I to say?

There was a genuine hotel. The Modesto. Hanno said he'd check
it out, went inside without asking me to check anything, came back in
ninety seconds, and his snow white smile announced that the accommodations were acceptable. We fetched musette bags from the rumble
seat and went upstairs. The room was spacious, the vast bed also, and
there was actually a bathroom with a tub on claw-feet.

Across the road awaited a genuine restaurant, swordfish, spuds,
sponge cake with icing. A neon sign nearby offered COCKTAILS, so
Hanno said, "How about we have a couple before turning in?"

"Not for me. Sorry, but last time I fucked up. Don't want to be a
spoilsport."

"Forget it," he said. "Anyway, we're all right."

"Sure," I said, "we are."

The bathtub beckoned, first real bath since—since I'd volunteered
to become somebody else. He told me to go ahead. A voluptuous
luxuriance, the water enveloping my nakedness so seductive, eyes tight
shut, then intimidating; suddenly the imminence of the bed made the
water run cold around my feet. I climbed out in a hurry, toweled
down, and pulled on my undies. His lay on the bed, the bedclothes
already turned back. He was naked, going in for his bath with a grin
like the lion tamer bowing to applause.

And I couldn't help myself, knowing it was worse than anything
in the world. I snapped up his shorts and pressed them to my face,
breathing in his odor, his whole being through the fabric, I felt, still
warm, deeply into my lungs, deep into the farthest reaches of the physical self, and shuddered with the ecstatic folly, the fear of this swollen
and delirious excitement—oh, my God!—and surrender, terrified he'd

catch me at it—and if he did!—trembling to put back his underwear precisely as I'd found it, clasping my hands onto myself as if to hide the awful evidence, drawing up above my piercing shame the secretive sheets.

When Hanno came out from his bath, all lustrous inside that magnificent skin, I could almost pretend to be barely awake, sighing, and I said, "Hi, pal. Pleasant dreams."

"Oh, yeah," he said, lying down next to me, "and all those hoppers eat an acre in five minutes. And Moses made the waters into dry land. All those dreams of milk and honey, *nicht wahr?*," drawing up tight above us the bed's benevolent covers, flicking off the overhead light and the room fleeing into potential anticipation. With which he exhaled aloud very slowly, as if to rise to a summit of release, turned ever so gently beside me, and his long, svelte leg touched mine all the way down to my foot.

Terrified for fear he'd feel me trembling, I tried to paralyze my body, all of it from my hair to my toenails, and my entrails too, tensed with the certainty I'd have to sustain this tension through the farthest limits of the night, waiting for God to put him to sleep, pretending all the time to have cheated the dark of compliance. So I waited, and the ability to wait became the immeasurable gauge of my capacity to live outside myself, inert as a stone. And what happened was that my love for him overpowered my lust for him. And eventually his breathing did answer my prayer to be saved from the moment of fear and longing, and his leg no longer touched mine, though the swollen erotic ache still pulsed oppressively all the same.

Nonetheless I drowsed. They say that no matter how fitfully you sleep you actually sleep even when you're lying awake all night long. That must be so, because when I came to in the crocus-colored morning hotel room, I was alone in the bed, Hanno all dressed in uniform sitting on a redwood chair beside the open window and smoking a cigarette.

"Pop to," he said, "brush teeth, shave, and there's a breakfast eatery across the street. I'll meet you in ten minutes. I have to check the oil and water. In this heat I could boil over." He stood up to go to the door, put on his cap, and nodded as he went out, leaving behind no intimacy.

After grapefruit, muffins, the marmalade, and the talk of Virginia City, of other days, other histories, and Asia, the Cape of Good Hope, and the movie version of *Of Human Bondage*, it turned out that Fresno was no more than a hundred miles away, and we were ready to go.

"Have to settle up at the hotel," I said.

Hanno said, "It's taken care of."

"But we have always gone fifty-fifty. I can pay my way."

"Taken care of, I said," he said.

"But you've taken care of everything," I protested with faint persuasion. "All the driving, the grasshoppers, and all the rest, Hanno."

"Forget it," he said.

Fresno was a dump, a market town of redwood siding and adverts for the fruitiest tutti-fruit this side of the Sierras. We tried some for lunch after the bologna sandwiches and hearts of San Fernando lettuce. It wasn't bad. There were signs showing the way to our destination, a tent camp on the seedy outskirts along the road to Sequoia Park.

"All those big trees," said Hanno. "They were standing before Aristotle invented science and changed the world."

"Genius always does that," I said.

He stared me in the face but said nothing.

The 856th was bivouacked in an uneven line of pyramidal tents. I unloaded my gear from the foot of the rumble seat, we nodded like the soldiers we were, and he said, "See you around."

"Sure," I said.

Karlo looked me up and down, shrugged, and drawled, "You made it. You're one lucky son of a bitch."

"Why's that?"

"The company's on red alert to ship out to the Pacific."

"Is that so? Where are we going?"

"Classified." He smirked.

"When do we leave?"

"Classified. You'll find out on the day we sail. It won't be long."

"Japs planning to use poison gas, are they?"

"Maybe. Those sneak attack sons of whores, you can count on 'em not to fight fair. A dose of mustard'd be just their style."

"Thanks."

"Anyway, kid, on alert you're excused from KP."

The grunts in my tent groaned when I lugged my stuff inside. I didn't blame them. As the number one complainer of the outfit I received no cheers. Nor was I eager to wait with them for the sickening day when I'd stare with eagle eyes at the Pacific.

Days melted together in the sweltering overheat of July in the San Joaquin Valley as we made ready for the orders that would come unclassified only at the fatal moment, our minds whetted like a felon's awaiting the hangman. While I feverishly searched the sprawl of tents for sight of Hanno, saw him nowhere, and wondered, wondered. What was it? Something wrong? Wrong, that is, beyond the all-encompassing wrong . . .

Then onto the torrid doldrums of contingency came Karlo one morning to say I was wanted on the double in the HQ tent. "Captain Ellis in a snit because he's got to talk to a goof-off like you."

Never before having been summoned before the company commander, I expected the kind of disciplinary reckoning that Karlo might have been reluctant to deliver. The captain sat in a heap of rumpled perspiration behind a messy field desk, an unlit cigar in the corner of his face, fixing a censorious glance onto the soldier at attention. He waited for an electric fan to swivel from side to side, rippling the overflow of sweat, before growling, "At ease."

I drooped.

"You were on detached duty to headquarters at Reno, right?"

"Yes, sir."

"Discharged from there for insubordination. With censure. Right?"

"Yes, sir."

"I'm not surprised. A rotten apple through and through. I received a memorandum to that effect. A lieutenant called Garlington. Saw him in the mess sometimes. A jerk. And when did you apply for ASTP?"

"I never applied for anything, sir. I don't know what that is, sir, ASTP?"

"That so? Well, I've got a paper here says you took an application test for this ASTP. Right?"

"Maybe."

"Maybe, sir! You're speaking to your commanding officer, Private."

"Yes, sir. Sorry, sir. I remember taking an exam. That's all, sir."

"Yeah? For a smart aleck like you, seems maybe you're as smart as you think you are. Got a high grade on that test."

"Gosh!" I exclaimed.

"Sir!" snapped the captain, mopping his face with a wad of soggy tissue.

"Yes, sir. Sorry, sir."

"Well, I have an order here requesting your release from this outfit to travel to Salt Lake City for assignment to some new specialized training program. Well, I can't do that. Would be a dereliction of duty if I did. Company's on red alert for shipping out to the Pacific, and a company on red alert's bound to maintain full strength under all circumstances till embarkation. No loopholes allowed. Understand that, Private?"

"Yes, sir," I assented, swallowing hard.

"You're disappointed."

"Well, sir, I admit a more specialized assignment might be—what can I say?—more challenging."

"That so? Think you have the know-how to take on a he-man challenge, do you? Think you're a better soldier than the hoi polloi? Personally, I don't think you'd be rightly fit to whistle a pig. And I hold your future in my hand. You know that? Right in my hand." And he held out his right hand with a smudge of dusty perspiration in the palm.

"Yes, sir. I know that, sir."

"Well, you can damn well be glad I do. Because I'm going to let you go. I shouldn't. Have to think up some excuse, but I'll find one."

"Thank you, sir," I cried in a burst of bafflement.

"Don't thank me, soldier. You want to thank somebody, thank Sergeant Stojanac. He said to better let you go. But doing you a favor's the last thing I wanted. It's doing the company a favor, because you're a really a rotten apple in a pretty good barrel of soldiers, worst nuisance, smart-ass troublemaker I've come across since I got in the service. So you'll be shipping out to Salt Lake City three days from today, first thing Thursday morning, 22 July. Dismissed."

"Yes, sir," I said, saluted, turned on my toe, and marched out of the tent.

There was Karlo. When I tried to thank him, he said, "Nuts," slapped me on the back, and added, "It's the best thing for you. The poop says we're headed for guard duty and KP till the war's over. So no regrets. Now, take care of your rear end."

Continuing on the lookout for Hanno, I went up and down the rows of tents on the far side of the main highway. He wasn't to be seen, and I started worrying I might not catch him before I had to leave.

It was almost—but luckily not quite—too late when I caught up with him in the oyster-colored twilight of my last day as he strode across the cinder parade ground.

"Hi there!" I called, and when he turned: "I've been looking all over for you."

"Oh, yeah? Well, I've been very busy," he said, a timbre of impatience in his tone.

"Oh? Is something wrong?"

"Wrong?" he repeated, lifting his head. "Wrong? What could possibly be wrong? You're imagining things."

"Sorry. That's not what I meant. Never mind. Only wanted to tell you I've got a new assignment. Out of the eight fifty-sixth. Some specialized training program. Leaving tomorrow morning. I wanted to say goodbye."

"Got another assignment myself. Back east. Not shipping out with CWS either."

"Lucky you. Well then, just wanted to say . . ." I ventured, with sudden faintness of heart. "Wanted to thank you. More than good times, I mean. That is . . . everything, you know, and thanks."

"Forget it," he said.

"Well then, just to say goodbye."

He paused to look with the twilit eyes and turned from the waist up, gazing over his shoulder, and said, "Goodbye." Then he was gone.

I went to my tent and lay on the cot. When one of the creeps came along, telling me it was time for chow, I said I wasn't hungry and please don't turn on the light.

Forget it? His watchwords . . . What precisely was *it*? Was forgetfulness his advice to the guesswork of the future? I promised myself, anyway, that I would never forget, though never then could I have imagined how *much* I would have to remember.

A PFC drove me and my kit to the Fresno railway station. The single coach bound over for Salt Lake City was hitched to the rear of a freight train, destined to be detached in Utah.

Six

AUGUST 1943

The lake was a desolate expanse of dead water, its edges encrusted with drying salt; the city, however, a well-tended locality of ample lawns and dignified residences beneath a well-enameled sky, all comfortably redolent of money. This came as a promising portent, with a freshening breeze down our necks, the good-mannered troop of us, twenty or thirty in a couple of ten-ton trucks. I'd not traveled alone in the stifling day coach en route from Fresno, and we welcomed being greeted by a polite first sergeant to the neat green campus of the University of Utah. It was in the U of U's spacious gymnasium, outfitted with rows of cots, footlockers, desks, chairs, couches, Coke machines, and other conveniences—like leaning towers of textbooks—that we were to be billeted.

After two well-fed days of idling we were summoned to the auditorium, where an obese major got up behind a lectern, whiffled a pile of papers, and told us what we were doing there. Army snafu, rampant as usual, had inducted too many men too quickly, overcrowding barracks but leaving many college dormitories depleted, so some sly general came up with a scheme to do both colleges and soldiers a favor by filling up empty classrooms with GIs who by passing requisite tests had demonstrated a fitness for intellectual calisthenics. In short, we were going back to college.

The name of this deal was Army Specialized Training Program, hereafter ASTP, the U of U having been selected as clearinghouse for prospective trainees from the western third of the United States. And within a week, ten days at the latest, each man would learn his date of departure for the institution of higher learning to which a supposed aptitude suited him.

Meanwhile we were free to wander around town, warned nonetheless to behave with careful decorum, respectful to a T of local mores, especially the virtue of women, their men severely uncharitable toward lapses of courtesy. I, to be sure, didn't care two straws whether a Mormon husband had one wife or twenty, the universe of my mind being measured entirely by the idea of Hanno's bursting through a supernatural door to knock me down again and again and forever into the next world.

Still, I dutifully walked the orderly streets, eyed the conventional dwellings of believers in highly unorthodox liturgical observances. More unorthodox, though—who is to say?—than sexual acts troubling my reveries? I visited the enormous, ostentatious temple to Latter-day Saints, who must have been saintly indeed to feel at home inside an edifice so monstrously vulgar. More credible metaphysical mystique, I thought, dwelt in Grand Central Terminal. The biggest church I'd ever been in, however, this one reawakened longing to see the great monuments to more ecumenical deities worshiped in foreign countries: Westminster Abbey, Notre-Dame de Paris, Saint Peter's, the Parthenon.

Impatient to get out of Utah, I had to wait thirteen days before my name was posted on a list of men assigned to a college in Boston, Massachusetts. Further cross-continent travel by train was not appealing, but the destination was. Boston, where I'd never been, scene of the seditious tea party, adjacent to a great university, locus of outstanding art museums, a celebrated symphony orchestra, Old Bailey burlesque hall, and habitat of abiding aristocracy.

Yes, the prospect of being in Boston, though Hanno would not be—Hanno being somewhere where I'd never see him again—was properly thrilling. Had I known what variety of thrills Boston would provide, I'd have done better to look forward to its contingencies with circumspection.

Seven

SEPTEMBER 1943–JANUARY 1944

The eastward train ride was less luxurious than the westward. No Pullman, no Billy, no poetic license. Sorrow at having left behind what lay behind. Some anticipation, to be sure, of seizing the opportunity of tomorrow.

My traveling companions were a jolly lot, an improvement on the guitar-playing, craps-shooting, Katzenjammer Kid malcontents of your by-the-numbers barracks. Not exactly supercilious bookworms or varsity sweater jocks, still they were college kids, complimenting one another on their collective escape from GI uniformity. One of the fellows I chatted with allowed that the beau monde in Boston was only too glad to remember Pearl Harbor because cocktail parties on Beacon Hill had gotten a lot better once the war was on. I had little to offer by way of participation in this anonymous vernacular but took note of the civilized pitch of talk among the thirty or forty soldiers in the car, whose leisurely gestures and confident smiles said nothing at all about foxholes or hand grenades.

Unwashed, unshaven, untoothbrushed, and undernourished, exhausted but excited, I got down from the train at the Back Bay Station. A friendly lieutenant on the platform seemed almost flattered by the smelly, dirty presence of all these privates, stuttering repeatedly as he read out the roster of those to travel to this or that locale in one of the waiting trucks. I fatalistically lugged my gear to the last one in the line.

The cocktail party connoisseur rode in the truck with me. A lanky, black-eyed, falcon-nosed fellow lolling on the backbreaking bench with patrician flash, evidently acquainted with the area, he said we were headed for Chestnut Hill, adding that that meant BC, which didn't mean Before Christ, by the way, but Boston College, though you might call it Ballistic Christ because it's run by Jesuit troops in skirts.

A small soldier crouched at the rear, half smile, half sneer on his heavy mouth, remarked that a person might think he was listening to the devil Luther.

The critic retorted that that was possible, yes, as the commonwealth hadn't said hello to Rome for three hundred years, and the Iroquois, you know, they were sensible people, and when they saw those paleface evangelists dressed up as women, well, they built a nice big bonfire and burned up a batch of them.

Must have been a really heartwarming auto-da-fé, said the crouching soldier.

The BC campus occupied a green, well-disciplined knoll among the genteel residences of Chestnut Hill, a prudent remove from downtown Boston. Our truck deposited us in front of an unsmiling pseudo-Gothic edifice called St. Mary's Hall, our dormitory. In the foyer a morose sergeant said we'd best go upstairs, find a bunk in any room where a bunk was free, bunk in with buddies, if any, stow gear, chow across the road at six o'clock.

Loath to risk another Teves fuckup or Hanno fantasy, I followed the conversation from the truck to Room 104, snagged the lower bunk by the window. There were three double-deckers, made up with olive drab blankets and *white* sheets, schoolboy desks and chairs, two deep closets and wooden, not wire, coat hangers, bright brass reading lamps, and leather wastebaskets with *BC* and a heavy gilt cross embossed.

We were safe and sound back in college, civilian life only a whim away. And my companions, Aaron Randolph and Tony Pelatti, would become my best friends throughout the Boston College adventure. Aaron the fancier of Beacon Hill cocktail parties, Tony the applauder of Jesuits burned alive by Indians. Two others moved in the next day: George Jansen and Billy Brush, bunking by the door, companionable but never friends because they were entirely absorbed in each other.

So there we were, and that day was the first of September, a Wednesday, and the coming weekend, of course, none other than the overexciting Labor Day weekend.

My parents, I knew, in order to logically celebrate that indolent holiday would still be in Paris. Not the City of Light, destination of my dreams, no, only a small hilltop town in the state of Maine, first locality in America named after France's capital in order to acknowledge help in our Revolution. Of all the places in my homeland, this was the only one I ever loved with a love that in all my life was comparable to my lifelong love for the great city of the same name in which, as it happens, I sit writing these words today, six decades later.

What on earth more natural, then, than to take advantage of the providential holiday by transporting myself to Paris? Mother and Dad had long ago bought a summertime home there. The town slumbered beneath a shimmering canopy of elms, its eighteenth-century houses largely occupied by well-heeled vacationers. In Paris, in short, dwelt escape from restraint, discovery of delight, and more, much more than ever the Count of Monte Cristo had stumbled upon.

Now, refugees from war-racked Europe had come crowding to America. Accommodations for so many being scarce, my parents, who had space to spare and a sense of civic responsibility, had taken in a couple. Monsieur et Madame Yakovleff had consequently come to stay in Englewood, and they traveled along to Maine in the summer. He was tall, stooped, despondent; she, younger, lively, spirit unbroken by cruel circumstance. The summer before my lunatic enlistment I had spent many vacation hours under the grape arbor chatting with Madame Yakovleff about French poets, painters, and politicians, speaking in French and acquiring consequently in that evocative tongue a certain conversational fluency, which fell in very nicely with my hankering after an exotic destiny and which, in fact, virtually determined it.

To resume my talks with a lady who came from the great Paris was an opportunity irresistibly alluring. I'd be glad to see Mother and Dad again, both having been thoughtful in sending letters of good cheer, let alone expedient checks, to a faraway soldier. I decided to try for a pass and to hitchhike my way home for the famous weekend. The pass was easily granted after I had heard an orotund introductory address by Father O'Brien, a portly priest in a billowy black habit.

From BC to Paris was only about 150 miles as the crow flies. An army uniform in wartime gave wings to unlikely hitchhikers. Two or three rides, I optimistically expected, ought to do it, and they did, the last leaving me in front of Paris's Baptist Church.

I walked along Main Street past the rows of Federal houses under the elms and found my mother among the phlox. Our embrace in the garden was a happy surprise after military forfeiture of expressive feeling. Dad came from the side porch with a pair of pruning shears, and we shook hands.

Around the croquet lawn Monsieur Yakovleff glumly ambled, followed zigzag by Flip-Flop, our pet rabbit he'd trained to keep him company in exile. Madame sat in a canvas camp chair under the grape arbor, as usual, a portrait of mature composure in the face of adversity. When I went to kiss her on both cheeks—*à la française*—she held in her lap a copy of *Sagesse*, and I thought she was wise indeed to seek the wisdom of quietude in the literature of her homeland as it lay under the dominion of diligent torturers.

I told Mother and Dad the tale of my devil-may-care escape from the implausible bouts of chemical warfare caused by an urbane display of intellectual know-how. Dad said that this was first rate and maybe I'd get into officers' training school. "Not if I can help it," I rejoined, adding with aplomb, "Everybody hates officers," forgetting that he'd been an air corps captain twenty-five years before.

I strolled with Madame Yakovleff through the tall grass of a nearby meadow, talking about the *other* Paris, the Café de la Paix, the Louvre, the Panthéon. Her daughter, Claudine, who lived on the avenue de Versailles, had aspired to be a ballet dancer but married a dentist instead. I must not fail to write letters, she insisted, telling her stories about the army. I promised to remember.

On the last morning I gathered handfuls of wild strawberries along the roadside, ate a couple of dozen right there, and stood for a while looking at the faraway White Mountains, musing. Of Hanno. By what wonderful benevolence of the supernatural might *he* materialize in this Parisian refuge? The twilit eyes. Last Chance Saloon. Virginia City. Forget it. Forget it?

I didn't have to hitchhike back to Boston. Dad drove me in the green touring car as far as Portland, where I took the direct Pullman to North Station.

The Army Specialized Training Program at BC was specialized mainly in that its curriculum consisted of a single subject: France, its geography, history, political administration, population, natural resources, industrial potential, economy, social structure, provincial organization, regional customs, cultural values, architectural styles, languages, dialects, art, literature, music, theater, cinema, foodstuffs, beverages, and heaven only knows what else, including the abundance of public toilets and their convenience as clandestine meeting places for secret agents.

Our professors were Jesuits, arrogant, autocratic, red-faced, overweight men in widows' attire, none of them friendly either with their students or with jollity. The single exception to this reign of pedagogical severity was a civilian teacher of colloquial French, Monsieur Gaston de la Hubaudière, a portly gent of waxed mustachios, well dressed in a velveteen smoking jacket and pearl-pinned pearl gray stock, a figure of fun even before relating, as he often did without prompting but with sniggering gestures of emphasis, how very nearly he'd been castrated by a boche bayonet at Chemin des Dames—*presque chatré, mes enfants*—during the Great War. He also confided that the most alluring prostitutes—*les filles de joie*—in Boston were to be found in the merry-go-round bar of the Copley Plaza Hotel, better known for good reason as the Costly Pleasure. We had a lot of fun with La Hu, probably got more practical information from him about life in France, plus off-color advice for off-duty fun, than from all the hermaphrodites in black, as Tony spitefully described the diddlers of the Society of Jesus.

BC must have lost all its undergraduates to the draft, because when we got there, St. Mary's Hall was stark empty, and we never saw a single male under fifty-five around the campus. A couple of hundred soldiers, devil-may-care and profane, as soldiers will be, filled up the three floors with replacements by no means eager to gratify the BC raison d'être of providing missionaries to save from hellfire people not yet graced by the good word of the Lord God's vicar on earth. Thus, with glum resignation, the Jesuit priests permitted us by and large to behave like normal college students, irresponsible, gleeful refugees from military ritual, allowed to rove fancy-free wherever we chose on every weekend from 6:00 p.m. on Friday till Sunday at the same hour. By bus or by thumb the ride from BC to Boston Common took thirty-five minutes.

Boston, America's patrician city par excellence—pace Philadelphia—seemed to bode well for fulfillment of pleasures naturally sought after by any young man who'd set his sights on satisfactions of the spirit. Boston, to be sure, was not for nothing known as the Athens of America, and one did well to be mindful that the cultural capital of antiquity had bequeathed to world literature not only *The Republic* but also *The Symposium*, the dramas of Sophocles, the comedies of Aristophanes and had honored as heroes such diverse figures as Alcibiades, Pericles, *and* Harmodius and Aristogeiton, those youthful Athenian lovers celebrated by Thucydides for having slain the tyrant who offended the honor of their love. All this borne in mind, the potential of Boston to provide Socratic enlightenment to American youths called for—shall we say?—reflection.

It was to introduce myself to America's most prestigious place of learning, Harvard University, that I walked across the Charles River footbridge that September Saturday, the water like ripplets of mica glittering under the breeze and some impressionist sailboats tacking upriver, buildings of Georgian brick, white cupolas on the far bank, the town of Cambridge. I'd liked to think I would have been happy at college there, where Henry James began writing, and maybe my shame might have found secret sympathy among soigné lovers of literature. Probably too soigné to tolerate a bumptious nobody capable of such poetic indecency as "Beethoven's Hands" and, anyway, a nonentity always ready to belittle his own aspirations.

I humbly wandered around the Yard, enviously watching the well-bred undergraduates in their J. Press sport coats and occasional servicemen wearing tailor-made uniforms, none of whom gave me the eye. Down an adjacent side street I found open a bookstore called the Grolier. In the window were piles of *The Hamlet* and *The Last Tycoon*. I went inside, the threshold giving a lift to my step, though this refuge from the madding crowd could not be expected to confer the consequences of Newbegin's. No matter. I'd not finished reading *Ulysses*, but it had done for me, and to me, all it could *not* to mention *Werther*!

An amiable lady with gray hair in a bun said to make myself at home, and more than enough was there with which to make something of myself. I came upon a book entitled *Three Soldiers*. The sharp coincidence of the title struck a chord, struck it so strongly as to deride the very idea of coincidence, as if that book, and no other, had purposefully been placed for me in that shop.

The story, when I'd read it, turned out to be powerfully relevant, but it bore little likeness to the sentimental fable by Remarque. The three soldiers are comradely, yes, but American, not at all prey to the militaristic tradition of Teutonic knights that bucked up Erich, Otto, and Gottfried against the humiliation of their homeland. Dos Passos's villains are the army and the mindless, degrading vicissitudes of warfare that destroy the creative nature of his hero. This denouement, certainly, seemed to be composed on purpose to speak to my situation, my longings, and my chances.

Aaron Randolph turned out to be a well-read admirer of Gibbon, for example, keen on the history of his hometown, which included cocktail parties sans cocktails, too an alumnus-to-be of Harvard, which he'd left to join the army, sometime enthusiast also of the Boston Symphony, of which his mother was a member of the board of directors and friend of Koussevitzky's. Aaron liked his booze, a glut of good food, and the bar of the Costly Pleasure, yes, but there was also the good alternative of debunking Carl Sandburg and Grant Wood or going crazy over *Gatsby*.

So we got to be friends before the end of September, Aaron and I. The maple trees were as red as rubies, and he took me to dinner at Locke-Ober's Restaurant, where we stuffed ourselves on oysters Rockefeller and other outré delicacies. His mother and sister, and he on the weekends, lived in a tall brick house with a bow front up Beacon Hill on Pinckney Street right by Louisburg Square, where all the grandest mansions stared at one another across a stately garden.

I never once saw Aaron's sister, Julia, who from the age of fifteen, so said her brother, had spoken only to the Cabots and the Lowells, while their father, Salmon Randolph IV, had dropped dead one day as he buttoned his spats, aged just fifty, felled by the sheer taedium vitae of his distinction.

The first time I went to Pinckney Street for lunch Aaron met me at the door with a bottle of gin cradled in his left arm. He said, "It's so smooth you don't need vermouth to make a perfect martini."

Mrs. Randolph came into the library while her son was readying the shaker, said, "How'dyuhdo," clasped my hand as if it belonged to her. She was tall, platinum hair worn short, powdered face, rheumy eyes, gracious nearly to the limit of etiquette, accepted a cocktail in a gold-rimmed goblet. We sat down opposite a couple of family portraits, aged dames in lace kerchiefs scowling at posterity. Conversation automatic about current events, Naples, Kiev, the duce's mountaintop breakout, and Mrs. Randolph recalled that at the party after his speech at Harvard, Winston had said Joe Kennedy was despised by all honorable people in London. As if the prime minister had in fact said so to her, which seemed perfectly plausible. We had another cocktail, and it's true they were marvelously smooth.

The dining room was long and narrow, more portraits, a sideboard loaded down with silver. Luncheon was served by a silent colored woman in a black silk uniform, and it was rack of lamb, floating island, and a wine that after two martinis was *too* smooth.

Afterward in the drawing room I was drunk, thought I'd never been so afloat on waves of perfection, if only Hanno could have been there, yes. And—my God!—at the end of the room in the bow window stood a harp, a fantastically beautiful contraption, carved frame golden in the autumn light, and I couldn't help myself, exclaiming, "What a beauty! What a marvelous thing!," waving my hand at it as if the others hadn't noticed it.

"Mother plays it," said Aaron. "If you ask her very pretty please, maybe she'll play 'Alexander's Ragtime Band.'"

"Wretched boy," said Mrs. Randolph, and, turning to me: "Are you musical, Mr. Lord?"

"Well . . . I like the classics, that is. I'd love to hear you play."

"I've been practicing a bit by Albinoni. Not too difficult. But I'm not Lily Laskine, you must understand."

She sat on a gilded chair in front of the window, her harp leaning into her shoulder, fingers hovering above the strings and music alive in the room like celestial harmonies. And then after an infinity of melody I patted my hands in the untouchable hush.

Aaron said, "Mama, that was, you know, it was really lovely. If Koussi had a grain of sense, he'd hire you in a minute."

"Foolish lad," said Mrs. Randolph, coming back to us through the silence her fingertips had left behind her, smiling, and added, "You boys had best go out for a good brisk walk. We wouldn't want the Holy Office to be examining two gay blades for sobriety, now would we?"

She kissed her son politely on his cheek, touched my hand, calluses on her fingertips, and said, "I trust we'll see you again, Mr. Lord."

Out in the street, gay blades really tipsy, we swung down Beacon Street and along Arlington past the Public Garden, where teenagers were cutting up in the swan boats, and I asked Aaron, "What in the world is the Holy Office?"

"Oh, a Vatican outfit masquerading as a sort of cover-up for the Inquisition. You know, Murder Incorporated in case you're a heretic. Our little roommate Tony probably thinks they've got him on their hit list."

"He's no lover of the Catholic Church, that's sure. Says the pope's only infallible about being in the wrong, hellfire for sinners except if they're beating up on the Jews."

Our walk as brisk as Mrs. Randolph had prescribed, a freshet of chill moving from the nearby Atlantic, and when we came to Copley Square and the Public Library, Aaron said, "Costly Pleasure straight on. How about a last one before the hermaphrodites smell our breath?"

I said, "Not for me. Too woozy for the merry-go-round. And watch out for the filles de joie. Might give you a dose of the clap."

"Don't panic," said Aaron.

We caught the bus from Back Bay.

Indian summer was a little late that year, bringing lambent afternoons, miniature whirlwinds of withering leaves, misty sunsets, wild evenings. To one side of the campus lay a strip of lawn secluded behind rhododendron hedges where I liked to linger now and then alone in the amethyst twilight, a select hideaway for meetings with myself. Then one evening an awareness that I was not alone stole across the grass: a figure in uniform, someone I knew by way of hello only, a PFC from down the hall you ran into in the washroom named Jerry Weinbaum, not in any of our study groups, a guy who laughed a lot, tall, not bad-looking. He said, "Hi there. Be dark in a few minutes. Mind if I walk along?"

"Course not. How you doing?"

"I make out. You?"

"Oh, sure. Everything's okay."

"Find Boston friendly then, do you?"

"I do, yes. Nice people. Make you feel right at home."

"Already found yourself a friend then?"

"One of my roommates, yes. Comes from Boston. His mother invited me to lunch last Sunday, played the harp; it was beautiful."

"Say, that must have been all right. Nice lady, huh? Don't hang out with the boys, though, do the bars, drinking, you know, hail-fellow-well-met thing?"

"Not really. I'm not too keen on the USO type, tell the truth."

"No kidding. Who is? That's not what I meant. I meant making out with guys you really get along with, you know, guys like us."

Then we'd come to the end of the lawn, so I hesitated, not knowing where such desultory talk could go—besides, it was getting dark—not giving a damn, pointless to chat with someone with whom I had nothing in common.

He said, "Do you mind if I ask you a question?"

"Not at all. Shoot."

"Are you gay?"

"Funny thing," I said. "That lady I mentioned, she said I was a gay blade. She meant somebody without a care in the world, I guess."

"Come on"—he cut in brusquely—"that's not what I'm talking about. I spotted you from the beginning. Takes one to know one. So fess up. I'm not the police. Wouldn't come on to you if I wasn't gay myself. Relax."

He put his hand on my shoulder while I was numbed by surprise and moved his fingertips gently to the nape of my neck, tickling my hair till I shivered and my legs were like danger in deep water.

"You like to make love to boys, don't you?" he said, and when in the trembling silence I didn't say no, he added, "Do you mind if I kiss you?" and when I didn't say no, he did.

And I kissed him back, letting go of time, place, myself, the swelling seizure of sensation, surrender, sudden nothingness of everything else, no longer knowing what or where or why, and his hands were all over me, fumbling with my clothes, nor did I understand how we were lying on the cool grass in the abrupt dark, so I mumbled, "But somebody might see us," in an ecstasy of fear.

"This is your first time, isn't it?" he said in my ear. "I can tell. I'll show you what it's like. You'll like it. Just let yourself go, baby."

So I did, and he did, and I did.

The ascent into oblivion was utter caesura of self. I choked against the lament of pleasure, the shock of life, as if I'd waited for it forever, neither vile nor frightening, it bit me exactly where—and how—the heartbeat of sensation, thoughtless and pure, drove my blood, the freedom of it ecstatic. So this was what it was all about. Climactic convulsion of everything. Yes. And I thought, "If only."

But there I was with Jerry in the confusion of our bodies in the grass, now pitch dark, and our clothes were a mess.

He said, "So you don't know what it means to be gay?"

"Apparently not."

"It's a password. We use it between ourselves so other people won't know we're talking about being queer. You don't know a thing about the gay scene, do you?"

"I guess I don't."

"How old are you?"

"Twenty."

"Late starter. High time you got to know the world you're going to spend your life in. I can give you a shove in that direction if you want. I'm not looking for a sex slave. You were a sweet fuck, innocent for twenty, that's all. Don't get me wrong, but you've got a lot to learn. I go into Boston weekends. Can show you around. You'll be surprised. I can give you the shove. You sink or swim, that's your business. Okay?"

"I guess," I said.

"Friday then. See you at the bus stop six-thirty, forty-five. Button up your pants, sweetheart."

Was what had happened apparent to my roommates? Aaron? Tony? They naturally knew that homosexuality was a quotient of the human equation, Oscar Wilde having taken good care to publicize the facts. Jerry considered me innocent; I could play that part for my friends breezily. When Aaron inquired about the weekend, I said I was going to cruise around town on my own, never in my jejune insouciance fancying that that described exactly what I'd do.

Jerry led me along past the Public Garden to the Hotel Statler, telling me never to forget how to get there, as this would be my jumping-off place in Boston.

The lobby was long and high, expensive, gold-plated, busy with wartime visitors. This was where guests registered for the weekend. It paid off to reserve a room in advance, Jerry said, because when cruising the bar, you'd want someplace to do it if you pick up a trick.

There was a portal to the right of the rear, the bar immediately beyond. It was packed with servicemen, several rows deep, standing against the long, crescent-shaped bar, too many to count, 100 maybe, maybe 150, most of them drinking beer from the bottle, loud with flighty talk and piercing laughter. Crowded tight together, jostling back and forth, not one lady or girl among them, only a handful of civilians.

"Yes," said Jerry, "they're all gay."

"But this is a public place. People who don't know could come in, couldn't they?"

"Oh, yeah. Straights stray in. It happens. But usually they notice something and stray right out again. I mean, we have a right to lebensraum, haven't we? Anyway, there's a straight seating area right up there to keep things looking honest."

Back a polite distance from the bar, up three or four steps behind a metal grille, were a lot of small tables, clients seated there, a good proviso of women among them, waiters in snappy jackets dancing around to serve them.

"But don't they know?" I wondered. "Can't they tell?"

"Hell, no. Decent people don't want to know. And anyway, they couldn't tell if their grandmothers sold snuggle on the side. It's an obstacle course getting to the bar to get served. Use your elbows. But watch out for your pants. It can get real feely in this crowd."

Elbows, knees, and "sorry" got us through. There were three bartenders. Jerry asked for Rheingold. Hanno would have said *das Rheingold*. I said Tom Collins.

A sailor in white sidled alongside me and said, "Hey, cutie, you must be new. I could blow you right out of the water."

Jerry said, "Fishing prohibited."

The sailor turned his back.

I said, "Is it always like this?"

"Wait till later. Later it's Revere Beach on the Fourth of July."

Some of the servicemen were exciting to look at, and some of them obviously knew it, glancing round the crowd with chancy eyes, semi-smiles of semiacquiescence, and the aura pervasive throughout was edgy-sexy readiness for anything. I'd never known the like or known myself like an element of it. I got another Collins.

An English marine lance corporal in dress uniform wedged along in front of me, said, "Hi there, Yankee Doodle, what say we make out belowstairs in the gents'?," his fingers fooling free and easy with the buttons of my fly.

Of course in the confines of the crowd it would have been difficult to see what he was doing, and he was good-looking enough, ruddy, bright-eyed, brawny in the tight-fitting uniform, and the incursion of his fingers roused me all right, though his breath in my face was brewery, and I knew perfectly well what the gents' meant; it was shocking that I wasn't all that shocked, yet I couldn't let myself go so easily so soon, and I brushed aside his hand, saying—but with a gasp—"Sorry. Some other time."

"You Yanks do play hard to get," said the marine.

Jerry was chatting up a lieutenant in pinks—yes, there were a few officers—but I bumped between and said, "Can't we get out of here? I need some air."

"Christ," Jerry gurgled, "hold on, will you? Let me say a word to Glen for a minute. I'll catch up with you in the lobby."

A nocturnal sweetness had come into the cooling air. We walked up Tremont opposite the Common, to Schrafft's, and had some pot roast and blueberry pie. Jerry told me I'd better settle down and learn what I wanted to do about what was inside my pants or I might turn out to be one sad and lonely faggot on the losing end of what was a fairly raw deal anyway. It was common sense speaking, I knew, but I felt the gnaw of worry I'd be found wanting when called to act on the lesson of my sexual ABCs.

"Back to the Statler?" I asked when we came out onto the sidewalk, a nip in the air. We were in the arms of October.

"Better try something else," said Jerry. "Now you know your way to the Statler you can touch base there anytime. Now's a good time for the Napoleon."

"Napoleon? As in Bonaparte? You must be kidding."

"Hell, no. Shit, ever since Alex the Great and his boyfriend what's his name, groovy guys in uniform are doable, and anyway, Alex didn't go in much for clothes, did he? Boy, oh, boy, those ancient Greeks really camped it up. The Napoleon's a gay club. Right down here."

In the darkling side street where dead cars cluttered the gloom, the houses all looked stunted, their doors steeped in secrets, to which our presence brought no enlightenment, and I wondered how the hell I was going to get out of this.

He pressed a button, a piercing light lit the doorway, a peephole popped open, and he said, "Hi there, honey child, it's your uncle Wiggly."

Honey child was a black six-footer wearing a purple T-shirt and apple green skullcap. "Hello, auntie," he said, "you bring me chitlins and okra, you come in, you bring your boyfriend."

"Just say my friend's friend's all," said Jerry, "trust him in your hands, honey, you give him a push. Me, I've got a date, gonna boogie with a looie at the Ritz."

"Yeow, boy, you do it," said the black man, catching me by the sleeve, "and we take care of friend's friend."

Jerry pinched my behind. "You're on your own, Jim. You'll be okay. See you back at St. Mary's." And he skipped away into the incautious dark.

Honey child led me inside. A staircase with a cherry red carpet and a pink droplet chandelier. He said, "You trot upstairs now like a good boy, find yourself any friend, you hear me, so hustle," and he gently prodded the small of my back.

In the high long room upstairs a comfortable crowd of men eddied along the bar; there was a huge painting of Napoleon astride a charger and a baby white upright piano against the other wall, a bald gent in a tuxedo tickling the ivories and singing "Mad About the Boy" in whispering falsetto.

"Are you?" someone murmured in my ear.

"What?" I exclaimed, turning. "What is it?"

"Like that?" said the stranger, a dark-haired, tan-cheeked young fellow in civvies, nodding at the singer, who was still singing about being mad about a boy.

"Are you?" asked my interlocutor again.

The entertainer flung up his hands, turning to face the crowd and gave a seated bow to the sputtering of applause, his face florid with makeup, mascara and rouge, and some of the red had rubbed off onto his teeth so that the show business smile was a bit Bela Lugosi as Dracula.

"Well," insisted my neighbor, "are you?"

Then I looked at him. Tall, slender, in a navy blue suit, eyes amber with an intense sapphire tint but smiling, friendly, dimpled cheeks, quite collected and calm. So I said, "Well, am I?"

"Mad about a boy? Must be, I'd think, hanging out in this place, no?"

I said, "Must be."

"Shall we drink to it?"

"Why not?"

He walked to the bar, his gait, it seemed, slightly askew, not quite a limp but not the automatic stride of youth either. It gave him an air, somewhat distingué, older than his age, attractive. Like a diplomat, I thought, on duty at the consulate in Palermo or Lahore. He ordered scotch and soda for two with that suave authority.

I said, "Why is this place called the Napoleon?"

"Why not? All his soldiers were in love with him. Stationed in Boston, are you?"

"Chestnut Hill, Boston College. Special training program."

"Cushy. Better off than GI Joe slogging around in the Italian rain."

"You bet." I laughed. "And you? You live here?"

"That's right. Just around the corner, as a matter of fact. I suppose you're wondering, aren't you? People do. I must be the only civilian in here. All these beautiful uniforms, and look at me."

What I saw was a handsome man about twenty-five years old, wearing a white shirt and a necktie matching his eyes. "So what?"

"I'm four-F. You may have noticed. The limp. Could call it the FDR exemption. Caught polio as a kid. Lucky, though. Only one leg affected, and not too bad. I can hop, but I can't skip."

"Well, then you're better off than the president. Lots of jobs in civvy street these days anyway. So you build airplanes or something?"

He smiled and offered me a cigarette. He was in control, as if appraising the terms of a plenipotentiary transaction. "I'm a sort of architect, pretty good with blueprints, you know. What's your name?"

"Jim," I said, taken aback by the quick simplicity of his superiority. "Jim Lord."

"Nice name. I like it," he said. "Jim. Mine's Gordon. Haney. Gordon Haney. You're on your own, are you?"

"Sure," I said, thinking Jerry would have told me, in any case, I'd better be. "I'm on my own."

"Like to come to my place for a drink then?"

I swallowed hard on his invitation, tensing to get it down, and it tasted difficult, but it was what I was here for, and I cleared my throat to say, "Yes. Sure. I'd like to."

Gordon gave me a very accomplished grin, paid for our drinks, and we went to the stairway past the portrait of the soldier beloved by soldiers, the singer having crooned into another song about wanting someone and being unable to say "no."

Nor was I there to say no, saying good night to variegated honey child at the door, stepping outside into a dark emotion of excitement and dread.

Around the corner turned out to lie several streets distant in the night now too quiet, and Gordon kept time with our steps telling stories of the city's history.

It wasn't too long, or long enough, before we came to his place. It lay down a walled passageway giving onto a courtyard where three trees still held a few faded leaves, and two small brick houses faced each other above an antique lantern. "Eighteen twenty-six," said Gordon, "built by a whaler for his twin sons, Ebenezer and Jedediah Spooner. We live on the left hand, of course, the Ebenezer House," as he unlocked the white door.

I followed up three flights to an attic room, narrow and snug with a sloping ceiling, a divan to the right with cushions heaped against the wall, a couple of chairs, a record player on a low table, orange lights turned low, and a glass door at the end opening onto a flat roof. He said to sit down, make yourself comfortable, take off your jacket and tie, take a deep breath. This room's designed for getting better acquainted. I'll make us a drink. And he went back downstairs. Undoing the top two buttons of my shirt, I wasn't afraid. I was terrified, knowing perfectly well why I was there, only wanting to be there. With this stranger, his gazellelike limp and capable eyes. Would he find me inadequate, clumsy, ignorant, timid, a fool, a mistake? I was ready for anything, prepared for nothing. And what had happened with Jerry would be no good to me now, because now I had to know *myself*, to be something, become someone I didn't know. Oh, God. And yet I wanted more than anything in all the world to hold the whole world in my arms.

Gordon came back, clinking glass in each hand, sat beside me on the divan, drinks on the floor, and said, "A little music maybe. Yes or no? Rocky Two?"

I swallowed. "What's that?"

"Rachmaninov. The Second Piano Concerto."

"Okay."

"Come on, Jim. Don't be nervous."

I lied, "I'm not, I'm not nervous."

"Yes, you are. You are. Here. Look at me."

He took my face in both of his hands, drawing me to him, to his mouth, kissing, searching with his lips tentatively at first, gently, then more tenaciously as I opened to him, responsive to his mouth in mine, yielding to him and succumbing to his awareness of what I wanted, the transport into the beyond of surrender, the physical entirety in his arms and my own holding on to him to save my life.

He held me back an inch from his face, our eyes like each other in the throes of vision, and he said, "Do you want to take your clothes off by yourself, or would you like me to do it?"

Someone else speaking for me said, "Yes, please, you do it."

He did it. Ever so slowly, so tenderly, button by button, easing away shirt, shoes and socks, pants, while at the same time guiding my hands to do the same for him, and he contrived too to turn off the nearby lights so we were in each other's shadow, and it was amazing, as if such gestures and facility had been born and bred in both of us from a time before we knew what we were doing, and we were naked together on the divan among the jumble of cushions, and it was all right, altogether, everything that he did to me, and with me, that I did likewise to him and with him, and I wanted ever so much to be more, far more, and *for* him, and it was, it was for him and because of him

when the crescendo of sensation became complete, then the silence of
our breathing, indeed.

Motionless, wordless, we waited. He handed me a glass. I held it
against my wet stomach. He lit a cigarette. Then there intruded a sound
as of a fluttering of winged things outside touching the door's glass
panes. It was raining. The universe beyond our own existed, thus another reality having been witness to ours.

"That was good," he said. "You know, you're very sweet to make
love to. Are you all right?"

"Yes," I said, wanting to whisper to him, "I'm all right, yes."

"I'm glad. I think it's raining. You can stay over if you like. There
are clean sheets and a blanket under the coverlet, a bathroom on the
half landing outside. Better to stay over unless you have to be someplace early Sunday."

He stood up, lambent in his nakedness, and I did notice then that
his left leg was thinner than the right, though not unsightly. Having
put out the cigarette, he gathered up his clothes and shoes in a bundle
under one arm, his drink in the other hand, and said pleasant dreams.
In the morning take a shower, shave. There's everything in the bathroom. Come down anytime you're ready. We get up early. Waffles for
breakfast on Sundays. And a glass of champagne. Nothing's too good
for a member of our armed forces. He laughed, amusement the
well-meaning answer to the muddle and misfortune of everyday existence, and turned away in a memento of sexual happiness and went
downstairs.

We? To be sure, he'd said "we" at the front door, but I could have
assumed he meant the two of us then. And why had he not stayed to
sleep beside the body it had been sweet to make love to? I wondered
in the sudden solitude, the flutter of raindrops against the glass speechless. The bathroom was almost overly immaculate, too well appointed
to allow you to feel at home, so you supposed you weren't supposed
to. I went alone to turn out the lights and go to sleep on the destitute
divan.

And then on the far side of the darkness there was a visualization,
something spectral, incorporeal, barely visible, hovering before my eyes:
Hanno's face, his face only, not his body, his face only, and his voice,
a whisper barely audible above the murmur of the rain, saying, "For-

get it," and then I lay in that alien attic in another world, alone, no forgetfulness coming to the rescue of the night.

An abrupt brightness, however, jerked awareness into the next day, the confusion of sheets and blankets, and there was cool sunlight but no naked body beside mine, and I suddenly ached for Gordon, anxious again for the relinquishment of everything we'd done together, the desire and the bafflement.

I shaved, took a cold shower, dressed, and went downstairs.

Voices and laughter came through from beyond the all-white front room. The farther room, also all white, was a dining room–kitchen, and Gordon sat at the square table in a blue silk dressing gown, opposite him in a canary yellow turtleneck sweater a man about fifty, maybe closer to sixty but very fit, gray hair crew cut, a superior air, thin smile, but cordial enough because the moment very clearly belonged to him.

Gordon did the introduction, my name first, then: "This is my friend Vincent. Vincent Wardour. The architect. *The* architect."

We shook hands, his grip masterful, brooking no recalcitrance and—emphatically, I felt—no rivalry. "Have a seat," he said, gesturing, "and have a glass of champagne." There was an open bottle in a chrome cooler.

I sat down on an uncomfortable chair, which was plainly the seat of taboo, putting me in my place at a table of triadic elements, two symbolic, the third superfluous.

Gordon poured champagne, made waffles, passed the maple syrup, filled the coffee cups, and performed with practiced aplomb as *mein* host, while *the* architect politely permitted himself to be waited upon. Eased by champagne, conversation flowed on the war, my prospects as an eventual participant, my impressions of Boston. Particularly of the city's architectural monuments. A pithy tutorial by Wardour. The Florentine palazzo on Copley Square, staircase and inner arcade, frescoes by J. S. Sargent. H. H. Richardson's Romanesque church, a vital departure from Gothic Revival. And of course the gold-domed statehouse on Beacon Hill, facade by Bulfinch, unfortunate statuary by Saint-Gaudens.

In no time it was midmorning, and I could say I'd have to be going, thanks for the breakfast. Gordon went with me to the door, kissed me—on the cheek—and said, "I loved being with you. Glad you could stay over and meet Vincent. Not many of my friends get the chance. If you're not shipping out of here soon, stop by for a drink some Saturday afternoon. Around five. I get together a bunch of friends upstairs, listen to music, shoot the breeze, get a buzz on before going out on the town. No need to phone. I'm in the book, though. H A N E Y. Any Saturday soon. Meet some kids you'll like, mostly in uniform like you. Okay?"

It was so overtly simplistic. I said, "Okay."

He patted me on the ass, and I went outside.

Walking back under the ghostly sunshine, violet air of Indian summer, I realized that the future had nothing to fear from my inexperience as to what was to be done about what was *inside* of what was inside of my pants. I could take care of it, and it would take an immensity of care of me. Overnight the sexual ABCs had run through to XYZ. I might have to refuel my alphabet on the primer of circumstance, but I wasn't afraid of experiment. Gordon had made me a gift of one night only. What machinery of satisfaction made him the lover of Vincent Wardour, and Vincent the architect of his days, if not of his nights, had nothing to do with me. He had shown a readiness to be my friend. The kiss on the cheek, the pat on the ass. I would, indeed, drop in of a Saturday afternoon. Meet boys with whom meetings might benefit the alphabet.

Aaron said, "Mother wants you to go to the Symphony with her Saturday afternoon. I have business to see to that day."

Mrs. Randolph said, "It's all Brahms, I believe. Are you partial to Brahms, Mr. Lord?"

"Oh, yes. After Beethoven, Brahms."

She laughed a trill. "Of course. The usual Schubert sandwich. Mr. Koussevitzky is partial to Brahms. But come. Hurry along, Aaron, your business will not wait."

Mrs. Randolph wore a sealskin coat. Outside on Pinckney Street waited a Packard with a colored gentleman at the wheel. We sat in the back, and as it was a blustery afternoon, Mrs. Randolph drew a fur lap robe onto our knees. "It's very kind of you to accompany me. My son has business to attend to in Randolph. Some dreadful people want to build something called a supermarket in the center of town, and I don't believe we ought to allow it. And Aaron, you see, is the man of the family now that Mr. Randolph is no longer with us."

"Randolph?" I inquired. "Is there a town too called Randolph?"

The chauffeur suppressed a chuckle.

"There is, yes, yes, indeed, that's where the Randolphs came from. Or you might say the town came from where they were. In any event, a considerable parcel of it is still Randolph land."

"No house on it?"

Another chuckle in front.

"Some," said Mrs. Randolph.

"I see," I said, though I saw only that the Randolphs resided in a sphere at which I could only gaze as a sort of latter-day vassal, that being their graciousness and my pleasure.

Symphony Hall stood way out on Huntington Avenue beyond that appalling monstrosity the Mother Church of Christian Science. Our seats were in the seventh row center.

"The highlight of this afternoon's program, I believe, is the First Symphony. C Minor. A popular staple of the repertoire."

It was. I hated it. At the hateful prep school the boys had all been compelled to learn to sing an anthem to a tune presumptuously pilfered by some music master from the final movement of that symphony. "Arise, sons of hell on earth blah-blah-blah . . ." in the ghastly school chapel where, when alone, I played on the piano the theme music of *Three Comrades*.

Having assembled in well-disciplined order, the orchestra rose when Koussevitzky came to the podium, bowed hurriedly to the public, and promptly got down to business, *Variations on a Theme by Haydn* the introductory composition. The First Symphony was rugged, rough-hewn, wrestling with the elements, as I was, waiting for the measures I dreaded, which didn't struggle out until the middle of the last movement, allegro non troppo ma con brio, far too much brio for me to hear with equanimity, but then I was once again in that dung-colored chapel, singing my heart out and panic-stricken till the end of time by my difference, which, after all, haunted Symphony Hall too till the final chord. Bang. I sat with my hands clenched, grinding my teeth. Koussevitzky had turned as red in the face as a pimento.

The last piece of the program was the *Academic Festival Overture*, a concert filler almost too familiar, nothing to fear from this one. Till suddenly there was something, too familiar, too evocative: "Gaudeamus Igitur," the heartfelt student song of yesteryear, young men arm in arm striding the cobbled alleyways of old Heidelberg, the selfsame song Hanno had spoken of sometime somewhere, as if he were bodily present in the auditorium, shocking me with desire and disappointment. Yet again. I closed my eyes against the vision of him sitting in a chair smoking a cigarette. My God.

As we walked away from the applause, the orchestra standing, Koussevitzky bowing, Mrs. Randolph said, "I was pleased to notice that you found the concert moving."

"Oh," I said. "Well, I did, yes. Was it *that* noticeable?"

"It was noticeable, yes. You are partial to Brahms."

"To Brahms, mmm," I said.

The Packard was in front. She said, "I'll drop you anywhere you like. Aaron, I fear, will not be back in time for dinner. Lawyers are unbelievably long-winded."

I said anywhere by the Public Garden would be fine. It was in front of the Ritz Hotel. She said, "I'm glad you enjoyed the concert, Mr. Lord. You seem a sensitive young man. My son will bring you to the house another time, and I shall play the harp. Good afternoon."

"Thank you, Mrs. Randolph," I said. A grande dame.

Spooner Place was not difficult to find, the Ebenezer House to the left. I rang. A marine, an unbuttoned barefoot bruiser, opened the door, studied my surprise, and said, "You must be for Gordon. He's upstairs. Come on."

I followed him, and the music came down before we reached the top. Rocky Two, I guessed, and it was. Gordon, a yellow turtleneck and blue corduroy pants, sat on the floor. On the divan lolled a soldier and two sailors, one of them British, wearing his navy blue bonnet down over the left eye. The marine stayed standing by the glass door, as if guarding against incompatible company. Gordon said, "Hi, Jim. That's Al who let you in, and this is Bill, Wally, and Ralph. Take a glass of wine. There on the table, rotgut from California. Squeeze in somewhere, get comfortable, take off your jacket. And your shoes."

I sat on the floor.

The boys on the divan yawned and ruffled one another's hair.

Bill said, "The Statler's good anytime after five."

Wally said, "The Napoleon after nine."

Al said, "Afternoons the downstairs gents' at the Museum of Fine Arts, good for a quickie and you can catch that great Gauguin."

"And the Duck Club," said Bill, "if you can get introduced to the doctor and want to have your face lifted."

"Or go really crazy," Ralph said, shaking his head, "that big house out on Commonwealth Avenue, Mr. Mad Africa, if you go in for the pee-pee gang bang."

I said, "But what about the police, let alone the MPs? Don't they know what's going on?"

"Of course they know," said Gordon. "That many gay servicemen you can't keep it a secret. So what? Are they going to arrest a hundred, hundred and fifty of Uncle Sam's soldiers and sailors every weekend on suspicion of going down on you? Not likely. And forgive a four-F for speaking frankly. They need food for their cannons, and the police aren't going to volunteer for the foxholes." He got up to fix the music but didn't change the record, started Rocky Two for another turn. "Vladimir Horowitz playing," he said.

"He's gay," said Bill.

Gordon went downstairs and brought back another jug of rotgut. We were all adrift on the ocean of silly freedom, opportunity, and self-confidence. Rocky Two reached one of its intermissions. Gordon sang.

A touching integrity to all of this, I felt, playful good humor in the face of nature, which hadn't necessarily done any of us a favor. It was sweet to be taken for granted for what you were, no question how you plead, not guilty till proved innocent, no judgment in lieu of argument, no confinement in the prison of your days. Bonhomie, however, was all very well. But I had promises to keep, other considerations in my head and between my legs. None of which, it was clear, was to be welcomed with warm embraces this evening in the Ebenezer House. So I said, "I'll be seeing you some other Saturday."

Gordon went down with me to the door, kissed my cheek, patted my behind, and said, "*Amor vincit omnia*, Jimmy. Go get it. And come back quick. See you." I said okay, and he closed the door.

It was quarter to nine. I walked down Washington Street, turned on Stuart, and there was a restaurant called Catania Café. On the wall opposite the front door hung a huge map of Sicily overwritten with lines, dates and decked with little flags. Syracuse, July 10, the Union Jack. Palermo, July 22, the Stars and Stripes. Catania in bold red capitals, August 5, Union Jack. Palermo, August 17, the two flags united. Of course. From this place the Allied conquest of Sicily had been observed day by day. With patriotic fervor. The entire island freed from German occupation after only thirty-nine days of fighting.

Yes, how excited would have been our roommate Tony Pelatti had he been here only two months before. Little Tony, as Aaron always called him. Though, to be sure, slight in stature, Tony furiously compensated by standing morally as tall as Childe Roland to his dark tower. No man had more vehement, more obstinate, more severe, proud, demanding, and demonstrative a sense of personal honor, its obligations and prerogatives, than Tony Pelatti. This made him frequently prickly but at the same time almost effusively friendly to those rare souls deemed deserving of his esteem. Why and wherefore I chanced to be one of these I never learned. Proximity may have bred affinity. Our desks were side by side, bunks one above the other, so we talked, and Tony had an abundance of unburdening ready for an attentive listener.

His parents, childhood sweethearts from a small town in Sicily, had fled oversea from misery and the Mafia, borne toward the Statue of Liberty by the tide of pre–World War I immigration. Giovanni Pelatti found employ in a leatherworking sweatshop on the Lower East Side, where he and Bianca shared tenement squalor with throngs of oppressed Italians. Bitterly resentful of brutal labor and bestial lodgings, Pelatti heeded the furious harangues of Emma Goldman agitating for anarchy and riot versus the ruling classes. Unwilling to fight for a nation that sanctioned the murder of workers and the lynching of Negroes, he evaded the draft of World War I and fled from New York City to chancy refuge among like-minded Italians in Braintree, Massachusetts. There on June 3, 1919, Bianca gave birth to a four-and-a-half-pound boy, immediately named Antonio Giuseppe Pelatti, the birthday celebration having grown boisterous when bad news ended it at ten minutes before midnight: sixty-seven suspected anarchists had been arrested on suspicion of complicity and bombing attacks on the homes of U.S. Justice officials. Several of Pelatti's guests, particularly his closest friend, a young fellow called Nicky Sacco, had cause to fear the proceedings of such officials.

The bad news that spoiled the celebration of Tony's birth turned disastrous a year later, when two men were murdered nearby and suspicion fell almost immediately upon Sacco—too quickly and too easily, everyone said. The police also arrested a sidekick of Nicky's named Bartolomeo Vanzetti. Evidence against both was circumstantial. But feelings ran high against them. Johnny Pelatti, intimate friend of the accused, a draft dodger with anarchist leanings, was also suspected, questioned, and called to the bar, though nothing could be lodged against him. The trial was a tragicomedy of racism, prejudice, and wrongheaded error, a mockery of impartial litigation, the bias of the judge egregious, of the jury overt, a verdict of guilty taken for granted, a sentence of death a foregone conclusion.

The nationwide clamor of outrage over the Sacco-Vanzetti case burst upon the front pages of newspapers, while radio commentators denounced the scandalous travesty of licit process. Petitions for retrial were thrown out of court; appeals for clemency, ignored. The life of Johnny Pelatti was blighted forever by the "case," and on the ghastly August day when the condemned men were taken to the electric chair, he turned his back on the future. His face fell apart, jowls hung flabby, and he began to stink, having refused to change his clothes, wash, shave, brush his teeth, or, finally, heed the necessities of natural functions or indeed eat a proper meal until, at last, his wizened body ceased to breathe. The diagnosis was self-evident. He had died of despair.

Bianca lay down in a paroxysm of bereavement, of which the fatal outcome, clearly, was her devout desire. Nor was its fulfillment long delayed. The priest said this was impious, that the Holy Father would never condone it. Sicily, however, in its insular and immemorial piety persevered in rituals that owed nothing to the strictures of Rome. Abashed, the priest took ten-year-old Tony aside, spoke solemnly to him of Jesus' goodness, God's wisdom, the loving charity of the church, and concluded by inquiring whether the innocent purity of childhood had by any chance been defiled by naughtiness, to which the little boy replied that he didn't know what that meant. So the priest set about demonstrating just what naughtiness was all about, whereupon Tony sank his teeth into the cleric's intrusive hand. Screams, rage, blood, though not very much of it, and the priest shouting, "This child is no good, no good, bites the hand that feeds the spirit," and Tony's piercing wail: "He touched my zi-zi. He touched my zi-zi."

The neighbors said, "A kid with that much spunk'll grow up to be a man with a mind all his own." They were right. But there was no scandal. Having become an orphan, Tony had had his choice of honorable Italian families vying to take in a child unhappily marked by the "case."

He attacked adolescence with a rage to master happenstance, to profit by the conditional and make the very best of the inevitable. Adults observed with wonderment his confidence in the future. A scholarship to State Teachers College at Fitchburg came as easily as a letter in the mail. Two-thirds of the students were Irish, hence Catholic, so Tony stared down their auld sod conceit, sniffed at the disingenuous horseplay of the frat houses, and ultimately awed both faculty and undergraduates by nailing to the door of the president's office a handwritten copy of the valedictory address he had earned the honor of delivering one week later, entitled "Perils of Priapic Priests." By noon the next day he had disappeared from Fitchburg forever. Antonio Pelatti was not a man to be trifled with.

Ten days after he had spurned a diploma, the world at large called to attention Tony's sense of honor. He volunteered six months before Pearl Harbor. That he was still a private when we first met, after more than two years in the service, was proof of Tony's prickliness. That he accepted with serene hauteur the army's indifference to moral sticklers was evidence of his equanimity. I came to admire both sides of that aggressively individual coin.

And I thought it was too bad Tony couldn't be sitting beside me in the Catania Café, with the victory map of Sicily on the wall, while I relished the tiramisu topped with ground pistachios. The prospect of my postprandial homosexual hunt would have given no pause: when he'd learned the euphuistic usage of the word "gay," he was seized by spasms of hilarity lasting half an hour. Anyway, having thought about Tony and his traumatic past throughout my meal, I found the allure of the hunt less urgent, and I imagined him all alone in Room 104 at St. Mary's Hall, and there he was when I arrived. We sat together, talking, till 2:00 a.m., and he told me about Sicilian verismo,

Giovanni Verga, and the grinding compassion of *The House by the Medlar Tree.*

I went to the Museum of Fine Arts. The Cézanne of a road turning through the trees toward a village, a surprising harmony of green, red, pale ocher, and blue, a flattering pattern in a powerful framework, seized upon your scrutiny like the grip of a hand. Then—I remembered the mention of it—I found the huge Gauguin Tahitian scene of a dozen natives ensconced forever in a smoldering landscape, a naked man in the center reaching overhead to pluck from nowhere a red apple, the whole thing entitled *Where Do We Come From? What Are We? Where Are We Going?* Compellingly relevant but unanswerable questions, a sentimental philosophy of life, of civilization and sexuality.

I didn't fail to recall that a visit to the men's room was reputed to be good for genital fun. The line of dead white urinals was about as fetching as a parade of tombstones, yet an elderly gent in a black mackintosh stood like a mourner at one of them, and he gave me the eye as soon as I walked in. Whether the eye was wary or optimistic I couldn't tell but really didn't want to find out. Still, recognizing desire, I had no good reason to offend it. When this stranger, gray-haired, wearing rimless glasses, flicked aside the hem of his raincoat, however, I looked aside, disinclined to encourage the brash disclosure of the exhibitionist.

He said, "Come on, soldier boy, I'll shoot the moon for you." Naive, slow to learn, I was shocked. A man of his age—he must have been at least fifty—how could he so submit to the mortification of lust? Walking out, I remembered having read that Sophocles in old age when asked how he stood in relation to the pleasures of sex had said that it gave him great joy to have escaped from that fierce and savage master. How just, how right, how sensible, and, indeed, how enviable. Leaving behind the museum, its masterpieces, and its questions—what *are* we?—I walked into the dusk on my way downtown to have something to eat in a hurry before turning up at the Statler.

The bar was mobbed, all manner of servicemen in uniform making ready for the onslaught of Saturday night, everybody drinking to the prospect of capturing someone for the time of their lives, a few enterprising gladiators already caressing prospective victims in the crowd. I had a couple too many, to no avail, and well after nine went along to the Napoleon, where honey child kissed my hand and upstairs "Mad About the Boy" was the foreground music of the soirée, and I asked a willowy American sailor whether he knew why the place was named for Napoleon Bonaparte. He didn't. Our conversation turned on a lot of nonsense that made sufficient sense for its purpose, which had nothing to do with talk. He'd been born in Boston, was in luck to be stationed at the coast guard base, could spend weekends at home with his parents. Name was Paul, as in Revere. He laughed. His face was like the face of a friendly teddy bear, crew cut the color of ginger, uniform just right: too tight. So there we were. His plans for the evening? Nothing special unless I'd like to come home with him. But what about his parents? Oh, Mom and Dad would be asleep upstairs, never heard a thing anyway. So it was okay.

We walked. Chilly dark. Saturday night good timers still a crowd at the corner of Newbury and Arlington past the Ritz. He took my arm. His home, a pretentious pile of sandstone with pilasters, corbels, and a couple of caryatids, was far out on Beacon almost as far as Massachusetts Avenue. In a bunker like this, I thought, the noises of illicit intercourse were unlikely to waken well-heeled parents to the shenanigans of their deviant offspring. Besides, I was by no means likely to be the first shenanigan. Paul's bedroom was rather too rakish for a kid his age, nineteen or twenty, the pineapple four-poster turned down and fire engine red pajamas politely laid out. We were in a hurry. The pajamas went flying, and we were naked in a luxuriant tangle of percale sheets. Afterward, still naked, he accompanied me to the door, said, "It was so good," put my hand between his legs, and whispered, "Something to remember me by."

"Yeah," I said.

I had to walk back as far as Exeter and Commonwealth to find a taxi, but when I reached St. Mary's Hall, Tony was still seated at his desk. He said, "Do you realize that Garibaldi was probably the best-loved leader of men of modern times?" We sat up for another hour while Tony told me about the Thousand Red Shirts, the conquest of Sicily, the triumphant battle of the Volturno River, and the noble asylum of Caprera Island.

There was a fellow, a corporal, rooming somewhere along the same corridor as we were. I occasionally ran into him in the shower, where he was decidedly worth looking over, a pretty baby face on top of six feet of Greek athlete. His name, I'd heard, was Bill Anson. He cannot have been in the French contingent, though, because I never saw him in class. It was the week after Paul when he spoke to me one evening after supper. "Hello, Lord, I'm Bill Anson. How are you making out?"

"All right, thanks. And you?"

"I manage. No fish for supper tonight."

"No."

"You have a thing for seafood, though, don't you? Really go in for it." And before I could say swordfish, he added, "Like it more than everyday meat, huh?" And he smirked as if at some bizarre idiosyncrasy of my appetite.

"Not so you'd notice it," I said.

Then he laughed out loud. "Oh, I noticed it all right. Saw you arm in arm with a dish the other night in front of the Ritz, looked like you liked it."

"Hell," I said, "you mean that kid, that sailor. I was walking him home."

"Sure thing. Paul loves to get walked home. Be careful you don't wake up his parents. Paul's not your everyday seafood; he's fillet of sole."

"I see," I said, "I see, I see. Sailors are from the sea. That it?"

"That's it. Gays eat 'em up."

"You take it for granted I'm gay."

"Takes one to know one. Spotted you long ago. Didn't want to intrude. But seeing you with Paul, well, why not? Do you mind?"

"Why should I? No, I don't mind."

"We've all got lives to live. How'd you like to join the Duck Club?"

"I've heard of it. But what is it?"

"Gay get-together downtown. Saturdays for tea. Well, tea and larks, cocktails, caviar sandwiches, a little recreation before you go out cruising."

"Why the duck?"

"The host's my friend. Dr. Duckett Smythe, the best plastic surgeon in North America, known to his friends as Ducky. You want in?"

"Okay."

He gave me an address on Beacon Street. Only a hop and a skip from the Ritz, he said, press the buzzer for Duckett Smythe, M.D., anytime Saturday from five to eight more or less, top-floor apartment, fine view of the Common. I said I'd be there, thinking this might be an enjoyable change from the Ebenezer House, Rocky Two, and Gordon's hand on my rear end.

Dr. Smythe was waiting on the topmost landing after four flights of beautifully carpeted stairs: a small man, about fifty, bald as an ostrich egg, suave face, lustrous eyes, aristocratic bearing, reminded you somewhat of Erich von Stroheim, that same rather melancholy air. He let me inside to a large room breathing of luxury, all beige, velvet couches and marble-topped coffee tables, five or six boys in various uniforms sitting around, smoking, with tall crystal-cut glasses in hand. The doctor introduced me to them all, names you forgot immediately, provocative glances, smiles, and hello. Bill Anson came in, carrying a silver tray of very thin sandwiches and a handful of tiny napkins. The doctor said, "Have a drink, my dear," and gave me a scotch and soda without having asked what I wanted.

From the double window you could see the bare treetops of the Common, Indian summer finished now, its dead leaves sere on the stiffened grass. Above the fireplace hung an oval painting in colors tan and black and gray, a beautiful Picasso of the period I'd already admired at the Museum of Modern Art.

"Picasso," said Bill, assuming I knew nothing. "Edward G. Robinson sold it to Ducky for five cents. Services rendered to Mrs. R. The doc has a host of clients in Hollywood, all those dames desperate for a nip here, a tuck there, you know how it is, my dear. Come sit, I want you to meet Paddy O'Higgins, a Canadian paratrooper passing through. Says he could be the great-grandson of the last viceroy of Peru. He's a wild one, Paddy is."

He looked it. Nothing regulation about O'Higgins. Trousers tucked into garish cowboy boots, tunic fitting him like a glove, epauletes, several ribbons, crimson kerchief around his neck, very long fair hair over the ears, a face too insolently handsome for anyone's good. But then none of Ducky's guests was plain. Except, I thought, for one.

"Well now," said O'Higgins, "you must be the stripling mentioned by Mr. Anson. Tell me about the miseries of your adolescence."

"It wasn't as awful as they say," I said.

"Sure, and it's bad manners to delude your elders, for I can see the sweet vestiges of sexual distress, don't you know? Incidentally, have you visited the farther reaches of the famous surgeon's abode? No? I'll take you round. Jump up. Follow right along."

No one cocked an eye as we went out.

A long corridor lined on both sides with drawings in gold frames led to a farther room. I paused to look, but Paddy said, "Don't dawdle. Come into the guest room. I think there are a couple of pornographic sketches by Jean Cocteau." He closed the door behind us and locked it. The Cocteau sketches were of strapping boys with outstanding erections. Paddy put his hands on my shoulders and said, "Do you mind if I put my tongue in your mouth?"

I didn't.

Presently he said, " 'At the fit hour 'tis sweet to unbend.' Horace. Let's go to bed. You taste of almonds and smell of the palaestra."

When we reappeared in the living room, the others behaved as though we'd been gone just five minutes. I gazed at the Picasso, thinking with admiration and longing and a kind of servile envy of the superhuman condition of genius, how its proximity could transform the world. Paddy said, "Your eyes are out on sticks, my dear. It's not distinguished to stare. I'll take you to dinner at the Ritz." Dr. Smythe as we left told me to drop in for tea (of which I'd seen not a drop) any Saturday at my leisure.

Paddy's attire turned heads in the restaurant. He talked about the power of literature to transfigure one's life, take Heinrich Schliemann, for example, and Homer, and Troy, and I felt the superior shiver of high culture, and we had chocolate soufflé for dessert. Outside in the frigid street, he said, "Cheerio, Giton. I have to go and jump out of an aeroplane. Imaginary succor for frog resistance to the boches. Thanks for the fuck." And he strode away into the adventurous dark.

Tony didn't give a damn whose nerves he frayed. Jesuitical duplicity was a frequent butt of his invective. He baited the professors incessantly, with the punitive result that his weekend passes were frequently suspended. He wrote wrathful letters to congressmen, senators, and left-leaning journals like *Partisan Review*. Nothing came of so much activity, of course, save that the flame of his fiery integrity stayed undimmed. How he talked! So much passion and pity and patriotism and playacting. He didn't make much inquiry into my private life, having more than enough to do to keep track of his own. In his frail frame he gathered myriad anxieties, betrayals, torments, plots, and battles to compound the all-inclusive entitlement of his honor.

It was not surprising, then, it was simply inevitable that Tony should have learned of the nearby presence of a famed opponent of Italian Fascism, a fierce adversary of its Roman Catholic hierarchy, now resident across the river in Cambridge, professor of history at Harvard, named Gaetano Salvemini. A ferocious enemy of the duce, he had been arrested by the Blackshirts and when freed had fled his homeland for the United States, where he composed polemical attacks on the Mussolini regime, lectured at Harvard, and betimes became a U.S. citizen. Tony wrote him a letter, presenting an account of his own political and moral convictions and requesting the privilege of an interview. An answer came, granting the request at a time convenient to both to be determined by telephone. It was the first Saturday in November. Allied forces in Italy were stalled at the foot of Monte Cassino, north of the Volturno River.

Tony insisted I accompany him. Opportunities to meet great men don't come often. Encounters with greatness are the civilizing milestones on the journey of a lifetime. Every man had a responsibility to himself to take such an opportunity. So I took it.

Salvemini's office was in an ugly building of old brick singularly unsuited, I felt, to the accommodation of a great man, the staircase stinking of a previous century. An acne-speckled undergraduate led us through an anteroom, knocked on an inner door, and clumsily opened it. Salvemini, however great, was short and frail, like Tony, but with an air of noble melancholy, wistful eyes, and gentle gestures of welcome. His office was a wonderland of books mingled with magazines, newspapers, and typescripts amid which he showed us to dusty armchairs and sat down between us, nodding as if to indicate that a tutorial might proceed.

Tony squared away with an angry denunciation of jesuitical iniquity, particularly pedagogical perfidy, citing for angriest disparagement the provost of Boston College, Father O'Grady. Salvemini listened with the sober concentration of a man who has heard many a tirade, and when Tony's passion paused, he acknowledged that the Society of Jesus had certainly been instrumental in extending papal authority across the earth and converting to strict Catholicism naive believers in other faiths, all of this, alas, of dubious benefit to mankind, the church, indeed, gravely censurable because of the connivance with the Fascist lack of principle.

What, *what* would history have to say? Tony wondered.

History, mused the eminent historian. One always tends to go back to Thucydides in order to go forward in mature consideration of mankind's behavior: the social, the moral, the spiritual aspects of evolving cultures in their rise and their decline. The beauty of history in its infinite limitation. Much as one may admire the ideas of one's countryman, Signor Croce, for instance, one can hardly agree that history is merely a form of thought, the culmination of philosophical lucubration. No. Hegel was mistaken. Monarchy is not the highest development of the state. History gives the lie to the idea that logic is the basis of the world process. You might say that this is illogic. Ignoratio elenchi. The beauty of history is the unintelligible specificity of the process.

And he pondered on to analyze the uses of art as a manifestation of thought in the development of historical discipline, thesis and antithesis, speculative but never abstract. The professor was delivering a lecture. Delivered with gentle and modest consideration of the audience. Tony did not interrupt. Nor, needless to say, did I. The monologue lasted fifteen or twenty minutes, imparting a sense of a relation almost physical with the substance of historical truth.

When presently a pause grew sufficiently prolonged, the signal that our time was up was clear. We stood. Salvemini said as he shook our hands that the war would put an end to Fascism and that we must believe in the right action of our commitment. But—but, he added, we'd do well in the end to beware of our shady friends, the disciples of dialectical materialism. Look them therefore in the eye with the eyes of Thucydides. We thanked him and went outside into the cloud-cluttered afternoon.

"Don't say a word," said Tony. "Silence is the full measure of respect."

When we came back to central Boston, I was anxious to ventilate

the matter of shady friends and made as if to speak. Tony instantly
raised a forefinger to his lips and whispered, "Respect!"

So we parted. I made my way to the convivial Duck Club on Beacon Street, there to admire the good-looking guests and the spellbinding Picasso. I mentioned to Dr. Smythe that I'd spent the afternoon
with Gaetano Salvemini, and he complimented me on my good fortune in having kept such illustrious company. Nobody else had heard
of the famous historian or, for that matter, I'd wager, of Thucydides.
After dinner at the Catania Café I went to the Statler and spent an
hour and a half in tenacious small talk before becoming acquainted
with an air force sergeant who drove me back with him to spend the
night in a dingy hotel room.

Between weekends we fooled around with books and maps and
papers and exams and orals and had a tolerable time of being taught,
Tony said, by lesbians disguised as priests. La Hu's flirtation with
castration continued to be good music hall entertainment, and he taught
us the slang of the rue de Lappe—*les apaches, les pouffiasses, et les
zigouilleurs du bas monde.* Room 104 was our fanciful theater of the
absurd, in which war played the part of the fall guy. Tony quoted incendiary passages from D'Annunzio.

It was football weather. Aaron invited me to the Harvard-Dartmouth
game. A former prof of his had gotten the tickets and would be sitting
with us. By name of Randal Phillips. Randy's the right name for him,
Aaron said. He'd tried to seduce Aaron, but they got along all the
same. Only in his thirties, speaks eight languages, including Esperanto.
After the game we'll go back to his room, get drunk on sherry, and
he'll probably make a pass at you. Don't suppose you mind.

"Is it that obvious?"

"Half the freshman class in my year was that way. Nobody gives a
damn. Do you?"

I shrugged. "Not that it would matter."

Randy Phillips wasn't bad-looking for a man of his age, somewhere
in his thirties. He wore a blue hat with a teal feather in the band and
spoke rather singsong in a tone of eclectic refinement. We had seats on
the Harvard forty-yard line, applauded and cheered the rough-and-
tumble, and it was almost cold. Randy had a flask full of sherry. Our
neighbors were on their second bottle of champagne, drinking straight

out of the bottle. There were many servicemen in uniform. It didn't appear to matter who won, though Harvard inevitably did and there was a tremendous lot of roaring.

Randy's digs were in Dunster House, indecently luxurious for an assistant professor, but Harvard, being the richest university in the world, could obviously afford it. There was a tiger skin on the floor. "A wedding present from a pal at Princeton," said Randy.

I said, "Are you married?"

"I was," Randy said, "to him. But we're divorced now."

An open fire made minor crepitations now and then. By the time Randy opened the second bottle of Xérès Extra Dry we were adrift on the after-six o'clock daze, and Aaron said he'd have to run along because Mr. and Mrs. Sears were coming to dinner, but, Jim, you stay on. I did. Randy said why don't we sit in front of the fire on the Princeton tiger wedding present of my divorcé? We did away with bottle number two and he tried to seduce me and I let him do it. Then he invited me to dinner in a Cambridge restaurant. We had a bottle of Bordeaux, and he talked about Berlin before the fall, Herr Issyvoo, W. H. Auden, *Professor Unrath*, *M*, and Marlene, and to me it all seemed like ancient history. I thanked him for the dinner and the drinks (though not for the sex), walked across the river in the chill, and never saw Professor Phillips again.

The first snowflakes lay lightly underfoot before the last oak leaves fell. Thanksgiving grew imminent, along with it the date of my birth, which fell on the Saturday following the appreciative day; I fought shy of celebrating either occasion with my family. My mother sent a check, and Dad promised a new wristwatch when I was discharged from the service. I spent the best and most thankful part of the Puritan holiday in bed with an Australian sailor who was happy to have run into someone fascinated to hear all about his boyhood on the ships sailing out from Coffs Harbour.

Some debris of the previous night's snowfall still lay on the sidewalks when I walked to Ebenezer House to take Gordon Haney out to lunch. In the afternoon, rather than Gordon's attic pillows, jug of wine, and Rocky Two, I opted for Duckett Smythe's luxurious couches, captivating Picasso, and—who knows?—perhaps a seductive stand-in for Paddy O'Higgins. But in place of Paddy I was offered a mere handshake to a nineteen-year-old 4-F movie star dressed up as a Restoration fop whose proboscis pleaded for one of the famous doctor's jobs. The other guests were companionable enough, and an abundance of the tiny sandwiches was sufficiently filling that when I left I wasn't hungry. Snow had again begun to fall, and I walked back across the Common down Tremont in the swirl of flakes to the Statler.

That evening for some reason—I'll never know why—I entered the bar from the rear of the raised mezzanine among the seated straight clients drinking at tables. Though I'd come to feel virtually at home at that hotel, I never before, and never after, entered the bar from that side. Not that it may have much mattered, yet it made a world of difference, for the moment of recognition became infinitely more piercing. Pausing for a moment at the brink of the few steps leading down to the bar proper, glancing with a prospector's eye across the crowd of faces below, suddenly—sudden as in the first tremor of cataclysm to come before one has time to be terrified—I saw a head above the others over to the right at the end of the bar and a profile I'd have recognized instantly anywhere on earth. And yet I didn't believe it. Not now. Not here. Not in this place of *all* places.

So I shoved and elbowed through the profane objections of the crowd to approach him, and yes, it was—it *was* . . . Hanno.

"What are you doing here?" I demanded.

He looked me in the face with such beautiful composure. He said, "Isn't that obvious?"

"But it can't be," I exclaimed, shuddering.

"Why not?" he asked. "Why can't it be?"

"Because it can't be," I insisted. "After all. It just can't. What *are* you doing here?"

"Well"—he sighed—"Jim. I'm doing what you're doing. This *is* a gay bar, isn't it?"

"Oh, my God, Hanno."

"Well, what did you think? Don't you realize that everybody has secret secrets? A hidden life. You have. I have. Didn't you ever wonder? All those days after the day I stepped on your foot? And nights? For God's sake. Wonder what it was all about?"

"Christ! Yes, I wondered. Well, no, not exactly. I didn't dare. Don't you see? I was so afraid, afraid of going wrong, ruining everything.

And there you were, you dared to take risks. That day you threw yourself down the hill by Lake Tahoe. And you decided. Where we went, where we stayed. I was just so afraid. Of you, really."

"Do you think I wasn't?" he cried, indifferent to inquisitive glances. "Hell. I was scared shitless. And yes, I took the risks. Why the hell couldn't you loosen up on me, Jim, give me a chance, for Christ's sake?"

"But, Hanno, you can't—you don't . . . mean. You're not queer."

"Hell, yes, I'm queer," he shouted, and the inquisitive glances around us grew uneasy. "What do you think? If you think at all. What the fuck do you think I'm doing in this den of iniquity?"

I gulped on that. No answer. So I said, "Please don't shout at me. I'm sorry. Then everything, I mean. Then everything . . . I don't know. What can I say?"

Hanno looked into my face. Those twilit eyes. And very softly he said, "Haven't you ever been in love?"

The sob seized my throat. That took a moment . . . "Yes," I said. "Yes, I have. I still am." And I let my hand rest on his arm. And again I said, "I still am."

He flinched away, so that my hand held the empty air. He said, "Don't."

"But why? Now that both of us know. Now that we've found out. When I said goodbye in that awful place, in Fresno, I thought I'd never see you again."

His face had gone hard. He said, "Well, you almost didn't."

"But now that I have. Now that we know. What luck. Isn't it, Hanno?"

"No," he said, the hard face in front of mine. "It's not luck. It's an everyday coincidence, is all it is, nothing more. For us it's too late."

"It's never too late. Haven't you ever been in love?"

"I was. I swear. But it *is* too late. Now. And you might as well know. I *am* in love. A man I met in Washington. I was in training near D.C. In Maryland. My German past, you might say, the Teutonic military thing, a sort of secret that finally caught up with me to do me some good. I had weekends in Washington. We met in the National Gallery." He laughed. "In front of a painting of the Good Samaritan by El Greco. Sort of a thing between Martin and me because he's in the same branch of the service I'm in. He could give me a boost for my assignment. And as a matter of fact, the only reason I'm in this place tonight is that I'm waiting for him here. Any minute now, or you might have missed us. He's flying up here to see me off. I'm shipping out Monday. Overseas."

I didn't, couldn't speak. Only then I noticed his sleeves bore the chevrons of a first sergeant. So I could say, "You got promoted. Congratulations."

Hanno said, "No big deal. About the rest . . . I'm sorry."

So I said, "That's okay. You're right. I might as well know."

"If you want to wait, Martin ought to be here any minute. If you'd like to meet him. We're going out to dinner. It's just as you like."

I didn't. To leave seemed unbearable. To wait was unbearable. I said, "I'll wait."

Silence between us as we waited became the only bearable alternative, while the crude clamor of the bar created an emergency partition between us. Hanno, at least, coped with silence by humming between his teeth that selfsame tune upon which I'd fastened so much emotion long before.

I couldn't help myself. I said, "That tune you're always humming. I remember. What's it called?"

" 'O alte Burschenherrlichkeit,' " he said, "*wohin bist du entschwunden. My God! I shouldn't have said that. I'm sorry."

"Why? What does it mean? I don't speak German. Had you forgotten?"

"No, I hadn't forgotten. It just slipped out. Well. It means, 'Oh, glorious fellowship, where have you vanished to?' I'm sorry, I should never have said that."

"It's vanished," I said. "Never mind. It's all right. It *has* vanished."

"Phew," said Hanno. "Here comes Martin. About fucking time."

Martin was a silver bar lieutenant in pinks, tall as Hanno, a few years older, holding up his garrison cap, lean face filled with his good fortune and smile, curly hair over the ears. Probably a little ill at ease as one of the few officers amid the mob of enlisted men. Still, he put a finger on his lips, then touched it to Hanno's mouth and said, *"Guten Abend, mein Schatz."*

Not constraining a flush of feeling, Hanno said, "About time, Lieutenant. I was worried you got bumped off your plane. Should have known you could show your magic credentials. But I had company while I waited. Some coincidence you chose this place to meet."

"It's famous for meeting people," said Martin.

"Right. Well, it is. This is Jim. I told you. My old buddy from the base in Reno, Nevada."

"Hi, Jim," Martin said, offering his hand.

I held it briefly and said, "Hi," wondering whether he could sense how I hated him.

"Thanks for keeping Johannes company."

Johannes? To me? I said, "Think nothing of it," biting the words.

Hanno said, "We'd better get going. I only have thirty-six hours left."

"Okay, Hanno," Martin said, giving me a semismile as if I owed subservience to his rank.

Hanno turned and, in turning away, the twilit eyes leaving mine, raised his arm as in a gesture toward a limitless horizon when he said, "So long, Jim. You take care, you hear me."

"Thanks," I said. "Thanks for everything."

"Yes," he said, and they went out together.

At least he hadn't said "forget it." Not that I could, or wanted to, or ever would.

They were just leaving the lobby. I followed. Outside in the tragic street the snow now was falling faster. The city had gone dead quiet. They went up the sidewalk under the sweep of the storm, Martin throwing his arm around Hanno's shoulders. Aghast and ashamed, lifting my face to let the snowflakes melt in my burning eyes, I drifted after them in the silence. At the corner of Arlington they turned left on Newbury, and I followed still, petrified with humiliation, raging at them both and at my ridiculous rage, my folly and my hopeless shame. Then far beyond me in the snow they hailed a lone taxi, got in together, and the sickening automobile veered away, red taillights fainting into the void.

After hurrying back to the Statler, I took the elevator to the seventh floor and cowered in bed in my blind room, remembering the quivering darkness in that room in Comstock Rooms in Hazen, Nevada, where I was drunk and sick with longing, and the healing hand on my forehead.

The drifts had made a secret wilderness. From the frozen window of Room 104 I looked down at my lost self in that snow-deep panorama of woe, where no sound, no motion betrayed the human helplessness.

Three weeks, and weekends, went by without my leaving the frozen campus of Boston College. A twenty-first birthday is presumed to open the door to the adult abode of a lifetime, the inhabitant expected to competently cope with the discombobulating riddles of existence. That's all very well, to be sure, but I was no swashbuckling protagonist prepared to cut through Gordian complexities and come to happy terms with the denouement. So the answer lay in the question, the question in the answer, while I looked out the window at a winter of discontent not made summery by memories of summer beneath the mountains of Nevada.

Berlin now was repeatedly subjected to merciless bombing day and night by hundreds of Allied planes. The British government announced that war criminals—"scores of thousands," it declared—would eventually be prosecuted "to the full extent of the law" and punished accordingly. "Sure," said Aaron, "but first you've got to catch them." In the Pacific the Allies invaded the Japanese-held island of New Britain. And next year, everyone agreed, the war must come to a conclusive crunch with the invasion at last of Festung Europa.

Tony said, "I'll tell you something. When I heard about the Crystal Night, I didn't sleep for the longest time. Of course we all know that the Greek civilization to which our own owes everything was paid for by slaves, the Romans crucified people to prove they meant business, the church burned freethinkers at the stake, the Puritans wiped out Indians, while gentlemen branded blacks with red-hot irons and so forth. But Hitler . . . Just think." He stood to his feet, shut his eyes, placed both hands over his ears, and muttered in a guttural semioracular voice, "We are living in *unthinkable* times."

"I thought so," said Aaron twenty minutes later as we walked through the ashes over the ice on our way to supper. And added, "By the way, Mother says, 'Has Mr. Lord tired of us?' So you'd better come to dinner on Saturday."

Mrs. Randolph said, "I was quite hoping Aaron could persuade you. I promised not to play the harp."

"But I was looking forward to that, I assure you. I'd be disappointed if you didn't."

"My word," she said, smiling, serene, with exquisite aplomb, "we wouldn't want that. Perhaps we can induce Aaron to delay the rendezvous with the gin bottle long enough for a brief pavane."

The light in the pale drawing room cast forward only a pearly penumbra onto the harp in the shrouded bow window, and Mrs. Randolph's fingers wove up and down on the gold and silver strings, the stately melody wafting decorously upward. To drowse, I thought, forever, all desire appeased, spiritual equanimity, the self suffused ad infinitum with repose.

I patted my hands together very gently but very sincerely when it was finished. "That was beautiful," I said. "What can I say? It was really . . . I can't tell you."

Aaron said, "*Arci bravo*, Mama. I'm going to send Mr. Koussi a postcard telling him you're better than Lily Laskine and if he doesn't hire you before the season is quite over, we'll cut down his allowance."

"Don't be asinine," said his mother. "Fetch the gin bottle and shake up some cocktails before we expire from thirst."

Aaron brought the mammoth shaker to the library, and we drank toasts to the end of the war. Mrs. Randolph reminded her son to see to it that the yuletide gifts to the underprivileged children of Randolph were delivered, as they always had been, before five o'clock on the twenty-fourth. "Your father delivered them in person," she added.

"I know," said Aaron. "But I'm not Mr. Nice Guy."

"Pity," murmured his mother. To me she said, "I suppose, Mr. Lord, you will be going to family for the holiday."

"I suppose I will," I said.

I walked back alone after dinner down Beacon and along Arlington past the garden and the Ritz, continuing on as far as the Statler. To find out how I was with myself, I admitted to the night. Taking a few paces back and forth in front of the entrance, I avoided faces coming and going. And it seemed, all in all, that I was okay. So I got into a taxi that came along and asked the driver to take me to Boston College in Chestnut Hill, where for a wonder I found Room 104 deserted.

In the parlor car from South Station to Grand Central a major and a first lieutenant in the smoking room, taken aback by the impudence of a private in a Pullman, gave me the glance. Fuck them. Fuck all officers, as a matter of fact, and most especially Martin X.

Dad met me with the Buick and drove me out to Englewood. Mother was waiting in the living room, where the tree was decked with all the baubles I'd known since childhood. No Yakovleffs. I knew already that they had eventually determined to no longer be beholden to charitable foreigners and had found employ as domestic servants for a British bigwig in Washington, Madame hopefully leaving behind her address in expectation of receiving mail from me. So I told my parents about Boston College, Aaron Randolph and his harp-playing mama, Tony Pelatti, his integrity and Gaetano Salvemini, the outré repasts at Locke-Ober's Restaurant, the Costly Pleasure Hotel, Mrs. Gardner's palazzo, and other innocuous sites of Bostonian interest. All of which my father capped with the true story of the ridiculous, disastrous Molasses Flood of 1919. Meanwhile my younger brother Peter was pounding away on the piano in his bedroom, the *Appassionata* by Beethoven. He didn't join us for drinks in front of Dad's impeccable fire but slouched sullenly down, the problem child aged seventeen, for dinner. My two other brothers, Ben, the eldest, and Teddy, two years younger than I, were both in the service, Ben in command of a minesweeper in foreign waters, Teddy recently volunteered for the paratroops, news I'd received with foreboding. So there were only the four of us, Mother, Dad, Peter, and I, to undo the ribbons and tear off the tissue paper of the packages under the tree Christmas morning. As I'd brought none and Peter, faithful to his Silas Marner neurosis, offered, as usual, nothing, all the gifts were affectionate parental presents, mine a Phaidon volume of Rembrandt's paintings, Peter's a set of books about the epistemological acumen of Ernest Rutherford.

On the Monday Mother and I went to New York to hear Rudolf Serkin play Mozart, Mendelssohn, Scriabin, and Ravel, had tea afterward at the Plaza, and talked about the beauty days at Paris Hill. Dad took his skates and drove up the Hudson beyond Nyack to do figure eights on the frozen river. Peter pounded the shit out of his piano. No one talked about the particulars of the fighting overseas, the jeopardy of warfare an unwelcome topic of conversation in a home having three sons subject to such peril. I went back to Boston on Tuesday.

Only occasionally in recent weeks had I run into Bill Anson in the corridor or showers, which suited me very nicely. The day after my return, the Wednesday of holiday week, he caught me by the hand, saying, "Hi, Jim, long time no see. Ducky's wondering if we're not good enough for you, or maybe there's a secret lover up your you know what. That it?"

"No such luck," I said. "Time goes by. Nothing personal. Say hello to the doc."

"Do it yourself. Big New Year's Eve dress-up party. He asked me specifically to ask you. Eight-thirty on. And don't worry about a costume. We got a mountain of dress-up stuff from Stage and Screen Costumes on Milk Street. So come as yourself, and turn into somebody else after you get there. Can we count on you?"

"Sure," I said, telling myself that in the hysteria of Happy New Year nobody would notice, or care, who was or wasn't present. "Will Paddy O'Higgins be there?"

"Never know with Paddy. Could be cruising Peru, making out with the ghost of his ancestor the viceroy. Always good for a surprise."

The surprise was the emptiness of Room 104 on Friday morning. Aaron was folded away on Pinckney Street, while even Tony had gone off to get drunk on free Pepsi at the USO with a WAVE he'd met at the movies and our two aloof buddies were eclipsed in each other's shadow. Leaving me alone to prove myself okay with myself in the nauseating nostalgia of tinny syncopation blaring from a record player somewhere down the hall playing "Chattanooga Choo-Choo." At quarter to nine, my ears pinched by the icy pliers of five below zero and having had two shots of Old Turkey at the nearby Ritz, I punched the buzzer button of Dr. Smythe.

The Restoration fop opened the apartment door. Disguised now as Randolph Scott in *Frontier Marshal*, complete with a silver star and brand-new Betty Grable nose, brandishing a rubber six-shooter, he said, "Stick 'em up, sweetie pie, your pecker or your life."

I said, "Shoot to kill," and walked past him.

Dr. Smythe was the nizam of Hyderabad in white crepe de chine, his headdress sporting a rhinestone the size of a golf ball. Behind him Bill Anson was a nearly naked Mowgli in a leopard skin loincloth.

The soirée promised exotic rounds of gaiety.

Bill said, "Come in the bedroom and take off your uniform. We got costumes galore. Who do you want to be?"

I laughed and said, "Captain Blood. What have I got to lose?"

The bedroom, indeed, was a riot of stage and screen disguises, boots and hats, wigs and ostrich feather boas, frocks, sarongs, pantaloons, jerkins, bathing suits, burnooses, loony outfits of wildest imaginings.

Bill helped me into tight breeches, a billowy blouse and even produced from a mound of headgear a tricorne that fitted me, a celluloid skull and crossbones pasted on it. I didn't for an instant feel ready to privateer a galleon, more prepared to walk the plank of mortification, but there I was, tricked out in the persona of a pirate, however dubious the windfalls thereof.

In the other room the other guests, a dozen or more young fellows were flopped about on the velvet couches, dressed up as cowboys, Lord Byron, policemen, gladiators, or ladies of leisure. Unprepared for the aggression of the unnatural, I wasn't much taken with men dressed up as women. Atavistic puritanical prudery suggested I get out of there. But the temperature outside was too cool, and besides, whom was I fooling? I was one of them. Making love to men was to be my life, no matter the sometime twinge of prudery, and there would be no getting out of that concomitant malaise.

The kid pretending to be a gladiator squiggled over against the golden-haired poet, making room beside him on the couch, patted the cushion, and said, "Have a seat, big boy. Who are you?"

"I'm a fake pirate," I replied, sitting down beside him. "You have nothing to fear. Who are you?"

He giggled. "I'm Ben Hur."

"Jesus!" I exclaimed. "I used to play with the Wallace kids when I was on vacation in Indianapolis. The general lived just up the street from my grandmother."

"Whadda ya know?" said Ben, indifferent as the real Hur had been to the author of his days and fame.

There were no tiny sandwiches. In their place a trestle table sagged with cold roast beef, horseradish sauce, turkey, jellied cranberries, Caesar salad, mince pie, angel food cake, champagne in silver buckets, and crystal decanters labeled "Burgundy," "Bordeaux," "Sauterne," "Port," "Scotch," "Bourbon," and "Rye." The versatile doctor must have worked his wiles on countless noses, ears, cheeks, chins, and jowls to underwrite a fete like this one. The music was interminable neo-Puccini welling from a rosewood record player. The Picasso was festooned with tinsel.

I ate a lot, drank a lot, breathed the stale smoke, went to the john, chatted with the stars of *Gone With the Wind*, waiting with good grace for midnight, sang and shouted for all I was worth, which was little when the lights went out, and it was—God have mercy on wretched earthlings—1944, and Ben Hur whispered in my ear, "Kiss me, you beautiful pirate, I think I'm in love with you."

I kissed him, and he kissed me, and it was the hard ingress down-your-throat mucous onslaught of the galley slave–cum–Roman soldier–cum charioteer hero to my stiffening surprise, at which I slid aside, withdrawing from so pugnacious an embrace. But he held on to me. He was surprisingly muscular. He said, "What's the matter? Don't you like me?"

"Sure I like you," I said. "It's just that—"

"It's just that we could go round the world," he said, pressing his hand into my crotch. "You into that?"

It was pointless to pretend his fondling had no effect. I said, "I'm into it. It's just that—"

"Shut up," he said. "I'll go see if the guest room's free. Buster and Teddy were in there before midnight. Ducky likes us to do it, you know."

"I know," I said.

He came back after five minutes to say the guest room was okay. As we went toward it, the doctor was in the corridor, and he said, "Be my guests, boys. Fellatio with the lights on. Who cares if the sheets are a mess?" and he pinched my right buttock till it hurt. I said ouch, and he laughed.

Ben Hur turned off the lights save a little lamp on a gueridon by the window. "What's your name?" he said. "I don't like to do it if I can't call you by your name."

"It's Jim," I said.

"Mine's Alex," he said, and he pushed me backward onto the bed. It was so easy, it was *too* easy, and I did it.

In the waxen-colored mornings my companion kept murmuring, "Jim, Jim, Jim," while his hands played over me, and I said, "Oh, Alex," and this time the daylight was on, and while we were doing it, I spied the nizam of Hyderabad in a far corner, furtively masturbating.

Having discarded my piracy and disinterred the GI costume, I found only Lord Byron asleep on the floor in the living room, his hair glutinous with cranberry jelly, and with the trestle table, coffee tables, couches, and carpets a spectacle of devastation.

I walked in the bitter air as far as Copley Square, had breakfast in the hotel, and took the bus back to Chestnut Hill.

Bill sought me out while shaving a couple of days later to ask whether I'd had a good time. I said, "Ben Hur won the chariot race."

"Alex is a winner," Bill said.

The priests strictly wished us a happy and well-spent new year. La Hu said *bon année* and the boches were going to catch it in '44 and the man with the mustache would be castrated, no mistake (*châtré pas d'erreur*).

The führer, however, remained defiant, boasted of deadly secret weapons up his sleeves, and promised to rain havoc upon the godless police state of his long-ago ally satanic Stalin. Soviet forces nonetheless relentlessly drove the Nazis from the last mote of Russian soil and crossed into Poland, where they came upon horrors confounding even to survivors of the Great Terror. And the fanatic warriors of the Rising Sun were forced by U.S. dogfaces to surrender the fortress of Saidor on New Guinea at a disastrous cost of men, plunder, and pride.

There did occur one occasion when the promiscuous lure of sexual emancipation almost initiated genital servitude. It began at the Napoleon. Mad-about-the-boy was doodling on the piano and I was moping over another Canadian Club when an ice-cold gush coursed down my leg. Shit on a stick! I cried to myself. Had I pissed my pants? No. Double shit! It was my neighbor, pawing my arm, all over me with excuses for his clumsy fumble, drink down my pants. "So sorry," he gasped, "I promise you. I can't tell you I'm so sorry. What can I do? Buy you a drink. Make it up to you, I swear."

He was a pimply PFC with a skull of musty hair and too old to be sporting pimples. I said, "Relax," removing my arm from his paw. "It'll dry out, and so will I; it's no drama."

"Listen," he said, replacing the paw, "let me make it up to you. I was just getting ready to leave. Going to a late-night party out on Commonwealth by the BU Bridge. How about I take you along? The more the merrier. I know the host. Plenty of drinks, and smokes too, in case you care for a little Mary Jane. What do you say?"

I said, "I don't know."

"Oh, come on. I owe you a good time, and you'll have it. Thought you pissed your pants, did you? I spilled my Pink Lady down your leg." He laughed as at a wisecrack truly riotous. "You not on for some gay fun? Cock-a-doodle-do, any cock'll do, don't be a shy sister."

We caught a taxi at the corner of Charles by the Central Burying Ground. His name was Larry, and he put his hand on my thigh as soon as we turned from Berkeley onto Commonwealth. I didn't bother to remove it. The ride was rather long, but the hand didn't advance onto private property. Our destination was a pile of crenellated fieldstone with a glass marquee over the front door and wrought-iron balconies at every window.

An immense colored man in a Prince Albert with a single diamond set into one of his nostrils opened the door. "Milady Larry," he said, "she scores again."

Larry said, "I aim to please."

We passed through a high airy hall past a fountain, water spurting from the penis of a bronze boy, and into a vast saloon, its walls wrapped in zebra hides hung with loops of red and green parrot feathers, outlandish furniture made from the horns of wild animals. A stooped, withered gentleman wearing a jet black wig, a mantle of monkey fur, and several diamond bracelets, speaking in the loud whisper of a reedy castrato, said, "Larry, my dear, what have we here? A neophyte novice of the amber stream?"

"Time will tell," said Larry.

"Reverence for life," said the gentleman. "But first a sip of the witch doctor's brew. Stirred it up myself, needless to say." Giggling, he patted the rim of an enormous wooden vat hewn, in all likelihood, from the bole of an ironwood tree. "Got the recipe from a blind sor-

ceress on the banks of the Ogowe on my way to see Dr. Schweitzer at
Lambaréné. Such a pet, dear old Albert. A saint, really. The natives
worship him. And there he is, year in, year out, playing Bach cantatas
on his broken-down organ at the edge of the jungle, don't you know?"

"We know, we know," said Larry, blasé about the legendary humanitarian of equatorial Africa.

Our host, not a man to be outdone by apathy, filled two wooden
beakers with his brew, handed one to each of us, and focused his
hooded eyes upon me. "And you," he inquired, "young man? Young,
young man? What might your name be?"

"Lord," I said, "Jim Lord," putting down my drink on an elephant's foot, and I thought, Jesus Christ, I'm in *Heart of Darkness.*

"Alistair MacCorkledale," he said, opening his skeletal hand.

I politely but briefly pressed the claw, thinking: How the hell can I
get out of here?, and said, "I'm afraid I'm not thirsty. Had more than
enough already."

Mr. MacCorkledale pointed a forefinger at the front of my pants.
"More than enough," he wheezed, "barely slakes the thirst of youths
your age. In Africa boys of eight years old can be ever and ever so
thirsty, don't you know?"

"We know," said Larry again. "We do know, Alistair. Those thirsty
little boys, so they say, caused the little accident, didn't they?"

"You are a beast," said Alistair.

Larry nodded, grasped my hand, and said, "Come on, baby, we go
play in the playroom," propelling me willy-nilly toward double doors
at the far side of the saloon opening onto a gloaming emptiness where
muted music of tribal drums rose and fell, punctuated by an occasional human yelp. "That Alistair," Larry went on, "ain't he a camp?
The darkest Africa routine. He overdid it with the eight-year-old boys,
so the natives grabbed him and cut off his balls. That's how he ended
up in the hospital of the crazy doctor. Well, we go along with darkest
Africa, and he gives with space for the mattress party. Come on, lovey."
He seized my arm and gave it a yank. "Take off your clothes."

"What?"

"Yeah, take off everything. It's a gang bang." And in less than a
minute he was naked, all his clothes tossed on the floor. "Come on.
Get in the swing. Everybody's in on it."

me, to satisfy, to fulfill already all the needs with which I could hope to cope, had, indeed, perhaps done too much. So I warily stayed away from Beacon Street, Spooner Place, the Public Garden, the nearby hotel, and its spellbinding bar.

The laze of days lasted only for about ten. Then one afternoon, a Friday, I was summoned to a ground-floor office in the administrative building. A friendly first lieutenant asked me to sit down and have a chat. In French. About France, the French, the Nazi occupation, the resistance, the collaborators, the French railways, radio stations, armament factories, the black market, the Free French, General de Gaulle, General Giraud, the Casablanca Conference, etc., lasting easily, informatively, and comfortably for a couple of hours. Whereupon the looie said, "That will be about all, Lord. You appear to be decently informed and getting along tolerably well in French."

I said, "I've always been attracted to everything French."

"Right. You're not so hot on factories, trains, and radio stations. Thanks for your time."

Despite the unfamiliar informality, I saluted before leaving and came upon Aaron in the hallway, awaiting his turn.

He came back to Room 104 barely in time for supper and said, *"Parlez-vous français?"*

I said, *"Les chemins de fer marchent mal."*

As it was Friday, we had halibut for supper, quickening an appetite for idle surmise, and both of us fancied that something strategically French, radio stations and trains notwithstanding, was probably in the works for our futures. The lieutenant had been too friendly to have *une simple causerie* up his sleeve. A hint to its purpose was posted Monday morning: we were both to be prepared for transfer to Fort Devens at 9:00 a.m. on Wednesday pending further assignment.

Tony took me aside. He said, "I'll never see you again."

"Don't say that," I said. "Who knows what the army's going to do?"

"The war knows," said Tony. "The war will do with us whatever the war wants to do."

"It's done plenty already," I said. "I can hardly believe how much when I think back about it."

"Think ahead. The war hasn't touched you yet. But it will, my

My eyesight concentrated on what everybody was in on: a mound of naked bodies in the dimmed half-light in the center of the room on an enormous mattress, bodies writhing on and around and on top of and below one another, the heads, buttocks, flanks, arms and legs, the hands clasping.

I backed away, stumbling backward over a settee of antelope horns, and ran to the front door.

Outside on the terrible sidewalk it was damnation and darkness. Frozen speechless, I walked all the way back to the Statler and got into bed—but not perchance to sleep—at three-fifteen in the morning.

A wave of anger and outrage swept America at the end of January following reports of Japanese atrocities. Thousands of U.S. POWs were alleged to have died on death marches to Jap prison camps, where countless others were tortured, starved to death, and murdered.

On the campus of Boston College in Chestnut Hill our matriculation as students of ASTP came to an end on January 29, an exceptionally sunny Saturday. I received a diploma.

The acceptable completion of my studies, at all events, however satisfying to the United States Army, did at least procure a semblance of military satisfaction for James H. Lord. It brought promotion from private to private first class. I became a PFC, a soldier in fact so lamentably low on the roster of rank as to be in his own esteem a nonentity of virtually less consequence than the universally unique private. I wore a one-stripe chevron on my sleeve, but it brought neither prerogative nor prestige. Aaron also received this honorary kick in the pants, though Tony didn't. Prickly adherence to a private code of right behavior is the surest way of remaining forever a private in any man's army.

The end of Boston College was not quite the end of Chestnut Hill, because we lingered on, all of us, in St. Mary's Hall, awaiting another assignment, laughing at the laxity of the army, not a little arrogant and complacent, hoping at the same time that a new assignment would not lead to the infantry, to a foxhole in the cruel Apennines or, still worse, to a beachhead in the pitiless Pacific.

It was for me, in any case, the end of Boston. Aaron continued to hide on Pinckney Street and said I'd best come for another visit before the provision of gin was quite depleted. I said I was sorry, and I was. But the city as a locus of enticement had done enough for me, and to friend. It will touch you to the quick. Wars do. Sooner or later. I know."

"But it hasn't touched you yet, has it?"

"Oh, Jim!" he cried. "Be serious. Do you imagine for a minute that these Jesuit inquisitors aren't at war with people like me? Class hatred. While you've been living in the Switzerland of bourgeois morality. But I don't pass judgment. I think. I wonder. I worry. About integrity. The man who handles war gets dirty hands. Innocence goes out the window. Have you given much thought, Jim, to guilt?"

"As a matter of fact, yes, guilt is something I've given a hell of a lot of thought to."

"Wait to see what this war has in store for you. When you look it in the face if ever you have to, and the landscape of life is shattered by guilt, then think on it."

"All right," I said, "if ever I have to."

A small truck came in the morning to carry Aaron and me and all our gear to Fort Devens. There we were led to a decent double room with adjoining bath in which we were to our amazement alone.

Aaron complimented the accommodations with a patrician nod and said, "I trust the secretary of war ordered this."

I said, "To put a feather in our hats and call it macaroni. The army must be eager to surprise us."

It was.

Eight

FEBRUARY–JUNE 1944

A surprise indeed was the brusque appearance of a captain in our quarters at 3:00 p.m. of the second day. His errand bored him, and he was curt. The following morning at 5:00 a staff car would take us to South Station, there to board a train for Baltimore. He dropped the orders and travel vouchers onto a table, turned to go, but I had the temerity to inquire as to our assignment. What that was, he snapped, we'd learn when necessary, which was not now, and he slammed the door.

At the Baltimore railway station a staff sergeant waited on the platform, listlessly waving a panel inscribed with our names. Follow me, he barked, leading us outside to a command car fit for a general. The sergeant was as bored by his errand as the Fort Devens captain, no less curt, ordering us to get into the backseat in a hurry, and he drove away with zero civility to his passengers.

Having left behind the suburbs, following a rural asphalt roadway that snaked through third-growth scrub, Aaron drawled, "Incidentally, Sarge, would you kindly tell us where we're going?"

"Classified," snarled the NCO.

After deserted mountain roads and ghostly fields it was deep dusk when we finally passed through a gateway toward lights and houses, and the driver became abruptly amiable, "Welcome to Camp Ritchie, Maryland," he announced. "The Military Intelligence Training Center."

Aaron and I looked at each other as if the oracles had knocked our heads together.

Adjoining beds in the assigned barracks had our names on them and were also marked "French, Class 17." The other occupants scrutinized us with hard-eyed vigilance. Military intelligence, for all we knew, might foster suspicion of the bona fides of strangers, especially should these appear well meaning. Or maybe mistrustful glances were prompted by scholastic snobbery, doubts that newcomers were sufficiently learned.

Camp Ritchie was a spacious conglomeration of neat white buildings in loops of paved roadway around a small lake along the modest mountainsides of the Blue Ridge. That this good-looking encampment might be on speaking terms with anything as arcane as espionage appeared, and had been well appointed to appear, as unlikely as the emergence from its lake of the Loch Ness monster. Passersby, moreover, were practically as rare as those who had really and truly caught sight of the Scottish subaqueous phenomenon. The only giveaway might have been the unpublished fact that the commandant of this woodland outpost was a brigadier general or, indeed, the regular appearance of his wife driving around and around the lake in a convertible roadster, her titian hair billowing in the breeze, smiling with unseemly broadness at the goggling servicemen. All in all, everything considered and everything to be considered were more than a lot; if BC had been like going back to college, Ritchie was like a spell at summer camp. Our counselors were officers in a state of pleasant relaxation, and the training was conducted under the conditions of sporting fair play.

I was amazed to find myself in a position to presumably be made fit for employment as a worker with, or for, or in military intelligence, as I had no knowledge of the uses of military mentality and no general intelligence that could be manipulated for the benefit of shooting wartime service. What had done the MIS trick for me was of course my romance with all things French, Baudelairean conversations with Madame Yakovleff under the grape arbor. Language, not intelligence, got me into the Military Intelligence Service, because shortsighted strategists planning the invasion of Nazi-occupied Europe had tardily seen that it would be expedient to have on hand speakers of the languages of the occupied countries in order to ferret out vital strategic information. The subsequent search for linguists must have been as frantic indeed, as reported in *The New York Times*, to have settled on me as serviceable material for the makings of a competent MIS man.

Such a man, at all events, it should be made clear from the beginning, would not be expected to have scratch in common with a product of the Office of Strategic Services, the legend-making OSS, whose operatives were expected to parachute into enemy territory, slit the throats of sentries in dead of night, and pass pouches of golden sovereigns to bearded men in the toilets of provincial hotels. None of that shoot-from-the-hip, risk-your-life-already action for us. Our doings and duties were all supposed to abide by the gentlemanly rules of polite warfare wisely, if disingenuously, set forth by the Geneva Conventions. To be sure, at the same time, if the occasion came along, it would be all to the good were we to apprehend any spies lurking beneath the living room rug, and should the fortunes of war occasionally call for unauthorized initiative, we might rip up the rug, and the flooring beneath it, in order to flush out dubious culprits, and so be it.

Training at Ritchie aimed to sharpen discernment: e.g., a man in a houndstooth suit and a deerstalker hat strides through our classroom firing a .38-caliber revolver, followed by a lady with a patch over one eye attired in a black satin cocktail gown, smoking a Sobranie cigarette in an amber holder and leading a dachshund by a green leather leash, followed by a harlequin in a red-and-white-striped outfit talking a blue streak in a foreign language, all three going out by the rear entrance in less than ninety seconds, after which we were required to describe in painstaking detail in writing exactly what had happened, what the three characters were wearing, doing, and saying, what their relations to one another had been, what purpose had been pursued in passing, what deceptions had been practiced, and what warnings of imminent trouble might have been suggested by their abrupt appearance. Our analyses of the incident were to be submitted within fifteen minutes, diligence of discernment being understood as an ability to see through artifice, disregard deliberate efforts to deceive, and recognize the modicum of falsehood in truth and the minimum of truth in falsehood. The intelligence service took for granted a talent to make inaccurate information accurate, to dismiss sentimental scruples, and to find out how to make killing people more efficient, and, if possible, more fun, for the infantry.

Our education was cunning, ingratiating, and cynical instruction in learning how to see through our own sly trickery while pinpointing the shrewd duplicity of an interlocutor. Naturally by way of recreation there were midnight marches through the mountains, risky scrambles around rocky escarpments and rollicking hours of target practice on the pistol range with .45 automatics. For added fun there was strict instruction in learning to drive dilapidated jeeps hurtling over dried-out riverbeds, under fallen telephone poles, and around artificial wreckage. Above all came indoctrination in the comfortable assurance that intelligence personnel were members of an elite cohort set apart from the dogfaced rank and file of foot-slogging soldiers. So we looked at one another with crafty but loyal smiles and went away on weekends to Washington, Baltimore, or a nearby waste of time called Hagerstown.

The frantic search for linguists having sought out mainly speakers of Continental tongues, there were German, Italian, and a few Mitteleuropean contingents at Ritchie, and around the campus you heard kraut rant, wop chatter, and Polack babble in the background and conversations in the languages of diplomacy and poetry, French and English.

Well, of course one didn't dismiss Goethe and Schiller, or Dante and Leopardi, Mickiewicz, or any of the great names of table and song. The very specificity, the weight, the personality of language lingered in the imagination, built there its stratagems of fantasy and measureless vistas of desire. Yes, and the haphazard phrase of German overheard in the PX excited inevitable imaginings.

Was it possible, was it not, after all, very probable, that *he* had passed through the Military Intelligence Training Center? Surely he had mentioned Maryland and added that his German, Teutonic, atavistic feelings had ultimately served him well. And the secret, furtive world of espionage would have suited him to a T, he who shied obstinately away from the trifling self-revelation of allowing so casual a vestige as a snapshot to document his identity. Hanno must have come to Camp Ritchie and left it, leaving me yet again alone and inconsolable.

Class 17 received much of its instruction in French. The man in the houndstooth suit wore in his lapel buttonhole the ribbon of the Légion d'Honneur, and you were well advised to notice it. The blue streak talk of the harlequin was in Breton. The leader of a midnight march bellowed, *"Traînez vos culs!"* We were ordered to talk frog, think frog, and fuck frog. There was zero fucking, however, frog or otherwise, going on at Ritchie, sad to say. I received—quite expectedly—kindly tutoring from an affable Frenchman named Régis, teaching me the particulars of French train routes and schedules, the frequencies and locations of radio transmitters, and the whereabouts of factories for the manufacture of automobile tires, electric lightbulbs, cooking stoves, and, incidentally, machine guns, howitzers, and heavy trucks.

Of the interesting fellow trainees in my barracks, the most interesting, if not perhaps the most jovial or rackety, was Garo Beglarian. He spoke, when he spoke, very quietly, not quite in a whisper but with a muted vehemence that recalled Tony's integrity. Apropos of nothing in particular, for example, he might say, "The defense of human dignity depends for full effect upon a recognition that the human animal is indefensible, and this, moreover—to situate us anent the French idea of the creative mind—despite Monsieur Bergson's intimation of a life force pervading all duration."

Garo was a philosopher, his locution decidedly Socratic, and we listened to him with a respect tempered by the embarrassing inability to follow the meanders of his dialectic. About the terrible turmoil of his past, however, there was absolutely nothing abstruse, and he spoke of it without restraint, with, indeed, passionate impeachment and recrimination.

With a name like that, Garo was obviously Armenian. His father, Parouir, had been a prosperous merchant of carpets in the town of Aralik hard by the Aras River in the shadow of Mount Ararat. Armenia through the ages had been ravaged by Romans, Persians, Byzantines, White Huns, Khazars, Arabs, and Turks and under Ottoman rule suffered severe discrimination. Serious persecution had begun in the 1890s and came to a ghastly convulsion in 1915 after the Ottoman Empire had allied its forces with the enemies of England, France, and Russia. Hundreds of thousands of Armenians, men, women, and children, were slaughtered by Turkish troops; towns, burned; villagers, left to die of hunger. Multitudes of others were forced in murderous marches over mountains, their route littered with corpses. The Beglarians were lucky, making their fugitive way overland by muleback to the Black Sea port of Batumi, thence eventually by ship to Marseille and finally to Paris. There the resourceful merchant shrewdly enrolled his only child in the elite Lycée Condorcet.

Fatigued and demoralized by the abominations visited upon this people, Garo's parents both expired without a whimper within one week of each other during the cruel winter of 1932.

Orphaned, bereaved, but philosophical, Garo inherited a sumptuous carpet that had been woven for the grand vizier Kara Mustafa, who extended Ottoman power to the very gates of Vienna. It paid for his education.

Nor did he require the intuition of a professional philosopher to decipher the National Socialist writing on the European wall. Having booked passage aboard the *Normandie*, he found lodgings on Riverside Drive, enrolled at Columbia, completed the doctoral dissertation in which he extemporized freely upon the supraliminal instrumentality of will and idea in the works of Tolstoy, Proust, and Thomas Mann, whereupon the writing on the wall exploded onto the front pages of the world's newspapers. It transpired that an Armenian refugee, especially one with academic eminence, speaking six languages fluently, could mutate into an American citizen by joining up, so Garo became a GI and gravitated to Camp Ritchie.

Not everybody was a philosopher. There were plenty of good-time Charlies too. Of these, one of the most versatile, exuberant, and competent I ever knew was Harrison Alliot, Jr., who slept in the bed next to Aaron's, across the aisle from mine. He said we'd better call him H and forget about the Junior, because he believed he wasn't, and hoped he wasn't, the biological son of Daddy Alliot. He was strikingly good-looking, dark hair, green eyes, and the irresistible smile of a cheetah, built like a Greek statue and, he merrily bragged, endowed by nature with "the biggest cock west of the Pyramids," a boast ratified daily by awed and envious stares in the showers. He intimated that since the age of sixteen he had been conscientious about sharing the largeness of nature's generosity. In short, many ladies in his life. Still, one Sunday evening he came back from a weekend in Washington and mentioned to me in passing that he'd spent all of the Saturday afternoon in bed with the daughter of a congressman and a marine guard from the White House detail. So I wondered.

The man H was loath to acknowledge as a biological parent was nonetheless as generous with the disaffected boy as nature had been. Daddy Alliot owned a couple of thousand acres of tangerines somewhere in California and sent munificent checks to Junior, who gladly cashed them and maintained that his scribbled endorsement of each, including the mandatory "Jr.," was a clear and sufficient sign of gratitude. Generosity, at all events, had been bestowed upon H not only by Ma Nature and Daddy Tangerines but also, as he smilingly let on, by dames elderly enough to be his mama and rich enough to lavish material bounty upon a youngster famished for affection. Some of these matrons even paid affluent attention to his military career, venturing as far as Washington, D.C., for the occasional nymphomaniac weekend. So much incidental lucre moved H himself to spasms of generosity, and it was often difficult at the PX to dissuade him from seducing every man present into accepting the extra Pepsi, BLT, milk shake, burger, banana split, or what have you.

"He's a gem," said Aaron, "a diamond as big as the Waldorf-Astoria, but a rough one." He laughed, adding, "Rough but ever so large."

It is odd, surely, that while my homeland was at war to destroy the Third Reich, do away with its criminal rulers, and shame the German people for their slavish adulation of the führer, at the same time I was deeply in love with things profoundly German, the music of Beethoven, the imagination of Thomas Mann. I thought of him often, asked myself unanswerable questions about his state of mind and the status of his writings in relation to the conflict ravaging *his* homeland. Luckily there was someone I could talk to or, rather, listen to.

Well now, Garo mused. *The Magic Mountain* is a snowfield of allegory. You're treading on nuance up there, passing across the thin crust of a distinction between what's philosophy and what's philosophical, and if that surface gave way and the crevasse below was very deep, you'd be plunged way, way down—over your head—in the fissure of conjecture. In any symbol there lie the lapses and temptations of the ambiguous. Some find it heavy going on the mountainside in the blizzard where Hans Castorp is lost to reality and humanity. One may take pleasure in the dialectical dance, an ontological pas de deux between Signor Settembrini and Herr Naphta, the juxtaposition of a humanist advocate of reason, the Enlightenment, and a fanatic partisan of violence and despotism, who commends torture and the Inquisition as access to spiritual redemption, Settembrini something of a windbag, Naphta a Fascist *en herbe*, and the pas de deux a three-step, thanks to the moral increment of Mynheer Peeperkorn—such a wonderful name—who selflessly contributes vitality to a philosophy of life by ending his own. All of this, to be sure—and all of it is decidedly a lot—is by way of leading to the salvation of Castorp's soul, a quite Germanic, even Teutonic soul, it's true, which in turn leads to the willingness of the protagonist to leave the mountain to its magic and go off to war, war that will lead to the defeat of darkness and the restoration of freedom to a benign and responsible populace.

I wondered whether Thomas Mann would think we do right by going to war.

Garo allowed that one may wonder, yes, what the old *Zauberer* would say about the redeeming potential of today's conflict.

I said nothing about fantasy suppositions of my own.

One of them came to a strange climacteric not long after my talk with Garo about *The Magic Mountain*. Maybe there was some relation between what happened to Hans Castorp in the snowstorm and what happened to me in the museum. It was the National Gallery of Art in Washington, standing in patient splendor on Constitution Avenue as if it were awaiting with clairvoyant assurance my compulsion to meet the Samaritan whose goodness had given such a "boost"—such aid and assistance—to a needy traveler. The painting by El Greco so crucial, evocative, metaphorical for Hanno and his good friend. I had no trouble finding it, because in that building, only recently made ready for visitors, there were not as yet very many pictures.

When I came face-to-face with it, I felt like laughing, because it was not the Good Samaritan, not at all, and the mistake would have been all too laughable had it not been unthinkable. What was it? I saw what it was and I saw what it wasn't, and saw that the mistake was *mine*, and my laughter swallowed itself with astonishment and bitterness, because the actual good man, not at all from Samaria, though in fact compassionate, was a soldier on horseback, the title of the painting— unbelievable, but there it was—at which I gasped: *St. Martin and the Beggar*. St. *Martin*! How could Hanno have thought? Or had he? Had they? The Freudian joke therefore on me! Had they, in truth, seen this painting, albeit definitely by El Greco, and a masterpiece, as the very up-to-date and apposite symbol of their own beneficent meeting? Why on earth not? If they were attuned to prophetic meanings. For what, in fact, was the painting a picture of?

Martin was by no means a saint. He was a grand military tribune in magnificent golden armor, with a lean, pensive, and appealing face, seated astride a noble white horse and preparing with his drawn sword to cut away three-quarters of the green velvet cloak that already falls across the naked, athletic, muscular body of a tall, dark-haired, and handsome young fellow grazing expectantly, and already thankfully, upward at his benefactor.

Oh, yes, it was easy to see what they had seen in the symbolism of that painting. A "boost" indeed. The name Martin deriving from the Latin *Martinus*, adjective for Mars, Roman god of war, personified by the good-looking officer come in time of war to benefit a boy whose atavistic aspiration, after all, had been to succeed to the gallant and noble military tradition of his forebears. Hanno touting the Teutonic cult of death-defying resolve to honor a soldier's code of duty. Siegfried, glorious warrior of the *Nibelungenlied*. Marshal Rommel of the Afrika Korps. And the military tribune in his armor and the good-looking beggar clothed in a handsome length of green velvet, to what destination may they have proceeded after that chance meeting outside the city gates of Amiens? Together or each on his own? The legend leaves their future up to them, which is a denouement, indeed, greatly to be desired.

The Samaritan then? How did he come into the picture? No likeness of him in the National Gallery, either by El Greco or anyone else. Had Hanno simply invented him, imagining symbolic relevance to the meeting of two men on the lookout for mutual benefaction? Or was this a malicious wrinkle in the Freudian joke, an unkind turn of the affective screw? I didn't know, but I did care. Had Hanno understood, hwoever, who or what he was bringing into the lover's picture? Well and truly beatified but unknown to fame, albeit the patron saint of drunkards, the Good Samaritan had been celebrated through the ages without the blessing of the Vatican but with biblical authority (Luke 10:30–35), which must be better. The parable tells of a traveler on his way from Jerusalem to Jericho who falls among thieves. They rob him, wound him, strip him naked, and leave him by the roadside half dead.

There comes down a priest that way, sees him, and passes by on the other side; likewise a Levite. But a certain Samaritan sees him and has compassion on him, binds up his wounds, brings him to an inn, and takes care of him. And on the morrow, when he departs, the Samaritan takes out two pence, gives them to the host, and says unto him, "Take care of him."

What was all that about? The wounded wayfarer lying naked by the roadside is taken to an inn and cared for there by the kindly stranger who spends the night and on the morrow pays the innkeeper for continued care. Is it gross irreverence to wonder what took place during the kind hours of darkness? Is it sacrilegious to imagine that the patron saint of drunkards might suppress something displeasing to holy canons of morality? What answer might Hanno be, or bring, or beg to such questions?

I ran out of the museum and took the first bus to Hagerstown. Public transport was not permitted anywhere near Camp Ritchie. I had a sort of dinner at the Mason-Dixon Café and afterward drank five or six Collinses.

Stumbling into the barracks, I found Aaron in bed reading *The Razor's Edge.* He said, "Truly it passeth understanding, the tiresome and naive things people will do in search of salvation."

I said, "Dante says you have to go through hell to get to heaven."

"If you can believe that," said Aaron, "you're already in heaven."

March melted into April. Monte Cassino refused to fall even as bombers reduced to rubble the Benedictine monastery within which the Germans had been fortified, and General Alexander said of them, "No other troops in the world could have stood up to it and gone on fighting with such ferocity." In Hungary at the same time, Nazi officials were busy preparing the deportation of 750,000 Jews to a Polish camp for expeditious extermination. A partisan in Rome tossed a bomb at a squadron of SS troops, killing 20 of them, and in reprisal the Germans shot exactly 200 hostages in the Ardeatine Caves. In the Far East, Allied forces operating behind enemy lines in Burma crossed the Irrawaddy River in an operation code-named Broadway, in order to fight, said General Wingate, "inside the enemy's guts."

At Camp Ritchie, meanwhile, we were quizzed about the importance of Trappes (a crucial railway switching yard southwest of Paris), the importance of General Henri Giraud (commander in chief of Free French Forces in North Africa and rival of General de Gaulle as leader of liberated France), and the importance of St. Tropez (an obscure fishing village on the Mediterranean coast and a possible beachhead). It was rumored that a grunt from Class 17 had made out with the general's wife, and we all assumed it must have been H, but he only yielded the feline smile of a leopardlike carnivore. An article appeared in *The Washington Post* reporting the sensational price lately paid at auction for a picture painted by Picasso during his Blue Period and commenting at length on the technical virtuosity and psychological penetration of the artist's work. I read and reread this tribute to his genius, and my imagination fooled with the idea that even a man of his transcendent creative superiority will drink a cup of coffee and walk out in the noonday sun like you and me.

It had certainly not been my intention to return to Washington, but then a letter from my mother rather pointedly suggested that that would be a kind thing to do. The Yakovleffs were unhappily employed there, he as butler, she as cook and housekeeper, by an overbearing British martinet named Sir John Dill, the personal representative of the prime minister to the Combined Chiefs of Staff. They would very happily welcome a visit for old times' sake from Jim if he could possibly slip away. So I did.

Monsieur and Madame were miserable, though resigned to one more of the misfortunes of war. It was a morose soirée. We tried without much success to evoke the happy moments under the grape arbor but did, at least, enjoy a luxurious dinner in Sir John's immaculate kitchen and drink his expensive wines. I promised to keep in touch with them via the army post office and if ever I reached Paris to call on their daughter. I did not regret going to see them and would later have reason to thank the fates for having arranged it.

Garo was seated on the toilet. "You find me at my best," he said when I came in to piss, "disposing of ideological waste. Such as torment one in the world of spiritual pain and unsatisfied sexual desire. Schopenhauer," he concluded, wiping, standing, flushing, and pulling up his pants.

"That old bore," I said, buttoning up, "no wonder he had no friends. Of either sex."

"He had a dog," said Garo, "but possibly neglected to preserve its name."

French, Class 17 had begun preparing for graduation. No more strangers firing revolvers in the classroom. No more guesswork as to the potential productivity of German armaments in the Renault factory at Boulogne-Billancourt. One last all-night make-believe combat exercise, however, up and down and around an adjacent mountainside, one company "attacking" an imaginary woodland redoubt, the other "defending" it, the outcome of this masquerade to be "decided" before dawn, accompanied by much noise, rockets, firecrackers, flares, and assorted gizmos.

We marched out one hour after sunset laden with M-1 rifles, backpacks, gas masks, picks, and shovels. I was in Company B, commanded by a creep from camp HQ who said he knew the terrain like the back of his fucking hand, a claim so false it led me to the infirmary. Company A was the enemy, marching onto the same mountainside from an opposite flank. As we reconnoitered our approach to the forest, darkness came down like lead, confusion stalked the troops, and bellyaching was general. The commander barked out a lot of bullshit. Sniper on the forward gradient. Eat dirt, you motherfucker, eat dirt. To which admonition someone bellowed, Fuck *your* mother, and eat shit. Off to the right, to be sure, there was a pop goes the weasel, and we fired a round of blank cartridges. Forward platoons blundered about in the underbrush, and in the distance somebody yelled, Casualty down, medics front and center. Our commander shouted, Mortar fire dead ahead. Foxhole drill. Dig in. The same someone called back, Asshole drill. Cop-out. Anyway, we hacked at the shale with our toy shovels.

H had a bottle of brandy, so we sat down for several swigs.

Aaron said, "Is this a take-no-prisoners operation?"

"Probably," said H. "Were you planning to go to the POW route?"

"Honestly, no," Aaron replied, "but I was thinking of turning. Doing the double agent bit."

I said, "As for me, I'm single, double zero operative, planning to get lost in the melee, shoot myself in the toenail. See you back at the camp."

"Not much pussy in these woods," said H, brandishing the empty cognac bottle.

I wandered off between the trees. Somewhere close at hand there was a monster boom, followed by a rat-tat-tat and a rat-tat-tat and then a chorus of simulated screaming. Anxious to escape capture and avoid stepping on a firecracker, I stumbled around, searching for somewhere cushy to bed down for the night. The darkness was heavy, air hot and humid, as if preparing for a storm to orchestrate the battle, and St. Elmo's fire flickered through the thickets. A little farther in the brush I nearly tripped over an invisible log, which moaned and cried out, "Watch your step, will you! Can't you see I'm dead? You looking to kill me."

I said, "Of course I can't see you, you idiot, it's pitch dark, and if you're dead, you're supposed to have a phosphorescent marker on you. I could have stepped in your mouth, for God's sake."

The let's pretend corpse said, "Drop dead, fuckface. Move out or I'll slice your balls off, got my knife on the ready."

To which I rejoined, "If you're dead, you can't talk, so shut the fuck up, or I *will* step in your mouth."

He groaned, and I stamped away in the dark.

This was more than enough of what could conceivably come about in actual combat, I thought, and the make-believe was too burlesque to go along with. Feeling my way across the ragged terrain, I came upon a patch of luxuriant leaves. Tossing away my pack and taking off all my sweat-drenched clothes, I settled with sighs of contentment, snuggling into the foliage, and fell asleep. Sometime in the depths of the night at its most vulnerable hours I started awake. It was raining. The storm had broken. Without thunder, without lightning, however, and the raindrops were warm, splashing down in a single jet, surprisingly, and I sat up abruptly, exclaiming, "What the *hell* is this?"

A voice above me said, "Jesus, I was just taking a leak."

"A leak hello," I shouted. "You're pissing all over me, you stupid son of a bitch."

But he said, "This is war, buddy. Aren't you supposed to be dead?"

"Of course I'm not dead, you jerk. Get lost."

He marched away, stumbled over something, swore, and was gone.

Fumbling, I found my underwear, wiped myself dry as best I could, and, bleary at the silliness, went back to sleep.

The dawn was noncombatant. Blinking against the first light, I rubbed my eyes and took a look at the surroundings. They were bad. My vegetal feather bed proved to have been a gleaming expanse of green poison ivy, to which I was extravagantly allergic and amid which I had lain naked all night.

Forty-eight hours later I lay in the infirmary. My face, my arms, hands, legs, feet, and private parts, my entire body front and back, were covered with crusted, oozing, unbearably itchy pustules, and every inch of skin was caked white with potassium permanganate. I looked like a leprous ghost. Aaron and H came to console "poison Jim" with shivers of hilarity.

Aaron said, "We're going to rent you out to the Ringling Brothers."

H said, "Show us your cock."

When I declined to, they laughed some more and left.

I was discharged from the infirmary on Friday. Graduation exercises for Class 17 were scheduled to take place the following Monday, May 8. My face was still caked with potassium permanganate, white indeed as the most serviceable clown. When I climbed to the platform to receive my diploma from the gingerly fingertips of General Banfield, the crowd howled, as if I by my commedia dell'arte makeup had intentionally meant to turn to derision this ceremony and all its purposes. Which, as a matter of fact, had I surmised but a mite of its outcome I'd have done very well to do. Mirth notwithstanding, I had become an accredited agent of the Military Intelligence Service. The diploma meant business.

The Military Intelligence Training Center
United States Army
Camp Ritchie Maryland
This is to certify that
James H. Lord 12183139 Pfc.
has satisfactorily completed the course prescribed for
the 17th Class at
The Military Intelligence Training Center

J. H. Huffman, Lt. Col.
Charles M. Banfield, Brig. Gen. Commandant
Shipley Thomas, Col., MI Director of Training
8 May 1944
Camp Ritchie, Md.

Exactly how satisfactorily, however, I had completed the prescribed course was a matter tactfully left cryptic by the diploma. A broad hint as to official satisfaction was nonetheless provided by the promotion in rank I received as a graduation present. I became a technician third grade, a T-3, tech sergeant, my sleeves improved by chevrons with three stripes above, one below and a *T* in between. This demonstrated discernment on the part of Colonel Thomas, for it was the lowest rank that one could hold as an MIS agent. I was pleased with it because I had no ambition to excel at winkling out secrets, extracting information from shadowy sources, or assuming abstruse responsibilities. Aaron apparently was more loftily motivated than I, as he received the rank of staff sergeant. He belittled the distinction, and I agreed. H did no better than I, which looked like the bounty of Lady Luck, while Garo made master sergeant because, perhaps, the authorities reasoned that they had best bestow superiority upon Socrates.

All this was very well, but what logistical assignments and duties were to be ours as agents of the Military Intelligence Service of the U.S. Army? That question naturally and insidiously preoccupied everyone, nor was it to be answered, if at all, for hamstringing months.

Camp Ritchie, meanwhile, having hosted our crafting as cryptos, no longer wanted us on its premises. Our beds beckoned to Class 18. Accordingly we were trucked to the Baltimore railway station and transported, without the least amenity due our status as elite personnel, to Fort Devens, Massachusetts, a stone's throw from Boston, albeit a stone the size of Plymouth Rock.

For some reason apparently perverse, the sexual inducements of the city failed this time to make me their creature. The Athens of America roused Garo to dialectical delight, of course, and he made a pilgrimage to the birthplace of the "radical empiricist" in Cambridge. H hung out in the Merry-Go-Round Bar of the Costly Pleasure, where his own pleasure found expensive wherewithal. Aaron insisted I accompany him for weekends twice to Pinckney Street, where I occupied the Salmon the First bedroom and Mrs. Randolph waggishly entertained us by playing "Alexander's Ragtime Band" on the harp.

The weather was stifling. Cassino fell at last on May 18, the surviving defenders chagrined but ever defiant, the mountainside a ghastly desolation of rotting corpses, blasted trees, and rusting wreckage, the monastery a heap of rubble.

In the late afternoon of the first Tuesday of June there came across the camp an unexplained hush of excitement, and in a magical moment every living radio divulged the wonderful facts. American, British, and Canadian troops were ashore on three beaches in Normandy. We sat up all night. By dawn our time 150,000 Allied soldiers were securing important bridgeheads. Casualties had been heavy but less than expected. German resistance, though fierce, was sporadic and surprisingly disorganized, as if the invasion had been unexpected, causing us to wonder what was wrong with Nazi intelligence.

Throughout the month of June we stuck by our radios, anxious to learn what was happening in the country where our training would eventually be put to the test. In vain, however, impatient for action, too ignorant to be afraid, we awaited orders to ship out. Besides, what harm, what peril could threaten the sly agents of MIS?

American forces, fighting from Omaha Beach through the cruel hedgerows and sunken roads of Norman farmland, had driven a pocket twenty miles deep into German defenses eight days after D-day, passing the towns of Bayeux and Balleroy, leaving in the latter the lovely château undamaged. Still, it became clear that the battle for Normandy would by no means be a pushover, and Patton warned it would be costly.

Far to the south in the insignificant village of Oradour-sur-Glane the entire population of six hundred souls had been herded by SS troops into the church and burned alive in reprisal for a resistance attack on German forces. The Russians launched their summer offensive and in one week broke the German line over a front of more than two hundred miles, a reverse from which Nazi forces would never recover. The enraged führer launched his "secret" weapon, the rocket-powered V-1 bomb, derisively nicknamed the Doodlebug by defiant Britishers despite disheartening damage and many deaths.

We waited and waited, confident but nervous in the expectation that our orders would be delivered without preamble. A clerk brought them on Friday, the last day of June, about five in the afternoon, while in Normandy our men on the road to Villers-Bocage, which lay in ruins, were fighting for their lives.

At dawn on Sunday, July 2, loaded like livestock into open trucks, we were carted to a far, malodorous dock in the port of Boston, there to say goodbye to our homeland, which some of us might never see again.

Part II

IN EUROPE

Nine

JULY–AUGUST 1944

The S.S. *Argentina*, grimy vagrant of the seas, redolent of overripe cargoes and nautical neglect, wallowed outward upon the Gulf of Maine. Fading behind us in the neutral afternoon lay the elbow of Cape Cod. I hung on to the rail and gazed back at the blue silhouette of home. So, ignorant of perils and treacheries, horrors and crimes, oblivious to the evil that works upon the innocence of any who come to grips with evil, no matter the goodwill of their intentions, I'd embarked at last upon the long voyage. Guilt is the keepsake of employment in a business that deals in death. That aspect, too, I failed to foresee beyond the watery horizon, where I was concerned mainly to glimpse the contours of starry-eyed eventualities. All adventure, of course, is concerned with going somewhere, attaining a destination, whether actual or spiritual, one remote from a point of departure. It will entail a search or a quest, which may lead to a definitive meeting with oneself. For this I was sensationally unprepared.

Meals of tasteless slop, eaten standing, were served to enlisted men twice a day in the fetid belly of the South American freighter, while in more spacious quarters above, officers, seated at proper tables, ate real food three times daily with decent cutlery, providing welcome cause for resentment. The tiers of bunks were designed for discomfort: lengths of canvas roped taut between steel stanchions, two deep and three high, cramped defiles between. Drowsing off in the airless half dark was not easy.

Our pitiable ship was part of a convoy. All around on the oily swell a flotilla of miserable vessels slumped against the waves, none allowed better progress than the slowest of the hulks, while sleek destroyers

cruised around and around in races of foam, sending depth charges
against nonexistent Nazi subs; the underwater war had long since
turned disastrous for Admiral Dönitz. I found Aaron and Garo sitting
on the starboard edge of the rear hold.

Aaron remarked that proper table manners were not needed on
the voyage. Garo mused about the waves. Below them lie the deeps.
Below the deeps lie the depths. And those who look deeply into
the depths will see the depths looking back at them from the abyss.
Truth, however, does not dwell at the bottom of things. So said
Democritus.

A democrat?

Garo laughed, for Democritus was known as the laughing philosopher, because he found human foibles so funny, and maybe the funni-
est foible of all is that Karl Marx wrote a thesis on him.

England, everybody promised, was our destination. Not North Africa, the Azores or, thank God, Italy, where cruel fighting continued
through the Tuscan mountains. And indeed, on our twelfth afternoon
afloat our destination did turn out to be England as the South American vessel came to dock in the battered brick harbor of Liverpool.

We trooped down the gangplank, and all the MIS men got formed
up in a column and marched off into the twilight through ruined
streets past hillocks of rubble to a railway siding, where a pitiful train
with many shattered windows waited. It was more comfortable than
the *Argentina*, broken windows welcome, as the July night was stifling. We were about forty men and a dozen officers, not nearly enough
to crowd the three railway cars reserved for us. It was dawn by the
time we reached our terminus, a town called Worcester, damaged but
picturesque. This was Europe, home to civilization, goal to the good
life, the destination I'd dreamed of. Worcester was not our final stop.
Trucks stood ready for the enlisted men; a few command cars, for officers. And we set off across the green and pleasant landscape.

So we came to Broadway, a beautiful, picturesque, charming, romantic Cotswold village set in the midst of sheep-grazing meadows at
the foot of a very high hill with a stone tower standing straight on top.
The broad central thoroughfare led gently down to a trapezoidal green
past antique houses of tawny stone with tall gables and leaded windows. The Military Intelligence Service had selected this lovely, peace-

ful place as its country HQ far from the ruins and dangers of London. Proof yet again of the privileged jurisdiction well exercised for the benefit of elite personnel. A number of houses had been requisitioned to lodge us, though not so many as to trouble the tranquillity of the place. Besides, MIS men were not expected to linger indefinitely in Broadway. Cross-channel assignments, if not actually threatening, were more or less imminent though the crump of artillery and bombs never disturbed that secluded spot.

Meanwhile the butterflies of July fluttered around the pinks and larkspur and fragrant mignonette in gardens designed when America still belonged to Britain. Aaron, H, and I were lodged in the same house, not a Cotswold classic but incomparably comfortable after the *Argentina*. Garo was billeted nearby, but a mere hundred yards distanced him enough from daily life that he no longer participated in our conviviality, and that was too bad, because his philosophical presence had brought to our camaraderie a dimension we missed without him.

Down the street, its width having doubtless given the town its name, stood a handsome, noble old hotel called the Lygon Arms, discovered by us in forty-eight hours. It had been efficiently spruced up to satisfy comfort-loving MIS standards, and the several well-heeled officers who had rooms there looked somewhat askance at the occasional levity of enlisted men. Meals beneath the cathedral ceiling of the dining hall were not bad, considering wartime rationing, and by some miracle there seemed to be plentiful reserves in the cellar, including prewar champagne. Two or three grocery stores offered surprising provisions at elevated prices. While waiting for assignments, we had nothing to do but enjoy the sunshine of an exceptional summer and ride rented bicycles around the countryside. What mornings, what afternoons and nacreous evenings, which thanks to double wartime went on forever. Even without champagne dreams awaited us beyond the wit of soldiers to say what dreams befitted a midsummer's night. And Stratford, as a matter of fact, lay but twelve miles away, and the theater presented plays. Never had I possessed such a wealth of well-being and the eagerness to spend it.

Indeed in a shopwindow one morning I saw something unprecedented: a small pyramid of peaches so perfect and blushful I remembered instantly the delight of boyhood picnics in the wildflower fields of Paris, Maine. Inside the shop, these fruit of the Hesperides looked even more alluring, and I asked the price. A gracious old lady wearing a pince-nez on a black ribbon named an amount so startling I said, "Each?"

"Each," she said. "But you'll not find another like one of these. For a military man I'll make it a little less."

So I bought one, took a bite of it right there in the shop. A marvel of sweetness, it was indeed incomparable, and I told the lady she was right, whereupon with juice running down my chin, I noticed through the shopwindow two small boys peering at the peaches and saw that they looked just alike, blue-eyed, blond-haired, pink-cheeked. They were twins, as a matter of fact, identical, dressed exactly alike, angelic in the duplication of their singular beauty and unparalleled sweetness of expression. Aged seven or eight, I thought. Beside them stood a tall light-haired lady, slender and pretty, unmistakably maternal, she too looking in at the peaches. Now, I had never before cared about good-looking little boys. But these two defied particularities. Looking at them was like seeing life's beauty looking back at itself in a living mirror, a glimpse that posed irresistible temptation. Buying two more peaches, I went outside and handed one to each child. They gaped, stared in bewilderment, held the peaches in their hands, and one murmured, "Oh, Mummy."

She smiled, and then it was simple to see how the sons had become beautiful. She said, "Really, Sergeant, you shouldn't have. Still, it is a splendid treat. You see, they have never tasted a peach. So rare now and so dear."

"Believe me," I said, "the treat is mine."

"It is very kind. All right, children. Their names are David and John." And they immediately set to munching. She held out her hand. "And mine is Katherine Scott."

We shook. "James Lord," I said.

"One sees soldiers cycling round about. Do you by chance have the use of a bicycle?"

"I rented one just the other day."

She bent down and wiped the chins of her sons with a handkerchief. "We don't live here in Broadway," she said. "We're from Birmingham, you see. Edgbaston, really. My husband's a surgeon there, but he didn't want us to stop on because of the bombing. We have a little cottage in a village called Willersey. A few miles across the fields. If you'd care to join us one afternoon for tea. Any afternoon you like. We're always at home. You couldn't miss the cottage, the only one in Willersey with a blue door. I hope you'll come."

"I'd love to," I said.

"Make it soon then."

"Would it be all right if I came tomorrow?" I asked, surprised by my eagerness.

"Please do. Anytime after four. At your convenience." The smile played from her eyes as well as from her lips, and the light in her face was shimmering.

As I strolled back down the street, I thought, What a world of promise, without the bother of slaying the dragon that guards the tree of the golden fruit.

I found the cottage easily and hardly had knocked before the blue door was open.

"Sergeant Lord," she said, "do come in."

"James, please," I said.

The boys were seated on either side of a squat table, and they giggled. "Shake hands with James," said their mother. They stood, looking downward, and held out miniature hands, which I self-consciously pressed. "And you must call me Kitty," said Mrs. Scott. "It's very low tea, I'm afraid. Wartime priority. I was just reading to the twins."

"Mr. Toad, Mr. Toad," the two cried with one voice.

She laughed. "Mr. Toad of Toad Hall, yes. You know, *The Wind in the Willows.*"

"I did once," I said.

"The poem, the poem," cried David and John.

"All right. One stanza. Then James must have a cup of tea." And she took up the book.

> *The world has held great Heroes,*
> *As history books have showed;*
> *But never a name to go down to fame*
> *Compared with that of Toad!*

"Mr. Toad, Mr. Toad," shrieked the twins.

The tea was strong, one lump of sugar and a single slice of bread and margarine. I thought how faulty I'd been to forget chocolate and chewing gum from the PX. My welcome felt so true that it dispelled any doubt as to the seemliness of presuming upon it by offering unobtainable tokens of appreciation.

The cups were empty, the bread and butter eaten. David and John sat in silence, musing upon the bravery and repute, so I assumed, of the Honorable Mr. Toad. Mrs. Scott looked at her wristwatch. She said, "Such a lovely afternoon. 'Tis a pity to sit inside. Shall we go for a stroll?"

"Let's," I said.

"To the stile and back," said one of the twins.

"Boys," said their mother, "we played hide-and-seek all the morning. From teatime to suppertime is time for reading, writing, and arithmetic. To your books if you please."

The twins went dutifully to their studies, their mother and I out the blue door into a perfect stillness. Not a cricket or the rustle of a waxwing was audible beneath the vivid air. We walked out of Willersey up a velvet hillside in the five o'clock sunshine.

Kitty said, "My heart leaps when I behold the life in these fields. Are you a Wordsworthian, James?"

"I suppose," I said, surprised. "That is, I had, or I thought I had, a feeling for nature. I remember when I was only seven or eight trying to write a poem about a bird flying from tree to tree in our garden. The poem was nothing, of course. I don't know why I'm telling you this."

"I know," she said, but before I could inquire, she went on. "The child is father to the man. I was in love with poetry too. My parents thought it was foolishness. Then I fell in love with Mr. Scott. His poetry is surgery. The human anatomy is lyric verse to him. But then only a surgeon can read the poem. I ought not to speak this way. Do you want to know why?"

"Yes," I said, "I'd like to."

Her smile was wistful. She said, "I'll tell you. There was something poetic in the moment of the peaches, when they passed from your hands into the hands of my children. Don't you see?"

"Yes," I said. But what I saw was that poetry, such as it was, had dwelt in my delight in the beauty of the twins and in the moment when I received from their four blue eyes the affirmation of delight's delight. So I said, "All the world's poetic license if you look into the depths deeply enough for the depths to look back at you."

She said, "The depths in ourselves," hesitated, then continued: "What I meant about Mr. Scott. The scalpel doesn't speak the same language as you and I."

"Maybe not. But excuse me. I can't help wondering. Why do you call your husband mister?"

"He prefers it. You see, in England a surgeon is not called doctor; he's called mister. An Anglicism. Many odd things in our country, you'll find."

"Oh," I exclaimed, "the odder the better," not knowing what I was saying.

"Splendid," she said. "Do you realize that you haven't once called me Kitty?"

"Haven't I? I don't know why. Here we are, anyway." I laughed, taken aback by the leap of intimacy. And I thought, What on earth are we doing in this field in England in the month of July in the sunburst afternoon?

She said, "It's a pity they missed him."

"Missed him?" I asked. "Missed who?"

"Why, Hitler!" she exclaimed. "Didn't you know? We heard it on the wireless. There was an assassination plot. A bomb. It went off, but by some unholy miracle he survived. Not even badly injured, so it seems."

"A pity," I said, "yes. My God, what a shame. Can't help thinking, though. They waited till it was clear they'd lost the war before they screwed up the courage to get rid of him."

"It's all so beastly," she murmured. "Perhaps we'd best go down. The twins will be growing impatient."

So we strolled back through the shivering grass to the cottage's blue door.

The beautiful boys rushed to their mother, threw four arms around her waist, and she laughed.

I said goodbye to all three, and Kitty said I'd best come back soon.

Riding the bike back to Broadway, I had never in my life felt a breeze so gentle and euphoric in my hair.

Aaron said that Julius Caesar had come to Gloucestershire, encamped up the hill in a place called Chipping Campden, only ten miles away, so by starting about six there'd be plenty of time for yon Cassius to look nasty, and what's more, he's a woman.

They were all women, a traveling troupe of female performers of Shakespeare, replacing actors gone from British stages to fight for Europe. Three of us pumped up the hill, and the performance, as a matter of fact, was rousing. These ladies bellowed effectively, especially Mark Antony: "O judgment! Thou art fled to brutish beasts, /And men have lost their reason." And so they had. And so they had. The conspirators who had attempted to dispose of the führer were being hanged by piano wire from meat hooks, their agony filmed for the entertainment of Adolf and his girlfriend.

I once rode as far as Cheltenham to hear a concert by a pianist named Soloman, who played Beethoven for two and a half hours, and rode back thinking of what Thomas Mann had said of that composer of all composers: "He dwelt in spheres where only the personal entity survives—a self painfully isolated in the absolute."

The Broadway shop had sold all of its peaches. But at the PX I filled my musette with candy and coffee, a few oranges, and a can of meat and potatoes.

Kitty said, "My word! I won't say you shouldn't have. You're too good. It's a joy forever, the thought, that will never pass into nothingness."

The twins' eyes feasted on the chocolate. They said, "Oh, Mummy!" as if they'd never seen any, and maybe they hadn't.

Kitty and I set out again for a walk up the slope onto the high fields. There we gathered together into the quiet radiance and a few distant sheep grazing in the silken grass and the sense of intimacy, the deliverance from the otherness of the world.

Katherine Millerbernd was born on the Isle of Wight, her father a notary public there, her mother a teacher at the grammar school in Ryde. Kitty found herself while reading Shelley, Shakespeare, Yeats and, when she was grown, rode her bicycle to the coast at Cowes to watch the royal regattas, awed by the yachts, their white sails crowding toward ports assured in a happier land than hers. Then one day at a crossroads the cyclist pausing beside her was Geoffrey Scott, who said, "I'm lost."

No *entrée en matière* could have been more appealing to Kitty, and she asked where he was wanting to go. He'd been searching for Osborne House, and she showed him the way to the last residence of Victoria.

Geoffrey was then well along with medical studies in Birmingham. They spoke of the queen empress, the beloved old lady of the diamond jubilee who had never ceased grieving for her handsome prince. Kitty was touched. They met again.

When he returned to Birmingham, he wrote letters. Kitty wrote back. Geoffrey returned to the Isle of Wight at Christmas, and the Millerbernds looked with approval upon the young doctor. It was a whirlwind romance, and like all the whirlwinds, it bore the potential of trouble.

They were married in the springtime, and Geoffrey became Mr. Scott in the autumn. His imperturbable skill in the operating theater rapidly recommended him to the first families of the city. The poetry of the scalpel, however, was not suited to his wife. The disparity set her to wondering, but then in the maturity of years came the twins. Geoffrey delivered them in an ecstasy of professional pride, named them, and declined to tell the mother which child was the elder by forty-three minutes. All in all, despite the terrifying miseries that beset the wide world, the war years in Willersey, when Mr. Scott came down but occasionally, may have been the best times for Kitty and her sons.

"And I'm glad I don't know which is the elder," she said. "As if forty-three minutes could make any difference to a lifetime. Well, mine has been uneventful, hasn't it?"

"I wouldn't say that," I said.

She offered me a short laugh. "Maybe I shouldn't have, everything being as it is now."

We wandered together back through the grass and the Queen Anne's lace to Willersey, and as we went, I thought she touched my arm, but I wasn't sure. I said goodbye outside the cottage, and Kitty, nodding, said, "See you soon."

Aaron said, "And where have you been slinking around in the countryside, may I ask?"

"I got acquainted with a family lives across the fields, invited me to tea."

"Well, H got acquainted with Lady Thingamabob, and we're invited to dinner at the Lygon, so brush your hair *and* your teeth and off we go."

Lady Thingamabob was forty anyway, laughed between every third word, wore a seed pearl choker and a diamond bumblebee in her hair, said we'd dine on bubbly and played her fingertips along H's thigh while we ate.

In France, meanwhile, the fighting went unabated from hedgerow to hedgerow, and for U.S. infantrymen its ferocity became a shattering experience: they had never realized how good the Germans were, how furiously they'd fight against superior numbers of men and machines even as eventual defeat became daily more certain. Caen fell, opening the way to Falaise, thence to Argentan, to Dreux, and finally to Paris. Still, the Wehrmacht, SS, and ragtag companies of raw recruits battled bitterly for every hillock or thicket as if the very substance of their being were at stake, which it was. And there were heaps of corpses in the apple orchards.

The weeks fled into weeks. If there were any gay soldiers in Broadway, they hid their guilty secret behind convincing esprit de corps. I was content to go strolling up the high fields with Kitty Scott, talking about the spirit of the universe. After the tea and bread and marmalade and the Water Rat coming to the rescue of luckless Toad, she told me that the following Saturday Mr. Scott would motor down from Edgbaston till Sunday tea and wished particularly to make the acquaintance of the American who had befriended his family, then, perhaps, I'd like to come to tea that Sunday, and I said I'd be happy to.

"But I should tell you," she said, "my husband is a very distinguished surgeon, a medical man, you know, very practical at analyzing symptoms, delivering a diagnosis, that's his profession, of course, and prescribing the right treatment. Well, his manner, sometimes, the way he goes about it, that may seem a bit—how shall I put it?—a bit blunt. Of course he says it's in the interests of everyone to be perfectly frank, no good calling a cancer a head cold. Still, some people might think it wanting in common courtesy. I only thought I should mention it."

I said oh, yes. However, I wondered. Was she apologizing in advance with a little too much feeling, a slight apprehension perhaps? I'd begun to wonder too about the true sentiments of the mother of the two little boys whose beauty I'd fallen for. Well, in truth I'd fallen for Kitty's own particular loveliness too, her sensitivity to the music of winds and the heartbeats of the grasses underfoot, an overly gentle temperament that she seemed to have crystallized upon me. And to which I was anything but indifferent, it's true. In our strolls in the Wordsworthian meadows above Willersey and the unspoken intimacy of mutual understanding, I felt the nameless acts of kindness—and of love—that become the best but unremembered parts of a good man's life. And I appreciated it, wanted it, but knew at the time I could not live up to it, never give satisfaction where satisfaction so naturally awaited and was due. Nor was it a trivial, meaningless thing. I was sorry but selfish. And there was the fault in the breathtaking summertime I was enjoying with Kitty in the generosity of her enjoyment. And yet enjoyment was all knowledge and desire in the fullness of that sublime summertime.

I said everything would be just fine as we came down again from the fields and along the road.

"It's fool's parsley," said Kitty, waving at the flowers in the ditch.

Facing a side street beyond Broadway Green stood an enormous topiary hedge of clipped yew shaped into a menagerie of fanciful animals, and beyond it a glorious garden, a parade of pale delphinium, and beyond the garden a grand house of honey-colored stone with a sundial in the pediment. There was something about that place, an aura, as if it acknowledged my notice, my curiosity, my vigilance—I can't say—and eventually I went beyond the green elephants into the garden and sat on a marble bench facing the distance. I went there frequently, in fact, took my notebook and wrote about what had happened and was to happen. And the simplicity was amazing by which it became as natural as the days, those summer vacation days of rapt blue sunlight, that that garden seemed to belong to me alone.

More amazing still when one morning a lady came from the house along the gravel between masses of boxwood. And there I was, the trespasser in the faultless garden. I stood up, blushing, ready to be rebuked. She was attired in black, her hair a halo of white, features pale, a pearl necklace, and I thought there was the suggestion of a smile as she said, "Please forgive the intrusion, Sergeant. I'd not meant to disturb your meditations."

"No, no," I stammered, "no, I'm the intruder, but—"

She held up her hand, a sapphire catching the light. "Please. Your presence these mornings, it's more welcome than you can know. I thought you might care for a glass of lemonade. By some miracle a lemon has come into my possession, and I thought, Ralph was very fond of lemonade. My son. I'd be happy to make you a glass."

"You're too kind. I should apologize. The garden, the hedge, it's all so . . ."

"Yes," she said. "My grandfather began the hedge. Come into the house."

The hall was high, with a double staircase, and I followed her into the drawing room, where she told me to sit down and she'd be back in a moment. The table in front of me was littered with small gold boxes. Between the windows on a gilt bronze gueridon stood a large photograph in a silver frame of a handsome young man in uniform, and before it on a patch of black velvet lay a gold medal, which my outstretched hand was preparing to touch when I heard behind me the tinkle of ice in a glass.

"That is Ralph's medal," she said. "Don't be timid. He would have been pleased for you to touch it. He was a very companionable person. Do sit down." She brushed aside several snuffboxes and set down the frosted glass of lemonade. "There you are."

"Thank you," I said. "I don't know how to thank you."

"You do that very nicely by sitting in the garden writing in your notebook. You are welcome at any time. Now I'll leave you to your thoughts." And she went out, closing the door very carefully.

The lemonade was marvelous in that warm morning. I drank it slowly. Whether or not my hostess meant to come back began to seem uncertain. The lemonade was finished, and silence plumbed the emptiness of the room, and I had no idea. It was noon, and I had promises to keep, so eventually I stole out as quietly as I could, leaving behind Ralph's photograph and his medal and the unforgotten heroism it had cost.

Several times I went again to sit in that garden, but the lady of the house never reappeared. I couldn't help wondering whether I'd been invited to have a glass of the lemonade of which "Ralph was very fond" specifically so that he might be remembered by another young soldier destined to participate in the same war.

The Falaise pocket was closed, St. Malo taken, while some German forces surrendered and the rest began a precipitous retreat across France. People started to say, and to believe, that the war would be over by Christmas.

That Sunday was one of the most beautiful of all the beautiful days of that beautiful summer, and I rode my bike to Willerscy with the odorous warmth of August in my face like a miracle. A small black Austin, an incongruity in that thatched village, stood in front of the cottage. I hesitated at the blue door, sensing I'd best prepare myself for the scrutiny of the doctor, the diagnosis of a medical man acute at discerning symptoms. Supposing that even if he didn't smoke, he might appreciate some American cigarettes, inasmuch as these had become international currency, I'd brought along a carton of Luckies, a can of powdered coffee, and some candy for the twins. I can't say I was exactly apprehensive, yet when I knocked three bangs on the blue wood in the ambient silence of a countryside holding its breath, they sounded like a signal in some drama rather than the happy forecast of a comedy of manners.

Mr. Scott opened the door: a man in a three-piece black suit, medium height, thinning hair, features as sharp as a scalpel, and eyes blue as its blade. Kitty hurriedly said, "Geoffrey, this is our friend James."

"Good afternoon, Sergeant," said the surgeon, offering a handshake, receiving politely with the other a carton of cigarettes, "How kind of you to come bearing gifts, though of course you are not Greek," and coughed, a brief laugh, "and naturally I don't smoke. One drop of nicotine in a barrel of water will kill a trout in ten seconds."

"I don't smoke either," I said, handing Kitty the coffee and Hershey bars to the twins, who hesitated, glancing carefully at their father.

"It's all right, boys," said the doctor. "Candy rots your teeth, of course, but just this once."

Kitty said, "James has been ever and ever so generous. We met because he bought peaches for the twins, peaches—can you imagine?— when we'd not seen a single one in donkey's years. And so dear."

"Very kind, I'm sure. But I expect the sergeant could afford the outlay. After all, an American private is paid almost as much as a British lieutenant. Shall we have tea? A low tea, to be sure, but high in honor of our guest."

So we all sat down around the squat table where the tea service had been set out. Kitty poured, and the twins spoke for the first time.

"Marmalade," they said. "Orange marmalade," added one of them. The other said, "Old Mrs. Miller next door said she hadn't seen marmalade since before the war, she said."

"James brought us two jars," said Kitty. "Do taste it, Geoffrey."

"How very kind of you," said Mr. Scott. "A forgotten delicacy indeed during these years we've spent fighting to save civilization. Our erstwhile colonists have reaped a very wealthy harvest in the New World whilst the Old struggles on alone. Now you've generously come to give us a hand at the last minute."

"Just as they did in the last war," Kitty interjected quickly.

"This isn't Earl Grey, is it?" he said, sipping.

"Everyday Ceylon. I'm saving Earl Grey for the victory tea."

"Well, we ought to have been drinking it all along in memory of Mr. Grey, who said, 'The lamps are going out all over Europe; we shall not see them lit again in our lifetime.' As cogent an observation now as it was thirty years ago."

"But we're winning the war," I objected.

"*You* are," said Mr. Scott, "You and the Communists. All we did was to make your victory possible by giving everything we'd got in order to stymie Hitler, and we did that, and what we had to give in order to do it was more than we could afford to. So now Mr. Churchill takes his marching orders from Roosevelt."

"Oh, Geoffrey," cried Kitty, "you do go on about politics."

"Indeed. It's strong medicine, but the patient is the British Empire, and the malady is gangrene, which means drastic surgery or death, so say goodbye to India, South Africa, Palestine, Burma, Hong Kong, and the rest till we're a second-rate nation and our only colony is some island in the South Pacific inhabited by a hundred people who'd sell their souls to leave it."

"How bleak, how fearfully bleak," sighed Kitty.

The doctor smiled, nodded, and said soothingly, "It is. But the alternative would have been bleaker still. 'Tis better to survive enfeebled and impoverished than defeated and enslaved."

"I suppose," said Kitty.

The twins looked from parent to parent with eyes the size of their teacups, small hands holding slices of bread and marmalade in midair as if a bite might be risky. And surrounding this uncertainty the adult silence held time motionless while the tea in the cups lost warmth.

When the occasion slowly regained some social momentum, Mr. Scott said to me, "Would this be your first time to visit England?"

"In person, yes," I said. "But we all look to England—in America, I mean—we look to England because England's where everything came from for us, the language, of course, literature, laws, traditions, et cetera."

"Very good of you to remember. After all, England in a sense is your spiritual homeland."

"I guess it is. I never thought of it quite like that, but you could say so, yes."

"I trust that you have found a satisfying welcome in our country."

"I have, I really have," I said, pointing around the small room at his wife and children, "I could say that the proof of it is being here, here under your roof."

"Right. Well now. You speak your mind to good effect. I like that. Kitty, of course, is a very special individual, sensitive, intelligent, and the twins are a chip off the old block, if I may so describe myself. And your comrades-in-arms. Do you hit it off with the Tommies?"

"Who's that?"

"British soldiers. Called Tommies, as the men in your army are called GIs."

"Oh, yes. Well, I'll tell you: it may seem strange, but I haven't had any reason to have much of anything to do with the soldiers in the British army."

"It doesn't seem strange. After all, unless I'm mistaken, in your very own army you have nothing to do with the Negro soldiers, call them niggers."

The fire glared in my face, even as I tried to quench it, and I said, "I wouldn't say that, Doctor. I think you're mistaken. Our country believes that all men are created equal."

"How comforting, for you, Sergeant. It's just as well you've had nothing to do with our Tommies. You might not find them friendly. They've done a lot of fighting. And a lot of dying. And here you are, fresh and clean and brash, money to spend, cigarettes and chewing gum, rubber-soled boots, comfortable uniforms, advantages unthinkable for a British soldier. For example, how many sheets of toilet paper do you use per day?"

"Really, Geoffrey," said Kitty.

"I don't know," I said. "Do you think I count them?"

"If you were a British soldier, you'd have to. I happen to know that your army allots twenty-three sheets per day per soldier. The British army allots three."

"Really, Geoffrey," said Kitty, "is this necessary?"

"Facts of life, my dear."

The fire in my face faded as quickly as it had flared. I said, "I'm sorry, but I didn't realize I'd have to be ashamed to come over here to give you a hand at the last minute, as you say, to win this awful war."

"I'll tell you something, young fellow. Every man who has a hand in a war, winning or losing or cheering on the sidelines, has cause to feel shame. War is vile, evil, hellish business. It changes men who have been at most capable of the occasional unkindness into men capable of the most appalling cruelty, sadistic monsters without a twinge of remorse. The infantryman murders his like, his brother, in an ecstasy of bloodlust, a heightened awareness brought on by rushes of dopamine and adrenaline. Some fighter pilot said that warfare was the most fun you can have with your pants on. The price of the good time is primeval guilt; it touches us all, and all of us had best be mindful of that."

I said, "Believe me, sir, I'm plenty mindful of the touch of guilt. Don't worry on that account."

"But I do," said Mr. Scott. "Understand me. When you spend your days incising or amputating or dissecting the bodies of human beings, then you become very intimate with the humanity of them, the spiritual in the physical, the moral of the medical. When you hold a human life between your fingers, then the guilt inherent in that power becomes at times almost unbearable; you think of a bombardier when he presses the button that will send ten tons of high explosive onto a village in the dead of night, well—what do you think of?— or an artilleryman or the commander of a U-boat." He emitted a hiccup.

"I understand," I said.

Kitty said, "Gentlemen, please, enough talk of the war, please. The tea has gone stone cold."

"Mr. Toad, Mr. Toad," cried the twins.

Scott said, "All right," and he took up the book from the hearth and began to read very distinctly with a surprising lilt to his voice, relating the waterland adventures of the madcap bufonid, escapes and trials, sufferings, such disguises and subterfuges and humbug . . .

My mind wandered away from Willersey, the cottage, Kitty, the twins, Mr. Scott, Mr. Toad, the Water Rat, backward and backward . . . to Hanno . . . where was he? . . . did he wonder where I was? . . . that night in Comstock Rooms when I was too drunk to realize that everything I longed for lay ready beside me . . . that folly . . . the Hotel Statler . . . guilt of the world at war . . . mankind's malfeasance . . . figments flickering on the walls of a cave . . . while on the seashore of desire a genius sits gazing toward the strand where death stands beckoning . . .

"And Mr. Toad says it's time for your nap," concluded Mr. Scott.

"Oh, Daddy," murmured the twins.

I stood up. "I'd better be going," I said, shook hands, patted the sleepy heads, and Kitty accompanied me to my bike.

"Please try to understand," she said.

I said, "It's all right. I'll see you in a couple of days."

"Please, James," Kitty said, and her hand rested for an instant on mine.

That summer vacation in the arms of England came to an end on the Monday morning. The fingertip of war touched us at last. Posted orders divided us arbitrarily into teams of six. To my dismay I found my name among five unknowns: First Lieutenant Edward B. Lynn, commander of Military Intelligence Team No. 456; Second Liuetenant Clinton W. Norton, second-in-command; First Sergeant Jan Zablocki; Sergeant William Brunet; Technician Third Grade Walter L. Babbs; and Technician Third Grade James H. Lord. A third grade technician, as I presently found out, was a negligible errand boy, jeep driver, mechanic, scrounger, and man of all the work nobody else wanted to do. This proved to be an enviable position, one for which my lack of ability was very well suited. H and Aaron were assigned to other teams,

and we groaned together over the imminent dispersal of the muske-
teers. Where Garo went we never knew.

Team No. 456 was to depart Broadway the following Friday, August 25, traveling directly south some hundred miles to Winchester,
there to join the Ninety-fifth Infantry Division on temporary attachment to its HQ company, awaiting eventual embarkation for France
from the nearby port of Southampton.

The goodbyes pretended to be casual so-long-see-you-around and
went as well as they were meant to. Except for Kitty and the twins,
who didn't hide regretful eyes and downcast frowns. I kissed David
and John and felt the guilty thrill of my lips against innocent faces.
Kitty and I walked on the field.

"Not for the last time," she said.

I said, "Oh, no."

But the war walked between us, its companionship unsparing, not
to be talked to. We chatted about flowers, the rainless days, and that
unique summer, when you think about it, more unique than any other
and the Wordsworthian gleam that spoke of something gone by, and
we strolled back to the cottage to my bike.

I said, "So here we are, Kitty."

"So," she said.

Our kiss was more than a courtesy before we drew apart and said
goodbye.

I rode back to peaceable Broadway with regret, almost with remorse
following me, like a shadow fleeing behind, Kitty's sincerity tinctured
with heaven knew what emotions.

Winchester, overshadowed by its huge cathedral, was a charming
old town, beautifully undamaged despite proximity to strategic Southampton. The Ninety-fifth Infantry HQ was housed in a hideous brick
building, a school—not the famous, fashionable public one—from
which students and faculty had been evacuated. A sweaty, overweight
major came down to tell us that we'd be in Winchester till embarkation orders came through, ten days or so, which we were free to spend
as we pleased, provided we kept out of trouble, especially girls and li-
quor, for discipline would be strict, curfew at 8:00 p.m., mandatory
blackout. Not much to do in town except visit the cathedral and a
couple of ancient ruins.

As for our function, whenever the Ninety-fifth Division caught up with the Germans fleeing eastward from Patton's tanks after the liberation of Paris, well, HQ would let us know. By way of conclusion, said the major with a wave, wafting BO across the room, we had the welcome of the division commander, General Twaddle. We kept faces rigidly straight, knowing already that the CO's believe-it-or-not name was Major General Harry L. Twaddle. And the major rapped about his own name: W. J. Flowers, adjutant general; second-in-command was Brigadier General Faith; chief of staff, Colonel Golightly. We appreciatively smiled as Flowers stamped out of the room, leaving us bemused by the leadership of Messrs. Faith, Golightly, and Twaddle, not to mention the odorous Flowers.

It had come time to take the measure of my teammates, to consider what manner of soldiers I'd be with if ever we stumbled upon the enemy. Lieutenant Lynn was stocky, weathered, mustached, East Coast sophistication stamped all over him, his uniform fitting too well, and so comfortably self-assured he could afford to be one of the boys when in fact, he was a playboy. Lieutenant Norton had been professor of French at the state university in Tallahassee, his eyeglasses gave him eyes the size of a spaniel's, and he apologized for his authority by addressing us with classroom courtesy. As for Sergeant Jan Zablocki, his name said everything: he was an only son of recently naturalized Polish parents, their misfortune having taught him its bitterest lessons, and as he often emphasized, he hated the Germans with such passion that "it makes my urine boil." Sergeant Brunet was everybody's friend, a laugher with rusty hair, the eternal halfback for the Thanksgiving Day game, loved to stamp up and down and brandish imaginary revolvers in derision of General Patton. T-3 Babbs was a cautious mouse, a demure student who spoke five languages with pallid circumspection; T-3 Lord, an impostor on earth who knew not whether his time had come or, indeed, whether a moment all his own might ever be timely.

I walked down the hill into the town of Winchester, its cathedral piers and arches sailing across the blue. The pavements were crowded with Tommies and bands of sailors, and I looked into their eyes, searching for suggestions or promises; but their eyes did not look into mine. There was a bookstore along the sidewalk to my right, a wild bouquet of dahlias in the show window, so I went in, for bookstores had already given uncommon twists to my itinerary. Among the fastidious stacks were several small booklets of poetry selling for only a couple of shillings. I selected T. S. Eliot, a familiar standby in cases of vicissitude.

Some days I went and sat inside the cathedral, immense and shadowy, custodian of the tombs of Saxon monarchs, idealistic humanitarians, and famous writers. They seemed to ask by what prerogative I made free to seek the company of such as they. The huge silence of the mythic edifice said, You have a lot to learn.

Ten

SEPTEMBER–OCTOBER 1944

The orders came at last light. We were to be ready by dawn, and all of us knew what for. Southampton lay a dozen miles due south. The embarkation area was a chaos of trucks, tractors, jeeps, tanks, half-tracks, command cars, drivers swearing and screaming, leaning on their horns, as if their impatience would win the war. So we had to suck on our canteens for hours in the trucks in the unseasonable heat, sweating and swearing with the rest. Camaraderie comes easy on the way to the war, and in the soil of anticipation seeds of friendship sprout overnight. The partnership of pals had been formed already by the time we reached Southampton. Lynn and Norton were united in the compulsory cooperation of rank, which I thought not much to the liking of the silver bar playboy. Zablocki's buddy was his gnashing hatred of Nazis, which he exalted as the boon companion of moral infallibility. Bill Brunet became my pal because both of us liked tomfoolery, disliked the nonsense of army esprit de corps, and relished occasions to stick out our tongues at it. Babbs was not the glad hand sort, though ready when necessary with mirthful squeaks of camaraderie. Thus the lines of *Burschenherrlichkeit*—but oh, without its hero—were drawn before Team No. 456 was charged for battle.

Summer died the day we took ship in Southampton for our final journey toward the war. The vessel was a worn-out tub called *James R. Randall*, who must have been a nobody to deserve the inglory of that hulk. It could never have held all twelve thousand men of the Ninety-fifth Division, but the HQ company, with General Twaddle in person, was aboard, plus several thousand other grunts of assorted ranks and assignments. As soon as all were loaded and counted, we cast off, drifted downstream a few miles, then dropped anchor in a file of similar ships in the center of Southampton Water.

Mr. Randall's ship was far too small to hold even the men and officers on board. How the latter were accommodated we didn't know, though presumed they slept in sheets, shit in private, and ate sitting down. Enlisted men had to eat and sleep on the deck. Even to dream of being comfortable on those welded steel plates was foolishness, yet we slept. Luckily no storm arose. As we charged away from England, the white cliffs faded behind us like the loneliest ghosts in all of history. It had come time to approach the European battlefields.

It was late in the afternoon when we shuddered to a stop, anchor chains sang, and the *James R. Randall* lay in sight of the French coast. My first view of France came as a piercing disappointment, for the Norman coastline resembles many another seashore, and I had been looking forward to a sight surpassing the capacity for surprise. That of course is why I failed to see a future of perpetual enchantment spread before me, because either genius or a lifetime of lucid hindsight is necessary to perceive the amazement concealed in the commonplace.

Sunset fell across the sea, red as the flare for danger, red shimmering heavily in the west, red as tides of blood on the dying water. And I thought of the thousands of soldiers come to this shore to die. Darkness fell like a precipice. Sleep was not ready when I was, and yet it came. The night, however, was abruptly interrupted by someone shaking my shoulder. It was the man beside me, to whom I'd paid scant attention.

I said, "What the hell?"

"Sorry," he whispered. "Could you just hold me for a minute? Please. Please."

This was no sexual plea I realized instantly as he held out his arms and I helped him into mine and in the tangle of blankets I could feel him trembling. "What's wrong?" I whispered. "Are you sick?"

"I'm so scared," he said. "I'll tell you. Please. Hold me as tight as you can. I'm so scared."

"Okay. It'll be all right." And I did hold him as close as I could, felt him trembling against me, and a sound as of a sob came choking from him, and I'd never known what it was to hold a human being in my arms in the desperate throes of his humanity, not a quiver of the sexual sense in it, no.

And his lips were so close to my ear that his words seemed to be mine, my own physical being expressing myself, his fear, and he said, "This is Omaha Beach, you know what it is, and my brother Jesse, he landed here that morning, never made it out of the water, I guess. Only nineteen, my kid brother." All this while he was shaking with tremors like the warnings of the worst, and I wanted to take them into myself entirely too, to hold his fear as firm and frightening as the end of everything and live with him completely, which itself was frightening, and I could feel my arms trembling while he was saying, "I don't want to die, I don't want to die."

"No," I said, "you won't. Don't be afraid. It's okay, everything, just lie still, here, it's okay, go to sleep now, please." And I held him closer than I could, his head down against my chest, our trembling together, as if we were one person only with our fear and the whole darkness joined into the fatigue of the night slowly falling asleep. Till dawn slipped like a splinter into cramped muscles reluctantly wakening.

After the anxious disentangling, shaking himself with the frantic energy of a wet dog, he said, "Now listen. What can I say?"

"Nothing," I said. "Don't say anything. I told you. It's okay."

"I'm no coward!" he blurted. "Get that straight! I'm no coward."

"No, I know that. None of us are. We wouldn't be here, would we?"

"Get it straight," he said.

I said, "Yeah, I've got it anyway. Now you take care, hear me."

He bit his lip and nodded deliberately, gathering blankets and scrambling up in the lukewarm air. And whether anyone had seen us in the embrace of empathy I didn't know. Besides, he was gone without goodbye in a minute.

We went ashore to Omaha Beach on barges in the midmorning of the fourteenth, a Thursday, the sand gleaming and clean, no enemy planes to strafe us, and the soldiers were singing. The beach was a turmoil of trucks, half-tracks, and bulldozers, the loading and unloading of mountains of supplies, the labor done by German prisoners, just kids most of them, "POW" stenciled in large black letters on their jackets. How poetic, how pathetic: these boys imbued with the nonsense of war's atavistic glory now reduced to chattel. As we marched up the sand, they kept their eyes fixed downward, and even on the beach where thousands of Americans had been killed by Germans only three months ago it was difficult to imagine these forlorn figures as enthusiastic killers. And yet their uniforms, however bedraggled, were the attire of guilt. At the top of the beach priority transport was lined for HQ company.

En route to our bivouac, about three miles back from Omaha, we passed through the shattered remains of a village called Trévières. Our vehicles raised whirlwinds of powdery debris, and the survivors in the rubble looked like dusty specters haunting the site of the un-imaginable.

Our bivouac was a lovely apple orchard a mile outside town, un-damaged and grassy, sloping down to a stream, clean and thigh deep, rippling over shiny pebbles. All enlisted men immediately got busy setting up our tents in measured ranks, large ones for the officers, py-ramidal for HQ, digging slit trenches, garbage pits to be prepared for very unlikely action. We were in the field, yes, but the war was no-where near it.

On that very same day, however, while we were making camp un-der the apple trees, U.S. troops in the Pacific landed on Peleliu Island, an action costing ten thousand American lives in eleven days, while shortly afterward Allied paratroops landed in Holland, aiming to seize the Rhine bridge at Arnhem, an operation that failed, leaving a thou-sand dead and ten times that many taken prisoner. In France after the liberation of Paris in late August, German forces kept on retreating eastward, while Hitler hysterically commanded his troops to fight to the last bullet.

The Ninety-fifth Division was one of the units of XX Corps of the Third Army, thus under command of the famous general George Pat-ton, celebrated for his no-nonsense principles of battlefield necessity and never mind shooting a few prisoners of war. His tanks were press-ing the German retreat, and Patton furiously requisitioned the excess fuel for them driven at suicidal speed on the Red Ball Highway by hilarious Negroes. The enemy formed a battle line in early October, running roughly from Arnhem and its fateful bridge on the north to the Swiss frontier at Basel, holding a considerable slice of eastern France, centered on the heavily fortified city of Metz.

Autumnal weather was benign, red and yellow days of indolence. I went for hikes along sunken lanes bordered by the high, blind hedges that had made the Normandy fighting murderous. Only bees and butterflies wandered with me. There were pretty farms along the paths, where I was welcomed like young Washington, given tiny glasses of burning alcohol and fresh eggs and gobs of butter in careful parcels. When I came back to the bivouac with this booty, Lieutenant Lynn exclaimed, *"C'est une prise de guerre!"* and said we must turn over everything to the mess of the HQ staff for their breakfast. Forget about ours. Well, if I could come up with butter and eggs once, I could do it again. And again. And yet again. And I did, and made acquaintance with the market later called black by carrying to outlying farms cartons of cigarettes and cans of coffee. The towns of La Viéville, Mandeville, even Rubercy eagerly emptied and readily refilled my musette bag, and the staff officers' mess didn't get everything. But the best repast was my freedom to stroll tunefully through the lilting greenery of the afternoons, whistling the *Three Comrades*' moody melody. Nor did I feel any fear for the future, and after that grim night aboard the ship facing Omaha Beach, held fast in Jesse's brother's frightened arms, I was never again afraid, which by no means proved I was not a coward.

Team No. 456 had been allotted two jeeps for the six of us and our gear. Babbs was the driver of one; I, of the other. Still on the waiting list for action, we were lazy and free, I drove down the lanes where I'd formerly walked, singing songs I'd sung when I was in love with the captain of the hockey team, sighing for him under the elms, and I was a hero to the farms in my white-starred vehicle. But the jeep, to be sure, was not my sole runabout to enjoy, Lieutenant Lynn the privileged occupant of the front seat at his pleasure.

So one evening he airily allowed that the next morning it would be well to set out promptly after breakfast, as he'd decided to go for a spin southwest to a town called Dinard on the Breton coast, where before the war he'd spent summer vacations. Vacations from what? I wondered. No kind of workaday employ, I guessed, as he'd obviously been a rich party boy, which made him cavalier about rules and regulations.

Dinard lay well over a hundred miles distant across devastated roads through bomb-blasted towns. We went through Carentan to

Coutances, both places in grim ruin. Driving alongside the ceaseless press of military vehicles, we came upon a couple of trucks loaded with German POWs standing packed together like cords of wood. On both sides of the road civilian men and women screamed at them, brandishing furious fists, and some threw shards of rubble.

The lieutenant said, "War's no bowl of cherries."

Later he said, "I know your name's Jim. Mine's Eddy. I think we come from the same background. Hotchkiss and Yale for me. When we're alone together, no use standing on ceremony. Okay?"

"Sure," I said.

Avranches, the next town en route, was also largely in ruins, detour signs pointing a twisted circuit southward, no warning for bomb craters. Eddy said, "This is where everything turned around. The Germans lost it. After Avranches, Falaise was a sure thing, Normandy was done for, the big retreat began, and now they have nowhere to go but home. Maybe try to stick things out at Metz, but basically it's all over, with the Reds bleeding them to death in the east, finished by Christmas."

Farther south in the shabby café of a town but slightly damaged, Eddy talked us into a meal of rabbit stew and red wine, for which the scarecrow proprietor refused to accept our fresh scrip, saying he could never sufficiently repay what America had done for his country. He kissed Eddy on both cheeks and shook my hand.

Then some ten miles farther along off to the right loomed the silhouette of Mont St. Michel, abbey-cum-fortress-cum-prison, sanctuary of faith in the Dark Ages. "It's not far now," said Eddy. And presently I was driving along a boulder-heaped coastline, the sea heaving and foaming through the breakwater, and we came to a place called St. Briac.

A line of villas stood down near the waves; one of them was larger than the rest, an ugly pile encrusted with weathered sconces, scrolls, and outlandish frippery. "A historic house," said Eddy. "The grand duke Cyril Wladimirovitch used to spent his summers there. I'd come over from Dinard sometimes to play bridge and drink vodka with him. A fine old sport. Could have been czar after the family was murdered, first cousin to Nicholas. He got out just in time. Left behind thirteen palaces. Managed to wangle a freight car, though, to sneak out the best things. Told me once it cost him a Botticelli to build that house and said nobody who hadn't known the imperial court before 1905 could have any idea what luxury meant."

Several miles farther along lay Dinard, damaged, and Eddy told me to stop at a large café on the promenade above the beach and wait in the jeep. He must have forewarned a clique of pals unseen since '39, because a hullabaloo of shouts, laughter, and stamping of feet instantly greeted his entrance. I waited in the jeep for more than an hour, grinding my teeth. Then a stunted redhead brought me a glass of white wine and said to join the party. A dozen women and men shook my hand, slapped my shoulder blades, laughed, smacked their lips, and said, *"Bienvenu, joli garçon, buvez sec,"* tossing back glassfuls, already high, and Eddy said, "Take off your jacket, Jim. They're going to give us a liberation feast."

It was an imposing repast: foie gras, lobster, crêpes flambées, white wine, red wine, champagne, coffee, and calvados. Lucky for me there was so much to eat. Otherwise I'd have been double drunk when it was time to go. Eddy, overcome with jollity, was plastered, reluctant to say good night. Once in the jeep he fell asleep, mumbling, *"Quelle fête! Quelle fête!"*

It was only the clusters of signposts that saved us from getting lost on the way back, but I had to drive snail slow in the dark. There was almost no traffic. At Avranches, Coutances, Carentan, we were stopped at roadblocks, with searchlights and machine guns, and treated as potential saboteurs. I had to wake up the lieutenant to flash his credentials and drawl out bona fides. A corporal at Carentan said, "Intelligence service, huh? Dumbbell service, I'd say, driving under the influence middle of the night."

Eddy roused to the offense, exclaiming, "Mind your manners, sonny, or I'll smarten you up. Drive on, Sergeant."

So I stamped on the gas, and we were not far from Trévières. The MPs at the entrance to our apple orchard asked where the fuck we'd been till two-thirty in the morning, and Eddy was awake enough to say, "Classified."

When I crawled into the pup tent, crowding Brunet, he muttered, "The hell you been, Jim-Jam?"

"Drinking champagne on the seashore," I said. "Want to smell my breath?"

"That depends." He sighed. "Anyway, you missed the excitement. Orders posted. Division moving up to the front five days from yesterday going to piss in Hitler's beer."

"Jesus," I said, "roll out the barrel."

Bill jerked his blankets closer. "Shut your mouth and close your eyes, Sergeant, you're asleep."

We had been goofing off in the apple orchard for exactly four weeks.

Eleven

OCTOBER–DECEMBER 1944

We left Trévières on the twelfth, a distended miscellany of olive drab vehicles hulking past bare fields punctuated by haystacks, tarnished streams, and stands of midget conifers while we crawled so slowly eastward you could almost count the treads of the tires in front of you turning at 10 mph. The itinerary made progress even slower, as we had to pass around blasted villages, follow twisting detours on country lanes so narrow the trucks tore away branches and wrecked a few walls. Tedium, however, was allayed by occasional crowds on the roadside, waving, cheering, brandishing makeshift American flags, tossing apples, plums, and chrysanthemums into the slow-moving vehicles, offering up bottles of wine, young girls running alongside the jeeps, some of them in tears, blowing kisses to the soldiers. Such spontaneous jubilation came as gladdening assurance that our presence in this European heartland was fitting and opportune, that our preparedness to fight was a moral indication of America's manifest destiny to see and to do the right thing, that we would win because the enemy didn't deserve to, Hitler and Hirohito cruel and evil men, and all in all, the cheers of the populace seemed to license for me the lovely surmise that the 675 days that I had already given to the army had not been squandered and that I might ultimately have it in me to live up to unpredictable categorical imperatives.

On the third afternoon of our low-gear crawl across France we came at last within sight of a monument to the immanence of French faith and glory: the silhouette of Chartres Cathedral, twin spires needle thin across the fields of wheat-colored stubble. And the following day much more, and more glorious. As we bumped along the paving stones of Paris's outer boulevards, I could see the Eiffel Tower, Pan-théon, Sacré Coeur, but nothing more, not the Louvre, Notre Dame, Napoleon's Tomb, and instead of bedding down on the Champs Ély-sées we made our bivouac in a nasty little place called Noisy-le-Sec and I was afraid the war would never offer me another glimpse of the city I longed to love.

Our cavalcade crept eastward. The villages were mostly intact, for the Germans were in such a hurry to save their own lives that they now had no time to massacre others. Day and night U.S. and British bomb-ers passed overhead unopposed on their way to pulverize enemy cities, factories, ammunition dumps, power plants, railroads, and a few prof-itless sites just for the fun of it. The country turned hilly, almost moun-tainous in places, mid-October grew cold, and the rains came, roadside ditches awash, and the bluster carried gusts through the jeep, soaking our field jackets. We crossed a couple of rivers. As we came closer to the fighting front, evidence of eroding morale and discipline appeared along the road: mounds of discarded equipment, abandoned clothing, even overcoats, and jerricans, used tins, shovels, bottles, thousands of empty ration packets, and festoons of filthy toilet paper.

As yet, however, we saw no sign of real war having been fought amid those gray fields and patches of leafless woodland, though we were only seventy-five miles from Germany the night we put up in an attractive, undamaged town called Nancy. It was there that someone remembered that while in the apple orchard I had shown a flair for finding opportune extras. Eddy told me to get busy to locate and req-uisition quarters as luxurious as possible for Twaddle and staff. In Nancy it was easy. I selected a palatial mansion, and the proprietors were flattered to move into their attic, leaving the noble rooms below for an American general. I invited my teammates and myself into a more modest residence nearby, its occupants an aged couple who served us warm champagne and stale cookies and soulfully remarked that in one lifetime it was sad to have seen three German armies march past their front door.

The next day, a Saturday, October 28, we finally heard a few intro-ductory flourishes of warfare. Driving north from Nancy along the left bank of the Moselle, following picket signs marked "95" through little places called Moûtiers and Avril, we could hear the intermittent medley of booming basses, kettles, tom-toms, and tenor artillery. On the blue distance livid puffs of smoke hovered onto the horizon. Eddy said, "This is probably as close as we'll ever get to the big shooting match."

Having left the main body of the division to bivouac in the woods around Algrange, HQ company moved on to Thionville, where XX Corps had previously set up its HQ, occupying already some of the finest houses and a small hotel.

General Twaddle had to settle for second best, and I found people less honored than in Nancy to vacate their premises, irascibly reluctant, in fact, obliging me to tell them that if necessary, a platoon of infantrymen could be dispatched to hurry things along, whereupon they morosely mumbled that the Germans had been at least polite. Eddy told me later that Twaddle had found an inscribed photo of an SS colonel in a bureau drawer. For our team I had no trouble locating two modest houses facing the Moselle.

After several days of SOP uncertainty Eddy was summoned by Colonel Golightly to receive instructions as to our duties, responsibilities, and prerogatives. Fluent speakers of French, we would be useful as agents, mainly in France, and at all times ready to interpret such conversations with French civilians or resistance fighters as could contribute tactical advantages. It might fall to us also to interrogate persons suspected of too-friendly relations with the enemy, potential saboteurs or spies, and to determine, whenever circumstances warranted, whether or not suspicion should entail more challenging and forceful investigation by interrogation of specialized ingenuity. And in order to emphasize that none of us was adequately authoritative, two French officers were assigned to assist, as it were, in any situation deemed by them to call for additional competence. As for prerogatives, we should feel free to take any initiative that seemed likely to prove advantageous to the order of battle. Such initiatives of course would lead us to range at our discretion throughout the division terrain, observing, questioning, speculating, listening, and consulting. And perhaps this was everything a military intelligence agent would be well, or well advised, to do.

The French auxiliary was an ambiguous, if not devious, lot. They came with papers all in order from XX Corps. Thus there was no argument with their bona fides, but their specific duties and/or responsibilities proved to be determined on the spur of the moment at their discretion, and they came and went in their own jeep, unsmiling, without prior notice, asking pointed questions or making laconic observations, as if our business were theirs, but on the other hand, theirs were not ours. The leader, called Jean-Pierre Rouvres, was a captain with a razor-blade face in a makeshift uniform, plus a yes-man lieutenant with sidelong eyes, baby fat, a snappy outfit and a diamond pinkie ring, Sylvain Parny, accompanied by a sullen bruiser in tight-fitting civvies known only as Georges, all three toting revolvers in leather bolsters stamped "US." They were not a nuisance, but the pleasure of their company was negative.

Eddy told me to take the jeep, get busy, and rustle up some wine, cognac, or rubbing alcohol for the staff, enough for us too, champagne, if possible. "And don't take any lip from the *marchand de vin*," he cautioned. "You know they all sold their wives and daughters to the Nazis and held back the best stuff for themselves. So sock it to them."

About my ability to do that I wasn't confident, drove around till I saw a sign, VINS ET SPIRITUEAX F. BELLEFELD, on a good-size shed, though a sign on the front door said FERMÉ. A serious pounding opened it up fairly promptly, producing a wizened gnome with a scowl and a knot the size of a cantaloupe melon between his shoulder blades. He looked me up and down, pursed his gray lips, and said nothing.

I said, "Wine. And cognac. For the American general."

"I have nothing," he rasped. "Those filthy Nazis, they took the last drop before you came to liberate us, thanks be to God. Come in and look for yourself, you'll see."

I went in, following F. Bellefeld down to the cellar, from which came up the dusty rustle of scurrying rodents, and in fact the grimy racks lay prostrate in their emptiness.

"You see," moaned the wine merchant. "Filthy Nazis seized everything, paid not a pfennig. I'm a ruined man."

"A pfennig?" I said. "We know you did business with the Nazis. Wine and cognac or I call the FFI, and they don't like collabos."

"Listen to me, young American," he whined. "For Nazis this piece of Europe is called Lothringen. Part of the German Empire. Yes, we did business with them or they would rip out your fingernails. And I, young American, am I not afflicted enough already?"

The Quasimodo lamentation was too facile to be effective. I told the sly hunchback to hustle some bottles or the Free French would trash his premises.

I was hard, he said, and only a sergeant. The Germans had sent a *Hauptmann*. The Free French of the Interior were Communist scoundrels.

He led me down to a secret cellar, tiers of bottles gleaming and plentiful, all of them, he pleaded, being saved for his old age, not to die in the poorhouse.

I took a dozen burgundies, several cognacs, the rest in champagnes, two crates full.

Eddy was euphoric, said it was outstanding achievement in the line of duty, and we'll go fifty-fifty with HQ. Tonight a bottle each for the team. Get tipsy, tune in on "Lili Marlene."

Zablocki said he'd save his bottle to celebrate when he'd killed his first kraut with his bare hands.

I drank all alone in my room facing the river, a few lights alive on the other side. I didn't get tipsy or tune in on "Lili Marlene." The boom of German cannons over beyond the nocturnal horizon bore their own lethal music, while far to the north a ghastly battle was being fought in the Hurtgen Forest, a vast snowbound woodland, the largest and most murderous action of the war. Deserters were said to be fleeing by the hundred in a frenzy of terror and shame. I flung my bottle of wine through the open window, but it didn't reach the water and fell with an ineffectual clatter onto the roadway.

Two days later we packed up to move out and in the afternoon drove about fifteen miles south from Thionville to a town on the Orne River named Moyeuvre, dirty and ugly, the center of an important iron-smelting area called the Briey Basin. I found accommodations for our team in a couple of houses along the main street. General Twaddle and his staff had managed all by themselves to get settled at a nearby place called Homécourt in an undistinguished château.

Relative closeness to the front made for a parade of volunteer information. These tellers of tales were an elderly and rather woebegone lot—a miner missing a leg, peasants wearing wooden clogs, a lady in a tattered sealskin greatcoat, another brandishing an ear trumpet, a ninety-year-old veteran of the battle of Sedan, an arthritic grandmother on crutches—each one of them impatient to report dubious goings-on in their neighborhood: lights from the attic window of the house next door flashing on and off at midnight, shadowy hurrying abroad after curfew by the blacksmith, suspicious disappearances of the grocer on a brand-new bicycle, girls too friendly with enemy soldiers returning at dawn from the east, farmer X in cahoots with Y, etc., etc.

A pretense of follow-up to these dubious allegations was SOP, and some of the supposed suspects, though none by any means suspicious, had to submit to a semblance of interrogation. A cheerful volunteer for interrogation duty, Zablocki alone asserted readiness and aptitude. Another candidate, however, was present and capable, the quiet, icy-eyed French civilian named Georges. Captain Rouvres pulled rank, calmly announcing that all interrogations would take place at the discretion of Georges. Zablocki's competence in the matter would be under advisement.

Eddy said, "If you say so."

Rouvres said, "Twentieth Corps's G-two says so, Lieutenant Lynn."

"Oh, boy," said Eddy.

Anyway, the few candidates for interrogation were such silly respondents to shady instances of malicious slander that nobody argued about procedure, and Zab relished browbeating elderly ladies.

Moreover, the actual espionage business assigned to us was childhood hide-and-seek compared with the perilous subterfuges essential for stealing enemy secrets. The Gestapo was famous for the ingenuity of tortures prepared for suspected spies. Little disposed to risk fingernails or testicles, we sat in our office in Moyeuvre, sipped yellow Chartreuse, and planned to recruit others to run risks in our place. The trick was to take advantage of the supposedly unoccupied no-man's-land between our front and the Germans. Called the combat zone, where killing enemy soldiers was the line of business, this area could stretch from a mile or two as far as ten and was strictly cleared of every civilian inhabitant, never mind what they had to leave behind, everything in any case liable to be reduced to rubble. The occasional stray was suspect. Our sly stratagem was to enlist a couple of neighborhood youngsters and persuade them to slip across the combat zone and sneak around the German positions, looking for unit numbers, tanks, artillery emplacements, etc., then slip back again and tell us what they'd seen. Our timorous amateur spies came back with confused, contradictory, and probably fictitious reports, which we didn't bother to send up to the corps G-2. It was all rather slapstick and anyway made no difference, as there was no fighting for the moment. Besides, the Germans were doubtless playing the same game.

Meanwhile my daily routine of doing nothing was quite decent—decent, that is, compared with the prospects of boys from the Texas panhandle or the Black Forest hunkering down in the mud hopefully out of sight of conscientious snipers. I drove around at random in the rain. And that was how I happened one afternoon to come upon a meaningless town called Jarny. Something was going on, as the street ahead was blocked by a noisy crowd. Leaving the jeep, I went to see what was afoot, and what I saw was that this was not a crowd but a mob, the distinction being the angry pitch of its voice, its agitation wavering and circling. I had no trouble approaching; my uniform made way. The commotion was a spectacle of ignoble bestiality: three young women, abject, pitiful creatures cowering, sobbing, stumbling barefoot, bleeding feet on the cobblestones, heads shaved bare, clothes torn from their breasts, and the scowling men and women shouting, shaking fists, spitting into their faces. It was a sickening sight, hideous and evil, and I shouted into the face of a stout matron sniggering and wearing a diamond choker, "What's the meaning, what do you think? This is an outrage."

And she bellowed right back at me, "They fucked with fritzes. They fucked with fritzes. They fucked with fritzes."

"Shut up," I cried, raising my hand. "Shut up. Where are the police?"

Her bellow became laughter. She gasped, "The police, you Yankee busybody. The police. There they are. Under your nose. There they are, the police."

And there they were, four brawny uniforms, kepis on pinheads and pistols in holsters, laughing, brandishing their nightsticks, and one of them throwing pebbles under the bare, bleeding feet of the weeping women, howling with the rest, "Fucked with the fritzes, fucked with the fritzes."

I clenched my jaws against the bile of disgust, spasms of pity and empathy. And oh, Christ, I might have fucked with fritzes myself.

Turning away from the nauseating mob, I fought backward against disgust and shame, careless of feet I walked over. And this? Was this too a mishap of war? Something to acknowledge and seize upon and all too willingly, perhaps, something of which to acknowledge the immemorial guilt.

I stepped on the gas to get out of there. And somewhere among the unfortunate, rain-sodden fields pulled to the roadside, the motor still running, pressing my face against the steering wheel, that sinister spectacle raging in my head. And to think—*to think*—I had run away from Beethoven, from Cézanne and Thomas Mann for this—*this*—as my grand denouement.

Our war came and went. The battle front, that is, was rubbery and amounted mostly to tentative skirmishing around Metz, twenty miles from the Ninety-fifth's line. But now and then, driving around the area, you came across evidence that real-life fighting was the business of the day: an occasional corpse. German, of course, because you never saw dead GIs, all these hastily removed by the Graves Registration detail. The first corpse you saw was the definitive, the unforgotten one, a heap of expressionless refuse yawning at the sky, absurd and breathtaking in its deadness.

Sometimes you also saw live Germans, drooping, bedraggled files of POWs, so hangdog and morose you could wonder whether they might not have preferred to be lifeless, having forfeited liberty down to the very meanest memento of intimacy. When taken prisoner, disarmed and standing in ranks at attention, each man was obliged to divest himself of all personal possessions, placing them on the ground at his feet. This done, his captors could pass along, assessing the lamentable piles of watches and rings, wallets, letters, photos, and all manner of vestigial trinkets. POW belt buckles too were sometimes taken as "souvenirs," and never mind the slippage of pants, because each buckle, though of cheap metal, was embossed with the motto *Gott mit uns*, a cruelly ironic slogan, because so many of the men destined to test its pertinence were doomed to learn too late that nobody at all was with them or ever would be. Of many wartime trophies, however, even including Luger pistols and SS daggers, the most prized was the Iron Cross medal, because it was rare and because it was prized by every German soldier, a central element in the Nazi iconography, worn by the führer himself as a symbol of Aryan bravery and atavistic Teutonic chivalry.

While helpless POWs watched their possessions, whether precious or worthless, being trifled with or pocketed by their enemies, you could see only too well how irreparably humiliated they were by the careless rape of their personalities. I felt for them. But what feeling precisely? Something germane to myself. Empathy? Was that it, melancholy and comforting? A disposition to make an abstraction of their mortifying uniforms. But how might I presume? A capacity to participate—*to participate*—in the sentiments of someone else? To comprehend his condition via emotions of my own? To look into life through the eyes of someone else? Well, not really. Besides, I hadn't seen anything yet.

When the rain let up one afternoon, I went for a routine spin. En route to nowhere, halfway along a hillside I pulled over by the verge, got out, and sat down on the withered grass. In the west a cleft was opening in the flamingo clouds, drawing up light from the world as sunset gathered. And I noticed something. Immediately to the right of my right boot, lifted among the brown grasses, one slip stood straight up as green as April, a single blade, amazing, and I fixed my whole attention onto it, as if it had sprung up that very morning solely for my contemplation, as if the tenacity of my observance, perhaps, were to illuminate a vital aspect of the origin of things through this mere wisp of greenery lit with life by the dying day. I felt for that leaf of grass a feeling wholly true to myself, and how remarkable, I thought: this must be one of those instances when all experience seems as self-determined as the beating of your heart and you wake up to the dawn of the future.

On October 19 the Ninety-fifth Division moved into the front line. Patton came to HQ at Homécourt in a cavalcade of flagged jeeps to deliver a pep talk to the division's officers. The NCOs were able to listen from the second floor of the château. The celebrated general was the very model of military swagger in his patent leather boots, riding breeches, pearl-handled revolvers, and stars on his steel helmet, standing on a raised platform with several hundred officers at strict attention before him. He needed no microphone to be heard.

"If you listen to what I say," he shouted, "you will come back alive.

If not, you'll be dead. Go in standing up. No digging. The division against you is the Seventeenth SS Panzer Grenadier, so young their balls haven't even come down yet. Remember that a dead soldier can't throw a hidden hand grenade. Rather shoot an enemy soldier than feed a POW." And more tough talk geared for no-nonsense doing and dying on the battlefield. And you could say what you liked about the bellicose general, but he certainly personified the notion that an ideal soldier is not only a doer of duty but a goer after glory.

To keep up with HQ, we moved forward from Moyeuvre about twelve miles eastward to a village called Maizières. The weather turned colder and, if possible, rainier, and we shook out the creases in our combat coats. But in our area, for the time being, there was next to no combat. All action was concentrated to the south of us, facing the city of Metz, which commanded the crossing of the Moselle River and had so far proved impregnable, protected by a circle of eight or ten sunken fortresses. Assault after assault was mounted against them and failed. The casualties were horrible, sometimes a thousand in one day. For the men on the line conditions were wretched, their equipment, their clothes, their bodies infused with rust, mildew, and mud. In some companies raw replacements threw away their rifles, ammunition, satchels and refused to fight for nothing. Commanders were frantic, and everyone wondered why Patton persisted when it had become plain that the engagement was intolerably punishing. But it was not in this general's nature to lower his sights, withdraw, or dismantle a strategy, and if that was intolerable, then that was war, and war was hell.

The front line, albeit inactive, lay slightly southeast a few miles in the direction of Semécourt, and I drove over there one day through the drizzle to take a look. A couple of MPs stopped me at the edge of a copse, demanding to know my business. So I told them I was an intelligence agent on a recco of the front line. They sniggered, glanced at each other with popped eyes, and one said, "Another tourist." They waved me through. The front was a mile or so farther ahead on the crest of a slope above a shattered stand of trees, and that this was indeed the front was clear, because the line of soldiers lay stretched in either direction as far as you could see, some of them down in muddy foxholes with scraps of tarpaulin stretched over them, others sprawled resigned to the drizzle, sucking on soggy cigarettes or listlessly clutching their rifles with condoms stretched over their muzzles.

A lieutenant munching on a cigar growled, "What the fuck do you want, soldier?"

"Intelligence reconnaissance, sir," I said.

"Shit," he said. "You're too clean to be worth a wet fart. Just do your thing and fuck off."

I tried to make my stride as purposeful as the pretense of bona fides, strolling along the line of prostrate, filthy infantrymen. Till one of them shouted, "Jim Lord, for Christ's sake. What the fuck are you doing here?"

It was Timmy Morreton. I recognized him immediately under his dripping helmet behind the smear of beard, exhausted eyes, and mud-caked field jacket. He was the best friend of my younger brother Teddy, in and out of our house all the time, in the same class at Princeton.

Squatting beside him, I said, "Hi, Timmy. What the hell are *you* doing here?"

"Shit," he said. "You know the army. I was fixed up in ASTP, but then there were not enough kids available to get killed, so they bumped us into the infantry."

"Figures," I said. "I lucked into their intelligence service. That means I have no IQ."

"Tough shit. I haven't changed my underwear for three weeks now. What's Teddy in?"

"He signed up for the paratroopers. No idea where he is now."

"Wouldn't you know? That's Ted. Always the one to volunteer, do the right thing while the rest of us ease along."

"The Eagle Scout, yes," I said. "Keep your fingers crossed for him. Where are the Germans?"

Timmy pointed his rifle. "Just over there in the woods about a mile. Dug in like us, waiting for the real stuff. We can hear them singing at night. No action since we got here."

Standing straight, I unslung my carbine, set it to my shoulder, and fired one round in the direction of the distant trees. I said, "I wouldn't have wanted to go through the whole war without firing a single shot at the enemy."

"You goddamn fool," cried Timmy. "The enemy? The enemy, for Christ's sake? You don't know fuck all. You don't come along in your clean clothes to shoot your wad for a joke and we're lying in the mud ready for the real thing, the works, the fucking war."

"Okay," I cried, "okay, Timmy, I'm sorry. I swear. I didn't mean anything wrong. How was I to know? Really. This crazy war."

"You're the crazy one," he said, pulling down the helmet above his face. "This war is what *we* fuck with. Get lost."

The soldiers on either side had looked up from the mud, hostile, muttering, spitting, and scowling.

Walking back, abashed, ashamed, I passed the cigar-munching looie, who leered at me and snarled, "Some screwball squeezed off a round down there? One of ours? Getting his rocks off for free."

I said nothing and hurried back from the line. The rain had started falling harder, and the GIs cowered beneath it. My jeep coughed, as if it realized I'd been in the wrong, guilty of misunderstanding the prerogatives of the military man.

Mail call one day brought through the rain into the monotony of Maizières a letter from Paris, focus of fantastic longings. It came from a woman named Claudine Goutner, the daughter of Madame Yakovleff, who had sent her my APO address, and she wrote to say that should I ever come to Paris, she would happily do anything she could to make as agreeable as possible a visit by the son of those who had befriended her mother and father. Aware that my use to the war effort, negligible though it was, would cease as soon as the front passed into Germany and that consequently Team No. 456 would be remanded back to MIS HQ near Paris for reassignment, I foresaw that I was likely at last to see the most brilliant and beautiful city in all the world. And it seemed to me immediately obvious that nothing could make a visit to that city so satisfying as to come face-to-face with the most extraordinary individual living there. So I wrote to Madame Goutner and requested that she find out where Picasso lived, go there, and tell the artist that before long he might expect to receive the visit of an American soldier named James Lord.

That this request might appear preposterous never occurred to me. I was, after all, a sincere admirer of Picasso's art, having fallen for it at age seventeen at the Museum of Modern Art in New York, enamored especially of the beautiful, sad-faced youths of the Blue Period, and had underlined in the exhibition catalog the artist's tantalizing statement "We all know that art is not truth. Art is a lie that makes us realize truth."

I was still imbued by the idea of genius, convinced that anyone with a sense of cultural affinities would naturally seize the opportunity to approach a man of genius. Thomas Mann, far away in America, was not at hand. Why not fix a wishful fantasy upon someone who was? I knew that an exhibition of Picasso's paintings had recently caused a riot in Paris. His art was familiar with warfare, violence, cruelty. That it should happen to be misunderstood, considered with contempt and derision by a large part of the public, made appreciation of it seem additionally judicious and edifying.

One afternoon when the rain couldn't make up its mind, Team No. 456, all six of us in our two jeeps, set out southward to have a look around, no particular aim in mind. I drove the lead jeep, Eddy beside me holding a map and Brunet behind. Coming up to the crest of a low hill, we reached a crossroads, the only sign there pointing to Plesnois, 4 km. I put the jeep into neutral while Eddy fingered his map as if we were actually on our way toward a strategic objective. And maybe we appeared to be, because below us in a shallow cleft crowded with bare thickets arose the hoarse grumbling, mechanized whine, and groaning crunch of heavy armor, and we waited expectantly for one of our Shermans to emerge from the underbrush. First appeared amid the dead leaves the long, slender snout of the cannon, swiveling slowly right and left, then the gray behemoth itself, a cross—not a star— painted on its flank, and the frightening 88 pivoting toward our hilltop even as we watched, and Eddy was shouting, "It's a Tiger. Everybody in the ditch. Now! In the ditch." And he leaped down, followed by Brunet, then Babbs, Zablocki, and Lieutenant Norton from the second jeep.

But it was all too fast for me. The sense of emergency too incongruous. My hands stayed riveted to the steering wheel; anyway, the motor ran on, while the German cannon fired and the crossroads exploded into a hailstorm of dust, rock, and rubble dust clattering onto the jeep and a rush of dirt in my face as I sat there staring at the fracas and Eddy was yelling, "Lord, you stupid fuck, get down into the ditch. You want to get killed?" though I thought I was all right and the Tiger already was lurching at right angles flattening the underbrush, ominous even as it crunched around to disappear into the thicket.

The others crawled up unabashed from the ditch. Eddy said, "You are one goddamned lucky son of a bitch. Could have got yourself killed. Bucking for a Purple Heart, are you?"

"It was too quick," I muttered, smearing dirt from my head and shoulders. "Didn't have time to get down, and anyway, I'm okay."

"Oh, yeah," said Eddy. "You have any idea what kind of luck you've had?"

What I knew was that I'd missed an opportunity. The war had given me a chance to be frightened, to taste the terror that stalks an infantryman like a real live tiger, to participate for a minute in the heartbreaking, ecstatic bargain of battle, your whole life subsistent in a puff of smoke. I felt a perfect fool and was ashamed.

A few days later a lieutenant colonel called McCarrenny from XX Corps sent a message informing us he would come the next morning at nine to find out what, if anything, our team was accomplishing. We spent out afternoon cleaning up the office, throwing out empty bottles, back issues of *Yank* and *Stars and Stripes*, emptying ashtrays, and mopping the floor. The Frenchies pleaded urgent business elsewhere.

The colonel was short, red-haired, with a pencil-line mustache, skintight uniform, well-burnished jodhpurs, and a black leather riding crop. Returning our salutes with a silent snap, he stamped up and down for effect, opening the drawers of the field desk and filing cabinet while we stood at attention. Finally he snapped, "At ease," and whipped the desk with his riding crop.

"You men stink!" he rasped in a thin, piccolo voice. "No results. No intelligence. No gung ho. No spies. You think this is fucking Florida, you're on vacation, get plastered, and screw all the broads. Not on your life. You know what you're here for, don't you? Well, do you or don't you? Answer me!" and he thrashed the desk.

"Yes, sir, we do," said Eddy with playboy flourish.

"Well, I'll tell you what you're here for," shrilled the colonel. "You're here to find out the enemy's secrets. You're here to catch spies. And you haven't come up with a ghost of a secret, you haven't caught the backside of a spy. Not one motherfucking result out of the bunch of you. And I expect results. Got that? Results!" he screeched, walloping the desk. "And I'll tell you something. On the way down here I had an idea. This coming week, I've decided to designate it as Catch a Spy Week, which means you have just one week to catch at least one real, live, breathing son of a bitch of a spy to put up against the wall in Nancy and bang, bang, bang. Do I make myself clear?"

"Yes, sir," said Eddy, "quite clear, sir."

"And I thought up a motto go to with it. 'Catch a spy, it's easy as pie!' Keep that in mind if you know what's good for you."

"Yes, sir," said Eddy. "Catch a spy, it *is* easy as pie."

"Well, do it! Or back you go with a blame on your service record. Do I make myself clear?" He yawned, battering the desk. "Attention!"

The furious colonel stamped out, brandishing his riding crop like an unhinged jockey.

We gazed at one another in a stupor of wonderment, seized by the slapstick burlesque of a senior officer whose orders we were bound to take seriously. Or were we?

"Catch a spy," said Eddy. "Pie in the sky, bang, bang, bang."

"If I may say so," said Zablocki, "I'd say our side has been a bit short on results. The colonel's cuckoo, okay, but he's got a point. No secrets. No spies."

"So?" said Eddy. "We put an ad in *Stars and Stripes*? 'Secrets wanted. Big reward for spies.'"

"Seek, and ye shall find," said Zab.

"Christ!" Eddy swore. "We'll seek. And if we can't find, we'll turn in Twaddle as a double agent."

And so Team No. 456 was organized into two search parties for the week of catching spies. Eddy and Bill took the first jeep, leaving me to mind the office. "In case Colonel Macaroni comes back to beat up the furniture," said Eddy. "And if you can rustle up some more wine while we're searching the sky for pie, do it. That's all you're good at anyway."

Consequently remaindered, so to speak, I stayed in the office, not unhappy, reading *The Hairy Ape*. The second jeep was driven by the taciturn Babbs with Norton beside him and Zab glowering into the rain in the backseat.

Three days passed without anything undercover turning up, much less apprehended, while I proceeded peacefully into *Strange Interlude*, which, indeed, it was fated to be.

In the fourth afternoon Eddy came back lugging four large portfolios found in the cellar of a wrecked château in the woods of no-man's-land. They contained dusty cadastral surveys and faded architectural elevations of obscure buildings, foxed and uninteresting. The old leather portfolios, however, if not their contents, might be worth having, Eddy thought, so he dispatched them up the line in case some souvenir monger might send down a condescending thank-you. But no nod came back. We drank a bottle of Château Anonymous and said, "Who cares?" Zab's anti-Nazi urine was now boiling over. He insisted on going alone to scour the combat zone for spy pie, and inevitably he turned up a couple of slices, blond and blue-eyed kids about eighteen years old who looked frightened enough to be the real thing, shivering in our well-heated office, their hands tied behind them. What evidence had given them away as Nazi spies? we wondered. Zablocki had the answer. They had been hiding in underbrush suspiciously close to our front line, an area where civilians were forbidden to trespass. Their story was that they came from a nearby town named Hagondange and were out to snare a few rabbits. They were too well dressed, however, to be farm boys or miner's sons well practiced in poaching. No meshes or twines for snaring had been found in their pockets. No indication, indeed, whether personal or official, to verify their identity. And their insistence that they neither knew nor hoped to learn the first thing about the war was too anxious, too nervous to be persuasive. There was nothing to prove their innocence. Or guilt.

"No rabbits?" said Eddy.

"Not even a rabbit's foot," said Zablocki, unamused. "But they haven't been properly interrogated as yet. I've asked Captain Rouvres for an assist."

"On what authority?" snapped Eddy.

The French captain provided his own answer by walking into the office, followed by the cryptic Georges, who dangled handcuffs in either hand.

"Wait a second," said Eddy.

"Rather not," said Rouvres. "The sooner suspects are questioned, the better the chances for results. Georges, take the prisoners to the other room."

Georges seized both boys by the nape of the neck and shoved them toward the farther room, an unused space with one high window, a few chairs, a table, empty knapsacks hanging along the wall.

"Go easy on those kids," said Eddy.

Rouvres said, "They were taken in a forbidden area. Suspected spies in civilian clothes are not covered by the Geneva Conventions. Their interrogation is a French matter and will be conducted by French personnel. If you wish to be present, that is your privilege. I am the ranking officer."

"Those are my spies," said Zablocki. "I caught them. I question them." He strode behind Georges into the farther room, followed by Rouvres, who slammed the door.

We looked at one another and waited. It was fifteen minutes, maybe twenty, when the first stifled whimpering came, then more slowly moans, followed by howls, and Eddy was at the door, pounding his fists on the cracked planking—it was locked—and he shouted, "Zablocki, you come out of there. That's an order. I won't have American personnel incriminated in this. Zablocki! You come out of there now, or I swear I'll break you."

The sergeant cracked open the door, peeking out, and he came through with sullen reluctance, leaving the door open for us to see inside . . . everything—the two boys naked, handcuffed wrists suspended above them from coat hooks, tears, snot, blood, saliva seeping down their faces—and I clamped my eyes shut to save me from the sight. Lieutenant Norton was shouting, "You frog bastards. I'll report you for this."

Georges had taken off his shirt. There were tattoos on his forearms. Captain Rouvres said, "Don't be ridiculous, Lieutenant," and shut the door.

We all went outside into the street, as if to dissociate ourselves from the outrage, for which we were collectively responsible, and stood around in distraught complicity. Lieutenant Parny sat at the wheel of the French jeep, smoking a cigarette in an amber holder, and he said, "Don't take it so hard, boys. It's the fortunes of war, kid stuff compared to the Gestapo: they string you up by your testicles, and then it's goodbye to Mademoiselle from Armentières."

Presently Captain Rouvres sauntered from the office, razor-blade features composed, and said, "That's it, gentlemen. The boys were sent across as German agents. We have confessions. You need to be concerned no further. I've taken the liberty of ordering up from the motor pool transportations to Nancy for final disposition and also called Colonel McCarrenny at corps headquarters to report. He requested me to convey his commendation."

"Very nice," said Eddy. "What about the boys?"

"Oh, they'll be put out of harm's way. That's a Third Army jurisdiction, all perfectly official, you know."

"I don't know," said Eddy.

"Well, to be sure," said the French officer, "you haven't had the Huns at your throats for centuries in order to learn the tough technocratic lessons."

But then, as an example technically to the point, Georges came outside, leading the two kids, dressed now but handcuffed, bruised faces in tears, gasping, "We're not guilty, not guilty, didn't do anything, got to believe us."

And who were we, then, to intercede in the machinery of military litigation, the jurisprudence of guilt—or of innocence? Not I, who wore the uniform of the right side with so unconvincing a right to it.

The truck from the motor pool arrived. Georges manhandled the boys into the rear and Lieutenant Parny climbed in after them, his baby face a mask of distaste. The truck drove away into the fading afternoon, and the boys shouted back, "Help us. We're not guilty. Help us please." But an immensity of oncoming dusk fell onto their entreaty.

Eddy ordered us never under any circumstances ever again to address a single word to the Frenchies. But we were practically finished with them as it was, or, worse perhaps, vice versa.

On November 5 fell the first snow of what was to become a very cruel winter, and despite the slush and despond, I thought to see in the mirror of introspection a person unthinkable two years before on my way to volunteer for the war. And here I was, a figure of moral happenstance attired in the guise of responsibility, pledged to serve a cause that the world of probity called good, a man, in short, who might be required to behave like a beast for the benefit of mankind.

And three days later, as if to corroborate the good and the responsibility, we learned that our beloved commander in chief, FDR, had been elected for a historic fourth term as president, an event as unprecedented as the conflict of which he more than any other man had determined the outcome.

On that same day the Ninety-fifth Division moved forward to take its place in the front line. We followed HQ across the Moselle River, which had been bridged in several places, and set ourselves up in a desolate little place called Vigy, heaps of manure on both sides of the single street. There was nothing strategic to do. No nonsense now about spies or secrets.

On neither side was the fighting in our sector severe, casualties moderate. Though we were settled well back from the combat zone, you occasionally saw columns of German POWs herded by a few GIs toward holding points in the rear, most of them young, all bedraggled, filthy dirty, and desperately glum, many hobbling on feet swollen from frostbite.

I was at loose ends. Eddy spent afternoons playing bridge with HQ officers from an adjoining division. Norton was on the souvenir chase, had liberated a swastika flag, an SA dagger, Gott mit uns buckles, and the dog tags from a couple of kraut corpses; he was not finicky. Zab kept sullenly to himself. Brunet pursued skirts despite regulations forbidding it, and several nocturnal absences suggested he made out with some of them. Babbs surprised his teammates by reading a tiny volume of the letters of Cicero in Latin. The weather turned bitter. Mud froze, then thawed, then froze again, and some of the infantrymen in their damp, foul clothes, cowering in the soggy foxholes, crept away in the dead of night, leaving behind their equipment and their fear and their loyalty.

The afternoon was useless. Icy rain flew in your face. I drove the jeep north and northeast through the woods in the direction of Gomelange and Valmunster. By the roadsides fighting must have occurred recently because a few contorted corpses in their nauseating uniforms still lay in the ditches. On the lookout for anything I could pretend would excuse my presence I saw a troop of soldiers one afternoon strung out in a clearing. As I drew abreast, a master sergeant beckoned me to stop.

"Lookin' for action?" he barked, tobacco slime seeping from the butt of a cigar in the edge of his mouth. Older than the usual, he had an angry regular army face, a greatcoat with fur collar, and a .45 automatic belted to his thigh in a tooled holster. GI attire at the front was catch as can, no questions asked.

"Military intelligence reconnaissance," I said.

"Yeah. Well, piss my pants, and who the cocksucking fuck we got to thank you for?" he muttered, and not waiting for an answer, turned to his squad of GIs. Behind them huddled ten or a dozen Germans, maybe one of the surprise advance units we'd been warned about. The front lay only a couple of miles east, artillery thumps audible far forward in the frozen rain. I turned off my ignition and got down to watch.

The sergeant shouted, "Okay, now get them POWs in formation, empty pockets."

The prisoners jostled into formation. At the head of the rank stood a young lieutenant in impeccable uniform, an exemplary type of ideal Aryan, face of a steel-eyed hawk. He watched his men soulfully set down their possessions in the mud, shed their belts, and unbutton jackets. He in turn gingerly spread before him a white handkerchief and placed on it a gold pocket watch and chain, a silver cigarette case, and a slender crocodile billfold. The sergeant had first choice of the spoils, at which he sneered till he reached the lieutenant. Watch and chain, cigarette case, and billfold having disappeared like magic into bulky pockets, he scrutinized the officer from boots to peaked cap and pointed at the Iron Cross medal pinned to his tunic, tapping it with a tobacco-stained fingernail, and said, "Take that off, kraut."

The lieutenant, standing stiffly at attention, said, *"Nein."*

Whereupon the sergeant snarled, seized the medal, and ripped it from the prisoner's tunic.

Not a tremor moved over the officer's features as he raised his right arm and slapped his captor smartly across the face.

The sergeant came up a couple of inches off the ground, as if raised physically by the force of the blow, roaring, "Shit-eating kraut raised his *hand* on me. That cocksucker touched me, put his *hand* on me," and he was rigid with the shock of it, staring pop-eyed at the German; then slowly he drew his pistol from the holster, caressing its muzzle for a moment, aimed it full in the officer's face, and pulled the trigger, at the same time uttering a wild, almost ecstatic cry as a geyser of blood and cartilage spewed back into his own face and he roared, "Touched his *hand* on me, I swear, oh, God," and he let fall his arm with the pistol, the young lieutenant lying dead before him in the mud.

The POWs stared in blinking stupefaction at their officer's corpse, gasped, and shook their arms.

Watching, aghast, I thought I saw what I couldn't think I saw, and yet there could be no mistaking, God knew. I did see what I was sure I saw: the telltale bulge in the sergeant's crotch and moist stain on his fly. He had come in his pants.

In the surprise and fury of the fray the Iron Cross had fallen into the mud. Looking down at it with haggard bewilderment, the sergeant bent forward, picked it up, rubbing it against the sleeve of his jacket, leaned backward, and hurled it into the underbrush.

Puffing and hawking, still spattered with blood, he turned, noticed me, and demanded, "What you staring at?"

I stood stock-still, speechless.

"You ain't seen a thing," said the sergeant with a widening sneer. "A thing. Prisoner shot while trying to escape. Happens. War's like that. You move off."

There were no answers. No questions. A single bullet had said everything once and for all.

I got into the jeep and drove back toward Vigy but stopped by the wayside some distance along and waited with the wind freezing my face, and then the rain turned into snow, silent and impersonal, endless, and the curves of my nostrils started twitching uncontrollably, a part of me foreign and hostile I couldn't control. The dusk began to swell with snow-driven enmity, and when I came back to Vigy, they said where've you been, Lord, you damn fool, it's a blizzard out there, and I said yes, I got lost, had a hell of a time finding the way.

The battle to take Metz slogged on day after day in the snow, casualties continuing heavy, Patton stubborn to reduce the fortresses against raging odds. Why the German garrisons fought so fiercely when it was obvious they had lost the war, well . . . that was the mystery of atavistic valor harking back to the age of legend.

Our operational utility received a tardy, farcical acknowledgment from the macaroni colonel, who sent a message of felicitation for the successful outcome of Catch a Spy Week. The boys had been condemned to death, sentence unfortunately commuted to imprisonment owing to insistence by the French general. Zablocki pouted. It had been obvious from the beginning that those kids were innocent. Orders came to move out from Vigy fifteen miles eastward through Befey Forest past Guinkirchen to Boulay.

Some troops must have bypassed Metz, because we could hear heavy artillery, either ours or their or both, over toward Creutzwald and the German frontier, while by day British bombers, flying low, passed overhead in untroubled formation to strike the factories at Saarbrücken. In a fluid combat zone the uselessness of Team No. 456 must have been evident to everyone, nor did we do zip for the sake of undeserved merit.

Though Boulay lay mostly in ruins, I'd found billets for our team. Mine was in the basement of a former grocery store, where I shared the vaulted cellar with the grocer and his wife and mother-in-law, a grizzle-haired old lady who muttered in her sleep. Sometimes I was wakened by an adventitious explosion shifting the rubble above, but my companions, accustomed to the intimacy of disaster, only sighed as they slept.

The Sunday afternoon of our ninth day in Boulay hovered overhead in late sunlight, no noise of battle having been heard since morning. Maybe the war had finished with this devastated town. A goof-off from corps HQ came along and said that Patton had finally entered Metz the day before, as several of the impregnable fortresses had fallen; blueprints of their structural particulars had made a surprise attack a pushover.

"So," said Eddy when I told him. "But well-bred spies don't boast when they've pulled off an ad hoc, do they? It'll be our secret setback to Herr Hitler."

When the grocer learned that Patton had taken Metz and the Germans were retreating eastward beyond St. Avold toward their frontier, his face overflowed with tears, and between yawps of joy he said he and his wife would prepare a victory banquet the following evening. I impulsively blustered that the next day happened to be my birthday, whereupon he seized me by both shoulders and kissed my cheeks, exclaiming that good fortune had done good work and they would do the impossible to make my birthday happy.

It almost wasn't an anniversary at all because a sibilant boom exploded not far from me the next morning in the street outside the grocery store, followed by a hailstorm of shattering shrapnel, miasma of dust, and clink of metal hitting my helmet hard enough to shock my jaws. A jagged shard of shrapnel fell at my feet. I picked it up. I dropped it, burning hot, took off my helmet to inspect the damage. There was none. So I had not, after all, been totally a tourist disguised as a soldier. But then. The war, of course, was not yet over. I again picked up the shard, no longer hot, a scrap of metal, lifeless, indifferent, not in itself purposeful. Yet it represented an intention, a missile meant to kill. I put it in my pocket. Then I went inside to the cavernous safety of the grocer's cellar in case the bombardment resumed. It didn't. I still have the shard of shrapnel.

In the Pacific, meanwhile, the greatest sea battle in history took place off the Japanese island of Leyte, destroying thirty-six enemy warships, crippling the Japanese Navy, and allowing General MacArthur to keep his vow that he would return to the site of surrender and humiliation.

The U.S. government published a detailed account of the mass annihilation of Jews at a concentration camp in Poland called Auschwitz. It had been known even before the outbreak of war that Nazi concentration camps were organized for unspeakable crimes, but the report of efficient German factories for industrialized murder appalled the coldest-blooded campaigners.

In Boulay the victory-birthday banquet was a sensation. So it seemed, anyway, magic deliverance from danger in the fairy-tale cellar lit by twenty-two candles. I had asked Eddy to join us. The grocer and his wife and mother-in-law were accompanied by a female cousin, a widowed neighbor, and the mayor of Boulay, eight in all, four ladies, four gents, as if we were sitting down, said Eddy, to a formal Thanksgiving Dinner—only four days late. Nor was there a murmur when the feast provided no turkey but, rather, brisket of pork, stewed turnips, and a delectable cake made of carrots. The mayor gave a speech, thanking Americans for having come—a second time—to the rescue of his homeland. Eddy responded by emphasizing it was the least one could decently do, France having given the decisive helping hand to our Revolution. We drank several bottles of champagne, which had lain buried in the grocer's garden, awaiting this unforgettable day.

Two days later orders came down for our entire team to report pronto to division HQ. When we got there, we found the temperature of optimism high. The Germans were retreating back onto their own soil along a wide front, suffering some four thousand dead or captured every day. HQ expected unconditional surrender to come before Christmas, two or three weeks away. Nazi V-1 and V-2 rockets, their "secret" weapons, were killing British civilians, true, but that gratuitous slaughter could not delay defeat, since American troops were advancing fast enough through the industrialized Saarland while furious Russian forces coursed brutally across Hungary and Czechoslovakia toward the German frontier. France was wholly free save for a pocket of perverse and futile resistance around the ruined port of Lorient in distant Brittany. Such being the operational situation, men needed to interpret military intelligence inklings, findings, or actual discoveries in the French theater were no longer useful to the Ninety-fifth Division. So Colonel Golightly advised us that vouchers would be readied in two or three days' time for travel to the French MIS HQ in the Parisian suburb of Le Vésinet.

Immediately, however, General Twaddle wished to see us all to say goodbye and, added the colonel with a wink, to pass out a surprise.

Almost before we'd had time to salute him the general told us to stand at ease. Very pleased, he was, he said, very, very pleased to congratulate us one and all, before our forthcoming departure for reassignment, on our outstanding achievement of the division mission in operations against Metz. In consideration of which exemplary devotion to duty reflecting great credit upon the service, consequently, it was his privilege and pleasure to decorate each one of us with the Bronze Star for meritorious achievement.

Eddy spoke for us all when he said with an audible quaver of voice, "Sir, words fail me."

"Actions speak for you, my boy," said the general with an avuncular grin. "God go with you all."

Gott mit uns, too, I thought, walking out of the general's tent into a sunset—I suddenly remembered—as cautionary as the one reflected in the sea off Omaha Beach only ten weeks before.

What could imaginably have been of sufficient strategic advantage to deserve decoration for meritorious achievement was never itemized, nor, I think, did any of us want to know. Was it the catching of the boy spies? Captain Rouvres and his shady accomplices had disappeared. We heard no more of the macaroni colonel. Nobody mentioned the lucky blueprints.

The Bronze Star came in an oblong black leather box lined with satin and velvet. In the form of a star, of course, probably of bronze, suspended from a red silk ribbon with a blue stripe down the center, marked on the reverse "Heroic or Meritorious Achievement." Accompanied by a typewritten notice:

Headquarters Ninety-fifth Infantry Division
APO 95, U.S. Army

G201   *29 November 1944*
Subject: Award of Bronze Star Medal
To: Technician Third Grade James H. Lord,
ASN 12183139, Headquarters 95th Infantry Division
    By direction of the President, and under the provisions of Army Regulations 600-45, as amended, and Letter, Headquarters, XX Corps, File AG200.b, dated 16 October 1944, a Bronze Star Medal is awarded to:
    Technician Third Grade James H. Lord, (ASN12183139), INF, Headquarters 95th Infantry Division. For meritorious achievement in connection with military operations against the enemy, from 8 November to 20 November 1944, in the vicinity of Metz, France.
    From 8 November 1944 to 20 November 1944, while the 95th Infantry Division was engaged in the attack and reduction of Metz, the service of Technician Third Grade Lord was distinguished by high professional attainment, and exemplary devotion to duty.
    By command of Major General Twaddle:
                                                W. J. Flowers
                                                Major, AGD
                                                Adjunct General

When this you read, think of an impressible kid wandering alone down the lanes of Normandy in search of fresh eggs and a bottle of calvados or eating carrot cake on his twenty-second birthday in the cellar of a bombed-out grocery store. And entertaining fantasies of conversation with a man of genius. But of military operations against the enemy, what conduct, what calculation, what account? And indeed, what enemy? What hurt had been done to me that I should take arms against? What guilt other than my own expiate? What profession? What attainment? Yes, once again from the secret hiding place of remorse rose the phantom caveat of the dead leaves on the cement sidewalk, after all, and of those blind raptures in the beds of Boston; who was to pronounce judgment?

To read and reread Major Flowers's Letter AG200.b. Something must have been amiss. More than amiss. Something was wrong. Vitally wrong, bringing wrong to spontaneous effect in the possession of this medal as a token of what, in a word, was queer: about myself and about the war, farcical and tragic. No one, to be sure, was accusing me of heroism, but medals awarded in wartime bear heroic intimations. The decoration of a dead British pilot revered in his mother's house in Broadway, an Iron Cross so precious to a German officer that its honor cost him his life: those were testimonials to reckless courage that for an instant makes warfare a credit to civilization. And in that crazy context, is it any wonder, holding in hand a medal to which I was not entitled, I fancied myself eligible to make the acquaintance of the most celebrated artist then alive, himself, as it happens, a master of clowning and pretense?

We said goodbye to the Ninety-fifth Infantry Division, stowed our gear and ourselves into our jeeps, and set forth through mean sleet for Paris, 250 miles westward across the internecine farmlands of a war that, unlike ours, had been fought for nothing. We spent one night at a decent hotel in Verdun facing the Meuse, another in Reims, where we drank a gallon of champagne, yet another in Meaux, where we sobered up preparatory to reporting, bemedaled and meritorious, to MIS HQ at Le Vésinet.

Twelve

DECEMBER 1944–JANUARY 1945

MIS HQ France was a French reprise of the comfortable Broadway hideout: a bourgeois suburb of Paris named Le Vésinet about a dozen miles due west of the Eiffel Tower, affluent houses set amid healthy gardens around a small lake. No danger of battlefront inconvenience here. The army reasserted its rationale with characteristic confusion. Nobody knew where anyone was to be reassigned, or when, or appeared to give a shit. Erstwhile teams were splintered. There was some uneasy poop about possible shipment to the Pacific Theater now that the European curtain was about to come down, Christmas Day only three weeks off.

Lieutenant Lynn abruptly discovered, being an officer and a gentleman, that to him I was no longer Jim, to me he would no longer be Eddy, and he disappeared forever into the officers' club, confirming yet again that all men are created unequal. Listed for billet in the Villa Ibis, a pink stucco pavilion overlooking the lake, I found Aaron and H already ostentatiously installed in Art Nouveau bedrooms, keeping an eye on three cases of Châteauneuf du-Pape. Having landed on the Riviera in mid-August, attached to the HQ of the Seventh Army, they had had a sightseeing tour of the Rhône Valley, the Germans hightailing it north, leaving behind hundreds of horses and several truckloads of wine. Of which we attacked a couple of bottles while I diverted my buddies with the comic relief, which they failed to find funny, of General Twaddle, his commendation, and the award for heroic or meritorious achievement. My devotion to duty may have been the stuff of jokery for NCO players of the intelligence game, but for those of higher rank and of official whim the putative prestige of decoration, being its own reward, deserved to be rewarded, and I became the rightful recipient of a three-day pass.

Thus, in the midafternoon of Sunday, December 3, I came out of the Gare St. Lazare for the first time. Albeit grimy and gray, Paris was glorious, everything I had ever wanted it to be, and I had wanted it to be everything I had ever wanted. All the sights were the most beautiful in all the world, and I gazed at them all. I also had an eye on beautiful young men, having forgotten for months how beautiful beautiful young men could be. However, I'd not forgotten that I'd come to Paris with the hope of satisfying a desire more spiritual than sexual.

At nightfall I made my way to 118 Avenue de Versailles, a drab address, where I found Claudine Goutner, Madame Yakovleff's daughter, her dentist husband, his parents, and her brother Pierre, who had just been discharged from the French Army. They greeted me with warmth in the dingy apartment, offering a glass of wine. My request had caused some confusion, for Claudine had assumed that I was already acquainted with Picasso, and when after considerable bother she had finally found herself face-to-face with the artist on November 13, he said, "But who is this James Lord?"

Picasso possessed a fantastic acuity for instantly perceiving distinctive and revealing features, and his question was incisively to the point, the point, indeed, as to which he would soon be asked to provide prima facie evidence, having himself been in search of it for half a century. Claudine was puzzled but polite; she had been merely instrumental: I could never on my own have located Picasso in three days' time. She invited me to stay for dinner. I told stories of the war, the fall of Metz, headlong retreat of the Germans, but took care not to mention the Bronze Star.

The rue des Grands Augustins is a short, antique street on the Left Bank close by the river and Pont Neuf, number 7 an imposing mansion of cut stone. A phlegmatic concierge snorted in response to my query, "Picasso? He won't see you. Stairs to your left at the top."

They rose narrow and circular two and a half stories to a stout oak door. I pressed the bell. Twice. Locks eventually croaked, revealing a pointed nose, eyeglasses, and a thin mouth, which asked what I wanted.

To see Picasso, I said. The door inched slightly ajar, disclosing an old man clothed entirely in black and wearing a black beret. My uniform was the object of his scrutiny; the field coat bore no insignia, because intelligence personnel sometimes had to pass themselves off as autonomous agents exempt from the symbolism and constraints of regimentation. He said, "You are American."

"Yes," I said.

"Ah, yes," he said, "an American officer, you come recommended by—"

"A lady named Claudine Goutner," I interjected, allowing ambiguity of attire to reason for rank. "My name is James Lord."

"You'd better come inside." He led me to a high, narrow room, gray daylight sifting onto an incredible accumulation of junk and treasure. His name was Sabartés, Picasso's secretary. He asked me to tell him about myself, a request instantly making for such an awkwardness under the circumstances, an awkwardness actually physical, that I turned for fear of making a misstep and on the uneven flooring loosely matted in hemp drugget made a real misstep, stumbling, and put out my hand to catch at an adjacent table. "You are ill," cried Sabartés. "You have been injured in the war."

"Yes," I said, surprised because the lie was the injury, yet it was not a lie because I had come to this place to learn that art is a lie that tells the truth. As for the *injury*, it had been inflicted when I fired one shot at my imagination and the naked boys were screaming behind the locked door, the sadistic sergeant firing his pistol into the face of the German officer, myself knowing such wrongs were committed careless of redress, guilty, in a word, of complicity.

When Sabartés moved as if to help me to a chair, I limped toward it in order to sustain the hoax of injury, not knowing exactly what I was up to but amenable at the same time to its childlike innocence. Though the injury was a contrivance, what it represented was sound. In short, I was true to myself. Of course my aspiration had always been to become an artist.

Sabartés asked whether I was in pain. I said no. He inquired about my role as to the vicissitudes of war, and I told him I was a member of the Military Intelligence Service, whereupon he observed that I must have had fascinating but dangerous experiences. Not really, I rejoined, attempting to suggest that the disasters of war had for me been all the more awful because I had been an onlooker well out of harm's way.

"I understand," said Sabartés, his forefinger wiggling in the direction of my legs. "It wouldn't be right for you to talk about military secrets."

I let that ridiculous surmise slide, though the eventuality of secrets appeared to please Picasso's secretary, who then got down to business by telling me that to meet his employer, I should come back two days later at exactly eleven o'clock. "In order to be alone with him," he added, having evidently assumed that privacy would be favorable for a meeting.

"I'll be on time," I said, rising, careful to limp toward the exit, maintaining the scam supposed to procure grace. Sabartés followed, and at the top of the stairs I thanked him for his consideration etc. and promised again to be on time, limping as I went down.

An aptitude for pretense and a readiness to resort to the virtue of false appearances might have seemed to present problems beyond the competences of a young man utterly unversed in the manipulations of a point of view that art takes for granted. But I didn't question the law of gravity or doubt the faculty of human nature to make the best, not to mention the most, of happenstance.

Two days later at ten fifty-nine I once more put my finger on Picasso's doorbell. Sabartés said, "You were wise to be punctual. Genius makes every moment momentous."

That dictum so magnified my diffidence I almost forgot to limp, following Sabartés into the farther room, where my presence proved my readiness to share his opinion, and then I became aware that someone had come in behind us, standing back by the window, and the secretary jerked about like a puppet on a wire, declaiming, "Here is Picasso!"

My inadequacy was breathtaking. To look like a fool, however, may have been the very best thing I could have done as I mumbled some nothingness and put my hand into the outstretched hand, aware of being scrutinized by the famous eyes.

"You wished to see me?" he asked.

I said, "Yes."

Stepping back a pace, the artist made a gesture toward himself with both hands, as if to demonstrate the obvious, which he then did by saying, "Well, here I am."

The fact was overwhelming, also my sudden surprise at the great artist's small stature. Though stocky, muscular, with a large, imposing head, he was much shorter than I was. Who would have expected such a great artist to be so slight?

"And what is it that you wanted to see me about?" he asked.

"I just wanted to see you," I stammered, blushing hard. And maybe it was immediate evidence of Picasso's uncanny power that my reason must have been the very best that anyone could give for presuming to intrude upon him. What surer virtue in his sight could there be?

He said, "Have you had your breakfast?"

I admitted that I had.

"Well," he said, "if you want to, you can come upstairs and sit with me while I have mine."

I said yes, blushing again, and maybe it was the fire in my face that did the trick, because a blush usually signals something the blusher wishes to conceal.

Picasso proceeded to open a door at the end of the room, while his secretary nodded like an entrepreneur pleased by the profitable outcome of his arrangements. The young soldier followed, limping, the very picture of one who has come to harm through the disasters of war, therefore *par extraordinaire* entitled to the consideration of a great man. Like many an injury, however, such a one as I pretended to have sustained could very well have been but the bodily manifestation of a hurt long before made wounding to the spirit.

We passed through a vast room filled chockablock with such a clutter I barely had time to recognize it all as sculpture before Picasso nimbly skipped up a circular stairway in the far corner. I followed. The room above was packed with paintings of all sizes, colors, configurations, placed on several easels and stacked one against another on the bare tiled floor in such profusion that little space remained to move about in. "This is where I do my painting," said the artist, waving at a pile of canvases.

I saw but could not speak.

Picasso said, "Sabartés tells me you have been injured in the war."

"It's nothing," I said.

"You limp."

I admitted that.

"Sit down, then," said Picasso, indicating a green wooden bench of the sort found in public gardens and parks. He sat beside me.

The breakfast consisted of one large bowl of black coffee and two chunks of bread, brought by a beautiful young woman, dark, full-breasted, with long, lustrous hair. She appeared not at all intimidated by the great artist, who chucked her under the chin and said, "This is Inès; she comes from mimosa country, land of wine and perfume, where men go mad with desire. Eh, my beauty?"

Inès shut her eyes, shook her head, suppressed some mirth, and wen away without a word.

"Now then," said Picasso, "tell me about the war."

Having blundered along the edges of battlefields, hung around in the undistinguished safety of and slept in the peaceful beds of liberated villages, what had I to tell a man of genius about the climactic chaos of human life? And why, having no insight to offer, had I insinuated myself into his studio to sit beside Picasso while he sipped his morning coffee and munched a crust of bread? That was the question upon which my existence now so patently seemed to hang. I had dreamed of men of genius, staking the fantasy of future fulfillment upon their example—and, if possible, their proximity—but now that the war had given me this phenomenal opportunity I had nothing to offer it but fear and false pretenses. As if the injury I pretended to have sustained were only now actually wounding me in the awful inadequacy of my presence beside the most prodigious artist on earth. I could hear the crumble of bread between his teeth and see the white stubble of unshaven beard, but the artist dwelt on the far, far side of an unbridgeable abyss, the chasm of his prodigy, which no one could ever cross, and his creative remoteness was alarming, as if his very ability to make art of mankind threatened one's survival as an individual.

The abyss yawned before me, ominous and menacing, but perhaps, I imagined, if I could peer into it deeply and tenaciously enough, I might one day have done something if not heroic, then meritorious enough to have survived the conflict without remorse. I had failed to be intimidated by the Tiger tank. Picasso was frightening. As if he in person embodied a state of war in which I might become a combatant.

I advanced a few superficial opinions concerning the corruption of people caught up in the lunatic circumstances of warfare. Also ran on about the hypocrisy and moral misery that prevail when patriotism invites men to murder one another with impunity and honor the enormity of their guilt.

"Yes," murmured Picasso. He said that the war years had been truly lunatic for him, because he had never been left so completely in peace. Denounced by the Nazis as degenerate and subversive, forbidden to exhibit, he had been free to work as he pleased. Since the liberation, however, he had been subject to increased annoyance, an exhibition of his paintings had provoked a public disturbance, and he constantly received insulting letters through the mail.

I tried to say how much I admired his work, which he took in with tolerant indifference, gesturing toward a pile of pictures as if they had mysteriously materialized as the result of some supernatural determinism, which indeed, his prolific prodigy seemed naturally to substantiate.

He said, "You have nothing to ask me then?"

"No, no, nothing," I apologetically admitted.

"Well . . ." He shrugged, stood, and went to the stairs in the corner. In the room below he added, "You understand. Other people are waiting. I must say goodbye."

"Oh, yes," I exclaimed, anxious not to seem too daring when I had been nothing else. In the farther room Sabartés was waiting with two or three other men.

The artist, however, did walk with me to the door and said, "You did well to come and see me. Now that you know the way, and the hour, don't hesitate to come again when your duties allow."

"Oh, thank you," I said, "I will, I will."

Sabartés went beside me to the stairway and, saying goodbye, added, "Take care in case of danger."

What strange advice! I said, "Oh, I've never been in the slightest danger," though I knew it was just then that at last I was.

Aaron and H, when I found them that evening in the Villa Ibis, were unimpressed when I let slip the news that their buddy had made the acquaintance of the greatest artist in the world. Soldiers, to be sure, are famous for being braggarts, tricksters, and liars, a fact gladly agreed upon by all of them, making it easier, perhaps, to pretend that they are not in the business of dying young. Mortality was much on my mind despite the actual slightness of danger, and death obviously obsessed Picasso, and my desire to meet him had certainly been dictated not only by admiration but also by fear.

When we applied the next morning for reassignment, Aaron and I were ordered to proceed by train to a town in Brittany called Quimper (pronounced *camp-air*) there to report for hypothetical counterintelligence duties, while H would travel by jeep to Dijon on assignment equally fuzzy. The train was scheduled to depart one day later, December 7 at 7:00 a.m. We missed it. A lovely stroke of luck. We laughed and said we'd take the next train. It left the following morning at the same hour, allowing us an extra day to enjoy Paris.

What manner of enjoyment I wanted I knew immediately. The longing had lain expectantly in wait, and if Picasso was the focus of it, I could have known he was the inevitable objective. It was by way of what Picasso did, as well as by virtue of what he was, that my purpose was to be served. The temerity of the thing was fraught at the same time with a sense of peril, but I could no more have discarded my idea than I could have thrown myself into the Seine.

Having left behind in the Montparnasse station both Aaron and my gear, I strode up the rue de Rennes toward the river, possessed for the first time in my life by the potential of portraiture. It seized me as fiercely as lust, and surely it had as much to do with the cravings of the flesh as with the dread of its extinction. For what is a portrait? No element essential to the continuity of life. If we assume, however, that it be a work of art, it possesses a durable existence all its own, not powered by muscles and blood, to be sure, but by a constitution that survives in sentient reality and contributes to our limited lives a vivifying intimation of eternity. And be this portrait an image of oneself, then a thrilling and irrational pleasure is vouchsafed not only by an apparent defiance of biological inevitability but also—and more marvelously to the point—by the sweeping and preposterous arrogation of a metaphysical supposition. You may die, but the portrait of you that is more you than you are will live on as long as art survives, redeeming from irrelevance the frailty and folly of human affairs. And how far more compelling, more exciting, and more sensible will be the prospect of your portrait in time of war, when life becomes so proximate to death.

Picasso being Picasso, after all, I didn't expect a painted portrait and wouldn't have time to pose for one anyway. A good drawing would do. And the shrewdness in my rashness suggested that even a perfect portraitist might be helped by having the materials of perfection thrust upon him. Providentially there was a musty shop on the quai Voltaire that sold supplies for artists. I bought a pad of drawing paper and a pencil.

Approaching the rue des Grands Augustins, I fell into the injured way of walking on which my access to the place now seemed to have depended from the beginning. As I took the first steps on the stairway, a door flew open above, and pretty Inès popped out. She gave me a smile, said I must want to see the boss, but it was a little too early and I might wait a few minutes in her place. The room was small, dim, low-ceilinged, walls resplendent with Picassos, several of them superb portraits of her, sudden proof that my purpose might be to the point. She apologized for the lack of coffee to offer. The boss himself, he who had connections, had a hard time getting enough. And I realized that if the occasion recurred, I must arrive bearing provisions for all the household.

The few minutes passed quickly. Inès went up with me, unlocked the door, ushered me inside. Sabartés was startled. I'd reappeared so quickly, he said, maybe it was my injury that prevented me from resuming duties. Not really, I said. The secretary told me Picasso was expecting several visitors. Was there any urgent matter that called for his attention? I admitted there wasn't. He went away to consult with his employer. I put down the drawing pad, doffed cap and coat, pretending to be at ease, while intimidation took my breath away.

Picasso burst into the room. "So you have been making advances to Inès!" he exclaimed.

"She let me in," I said. "That's all."

"What a story!" he cried. "No wonder you are in the secret service."

Sabartés came in with several men, and Picasso led us upstairs to the painting studio, where he and his visitors stood to one side talking, while I was left alone to admire the piles of paintings, which I made free to handle with daring. Sabartés went into another room. After a while Picasso came over and said, "When the others leave, you stay."

The secretary reappeared presently and whispered to his employer, whereupon we all went back downstairs and the visitors departed. Picasso said to me, "You will have lunch with me and a friend."

I said yes, thinking only of the opportunity for the portrait, never pausing to wonder whether the artist might foresee some pièce de résistance of his own. He went ahead to the stairs, and I limped after him.

In the street, in the open air, he seemed smaller. In his studio, where everything pertained only to him, his stature, though slight, seemed immeasurable. Here it was different. Picasso was no less Picasso than before, and by the very semblance of being small in the perspective of the city he seemed at the same time to be immense, limitless, and, in a word, terrifying.

My chance had come to a crisis. I said, "I have something to ask you."

The artist spun around, his eyes shooting at me. "What is it then?" he demanded, as if he'd been waiting only for this.

I was in a void. I said, "I'd like it very much if you would do my portrait," adding quickly before the end could come, "Just a drawing, that is."

He immediately said yes and of course, whenever I wished, though not just then, holding out both hands, palms upward, not just then because he had at hand none of the necessities. A pity.

But I had the pad of drawing paper, a pencil.

Picasso had turned away. He was waving at someone, a woman, who stood waiting at the nearby street corner. He kissed her, introduced me. This was the famous Dora Maar, his mistress since the time of *Guernica*. She did not look pleased to see me. He said he'd be happy to make my portrait. In the restaurant.

Picasso and Dora sat side by side, I facing them. They lit cigarettes and chatted in Spanish. The meal materialized without having been ordered, beef and sautéed potatoes, Camembert, baked apples, red wine, though I was not hungry for food and my time was running out. I pushed pad and pencil toward the artist. I said, "If you could do the portrait."

"I'll do it immediately," said Picasso, taking my chin in his hand, lifting it slightly and turning my head to the right. "Good. Now don't move."

He studied me for a moment, no more than a minute, then drew very fast on the page. It was done in three minutes, four at the most. "There you are," he said, holding across the pad so I could see.

I didn't see. Not so quickly. The magic of the effect was too overwhelming. Where there had been nothing, suddenly there was something, by which I was possessed.

Picasso asked how to spell my name in order to dedicate the drawing, signed and dated it, and handed back the pad, which I put down on the chair beside me. Oh, he made in his lifetime tens of thousands of drawings, to be sure, and many, many of these were portraits of people he knew far better than he ever knew me. But genius is wont to fight shy of conquests that are too easy. To capture a likeness is one thing; to accept its surrender is very definitely another.

When Picasso stood up, Dora and I did likewise. No bill was presented; no money changed hands. I learned later that the artist paid for meals with drawings that were done in the restaurant between the hors d'oeuvre and the entrée. We said goodbye in the street. Alone, I limped back along the rue des Grands Augustins toward the Seine, the pad in my hand, aware that I held an element of lived life that I could look at even as it looked at me according to my discernment and *its* demands.

I was disappointed. In my diary I described the meal with Picasso and Dora but about the portrait said only, "A quick little sketch dashed off during lunch." It's true Picasso's attention and creative faculties clearly had not been engaged to serious effect either by his model or by his drawing while I sat before him in the restaurant. I saw in my portrait principally evidences of haste and indifference, its inadequacy, not my own.

And yet in the catalog of the 1939 exhibition whereby Picasso had first excited me I had also underlined this statement by the artist: "A picture lives life like a living creature, undergoing the changes imposed upon us by our life from day to day. This is natural enough, as the picture lives only through the man who is looking at it." Perhaps, then, I would later be able to offer myself, and seek from the artist, another likeness of the young soldier. I had had temerity enough that morning. Why deny the future a chance?

Quimper is the last locality of consequence at the southwestern tip of the Breton peninsula, only thirty miles from the fingertip of France

in the Atlantic Ocean, hence a place of mists and rains, though mild
enough, thanks to the Gulf Stream, to foster palm trees and camellias.
It is laughably known among urbane Frenchies as the most excruciat-
ingly provincial of provinces, backward, bigoted, and benighted.

The train was a movable wreck of rotting coaches that stank of piss,
shuddering at ten miles an hour over roadbeds blasted by Allied
bombs. Aaron and I were in dubious luck in a grimy, greasy compart-
ment by ourselves. We stopped at every mud puddle en route so that
the passengers could get down and shit in the bushes. Hawkers sold
stale sandwiches and vile wine. The aisles were thick with garbage before nightfall. The journey lasted a lifetime.

Unwashed, unshaven, and exhausted after thirty hours of brain-
bruising travel, we were welcomed on the Quimper station platform
by a well-dressed, languid corporal, aged at least forty. He said we
must be the ones he was waiting for, having been the only GIs aboard
the train. His name was Leahy, Francis Leahy, and we shook hands
before he led us to a brand-new jeep.

We drove at timorous speed through empty, soporific streets. The
absence of a single pockmark or splintered windowpane celebrated
wartime unimportance and safe distance from fighting. Scenic variety
was provided by a minor cathedral—rather nice twin spires—a few
half-timbered houses, and a modest river in the center of town. Our
destination on a hillside of the western outskirts was a small pseudo-
château, ludicrous domicile in this land of humble Breton cottages. It
had been built, said Leahy, but never quite finished by a collaboration-
ist merchant of machine pistols who hightailed it out of town with his
Nazi girlfriend two weeks after D-day.

Seated in the dining room behind a hulking desk heaped with official papers, none of them stamped "secret," awaited a staff sergeant
dressed for parade save for the pearl stickpin in his necktie. Jet black
hair slicked down with Vaseline, he sported a Wild Bill Hickok mustache. His up and down glance meant to say at ease, but he didn't
have the brass to come out with it, instead said, "Jars," as if his surname were sufficient stress of seniority. When neither of us spoke up,
he added, "Welcome to Quimper."

"Thanks," said Aaron.

"Hope you had a comfortable trip."

Aaron said, "Bliss it was to puke your heart out in that train."

"Funny man," said Jars. "Which one of you is Lord?"

"'Tis I," I said.

"Yeah? It says here you got a Bronze Star. A hero in our midst? What did you do to get it?"

"Nothing."

"Jesus!" gurgled Jars. "You gonna be a pain in the ass? I don't give a fuck you licked the general's ass to get a medal. You and your buddy are five hundred miles from the action now. No medals gonna get handed out by me. So hear this."

He squared his shoulders and caressed his mustache with both forefingers. "We are the only Americans within fifty miles, and it's up to us to defend the good name of the US of A so as the frogs respect us. They've already forgotten we saved their backsides, think de Gaulle did the job single-handed. But they'd better respect us they want to keep on chewing our gum and smoking our ciggies." He spoke with resonant pitch and rhythmic inflection. Leahy later told us that before the war Jars had been a radio announcer in Buffalo, New York.

"Now," he continued, "there's not a hell of a lot to do. The only krauts left round here are those stupid motherfuckers forty miles down the coast at Lorient, surrounded since four months and too damn Nazi to surrender. So let 'em eat rats. You take care of the jeeps, drive up to Morlaix once a week, stock up at the PX, check in with Lieutenant Crisp. We keep on decent terms with the local FFI, pretty trigger-happy, but that's their business. We live well, you'll see. Plenty to eat. Girl comes in every day to cook and clean, do the laundry, shine your goddamn shoes, name's Sylvie. We get lobsters pretty often, courtesy of our friend, the baron de Chaussepied, you'll meet him. Drives the only civilian car—a honey—in the area, runs it on calvados. Owns a castle and a thousand acres of apple trees down the river. And by the way, fucking local girls is verboten, so if you do it and get reported to the prefecture for rape, watch out, because the frogs have fallen in love with the death penalty since taking over from the Gestapo. Aside from that, live it up."

Jars's well-enunciated exposé of the routine to come in Quimper promised little merriment. He added, "Francis, kindly *usher* our new recruits upstairs," smirking over the verb. Jars was no gentleman. We learned later from the Baron Shoehorn that in the real world Leahy had worn the uniform of an usher at the Warner Brothers' moving picture palace in Chicago.

As for Jars, his familiarity with the French language and with the French nation came as a windfall of the First World War, his father a doughboy from Tonawanda, his mother a mademoiselle, not from Armentières itself but from the nearby village of Houplines, marriage celebrated in the *mairie* of Choisy-au-Bac, only three miles from Compiègne, on November 12, 1918, ink on the armistice barely dry. Their son and only child, Florent Wilbur Jars, was born romantically premature on the Fourth of July 1919 in Le Havre, awaiting the homeward voyage to Buffalo. Going by the surname Jars, it may try a man's temper to bear a forename like Florent, while Wilbur, albeit evocative of evangelical Wilburites, is hardly a moniker that goes with glory on the football field, the silver screen, or the fighting front. So Jars was Jars, sometimes Sarge, in extremis Will, though under no circumstances ever to be mistaken for anybody's buddy.

The billet to which Leahy courteously ushered us was the top floor of the phony château. Two small bedrooms, a washroom and toilet opening off a narrow landing and appointed as if for penitentiary detention: one cot, one table, one chair, one footlocker per room, one cake of soap, one roll of paper toweling, one of toilet paper. Leahy said, "Not the Ritz. But there's hot water. Anyways, it's a sight better than a foxhole. Not that I've ever been in one. My age it's a miracle I'm in the army. Only because I picked up French as a kid, my folks French speakers from Montreal. Jars and I got the downstairs, the ground floor's for office and sitting around. That's about the hang of things. We get the *Stars and Stripes* and *Yank*. Mauldin would see double he got a peek at this place. Anything I can do, sing out. Quimper's big on boredom, you'll see."

By what bizarre back door of the espionage outfit Jars and Leahy had been brought to this unlikely and unnecessary outpost of the counterintelligence dumb show beggared speculation. Jars spent hours muttering into the telephone, but nobody ever called him. Occasionally he walked downtown and came back with a feline grin, allowing he'd been invited by Captain Smadja of the FFI to attend the execution of a local boy who'd driven the German general to a whorehouse in Brest. Or maybe his contact with the spy world was via the outlandish baron Nicolas de Chaussepied, who came regularly to call in a canary yellow convertible Delage. I once took a surreptitious sniff of the gas tank, which actually did smell of calvados. His ridiculous name and title were supposedly the legacy of a great-great-great-great-great-grandfather who had been granted the honor of aiding the Sun King to slip on his red shoes in the morning. He always brought with him a few bottles of Côtes de Beaune 1926 and a couple of lobsters, which he and Jars persuaded to race across the kitchen floor by pinching their eyes with a pair of pliers. Aaron and I were even invited to taste the remains of these miserable crustaceans following their merciless immersion in the cauldron. After a bottle or two of burgundy Shoehorn and Jars used to whisper and giggle, and Aaron imagined they were trading strategic secrets, but I believed their sole strategy tended to be taking advantage of the black market. Leahy was an understudy to the antics of his boss and the baron, and if they amused, or even interested him, he seldom spoke and never smiled.

Of the two bedrooms on the top floor I occupied the smaller. Its window looked out across a vista of spare fields dotted with tiny white houses, curlicue wisps of impoverished smoke soiling the sky. Not the lost land of Lyonesse, though dreamed-of sometime romance, remembering epic adventures—a blue car aeons ago.

In preparation for more useful dreams I would also represent to my imagination the moment of exaltation and deliverance when I would come into possession of another portrait of James Lord by Picasso. Never did it occur to me I might not find myself once again in the presence of the great artist. Nobody, I thought, having known him at all, could ever afterward foresee a time when Picasso would cease to be present in the perspective of things to come.

Jars, when he said there wasn't a hell of a lot to do in Quimper, had for once said something replete with pertinence. You walked along bourgeois sidewalks beside speechless houses that scrutinized you with mistrust behind blind windows. In the Café de l'Épée you sat for a deadly half hour in front of one glass of Cinzano while unshaven, unemployed, alcoholic fishermen sullenly stared and irritably waggled their wooden shoes. A lady walking a dachshund as withered as she was shuddered in a spastic dither if you nodded politely in passing.

There was the cathedral, yes, Gothic, fifteenth century, though the spires were nineteenth. The interior brooded beneath an uprush of granite vaulting, while obese priests yawned in the confessionals, waiting to fondle little boys' private parts.

So I volunteered to take one of the jeeps for the periodic run to Morlaix for replenishment of supplies at the PX. It was the dreariest of trips through the uninhabited, uncultivated uplands, forlorn expanses of broom, gorse, and heather, occasional outcroppings of granite scaled with fungus. At crossroads here and there stood a grim stone crucifix to remind wayfarers of life's unforgiving terminus. I passed en route one car, one truck, one wagon drawn by a dying horse, and one cart drawn by a man who looked like the best friend of the reaper.

Morlaix was not much. Bourgeois stupor, stultifying residences, and comatose stares, the only notable landmark, a high, slender viaduct across the center of town built by a railroad robber baron.

The PX had everything, even radios and electric toasters, a miraculous prodigy of unnecessary necessities, wonderland of would-be-plunder for a black marketeer. I stocked up on all the items on Jars's list. Mindful of potential profiteering, cigarettes being worth more than money, coffee also priceless, I took three cans of Maxwell House instead of two, plus a couple of extra cartons of Luckies. The checkout kid, a PFC with a nasty attack of acne, gave my stuff a petulant okay without a lookover, and I signed the receipt as per F. W. Jars, MIS Quimper.

Lieutenant Crisp was bored shitless and said so as soon as I stood at ease. "Shitless," he repeated. "Morley is the last roundup. Why MIS wants an outpost in this privy of civilization, you can tell me maybe."

I couldn't tell him and shrank from trying. He was the nervous type, thin-lipped, prematurely balding, cuticles nibbled raw, the sort who probably thinks constantly of fucking because he's done so little of it.

He exhaled through his nostrils and said, "If a spy farted in this town, it would sound like heavy artillery. What about Kwimper? Much action down there?"

"No, sir, not lately."

"Don't sir me, Sergeant. This place has got to me. I could almost settle for an SIW."

"A what?"

"Self-inflicted wound. Real popular at the front, I hear. So what does Jars do for R and R?"

"Who knows? There's a baron who comes for dinner. He runs his car on calvados."

"Brings lobsters. I've met him. A creep. Now, *he* might be a spy. Perfect cover. But what I mean is what does Jars do for pussy?"

"I'm sure I don't know," I said, adding, "but I'd better be moving or it'll be dark before I get back."

"Yeah, okay. Well, you needn't hurry, because it's dark day and night in this hellhole. And tell Jars don't beat your meat too often 'cause it'll make the palm of your hand sprout hair."

Not bad advice, I thought as I drove homeward over the bleak and savage moors in a purling mist.

"So how was Morlaix?" Aaron inquired.

"Well, there's a terrific viaduct across the center of town, but it's come out of nowhere and leads no place. If you get the picture. PX chockablock with goodies for the *marché noir*, and I brought us a couple of cartons of ciggies."

"That's wizard, Jim, but better hang on to the cigs because the money's not worth anything."

"I know."

"Didn't run into Fred Astaire, did you?"

"Just missed him. But Lieutenant Rice Krispies was good for a laugh: his brain is stuck below the belt, wondering what Jars does for pussy, and he swears that beating your meat makes hair grow in the palm of your hand."

"Gee whiz," said Aaron. "That's what they used to tell us at Groton. So I conducted a few experiments to find out if it's true, and I'm sorely disappointed to have to tell you it ain't."

Jars asked how Crisp was getting along.

I said, "He appears to be having the time of his life."

"The poor son of a bitch," said Jars, "he must have cashed in on his marbles, due for psychiatric therapy, they give you an enema morning, noon, and night, wrap you up in wet sheets and turn on the electricity till you wish you were dead, but they say you've never felt better in your life, so you get reassigned to the Pacific because there's nothing like a change of scenery to buck up the morale of a goddamn fuckup like Larry Crisp."

"Anyway, he said to give his regards to the baron."

"Ha-ha-ha," said Jars. "Next time you go to Morley tell Crisp to come down for the lobster steeplechase, and we'll give him a taste of the pliers."

"I'll be glad to," I said.

Aaron did not mope. He was reading *Valmouth* and howled with laughter. Jars, who probably did not know how to read, listened to the radio and played checkers with Leahy, who cheated and told Sylvie what to cook for the next day's meals. Monotony and ennui haunted our paradoxical status like the pietistic ghost of St. Corentin, Quimper's first bishop, who had presided over the superstitions of that rude settlement in the fifth century A.D. I went downtown in cloying mist, damp but not wet, smelling of distant manure and rotten apples. The luxurious romanticism of France had flown into the blur, and I felt the choke of boredom slowly stifling the pitiless street.

The bad news came over the radio. A totally unexpected, incredible, massive German counterattack had been launched through the Ardennes Forest against thinly held Allied lines. Christmas was but nine days away. The war would not be over in time for Willie and Joe to feast on victory turkey in their foxholes. Here in Quimper we might have been on the other side of the earth.

Something unusual occurred the very next morning while the four of us were munching bran flakes in silence. Baron Shoehorn came knocking. Jars leaped up and rushed to the door, went outside, whispering with the agitated nobleman, rushed back in to snatch his raincoat, and the two men drove off in the baron's roadster.

Leahy said, "You could knock me over with a feather."

"Ostrich?" said Aaron.

"You'll find it's unlikely a laughing matter, son," said Leahy.

He was right. They returned before noon. The German counteroffensive, half-tracks and tanks, advancing rapidly in driving snow against slight resistance, had surrounded an American troop of about a hundred men, who surrendered, but the SS murdered every last one in cold blood. This had happened, this massacre, it was confirmed, near a place called Malmédy. They'll claim, said the baron, that it was a tactical necessity, and the men were shot while trying to escape.

"We'll catch the commanding officer someday, believe you me," said Jars, "and shoot him down like a dog. In Times Square."

Aaron and I didn't go downtown that afternoon. It was a misfortune of war, of course, though murder most foul. And the appalling incubus of guilt that would pursue all accomplices—every man in uniform?—even unto the safekeeping of dreams, the havoc of nightmares running true to life.

I drove again to Morlaix over the heartless uplands and stocked up double, if not triple, at the PX. The pimply PFC at checkout said, "You layin' in for the gray market, Sarge, I'd bet my bathwater on it."

Bathwater? The word ached in my ears.

"Not so you'd notice. Sergeant Jars entertains."

"I'll count it okay. But next time I want my cut, and I'd better get it. Crisp would crucify us both. Ten percent."

"Okay, okay. This is for Mr. Jars's army."

He grinned. "My name's Jonas, tell you the truth, hail from Murfreesboro, deep Tenn."

"Swell," I said.

And I didn't offer my respects to the shitless lieutenant, who had by now probably grown tresses in the palms of both hands.

Christmas Eve in Quimper. Five hundred miles safely removed from the Battle of the Bulge, the Nazis still advancing in snow white uniforms and rime-encrusted tanks, GI corpses scattered in the frigid air, a single village, called Bastogne, still in Allied hands, though surrounded and refusing to surrender. Were we embarrassed to be safe and sound so far away, listening to the abominable Bing crooning Irving's workaday carol? Hardly. The lobster torture races were over, winners and losers boiled alive, carcasses picked clean, washed down with a magnum of Corton Charlemagne 1926.

Nicky Shoehorn, quaffing the excellent calvados he'd also brought along, the same, I expect, used to fuel his canary runabout, vented enmity of communism, its works and perfidies and plots and fanatics.

The party, he swore, true to its false face, fully intends to run things in this country, setting up secret networks all over the place, especially in armament factories. General de Gaulle is holding hands with Colonel Rol, a true-blue Commie, and who knows how many MAS submachine guns are stashed away in Malakoff waiting for a showdown on the Champs Élysées? And right here in Brittany, who can count on the FFI? The June moon arms drop for the Morlaix area set down four tons of matériel, guns enough to arm a regiment, and where are they now?

Jars said, "And there's not a single weapon in this house."

I said, "I have a pistol." A statement accorded neither consideration nor inquiry, though factual, and possession of a firearm illicit.

The baron said, "A telephone is the only weapon you folks need. Just call me in case of emergency, and I'll take care of it."

My pistol was a Walther P38, lifted from a depot at Bouzonville, where thousands of weapons confiscated from the populace were heaped in a boilerplate factory.

The day after Christmas the cloud cover above Bastogne evaporated, our planes began bombing the shit out of the panzers, and the bulge slowly shrank back into the forests, leaving behind seventy-five thousand Allied casualties as evidence that the Teutonic warrior, albeit facing defeat, would still do battle because fighting was his raison d'être.

New Year's Eve loomed, occasion for a lonely drive in mist-cum-rain over uninhabitable heaths to Morlaix. The PX was bestial, packed with brutish celebrants-to-be or black marketeers on the make, of whom I was a puerile accomplice. The shoving and grunting at the checkout counter evoked a cattle drive, and I muttered to Murfreesboro, "Do you cut ten percent on every sale?"

He passed his baccy to the other cheek, said, "I've got a right to be happy too," and let slip a drool of khaki saliva onto the floor. "Gonna go to college and make a million as soon as I 'scape this outfit."

"That's the spirit," I said, signing the chit, as usual, F. W. Jars, MIS HQ, Quimper. Where the money came from to pay for so much priceless merchandise I'd no idea, or ever inquired, nor did Florent Wilbur ask for an accounting, which was strange for such a fault-finding asshole.

New Year's Eve. No merrymaking for Private Lord. Aaron was being shown a good time by a sexy demoiselle who had asked him for a cigarette on market day two weeks ago. Jars and Leahy were guests of the baron at his early-twentieth-century castle overlooking the Odet River at Ploemeur. To have been excluded from these industrious jollities was no privation. At my back lay Europe, its culture racked by the chaotic disorder of mankind's tragic masquerade. And who was I to pretend to grasp a glimpse of meaning in such unmitigated darkness, I an inferior soldier devoured by unimportance?

Picasso peopled my reveries. The portrait dashed off in the restaurant was a continuing disappointment, an incentive to yearn for another from the same hand. I lay awake, concentrating upon the memory of the artist's studio, the dynamism of his gaze, the knowledge of his genius fixed to summon again from the void my immemorial image. And the very tenacity of those reveries became the simple assurance of their eventual satisfaction.

Seizures of boredom sometimes led me to fish out from the depths of my duffel bag the illicit pistol and twirl it around like a dashing gunslinger in a B movie. And in fact, one afternoon of truly excruciating ennui I loaded it with a few blank cartridges, stepped out onto the landing, and fired several rounds into space, shattering the exquisite tedium of that day and leaving the smell of cordite heavy in the dead air.

Inevitably Jars came screaming into the stairwell. "What the fucking hell? Oh yeah, Lord, it's you. I should have known."

"Shooting to kill," I said.

"It's the last straw, you creep. I'm telling you. Bring that gun down here. You're not allowed to have a weapon. Only I'm allowed to and I don't have one."

I skipped downstairs and handed over the Walther. "A souvenir from the front," I said.

Jars scowled, squeezing his bloodless lips, lizard eyes squinting. "I've had about all I can take," he snarled. "So get real careful. One more fuckup, and you're finished. I'll send you back. I mean it."

Leahy said cluck-cluck.

Aaron also clucked when he came back from having his rocks off with Mademoiselle. I'd better watch my ass, he said. Jars was a vindictive prick. And Quimper offered a hell of a lot more creature comforts than a pup tent in the snowfields of eastern Belgium.

As for creature comforts specifically, my epidermis had been troubling me for more than a week, chest and thighs livid with pimples that suppurated sometimes, itching outrageously at night. It was only scabies, not a serious threat, but a cure could not be had in Quimper because of the wartime scarcity of benzyl benzoate. To find that, I'd have to go fifty kilometers away to Quimperlé, where a U.S. field hospital was part of the contingent containing the port of Lorient, where the Germans, surrounded, still stupidly refused to surrender.

That night the thermometer took an unprecedented plunge. Pure frost lay like tinsel on the morning grass. A wan wintry sun, however, shone from the milky sky. It was bliss to be alive in that innocent dawn. So I took one of the jeeps without alerting a soul and set off upon my embarrassing errand. Oh, to be free and singing in the rush of the newborn scenery. Not another vehicle on the road. I stepped on the gas.

At the crest of a shallow valley the asphalt below shimmered in the white sunshine, while on the far side it was dead black in the shadow of the rise. I was on it before I could see the transparent glaze of sheer ice, the jeep took a slewing skip, and I made the very worst move possible by slamming on the brakes. The jeep lurched crazily and veered, plunging against a heap of huge logs as solid as a stone wall in the roadside ditch. I was thrown out backward onto the road, my shoulder and my knee pounding with pain. I didn't know where I was or what the passing time was—before I realized, lying on the fucking ice, I was waiting for something to happen.

It happened after a few minutes, or an hour or more. A civilian four-door black sedan very cautiously coughed on the downward slope. I raised my one arm. The car swung slowly away from me as from something wrong on the road, passed by on the other side, and disappeared from sight.

"Didn't they know?" I demanded of the empty morning. That there was a war on? A U.S. jeep tilted askew against the logs on the roadside, its right front smashed, radiator gasping, and plumes of steam adrift on the windless air, a wreck, the driver in uniform prostrate on the ice already beginning to melt.

Later: I was actually in pain. Another car approached. And stopped. A young fellow in a fisherman's outfit, a yellow slicker that creaked when he moved, bright teeth as he leaned above me and said, "You wounded, Yankee?"

"I don't know," I said. "Don't think so. It's my knee."

"Come then," he said, "get on your feet," seizing my arms and lifting. He was very strong, rough, but the pain hit my knee like a hammer. "So where you going?" he asked.

"Quimperlé."

"Oh, can't drive you that far, no, have to take the turn for Port Manech in time to catch the tide but let you off by the crossroads where the café has a telephone. Your jeep looks a proper wreck, bad luck, because without those logs you'd have gone safe into the ditch." His car was a rusty Citroën, heaving and belching, and he drove it hard.

We came to the crossroads soon enough, a few houses, the café at the corner. The fisherman smiled as I got down and wished me a good day.

In the café a trio of grizzled old-timers gawked when I limped inside, asking to use the telephone. Jars answered. I told him what had happened.

"You goddamn son of a bitch," he howled. "Wrecked a jeep and never asked permission to take it out. This is the last fucking straw. I've had it with you, Lord, you horse's ass, had it and had it. Told you to watch yourself. Well, now I've had it. You're through, washed up, finished. Get that into your head, you creep."

I said, "You realize I could have been killed."

"Good riddance if you were. And as far as I'm concerned, you might as well be. Dead and buried. So where the fuck are you and I'll send your buddy to pick up the pieces?"

I asked the man behind the bar, and he said, "Halfway between Rosporden and Bannalec on the main road, café called Le Dolmen de Riec."

Jars said, "Typical, you freak. Just you wait!" and hung up.

I sat down at the rear of the dingy room and, when asked what I'd have, said, "Calva." I sipped it very carefully while waiting for Aaron, aghast at the absurdity of my situation.

He arrived after I'd downed another calvadoes, asking immediately if I was all right. Enough to stand, yes, though I limped, an honest injury this time. I thanked the man behind the bar, an old salt gone to the dogs who declined to be paid.

In the jeep en route to Quimperlé Aaron said, "I saw your wreck back there. Looks total. Wilbur is going to be angrier than he thinks he is. Not as if he's going to be out of pocket himself. He's around the bend anyway, says he's going to get you recalled.

"A man who can't take a joke," I said. "Maybe the Shoehorn can soothe his nerves."

We found the field hospital, where a good-looking medic felt my knee, said nothing was broken, and gave me the ointment for my itches. We had something to eat in the hospital mess. On the way back to Quimper the sky turned hostile; dense cloudlets scudded across the afternoon, storm shaping up in the west.

Jars said, "I don't want to talk to you. You're finished. Not only here. Finished. For good. Pack your gear. I've already settled it with HQ Rennes. You take the train tomorrow at eleven hundred. An MP will be waiting at Rennes Gare. Dismissed."

"But—" I said.

"Dismissed!" said Jars.

Aaron, driving me to the station through the medieval mist, said, "Don't fret, Jimsy. You'll outlive it all." Aaron waved his cap, as the train lurched away from the platform, and Quimper diminished backward into the Breton void.

Thirteen

FEBRUARY–MARCH 1945

Rennes was in ruins. The blasted wreckage of ancient buildings dusted with snow hung dangerously above streets cramped with rubble and mounds of filthy slush. It was freezing cold. People said that this was the worst winter in fifty years.

I had expected an MP, maybe with handcuffs, awaiting me at the station consequent to Jars's rage. Instead there was a cute PFC holding a card inscribed "Sgt. J. Lord." He told me that Major Aldrich had arranged transport to a barracks, seized my duffel bag, led me to a jeep, and said, "The major expects you to report to HQ at eleven hundred tomorrow morning. Okay?"

"Sure," I said. "By the way, is the major—Major Aldrich, that is—is he MIS?"

"I'll say," said the private, swerving to avoid a heap of rubble. "He's head of intelligence for all of the Western networks. Didn't you know? But he might fool you. Better be on time."

I was. MIS HQ had been a bank before the artillery hit it. Enough had survived intact to provide offices evidential of affluence. Major L. W. Aldrich's door was coffered oak, the name on a bronze plaque, and I knocked at one minute before eleven. "Come," cried a quick baritone.

The Louis XVI desk stood ten paces away. I marched to it as smartly as I could while limping and saluted, expecting to be told at once to stand at ease. I wasn't. The major took his time studying me frankly up and down from my boots to the angle of my cap, which allowed me to covertly do the same. I thought I'd never before seen an officer of any rank so elegantly attired. His bespoke uniform fitted perfectly to a slender, if rather straight, physique, which gave him his air of unas-

suming dignity, distant but not arrogant, perhaps slightly morose, features modestly good, eyes so pale as to be almost colorless but vigilant,
and apricot-colored hair clipped very short.

"At ease, Sergeant," he said at length, fingering several typewritten
pages. "I have this report. Quimper. Your service record. Frankly, I
don't know quite what to make of it. Probably you should clarify."

"Yes, sir," I said, "if possible. I'll do my best, sir, to clear things up."

The major waved a pale hand. "You'd better have a seat. No point
in standing about all morning. I see you have a gimpy leg. Combat
injury?"

"No, sir," I said, settling into one of the two armchairs in front of
his desk. "My jeep skidded on ice. I got thrown onto the road and
hurt my knee."

The major sighed. "Oh, yes. Wrecked the vehicle. I heard that.
Seems you're something of a problem child. Decorated under combat
conditions, however. But then what? This Sergeant Jars talked me into
a coma concerning you. Inattention to duty, delinquency, generally
guilty of insubordination, God knows what, doesn't sit very well with
a Bronze Star."

"No, sir. All I can say about the medal is I don't know why I got
it. Nobody on the team knew why any of us got it."

"That's the nature of combat commendations. You're in the intelligence service. The whole point, I presume, was that you *shouldn't*
know. The why and wherefore of the espionage métier is to know as
little as possible."

I said, "Yes, sir."

Reaching inside his jacket the major fastidiously extracted a slim
gold cigarette case, from which he selected an oval cigarette, then held
the case across to me, inquiring, "Do you smoke?"

"No, sir, thank you, sir."

"Don't sir me to death," said the major, lighting his cigarette with
a gold lighter. "Where are you from, anyway?"

"Englewood, New Jersey."

"Englewood? Don't the Muhlfelds live out there?"

"Yes. I was in school with their son."

"That's nice. And now you've been in Quimper station. Jars, Leahy,
you, and your buddy. I forget his name."

"Aaron Randolph."

"Right. Aaron. Boston. The Randolph Randolphs. She plays the harp. Friend of Mrs. Jack. And young Aaron. Did well in Quimper, did he? No difficulty with Jars."

"Not really."

"You didn't find the posting compatible? What with the dashing baron and his inexhaustible wine cellar?"

"That phony," I said.

"Actually rather grand lineage, slightly *fin de race*, it's true, but resourceful, very sly boots. No wonder the product was picturesque, what with such a colorful cast."

He picked out another cigarette from his gold case, again offering one to me. "They're excellent, you know, worth a fortune on the BM; my godmother sends them over by the pouch."

"I don't smoke."

"Oh, God. I suppose you'd better call me sir, after all. What on earth am I to do with you, Sergeant Lord? As an agent I'd say you're still in diapers. You've got to grow up in a hurry, get tough, heartless, a bastard in wolf's clothing. Didn't they teach you anything to be ashamed of at Ritchie?"

"I don't think so, sir."

"Well, you're a proper case for study, you really are, and I'll have to ask around. I'm not suggesting you do your homework on the POWs, mind you, most of them are immune to abuse anyway. Maybe you could manage to get a few of your own teeth knocked out." He smiled with his thin lips but gave no quarter in the narrowing gaze. "Enough chat for one morning. When I can invent something, you'll hear from me. Meanwhile, if you get bored, don't go firing a Walther into thin air in the barracks."

"No, sir," I said. "Besides, I surrendered my weapon to Sergeant Jars. He's probably using it to shoot himself in the foot."

"Dismissed," said Major Aldrich.

I lay on my cot. The soldier in the adjoining cot said, "Whyn't you take a look in the USO?"

"How'd you like me to break your arm?" I said.

The soldier said, "You King Kong?" His face was speechless, numb, eyes wan with exhaustion and amnesia.

"I wouldn't hurt a fly," I said.

"Nobody would. The kraut who shot me in the leg, he was as close to me as you are, almost, I swear, and it broke his heart to pull the trigger, I could tell, and two minutes after—that's what happens—he got shot in the head, and his brains splattered all over me. I thought I'd die."

I went to the hospital for an X-ray of my knee. The nurse said, "Never fool around with a knee. It's a tricky articulation. Torn femoral-tibial cartilage. It may bother slightly for a while, maybe forever. Who knows? No Purple Heart this time."

In the western Pacific the volcanic island of Iwo Jima had been assaulted by American marines with maximum firepower, but the battle for eight square miles of barren gorges and escarpments was to be one of the bloodiest of the war. In Budapest, meanwhile, a German force of sixteen thousand struggled to break through the Russian lines, but only a few hundred got away.

Sometimes truckloads of German POWs passed through the ruined city. Drenched by the freezing rain, ragged, dirty, sullen, their faces shrunken, vacant eyes, packed like cargoes of commercial live-stock on the way to the abattoir, they must have known they had nothing to fear, for by and large we respected the Geneva Conventions. Still, the war, warfare, the disasters, the atrocities, the wounded and the dead, the crimes against mankind. Were there no criminals? Were they not afraid, these nefarious prisoners? What heinous leader had betrayed them to their enemies? Had they supposed themselves invulnerable, Gott mit uns?

Watching them trucked down the battered fronts of the canal, what I mainly felt was pity for such haggard remnants of humanity, an empathy that came with neither sense nor ratiocination, feelings disguised as thoughts. But what, then, if *I* were one of *them*, guilty as they in their theoretical innocence, prepared in the tragicomic enactment of rectitude to assume the full measure of the inevitable? What indeed! A transient will-o'-the wisp of supposition.

Anyway, no matter what fugitive fantasy of POW fate followed my view of these truckloads of Wehrmacht dregs, it was not shared by the French. They shouted insults, shook their fists, spit, and threw snowballs, sometimes with rocks or shards of glass inside. And polite women carrying umbrellas said to me, "Why you Yankees so good to Nazi monsters?" To which I could but rightly reply that this was none of my responsibility, an answer that did nothing to mask allowance for the irrational. Of which, moreover, my daydream of empathy made, perhaps, an excess of allowance.

It was perplexing, almost unnerving during this time—irrespective of POWs, of course—that though surrounded entirely by men, whom I saw not only clothed but naked daily in the showers, I felt no sexual hunger for any of them despite a nagging awareness of which ones were attractive or might even be gay.

The purgatorial interlude in Rennes lasted only nineteen days. The cute PFC who had met me at the station was Major Aldrich's driver-factotum. I saw them several times speeding around town, laughing their heads off, and I wondered. His name was Peter Fahnestock, curly haired hero of the tennis court, cherry blossom cheeks, and a twinkle. It was Fahnestock who conveyed the major's command to report again one morning at eleven.

The gold cigarette case already lay before him on the satinwood desk, and he immediately told me to stand at ease. Otherwise it was as if I had just stepped out of the office two minutes before. The major steepled his fingers. "I suppose," he said, "or I don't suppose you speak Bulgarian."

"No, sir."

"Or Hungarian, or Polish, Greek, Russian, or Czech. Turkish. Danish. For heaven's sake." He shut his eyes and smirked.

"No, sir. I'm sorry."

"Don't be. Nobody in his right mind speaks that many languages, unfortunately for the people who speak only one or two of them. Oh, those wretched Nazis have left us in an awful mess. And you in particular, Sergeant. You might as well sit down."

I did, and sat with misgivings.

"Your situation has been under advisement. Now, mind you, we haven't put much stock in the strictures of Wilbur Jars. Still, things are a bit sticky. French network agents are going begging these days. So you'll have to make the best of your new assignment, which is likely to leave Quimper seeming like Biarritz at the height of the season. But I had to wiggle to get something even this good. Better than taking your chances in Pacific Theater bingo, and the fact you have the Bronze Star on your record, that actually turned the trick. So better not belittle your merit in the future. Hear me?"

"Yes, sir. I'll try to bear it in mind, sir."

"Damn it, Sergeant, don't sir me to death. And have a cigarette."

"I don't smoke."

"You will. You'll smoke. You'll burn. You're a very combustible young fellow, you are. Not that it's any of my business. My business is to send you to Épinal. Apply downstairs for papers. In Épinal see a Colonel Wendell, his office in the Hôtel de Ville. He'll fill you in. Said to be a hotshot from Hollywood, got his commission by knowing Harry Hopkins. So there you are. Good luck." He stood and held his hand forward.

I reluctantly shook it and said, "Thank you, Major."

The trip took sixty hours, via Laval, Angers, Tours, Bourges, Nevers, Creusot, Dijon, Langres, and at last, when I was speechless with fatigue, famished, tongue swollen with thirst, unbelievably constipated, I arrived at Épinal, a town cut in half by a river, many buildings bombed, shattered walls painted with large red letters MERCI USA. Snow lay up to my ankles. The Hôtel de Ville, thank God, wasn't far and was undamaged save for the pockmarks of machine-gun fire across the facade.

Wendell was an oak leaf colonel sporting a gargantuan cigar, its curlicue of smoke whirling around a full moonface ornamented by a predatory smile. He exhaled an air of worldly contempt, said, "I didn't ask for you for this part. Somebody's got to play it. A Z production. Cast of thousands. Never mind nobody can speak a word of English. Tough it out, kid, tough it out. Those extras give you pain, give 'em worse. Make 'em howl. Never been on location myself. Word is that it does stink. But that's the scenario. Improvise, baby, improvise. You'll be okay. Get me?"

I didn't "get" him and didn't wish to, but it was clear I was about to get gotten, so I said, "Yes, sir."

"Good kid. You go down to the motor pool, grab some stooge to ride you up to the camp. Hell on wheels in this weather, not Palm Springs. Fuck, there's a war on. Report to Major Weinstein. He's waiting for you. Some kook. So long, baby."

"Thank you, sir," I said, saluting him and the suspicion that this assignment was about to make both the war and myself queerer than anything so far.

The corporal at the motor pool said an MP would probably drive me for a carton of Camels. It was only nine miles. But the camp might as well be on the planet Mars. Boy, oh, boy, you must have made poo-poo in the general's socks to get this assignment.

He gave me the Bronze Star, I said.

The corporal said he wouldn't serve in that camp for the *Silver* Star.

I went to try my luck with an MP, offered him half a dozen Camels. He was eighteen years old, had shaved only twice in his life. He said, "Jeez, Sarge, I don't even smoke. Sure, I'll give you a lift. Listen, it's pretty bad up there. Smell it before you can see it. Garbage detail takes out the corpses every morning."

I said nothing.

The road was pitted with craters, making for slow, sinuous progress up through a dark forest. A sloppy sign presently pointed to DP CAMP 5 MI. So *that* was it. I knew what—or should I say who?—the DPs were.

Displaced persons.

American troops had broken through the Siegfried Line, while Russian forces had cut a breach of more than a hundred miles along the Oder River. The Germans were everywhere in retreat, though furiously defending every bog of their homeland and obdurately refusing to surrender. From all the cities, villages, countrysides, factories, and prison camps of all Europe at the same time hundreds of thousands and eventually millions of persons imprisoned, enslaved, bamboozled into servitude, or, indeed, coaxed into military complicity by the Nazis suddenly found themselves free, fleeing at random, frantically in search of havens and houses and livelihoods and friendships that they knew at heart had been lost forever. They spoke a hundred dialects and languages. Multitudes hailed from places so obscure that they had forgotten where those were; some had been so brutalized that they had forgotten even who they were or what they had been.

Uncountable and uncontrollable hordes of them had swarmed across Europe into a strategic nuisance so troublesome that it had to be taken care of somehow, and just how it was to be taken care of was not, incidentally, *everything* considered, a matter of necessarily decent, though urgent, procedure. What mattered was to try to find out from what locale these persons had originally been displaced, why this had occurred, where they had been relocated, what they had done, endured, and witnessed. And most important, whether or not the testimony of each individual was the truth, because a great many people had a great deal to hide, countless atrocities having occurred, and fitting punishment of the guilty being a matter of grim force majeure. German was the lingua franca of the displaced population, and this encouraged the suspicion that many of them might be deserters who had shed the Wehrmacht or SS uniform in order to pose as innocent scapegoats of wartime misfortune. In short, the DP problem was an appalling and miasmic mess.

And why I, James H. Lord, 12183139, should have been assigned to have a hand in it seemed on that February afternoon in the midst of the forest a daunting and unfair twist of the mess itself. Then I smelled it.

"Just you wait," said the MP.

It was an acrid stench on the freezing air, as of rot, putrefaction, excrement.

A large sign above the road: DP CAMP DO NOT ENTER IF UNAUTHORIZED. Fifteen-foot steel pylons festooned with coils of barbed wire closed off an area larger than you could see. At the gate an MP brandished his white baton. My driver told him I was from Colonel Wendell for Major Weinstein. The MP raised the red and white barrier. Beyond lay a world of mud with a few muddy boardwalks leading from one to another of half a dozen time-darkened brick buildings, which once had housed a bicycle factory. In front of the largest the American flag fluttering from a white staff was the only sanitary thing in sight. I was set down with my gear beside it, and the baby-faced MP had vanished before I could say so long.

The stink was so foul I thought I ought to vomit, but couldn't, staring as I tried to see where I was and what was where I was. Down a muddy decline there was another gate, this one tall and doubled with crisscrossed lathing intertwined by barbed wire and added pylons on both sides, a makeshift entrance to a prison that meant business. Inside in the mud under the spitting sky, no shelter save a long, low wooden shed.

The inmates of the camp, the DPs, men only, mostly in rags, their eyes eerily alive, faces cadaverous masks of hunger, claw fingers brandishing tin cans, pressing against the gate as if it were open, a shivering mob enormously murmurous gathered into this nauseating stench while all I could do was turn away to the HQ building.

A master sergeant inside, lolling behind a desk, the bottle on the floor beside his boots, slurred, "Whatcha doing, bub?"

"Major Weinstein," I said.

He shifted a prognathous jaw, shut his eyes, waved his cigarette at the upstairs, and bawled, "Uppadair, uppadair."

The major's door hung open. He was fiftyish, a few black strands glued to a naked cranium, cigarette permanent in the right corner of his pulpous lips, jiggling up and down when he spoke, a rusty stain streaked up his cheek so that the right eye fluttered half shut. He told me to get easy. So I was counterintelligence? Know how to make kraut suspects talk? Modern interrogation techniques?

These DPs? Mostly phonies. Krauts dressed up as refugees, throws away his uniform, says he hated Nazis, despised the Führer, just wanna go home to Bertha and the Hitler Boy Scouts. The Jews? Some of my best friends were yids.

Don't fall for all that malarkey. Make 'em sing. What they did, where they did it, and why and how. Smack 'em in the kisser. Give their gonads the third degree. No time for cocoa and cookies. More coming in every day, roads so clogged with 'em our armor can't hardly make it.

While he stopped to light a fresh cigarette from the butt of the last one, a staff sergeant slouched in, six feet two or three, a purple birthmark the size of an eggplant along his left jowl, a length of green rubber hose stretched behind his buttocks. He said, this the new intelligence interrogator?

Oh, yeah, said the major. Hey, Sergeant Lord, meet Rog Zeleeny. Rog rules the roost around here. He'll clue you in. Lord is counterintelligence. Knows how to make a suspect sing.

The problem, however, to which Rog might provide the clue essential to a solution was not a mystery, being the camp itself, his prerogative to run it and its fitness to determine what locus in life, if any, might be made to suit the displaced inmates. Their displacement was like a disease. That camp in the Vosges Mountains was like a sanitarium that kept the sick in disciplinary isolation and their experiences like the epitome of an ailing world. And the whole place, I suddenly imagined for an instant, was like a hellish version of the Berghof, the sanitarium of Thomas Mann's mountain, where characters from all corners of the world gathered to ruminate and theorize and debate the meaning of malady itself.

Rog led me to a billet on the second floor of the adjoining building, sat me down on a cot, and clued me in. First, a newcomer to his camp is allowed one puke his first time on the far side of the wire, and one puke only, so he gets *that* out of his system and the inmates see how he feels about living with their shit, because you're actually walking in it.

Next, and let this be clear clear, a DP is no POW, so none of your convention Geneva Red Cross pussyfooting bullshit. Okay. These phony freeloading sons of bitches got picked up wandering around, mooching and stealing, sob stories off the trolley, speak no language anybody speaks, so the trick's to make 'em talk, interrogation, no fooling, make 'em squeal, make 'em sing hallelujah till it hurts, and brother, *make* it hurt is the way to hear the truth, where they came from, what they were up to. Then maybe let them go. Big maybe.

A new batch every day, so's if we don't move 'em, they'll have to sleep standing up or drop dead in their own shit, like they do anyway. So . . . interrogate, interrogate, interrogate. 'Tain't a camp for displaced persons, 's a camp for desperate persons. They say anything to get out of here. Lots of these guys probably killed Americans. Make 'em talk. Tough job, you gotta be tough. Use your fists. They won't hit you back. Use the rubber hose. You're not the Secret Service here. We're in a hurry. Fill in a file card for each man.

"Okay," I said, "but how can I make 'em talk if I can't talk to them? All those languages."

"Interpreters," said Rog. "They all talk a bit of German, and something else, or pretend they do. They're men in there can interpret shit into Shinola, you give 'em a Hershey bar to handle the rough stuff if you get tired, beat the living daylight outta D fucking Ps."

I said, "That sounds like torture, and we don't do that."

Rog grumbled. Wise up, sonny. We don't do it, but they ain't us, all those funny skin faces, and anyway, ain't like we do it for fun like the krauts do, we just sort of kick 'em in the crotch to keep the balls rolling, see what I mean? So I guess that's the size of it. You're twelve interrogators. Somebody'll take you down to the shed tomorrow. Me, I don't go to the far side of the wire. Anything comes up I'll clue you in. Okay?

"Sure," I said.

Rog thrashed the cot with his rubber hose, smiling so the eggplant jowl looked about to burst. He hawked some phlegm. Make sure you're sure, boy, 'cause I keep an eye on ya.

A corporal wearing muddy boots and smelling like a slit trench came in and flopped onto the cot adjoining mine. Short, stocky, bald, he had a lopsided head, his face looked as though an elephant had stepped on it: flat nose and little chin but metallic eyes pierced with dark intelligence, a presence softened by sly kindness. "Stassoff, Ossip," he said, holding out a puffy hand, adding as I shook it, "Don't ask. My parents got out in '17 through Odessa. I was two. They made it to the U.S., still in the Bronx. So that's why I'm here. Speak Russian, German, Spanish, Italian, Yiddish, a little French. Dad was a professor of philology in Petersburg. Now NYU."

"Maybe you can help me with some of these so-called interrogations. I only speak French."

"Nobody can help you. You're holding a lot of fate in your hands, my lad, and you don't have the first idea of what it's all about. If the occasion presents, maybe I can make it a little less painful. I suppose Rog the Dog clued you in."

"Yes." I sighed.

The Russian was right. I didn't have a clue to the mystery that enwrapped me like a boa, constricting the life inside, and the idea of the war gripped my bowels like ice, and I was afraid.

In the morning Stassoff came with me and the ten other interrogators, sullen stragglers, spitting and bitching, down to the gate; an MP with wads of cotton in his nostrils opened up; and we entered the camp proper. The impulse to puke was close to irresistible, but I swallowed against it, knowing the others were ready to jeer, and the DP mob parted barely enough to let us pass, their stench an atrocity. The interrogation shed had been thrown together out of odd lots of plywood, twelve U-shaped stalls along an open corridor, each with one window, a table, a chair, two stools, on the table a pile of yellow printed cards, a dozen pencils, a pencil sharpener, a length of green rubber hose.

Stassoff explained. "You interrogate the subject, call for an interpreter, if necessary, fill out the card: name, date and place of birth, familial circumstances, also dates, locations, and descriptions of occupation both before and during the war, destination, if detached from camp. If release is recommended, write 'Release' and sign, if not, write 'Vesoul.' That's a camp fifty miles to the south where more meticulous interrogations can be pursued. As for the hose, you have to live with it."

"But, Ossip—" I said.

He said, "Darkness at noon," though it was eight o'clock in the morning.

I didn't know what to do, sat down behind the table, aware that the vital questions would be addressed to me. From beyond the poor partition of my stall I could hear a confusion of babble, shouts, or shrieks, yelling, pounding, the echoes of the fall into the nowhere of adversity.

A black-bearded, simpering lobo of a fellow, gap-toothed and lean, sauntered in, said he could interpret eight languages, sucked his lower lip, adding he'd handle the rough stuff in case I was short on guts. Well? I shrugged. And the first interrogatee was a boy about sixteen, ugly as a saucepan, caked with mud, said he was French. Name? demanded Lobo. Pierre Walser. That so? And Lobo landed a powerhouse punch to the kid's solar plexus, sending him to the floor. I leaped up, shouted, "What the hell?" and Lobo said, "Getting acquainted, loosens up the tongue." I told him to get out. He sneered but went.

The boy pushed himself to his feet. I said, "Sit on a stool. I'm sorry."

He said, "Everybody knows it's coming. You expect it. The Germans had clubs; they had whips and dogs."

I asked him to tell his story.

He was from a farming village called Bouzy, drafted by the Nazis for work in a factory making artillery shells. When the Americans came, everybody ran away. He headed for home, but the roads were overcrowded. Then some more Americans picked him up, brought him here, that's weeks ago, worse off here than on the road. Not enough water or enough to eat, sleep in the mud and more than mud, somebody dying every day. Begged to go back to Bouzy, never did anything wrong, and you could beat him as much as you want; anyway, the Germans did worse, they did much worse.

I said, "All right, all right, you can go home, I'll sign your card release, I promise." His eyes glistened as he went out.

For a time I sat still, staring into the middle of disgrace. Never before had the clutch of corruption been so severe, clawing at awareness for the medium of vindication, the lonely strife of clairvoyance.

So I swallowed my struggle, went outside, and called at the crowd that I'd take any speakers of French. A dozen or more crowded clumsily inside. I took them at random, questioned, listened, wrote "Release" on every card, observing that all seemed surprised not to have been mistreated and stupefied to be released.

When the siren sounded for lunch, I wakened to fatigue, waiting to watch my colleague interrogators, glowering angrily as they strode outside, their features stricken masks of malevolence. Ossip came along at the last and walked with me to the mess hall. We sat apart from the others. I told him what had happened. He said, "Be careful."

"But this place can't be dangerous."

"I'll give you a bit of advice. It's all very well to be compassionate, but beware of being lenient. Too many recommendations for release from a single interrogator could attract unwelcome attention."

"But that's what this place is for," I protested, "to help displaced persons find the right place?"

"Right is a rubbery judgment. Major Weinstein's verdict would surely be less pliable than yours. And the notion of help doesn't coincide very nicely with an area where men are held behind wire with too little to eat or to drink."

"You remember what you told me yesterday: I'd be holding a lot of fate in my hands, and maybe you could help make it less painful. I'd be grateful if you could. Because it *is* painful. Look at the other interrogators. You'd think the pain's been too much for them already."

"Oh, it has," said Ossip. "But it's not the pain they endure. It's the pain they inflict."

"But they're Americans!" I exclaimed.

"Lucky thing they're not Turks." Ossip snickered.

The camp was a roaring miasma of humankind, heads, arms, fingers flailing, shouting, jostling, elbowing and kicking, furiously attacking the raised cement platform where two men like themselves frantically struggled with long-handled ladles to slop out into waving tin cups or bowls, or even one or two wooden shoes, some russet-colored slop from cauldrons of corrugated metal. And in their frenzy to eat many were so desperate they dribbled and spilled their watery ration into matted beards and down their tattered clothing.

"I don't believe it," I cried.

"Misery is the child of ignorance," said Ossip.

Thirst of course went hand in hand with hunger for the DPs. Along the west side of the wire, a shallow trough of rusty metal ran at waist height for about a hundred yards, into which midmorning and mid-afternoon a gush of gray, turbid water ran for fifteen minutes. It was with the same bestial abandon as for their rations that the men attacked the trough, howling, gulping, splashing, soaking in the battle of thirst.

So from that first day the numbing drain of sand in the hourglass of circumstance timed my crossing of the odious frontier of responsibility. To try to interrogate, with or without brutality or interpreters, random prisoners—what else were they?—in order to determine if any had been guilty of the crimes and atrocities of war: What guilt of mine might this atrocious license entail?

Day after day, day after day, ten or sometimes twelve hours. I never used the rubber hose, though I listened helplessly to the nearby effects of its use, and my silence was their accomplice. I dissimulated; I malingered. And yet there were times, there were times and again when the toil against the Sisyphean rock posed its ultimatum, for how in this underworld of unforgiveness could I presume to come by forbearance? What was *I*, after all, in relation to the suffering, degradation, and despair of so many? The paleontologist of their plight? Linked in imagination by a disposition to identify one's own predicament with a general adversity? Well, no, of course, not for an instant could I compare my poor sense of oppression with the surrounding sea of wretchedness. Empathy in such conditions is a luxury; one feels compassion inasmuch as one's own crisis emphasizes how needfully we acknowledge that we are all mortals together.

Thomas Mann was much with me during those despondent days of rain, mud, and inhumane extremity; the idea of high art contrasted with this quagmire of barbarity. Even before fleeing from college I had sometimes thought of writing to him and had even obtained his address from a friendly professor of literature who had published in the *Saturday Review of Literature* an essay on Mann's use of the literary leitmotiv. So I knew that the author, who had grown up beside the Baltic Sea, now resided on the Californian shore of the Pacific Ocean. And I couldn't tell what came over me one evening after a perfectly routine but profoundly harrowing day that led me to sit down and write the following postcard.

Dear Mann,
    I have for a long time had the intention of writing to you, since there are some things I feel I want to say, but a soldier's life is not full of time for the composing of such letters, so I write now this card to say that I am thinking of the letter and will write it as soon as I have time. Until then, I remain
                                                                Yours Sincerely,
                                                                James Lord

Despite the callow and impertinent presumptuousness of this gratuitous communication, I mailed it, having then been at the DP camp more than two weeks.

The fighting for Iwo Jima continued bloodier than ever, though the famous photo of GIs raising the Stars and Stripes on a mountaintop had already gone around the world. Roosevelt, Churchill, and Stalin conferring at Yalta had carved out the postwar zones of influence to be theirs across the globe after the unconditional surrenders of Germany and Japan. I told no one that I had written to the most eminent man of letters then alive.

One morning a Russian came before my desk: gaunt, the flaccid physique of a famished athlete, and something slightly wrong about the face, lopsided but not scarred, younger than he looked because his wasted appearance was ageless. We knew that the occasional Russian turned up in camp, and German mistreatment of Soviet POWs had been infamous, millions starved to death.

I called down the corridor for Ossip, who came along, questioned the fellow, and told me his story. Name: Balinski, Leonid, born Kiev, 1924, enlisted in a Guards Shock Army, survived by miracle the winter siege of Stalingrad but taken prisoner by the Germans in the town of Maków, north of Warsaw, '44, sent to work in an underground factory making spare parts for airplane engines somewhere in Germany, escaped with several comrades by killing a guard and two dogs, walking only at night, guided west by the stars and stealing food from farms till they reached the Americans, at Épinal now for many weeks.

"What do you say?" I asked Ossip. "The case is special. If I write a release, where will he go? What will he do?"

"He can drive a taxi in Paris," said Ossip. "Must be a few czar's cadets still driving who could give him a hand. *But* Russians are a tragic race. Murdered and starved to death millions of their own people. Hitler and Stalin, Stalin and Hitler, a match made in heaven, husband and wife, wife and husband. If we let him go, the NKVD will catch him, call him a deserter, and kill him. If we send him back to Russia—and there's a caveat for doing so—they'll say he's a traitor, worked for the Nazis, a bullet in the nape if he's lucky, Sakhalin if he's not. Ask Solomon to decide."

"Well, why not ask him, Ossip? Tell him we'll see to it he gets back safely to Kiev."

Ossip shrugged, spoke a few phrases, placing his hand on the boy's shoulder.

I saw the color sink from his cheeks, a scar suddenly stood out on his jaw, and he began to tremble. *Nyet*, he whispered. *Nyet*, he repeated, *nyet, nyet, nyet* till he was shouting, hands clasped over his eyes as he fell to his knees and began to sob, gasping *nyet, nyet* again and again, reaching under the table to seize one of my feet and kiss the toes of my boot, weeping.

It was frightening. Terrible. Dostoyevsky. *The House of the Dead.* My eyes were also overflowing. I turned to Ossip. So were his. I cried, "For God's sake, get him to his feet. We can't just sit here and cry. Do something. Take him outside. Tell him we'll do what we can. He won't have to go back to Russia. Everything will be all right. Yes, he can drive a taxi. Go on."

Ossip lifted his compatriot under the arms and, as they lurched out, murmured gently into his ear.

Alone, I wiped my cheeks and clasped the incredulous air for support, which was not forthcoming. In its place came a racking howl of pain through the partition from the adjoining stall, pursued by a huge thump, moans, and babble. I ran around from the corridor. A DP lay crumpled on the floor in a puddle of piss and shit. Another DP stood above him, lifting the knotted branch of a tree. "What the hell!" I cried. "You can't do this," though it was clear he could.

Behind the table sat a corporal with a toothpick in the corner of his mouth and the rubber hose distended between his fingers. He said, "Says who? The major wants results. This kraut is Wehrmacht if there ever was one, maybe Waffen SS. Claims he was drafted, Hitler Jugend anyway. Saw nothing, knew nothing, did nothing. Then why's he hiding out in DP camp? Maybe he forgot he had a hand in the Malmédy Massacre. So we give his memory a jog. Anyway, seems I heard somebody bawling on your side of the wall just now. So go do your deal, and I'll carry on with business here. Get me? So long."

It was hopeless. I waited in the corridor for Ossip. His frown said too much, but I was the hostage of expectation, so "What did you say?" I asked.

"I quoted some Lermontov, told him we'd find a way to keep him in the West, have a new life after the war."

"Is it the truth?"

"No, but I'll tell you. His tears weren't only tears of terror. They were tears of longing too. Exile has always been the worst fate for a Russian. My parents, they walk down Flatbush Avenue, they think they're on Nevsky Prospekt. When he gets back, Leonid, maybe they will send him to Siberia, and Siberia is Russia too. Write 'Vesoul' on his card."

I did it, and then I was done for. Keeping my eyes on the mud, I went through the crowd, wondering where they kept DP corpses till the garbage detail came in the morning. On the boardwalk side of the wire I came abreast of Rog. He said, "Taking off early, eh? Going on sick call?"

"I ought to. I'm so sick of what's going on in this camp. I'm sick to death. Do you realize? Right now in that shed, I'm telling you, they are beating some kid with a stick of wood, he's on the floor, shit his pants."

He nodded. "We're winning the war, aren't we?"

Turning away in my weakness and regret, I climbed upstairs and stretched out on my cot. Did my country have an infallible role to play in the history of nations? As if our ancestors in the wilds of Massachusetts had begun a new, fresh, innocent chapter in the story of civilization? Written and ratified by the bona fide deity of the Pilgrim Fathers, bequeathing to us the manifest destiny of a duty to correct the political errors of mankind.

U.S. forces captured intact a bridge across the Rhine at Remagen. No enemy had crossed into the German homeland since Napoleon's imperial progress on the way to Austerlitz 140 years before. Thus began the final fatal act of the Nazi Götterdämmerung, and the mortal man responsible, crazed by what he'd wrought, unwittingly acknowledged the enormity of it all by firing his favorite field marshal, Gerd von Rundstedt. In the Pacific American bombers dropped two thousand tons of incendiary bombs on the Japanese capital in less than three hours, causing a firestorm so violent that sixteen square miles of central Tokyo were destroyed and over a hundred thousand civilians killed. Worse was to come for other cities, but the merest mention of surrender was hateful to the fanatic fidelity of the Japanese to their emperor.

My overriding concern became the cumulative chronicle of DP accounts of their experiences, their adventures and sufferings endured at the whim of the war. It was a stupefying, incredible, but factual narrative of lives rendered as an everyman allegory of wonder and horror, fortitude, charity, cruelty, evil, faith and disease, lust, laughter, madness and death, all of that and more, the rivers, the meadows and villages, valleys, factories, mines, highways, and mountainsides of Europe. And in the likeness of every account there was the infinite variety that made of personal identity a dizzying world of ineffable variety. Nor did it matter one whit whether I could understand every word of the murderous interpreters as I came to read the faces of the men who spoke impetuously to my eyes.

The interviews went very slowly. You can't hurry the history of metabolism. I felt an imaginary rebirth in the trustful zest with which these strangers became companions of my longing to make amends: to become one of them, so to speak, which was the impossible portion of my pity. But they never appeared offended by my curiosity, and I squandered fair prospects that were, in fact, pointless. So it seemed at times that the emotions of these dramatically displaced persons brought me face-to-face with the self I had long ago condemned and yet aspired to someday set right with the dictate of conscience. I wrote Release Release Release on their cards. My colleagues, needless to say, viewed with contempt and animosity my perverse concern to hear the DPs' stories and probably for spite sent many to Vesoul with bruises intended for me.

That implacable winter of '45 persisted without amnesty well into March. The cold-crazed DPs stood all night knotted in clusters of interlocking arms and legs static under the floodlights for the sake of collective warmth like cadaverous statuary. Come morning they leaped and flailed the air against the threat of sluggish blood. And if there were frozen corpses in the frozen mud, and there were, they were hustled out of sight by the garbage detail. The mud thawed slowly. By late afternoon few solid islands remained in the putrid slush, so that exit from the camp proper varied unpredictably if you hoped to keep the excrement from slopping over into your boots.

Which is why I almost stepped on the man's head, and would have had he not moaned as I raised my foot; he was practically indistinguishable from the slime. Leaning down to him despite the stench, I touched his hand, cold and lifeless, but the eyelids shuddered, and violet lips whispered, *"Aiutami aiutami aiutami . . ."*

I didn't understand. But the plea was all too clear. I said, "I'll call a doctor. *Médecin.* Quick. *Le docteur.* You'll be all right," and took a couple of bits of chocolate to put in his mouth. He spit them back, however, his teeth blackened stumps, his skin like wrinkled rice paper clinging to his skull.

Stepping across the morass through the gate, I clomped up to sick bay. The waiting room was empty. I shouted, "Doctor! Come quick. An emergency." Several minutes passed. I shouted again. And again.

The inner door cracked open only slightly; the doctor, a captain, peered out and muttered, "What's the ruckus? Sick bay's been closed for an hour."

"This is urgent," I cried. "Urgent. One of the DPs in a very bad way. I think half dead."

"They all are," said the doctor, opening the door, buttoning his shirt. "Nothing I can do unless it's typhus, and even that would have to wait till tomorrow."

"But why?" I exclaimed.

"I'm off duty as of one hour ago," said the irritable M.D., coming into the waiting room now, buttoning his shirt to the chin and preparing to put on a tie. "Going down to Épinal in half an hour. Have a date with one of the nurses. No way I'm going to miss it. More than a month since I've had a good fuck."

"And what if he *is* dying?" I said.

"I wouldn't go down into that filth if *you* were dying. That's it. A miracle you're not dying, matter of fact, hanging out every day with those specters, it's asking for infection. Tell you what. I'll give you a few aspirin, a bottle of good water, and you can be Florence Nightingale." He went back inside and returned quickly with the water and a tube of aspirin. "There you go. Good luck. You've got the whole world in your hands."

"Son of a bitch!" I exclaimed. "For quacks like you the Hippocratic oath is obviously a crock of shit."

"Wait a minute, soldier. You're way out of line. You're speaking to an officer."

"Yes, sir," I said, snapping a salute, "right you are. For a minute there I thought I was speaking to a doctor."

"You forget yourself, Sergeant. I could put you on report for this."

"Do it," I replied, and went out with the water and the tube of aspirin.

My patient lay where I'd left him, the others looking down from a careful distance like mourners at a spectral funeral. I crouched beside his head and pushed two aspirin between discolored lips, pouring some of the water after them. He swallowed but immediately coughed up both the pills and the water, his face twitching spasmodically, and murmured a word. I thought it was a name. But how would I have understood? I took one of the flaccid hands. The sullen sky let fall a few huge drops of freezing rain. The wait was not long; it was interminable, since I feared for myself: the man within humanity was dwindling away. He coughed once or twice, a hacking metallic rasp, the head wrenched upward in a spastic rictus, his hand fell from mine, and that was all. As I walked away, the mourners closed around the corpse preparatory to serving necessity.

When I described to Ossip what had happened, he said, "All the world has bad places, and bad places naturally produce bad people, and the worse the people become, the worse the places get, and the worst places produce unthinkable consequences. Now, this camp is not a good place. It is a bad one, and bad people in it. But I think, my friend, I have a terrible suspicion, as if the devil himself is waiting around the corner, I seem to foresee much worse than Épinal, worse even, if possible, than the worst, and I tell you this because I have listened to some of the men in this camp, and what some of them say is so unbelievable that even if I believed only the believable part, that would be hell on earth, which *is* unbelievable."

I said, "I'm afraid I don't know what you're talking about."

Ossip tilted his lopsided head to one side and said, "I too am afraid I don't know."

It was not to be very long, however, before both of us, as well as the incredulous world, found out that the believable part of the unbelievable did, in fact, beggar belief, which would make hell on earth as credible as $E=mc_2$.

Meanwhile, the war rolled on. In East Prussia the Red Army battered weakening German forces that refused to surrender, accepting annihilation instead, and I decided, having said I'd think about it—without, in brute fact, having the faculty to think about either its substance or implications—to write to Thomas Mann the letter I'd already threatened to send him. Oh, yes, the decision was wildly pretentious and impertinent, withal nonetheless a measure of callow and therefore honest audacity. Before writing, I thought and thought, then wrote without thinking.

March 24, 1945

Dear Mann,

Some weeks ago I wrote you a post card in which I stated my intention to write to you at a time in the future. I should surely have written before now had I not been caught in the relentless grasp of the idolatrous chauvinism and inane, pagan symbol-worship which are standard procedure over here.

At the time when I wrote the post card I might conceivably have written a joyful letter in which all the presumed ideals of my age would have been conspicuous. And I would have asked some questions and proposed perhaps a naive idea or two on writing, the avowed purpose of my communicating with you at all. But since then the futility and hypocrisy and emptiness of this whole undertaking have been forced so intensely into my mind that there is little place for other things. There is now no basic difference between what we are fighting for and what we are fighting against, and it is a hard shock to know it. But anyone should have been more objective than ever to imagine there was any truth or integrity in what went on here.

But that is not all—it is the utter game that I abhor, because there is no good anywhere. The few isolated points of real value serve only to make all the others, against which they fight for existence, seem sordid and hideous. Civilization has become a great number of loathsome beasts; and the rapacious, slavering maw of every one is just half-filled as it devours the body of every other one. A sight it is which would have made even Caligula creep away in horror and revulsion, for it is their greatest pleasure and sense of fulfillment so to act. It is at moments such as this that one most fully understands what it was which motivated Simeon Stylites. The wasteland, space, and nothingness have now become what is most beautiful to me, while the world and its people I wish only to leave to their monstrous orgy of masochist self-mutilation and destruction.

I will not ask that you make yourself excuses for my bitterness, since I feel it is just. I wish only to say that I wrote to you rather than others as I do because of my great admiration for what you have done and because I think that you might well realize what I mean to say and probably have failed in any way to express.

Sincerely I send this, if nothing else.

James H. Lord

Pitiful fuck, snarled the major, his cigarette flapping up and down. Got to be the saddest sack ever come this way. I'll swear. Want to know something? he shouted, leaping out of his chair so violently it fell over backward and the cigarette slipped from his mouth.

I replied, Yes, sir, still standing at attention while he snatched another cigarette from a tin box and lit it.

Then I'll tell you something. You're no good, worse than bad. Too slow. Too soft. We need people here can dish it out. You can't. Don't have the guts. Talk back to officers. Dr. Dana. I ought to bust your ass. We had to double-check every DP you recommended for release last ten days. And I'll tell you something, you stupid fuck. One of them we got through loosening him up, you know, turned out he was a guard some place called Flossenburg concentration camp. How many Jews he murdered you couldn't count 'em, goddamn war criminal, you'd have let him go so's he could murder a few thousand more before the war's over, you pitiful asshole. I had my way I'd send you to the infantry. Kill some Germans, get a little backbone to ya. Instead you're going back where you came from. One hour. Signed the papers ready to go. Jeep on order. So pack your bag and get your motherfucking ass off this post before I say kill. Dismissed.

While I was stuffing my duffel, I looked out for Ossip, but he must already have gone down to the interrogation shed, that gateway to abandoned hope. So I couldn't say goodbye to the only man in that place manful enough to face it with knowledge and to persist when persistence led nowhere.

The jeep was ready, the driver, a fawnlike kid, raced the motor, said his dream was to do the Speedway in Indianapolis, and swore God must have given me the good luck prize from the Cracker Jack box to get me out of this hellhole. I said, "Anyway."

As we drove beyond the stench of the camp down through the forest, I wondered whether my letter would ever reach Thomas Mann.

Fourteen

MARCH–APRIL 1945

Major Aldrich had moved up in the world of wartime mystique while I moved down. His office occupied the entire floor of a flamingo-colored villa by the lake in Le Vésinet, making his former accommodations in Rennes seem squalid by comparison. PFC Fahnestock, also risen in prestige and rank, cute, twinkling, and dimpled, presided over an outer room, a sergeant now, slickly tricked out in an Eisenhower jacket. He said, "Major's expecting you, but better knock. Incidentally, you look like hell."

"Just come from there," I said. "Twenty-two hours on the train even you'd lose your bloom, believe it."

Still a fashion plate, and Louis XVI desk ostentatiously the same, Aldrich waved his gold cigarette case toward an armchair and said, "Sit, Sergeant. You are a very talented young man."

Astonished, I said, "Am I, sir?"

"Very. You seem to be inhabited by a unique faculty for antagonizing your superiors. First Sergeant Jars. Now Major Weinstein bellowing down the telephone. Perhaps you'd care to comment," he inquired, opening the elegant case, selecting a cigarette, and blinking.

"Yes, sir," I said, "I would. You have no idea, if I may say so, sir, not the least idea of what's going on in that DP camp. We are supposed to be helping those men, their lives have been ruined, these are people who have lost everything, homes, families, livelihood, everything, clothes, food, water, they're dying up there in the mud with nothing to hope for except maybe a little kindness, and what they're getting is the shit beat out of them supposedly to learn who they are and where they came from. I can testify to it, that's hell on earth, and

Major Weinstein couldn't care less, he thinks they're war criminals, and the doctor, Captain Dana, he can't be bothered to take a look at a dying DP. We're not supposed to tolerate things like that."

Major Aldrich fastidiously extinguished his expensive cigarette. "My boy," he said, "I gave you some advice awhile back, advised you to study how to be heartless. You haven't learned, and I'm sorry, because I can see through your worry. Yes, there are things we don't do, and there are things anybody *can* do if an earthquake or a hurricane or a war comes out of the blue and suddenly nobody is the person he was yesterday, and you might as well complain to the tremors or the wind as to the fellow who fires the machine gun or beats the shit out of a prisoner. The idea of knowledgeable moral choice between alternatives is moot, you know, whether your heart is in it or not. Does this help? Because I'd rather like to help, because I think we have more in common than you might suspect."

"You're very kind, sir," I said sincerely, "and I appreciate that, but the trouble is I had to live with it—the earthquake if you want to call it that—and it came to be part of me. I can't mark it up to historical inevitability and forget about it."

"I see. I see quite a lot, as a matter of fact," and he opened his cigarette case and inspected its contents as if some enigma were hidden there. "Well, there's no knowing about the liabilities of being alive, which life itself compels us to live through, now is there? Here," he said, holding across his cigarette case, "have a cigarette."

"Thank you, sir, but I don't smoke."

"I know it," he said, "that's the point. Have one anyway."

"All right." I took it and stuck it in my mouth, and Major Aldrich leaned across, clicking his gold lighter, to light it. The taste was smoky, pungent, not unpleasant but foreign, though I didn't cough and puffed conscientiously till I'd deposited sufficient ash in the ashtray, then stubbed it out. Neither of us had spoken.

"Now," he said, snapping shut the cigarette case, "what am I going to do with you? I'll have to poke around. We don't want you bearing the cross of first causes, do we? Something will turn up. While you're waiting, try to find a congenial watering hole on the Left Bank."

"Thank you, sir."

"My name happens to be Laurance. Not that you'll have occasion to call me by it. That too is a consequence of the earthquake. Good day, Sergeant."

Picasso had by no means been forgotten during those harrowing weeks, or my purpose in wanting to see him again. To replace the little sketch, done in December, with something more worthy of a creative future, I'd have to explain its necessity and felt that a misfortune best left unexplained would have to do the trick. A man famed for transforming junk into art would be unlikely to argue with a nameless and faceless mishap.

Luckily the convenient art supply shop was open, and I selected a single large sheet of drawing paper and a good pencil. Thus prepared, I set out for the rue des Grands Augustins, bearing also a bulging musette bag.

"We've been wondering," said Sabartés, "whether you would ever come back." The plural pronoun sounded promising, and he made no mention of my portfolio holding the drawing paper. I put it on the table, at the same time bashfully hefting the musette, as if embarrassed to presume that a few privileged items might cause my presence to become likewise. We were still busy with chocolate, cigarettes, soap, and coffee when Picasso strolled into the room.

"Here you are, here you are!" he exclaimed, grinning as he tugged playfully at my cheek. "Let's go have breakfast. You can flirt with Inès."

We went upstairs and sat on the park bench. Inès was there with breakfast, but no flirtation ensued. Perhaps she was more perspicacious than her boss. By the window was propped up an enormous canvas. I hadn't seen it in December, and the image it bore leaped forward immediately: a jumble of dead bodies, limbs disjointed, buttocks, bellies, breasts twisted and contorted, gruesome faces, a pair of huge hands lashed together at the wrists, a vision of odious atrocity. It instantly evoked spectacles I'd seen all too recently, the prison camp packed with men huddled in fetid mud and their own festering filth, some next to death. I was dumbfounded. How could he have known?

Picasso sipped his coffee, thanked me for the gifts, and said nobody thought to bring him toilet paper. Sabartés came upstairs to say that several men were waiting below. There were three edging tentatively by the long table. Picasso introduced me, having got my surname well in mind, and it seemed to amuse him to pronounce it with a guttural roll of the *r*, "Lorrrd." I'd noticed he always referred to others by their surnames, even Sabartés, whom he'd known for half a century. The others paid no attention to me. The portfolio of drawing paper lay on the table beside my musette bag, now empty. I don't know what reckless assumption of self-intoxicated prerogative seized me, but it was the simplest and most obvious thing on earth to touch Picasso's arm, interrupt the conversation, and say, "Would you do a portrait of me?"

Not at all taken aback, the artist said, "But it's done already."

"A misfortune befell it," I said. Hadn't Picasso himself said that art is a lie that makes one realize the truth? He didn't inquire about the misfortune but fixed his eyes on me. Stepping across in front of him, I brought out the sheet of drawing paper and from my pocket the pencil, aware all the while that the others were observing this as if in a trance of stupefaction.

Picasso took the paper and pencil and held the sheet up to the light. "Bad quality," he said, shaking it, "and too large." He folded it quickly in half, the crease hissing under his fingernails. "Then sit down over there," he brusquely instructed me, "and turn toward the right." He sat on the other side of the room, paper propped on the portfolio from which it had come.

I was hardly conscious that he studied my appearance. The pencil started rasping on the paper, slowly, slowly at first, then faster and faster, and I was only aware that I wanted it to go on forever, feeling that the longer it continued its work, the surer I could be that the outcome would live up to the mystery of my hope. But before I could even apprehend that the experience was an event, much less that it had meaning, it was finished. Picasso stood up, tossing the paper onto the table, and said, "It's done."

The others crowded in front of me to look before I could catch a glimpse, and Sabartés cried out, "The latest masterpiece!"

Then I saw the drawing, and I was baffled. Maybe Sabartés was right, but I was embarrassed by what he'd said, realizing that I hadn't known what I wanted. I'd wanted a portrait of myself by Picasso, and this was it, signed "Pour Lord, Picasso, Paris, 27.3.45." But if Sabartés was right, then this was more than a mere likeness and surpassed by its very nature the identity of the model, reducing him to an incidental effect but by no means a cause. How mean is the hunger for eternity in youth. Certainly the drawing looked like me, was adequately large, its lines vibrant with life, in no way ever to be a disappointment. Clearly, the artist had seen in me that morning a being very different from the one who had come unbidden to ring at his door several months before. I awkwardly endeavored to express some manner of thanks, but Picasso dismissed this gently. I put the drawing into the portfolio, preparing to leave, and as I turned, forgetting my resolve, submitted to the sudden twinge in my knee and limped toward the door.

"Oh!" cried Sabartés. "You haven't recovered from your wound."

"I have, I have," I protested. "I made a misstep is all, only a misstep. I'm quite all right, I promise you."

Picasso pinched my cheek, said, *"Au revoir, mon garçon,"* and turned back to talk with the others as though I were taking away under my arm nothing that could ever pretend that that drab day in March might forgive the faults of the future.

To find a congenial watering hole was not my first priority. All of Paris was the place I wished to find affable and friendly. Every day, left in peace by Major Aldrich's goodwill, I took the train from Le Vésinet to St. Lazare and lazily ambled around and about, admiring everything. Having for so long disregarded the tingle in my trousers when observing the contours of theirs, I kept my eyes open for attractive boys too. But I didn't try anything. The time was not prepared. Besides, I was in love with Paris, and I had my portrait.

One morning in the studio on the rue des Grands Augustins there were more visitors than usual. Sabartés shrugged. But Picasso got around to me eventually, and I said good morning. He said, "Do you know Gertrude Stein?" When I said I didn't, he added, "You should. You're both Americans. It will be interesting. I'll call her right now and arrange it. She lives very near here."

After taking up his telephone, dialing, he said, "Gertrude. It's Picasso." And after a brief greeting: "There's a young American soldier here who wants to meet you. I'm going to send him over."

A toss of Picasso's head, sweeping gesture of the left hand. "Well, it doesn't matter if it's time for your bath. I'm going to send him over anyway."

Guiding me toward the door, he said, "You'll see. Gertrude is a very interesting woman. Then there's her friend, Alice Toklas, too. Everybody ought to know them. It will be interesting."

Outside in the street I wasn't so sure. To me an introduction by Picasso may have seemed a categorical imperative, but Miss Stein was apparently of another mind. Picasso himself, however, had not proved too formidable. So I went along to the nearby rue Christine, a fine but short street lined on both sides with stately mansions. The Misses Stein and Toklas lived at No. 5 in the middle of the block on the south side. The courtyard was distinguished by a cheap shed, but the staircase still had its antique balustrade of wrought iron. My finger on the bell button created a distant tinkling, and I waited, mirrored as an awkward presence in the highly varnished door.

It opened, disclosing a small, stooped figure attired all in gray, a beaked nose, dark bangs above dark, direct eyes, and a dark wisp of mustache. This was Alice B. Toklas. She said, "You're the young man from Picasso, aren't you? Then come in."

The entrance hall had height, light, and a quantity of unframed paintings—obviously by Picasso—hung against the white paneling. Impossible to appreciate the profusion without showing how over-awed one was—and maybe meant to be. Miss Toklas took me through to the salon, asked me to sit down, and said that Miss Stein, who was having a bath, would soon join us. But she was already there. Whether present physically or not, whether alive, indeed, or dead, Gertrude Stein always inhabited that room as long as it contained all the possessions that so vividly, historically, and imperatively substantiated her presence, her prescience, and her prominence. These, of course, were the pictures. Where the pictures were, Gertrude was.

The pictures were by Picasso. A few by Juan Gris, Marie Laurencin, or Sir Francis Rose only emphasized that those that mattered were by *him*. The celebrated portrait of Miss Stein hung above the fireplace against the inset mirror of the chimneypiece. Opposite the two tall windows hung the famous Blue Period painting of a nude girl holding a basket of red flowers. Above a bulky commode between the windows hung a large cubist picture. Opposite Miss Stein's portrait from across the room a muted nude woman of the Rose Period gazed passively outward, her hands joined. Among these four most important paintings hung other, smaller ones, a dozen or more, all of exhilarating quality, still lifes, figures, and landscapes of the early cubist and Negro periods.

I sat on an overstuffed sofa upholstered in shiny brown horsehair, Miss Toklas facing me in a small armchair. She made a few observations about the military life, then added, "Miss Stein and I are very fond of General Grant."

"Oh? What outfit is he with?" I asked.

"General Ulysses S. Grant," she replied severely.

"Oh, yes," I said, meaning, Really?

"General Grant is one of the greatest figures in American history," said Miss Toklas. "We quite prefer him to Lincoln."

I said, "Oh!"

Presently through the ensuing silence a shaggy, white, but not very clean French poodle plodded into the room—Basket, the famous dog. Then Miss Stein came in, her step heavy, magisterial. At once and always her figure in those shapeless tweed suits made me think of a burlap bag filled with cement and left to harden. Little taller than Miss Toklas, she was so sturdy and solid within herself that she seemed very large. The bold head, hard, short gray hair, and deeply creased features were imperial. As I rose, I was afraid Miss Toklas might tell her friend that I'd failed the General Grant appreciation test.

She simply said, "Lovey, this is the young man from Picasso."

Having said how do you do and shaken hands, Miss Stein told me that she had to go out to do some errands and walk her dog for half an hour, which was all the time she had to spare, if I wanted to come along. Not an invitation but an ultimatum. I instantly said I'd be happy to. She attached a leash to Basket's collar and went toward the door. I followed, lacking only a leash, I thought, to be dog No. 2.

In the stairway Miss Stein matter-of-factly said, "Now tell me everything about yourself." Her voice was resonant, expressive, the voice of authority.

"There really isn't much to tell," I diffidently replied.

Miss Stein stopped, her hand on the faceted glass newel knob at the front of the stairs. "Now listen to me," she said, "if that's the sort of answer you're going to give when I ask you a question, then it's quite obvious that you and I will never have anything worth saying to each other and you might as well run along this minute."

Appalled and yet determined, if possible, not to be found wanting in this crisis of identity, I said, "All right, I'll tell you about myself. I'm twenty-two years old. I was born in Englewood, New Jersey, and I went to school there until—"

"That's very interesting," said Miss Stein, pulling her dog along behind her as we stepped from the courtyard into the street. "I happen to know already a young man from Englewood, New Jersey. He takes very beautiful photographs, and his father was a clergyman in Englewood." She continued for a time to talk about the young man, whose name was George Lynes, then moved to another topic, which led to another, another, and yet another.

I was not required, or invited, to talk further about myself or to talk, in fact, very much about anything whatever. Miss Stein did all the talking while we walked up to the rue de Buci and along the boulevard St. Germain, stopping occasionally to make purchases for the string bag I carried. She told me about Paris, France, the French, the war, and, above all, her impressions, feelings, and ideas.

She talked well. One of the sources of her charm, I thought, was her plain, almost childlike absorption and pleasure in her own being, her assumption that the whole world was just as she believed it to be, a comforting conviction, and she communicated that sense of comfort to others. The responsive quality of my attention must have seemed acceptable, for when we made our way back to the rue Christine, I was invited to return as often as my military duties might allow. Never one word about Picasso, his portrait of her, his paintings in her possession, or, indeed, about art in general.

I reported to him a couple of days later that my meeting with Misses Stein and Toklas had been pleasurable. He did not seem concerned to hear the first thing about it.

Two days later I received a notice requesting—requesting!—me to appear before Major Aldrich the following morning at eleven. Fahnestock, as usual, in the other room, said, "Hi, Sergeant, you're looking better for a change."

He, I thought, was not looking any better—so good-looking he hardly could—but flashier, a gold identification bracelet on his right wrist, and I deigned to say, "Thanks a lot."

Major Aldrich—why had he bothered to tell me his first name?— was changeless. He said, "At ease and sit down. I think I've turned up just the thing for you. In Dijon, a splendid town, once the capital of the dukes of Burgundy. I happen to have a friend there, Captain Jones. You ought to like him, very urbane, one of the New York Joneses, a relative to Edith Wharton. You know, *The Age of Innocence*." He laughed, toying with the cigarette case but didn't light up. "He'll look out for you. He's posted to Dijon to do the honors for General Giraud. Even though de Gaulle got rid of him, the higher-ups think he has some decorum coming, so they have a carnival HQ set up. But you won't have a thing to do except maybe shine your shoes and keep your hair cut. A welcome change from DP camp. Sergeant Fahnestock has your orders; pick them up on the way out. Oh, and you can tell the captain he owes me one. Bon voyage."

"Thank you, Major. I don't know how to thank you, really."

"Forget it," he said.

If only he hadn't said that, Forget it! How could I, never had, never expected to; Hanno, yet again, always walking with me in Virginia City, the roseate prelude to that sunset, blinded eyes in millionaire mansions, the tarnished opera house, songs of yesteryear from the heart of nowhere, Hanno humming? "O alte Burschenherrlichkeit," yes, and the color of his torso in the shabby bedroom, shoulders of Parian marble, the glint already of irrelevant dreams as he said goodbye in Fresno.

At the railway station in Dijon five or six jeeps were lined up in front like a rank of taxis, privates slumped behind the wheel, waiting stoically for nothing to happen. I asked along the line for Captain Jones and was greeted with a yawp and "You're two hours late."

"Sorry about that," I said, "but in case you didn't know, there's still a war going on."

"Okay, Sarge, got an extra pack of Luckies, have ya, for waiting round?"

"You the kingpin of the black market, are you?"

"Naw. Just another odd-jobber aching to get by is all. Black market? Everybody does it. Lemme help ya with your gear."

He drove me to the Hôtel du Chapeau-Rouge, indistinguishable in drabness from its neighbors. A PFC with a face like corrugated cardboard showed me upstairs to a room furnished for the nineties, opening onto an air shaft, a bathroom with a rusted tub on claw-feet.

"Single occupancy," he said, "orders of the captain. He said to meet him nineteen hundred by the polar bear."

"And where is this fucking bear?"

"It's a statue. In the park facing the Hôtel de la Cloche. Not far from here. Can't miss it. I'll give you a map of the town."

Captain Jones was the captain of the football team, could almost have—and only yesterday probably had—stepped right out of the varsity locker room at New Haven, curly-haired halfback, shrewd eyes, broad shoulders and slim of hips, the reckless grin, attired in clothes cut to his figure by J. Press, a winner and knew it.

One of the New York Joneses decidedly, and knew that too, related to the well-known novelist Mrs. Wharton, a lady of high principles and high society, née Jones. Anent the age of innocence, he'd clearly left it far behind though not yet thirty, in all probability a sexual winner, his lush mouth smiling upon teeth as white as the life-size polar bear poised before us in the park where we sat side by side on a bench.

He said, "How do you like my favorite bruin?"

"He's frosty," I said.

"He's named Baffin," said Jones. "After the pilot of the Northwest Passage, who must have been one of the first sailors ever to see these Arctic beauties."

"Reputed to be savage killers."

"Beauty *is* a killer. Larry asked me to watch out for you. How is he, by the way?"

"You mean Major Aldrich, I guess. He seems to be okay. Very kind to me. Told me to tell you that you owe him one."

"Did he now? Well, he *is* kind. I hope you're decently lodged in the Red Hat. It's not the Ritz, I know. NCOs can't be too choosy. But it's not too ticklish about middle-class morality. Better than DP camp. That pretty bad, huh?"

"A penal colony."

"Well, here you won't have any responsibilities. The rest of us keep General Giraud happy, as he doesn't realize yet that de Gaulle docked his testicles. The town is attractive; you'll probably find what you're looking for to keep you happy. If there's anything I can do personally, let me know. And one evening I'll take you to dinner at the only good restaurant in Dijon, the Trois Faisans. So there we are." He stood up. "I'll be off. See you soon." And he strode out of the park with varsity swagger, his trousers below the hem of the Eisenhower jacket rather tighter than Ike would have deemed regular.

Dijon indeed was an attractive town, containing more than enough palaces, cathedrals, museums, mansions, and monuments to keep me happy. My favorite was the Church of Notre Dame, its facade a Gothic forest of columns and statuary, the interior rather gloomy but sacred. I strolled the cobbled streets under an improved sky and often had breakfast in an antique café presided over by an aged crone who kept a pet rooster that hopped about under the tables. She said she could remember Napoleon III, parading on horseback through the city before the Huns came, and Clemenceau, riding in a motorcar after he had chased them away. And here we were, we Americans come to chase them away once again. She was well over eighty and as lively as her rooster. Usually I was the only client, spending tranquil mornings writing in my diary.

I had also begun to write a play. Though hardly daring to compete with a masterpiece, the Freudian-Dionysian tragedy of *Desire Under the Elms* had eased the notion that I try my hand. The plot was drawn from an incident reported in the newspapers while I was in Quimper, much commented upon by the baron. A young Frenchwoman, who happened at the time to be pregnant, had been raped and murdered in the obscure village of Pluguffan by FFI ruffians. Charged with murder, they said the girl had been mistress of a Nazi soldier father to the unborn child. Her elimination therefore was a patriotic act of retribution for dishonor brought upon the homeland by a wanton slut during France's time of ordeal.

That this was nonsense and criminal slander became quickly clear upon testimony by the neighbors, who established that no German soldiers had ever been in Pluguffan and that moreover, the father of the unborn child had been a respected member of the resistance arrested and executed by the Nazis several weeks before the murder and had been envied and defamed by the killers, who were opportunist latecomers to the FFI. The court, however, solicitous of the reputation of the Forces Françaises de l'Intérieur, found for the guilty and pronounced them innocent. I entitled my effort *Such Costly Blood*.

It was only a week or so after my arrival in Dijon. I'd heard nothing from the captain. Walking across the square in front of the ducal palace, I was astonished to encounter a master sergeant who was crying, his face openly streaked with tears, and he passed by without speaking. A couple of other enlisted men straggled past me, silent and glum. Then another, this one also weeping. I stopped in front of him and said, "What's wrong?"

"The president's dead," he muttered, and passed by.

I couldn't believe it. FDR dead. The war without him, it wasn't the same fight. How could it be? Three more GIs came along, and I said, "Is it true?"

They nodded. The president. Dead at sixty-three.

The days were given to disbelief and grieving.

I was ten when he gave his first speech as president. I'd heard it over the radio at the Litchfield School for Young Boys, when he told a frightened nation we had nothing to fear but fear itself. So he came to stand in the imagination of his countrymen for the strength of humanitarian, liberal, and democratic resolve. He personified purposeful confidence and idealism. More than any other statesman of his era he possessed the intelligence, charm, audacity, and vision to inspire a free world. His moral superiority brooked no comparison. No wonder the Goebbels gangster gloated and Japs celebrated. But Roosevelt's legacy to the history of mankind was soon to bring unparalleled disaster upon both.

The war was incredible. It had made me its creature, a dreamer pretending to have his wits about him, having fired one shot at an unbegotten enemy. Oh, yes. The war was *that* queer. It created a co-incidence worthy of genius and of hope against hope. I received one morning at mail call a letter sent from 1550 San Remo Drive, Pacific Palisades, California.

April 11, 1945

Sgt. James Lord
12183139 U.S. Army
Hq. ge., BD, Con. Ad. Sec.
APO 517
c/o P.M. New York
Dear Mr. Lord,
    I received your letter and thank you sincerely for the confidence with which you have disclosed (in a particularly darkened hour, I

think) your pained and worried sentiments to me. Believe me, I can fully understand your feelings; I tell you this with all emphasis, though very shortly, as urgent work keeps me from answering your letter in such detail as I should wish.

This is the tragic state of affairs: For a long time, and partly for very bad reasons, the democratic nations have not resisted the evil of facism [sic]. They are doing so now, but the means by which they must do so is war, and this expedient, unavoidably, has a corrupting effect upon him who handles it. It is the effect you write about in your letter with such passion and such understandable abhorrence.

However, to me as a European and German, the defeat and annihilation of the detestable powers which have plunged my native country and the whole of Europe in such misery, is [sic] of the foremost importance. The victory of the United Nations in this war is my greatest concern. I deeply appreciate the sorrow you feel about the damage inflicted upon your own people by the war. But I have faith in America's fundamental soundness and power of resistance against these moral detriments, and I wish that this belief would also help you to overcome your momentary understandable worries.

Very Cordially Yours,
Thomas Mann

Thomas Mann. From the other side of the world. A world of his own made actual by art, its inhabitants created by an intellect of genius, a humanist of high attainment, master of mankind's imagination. Addressing with sober wisdom, with heartfelt compassion and simplicity the boyish outburst of a brash and anonymous soldier, one among millions. Clairvoyance indeed would have been required to discern true passion and spiritual abhorrence in the self-indulgent excess of my letter. War, perhaps, pardons intemperance. It does indeed have a corrupting effect upon him who handles it, who is handled *by* it. The creator of the snow-drenched brilliance of *The Magic Mountain* no longer foresees for his protagonist the awakening of war as a transcendent redemption. Now the annihilation of those in the wrong is paramount. Never mind for the moment the painful issue of knowing when war—supraliminal of tragedy—can be considered good or simply necessary or utterly unjust, no matter how cruel and brutish the tactics practiced.

I reread and reread the letter, while the old lady's pet rooster scratched and dawdled beneath my table. Thomas Mann in this quaint café in the antique capital of a wine-soaked duchy. What a congeries of heroes. It seemed unlikely the world-famous author had ever set foot in Dijon, but the people of his invention, unintimidated by the rooster, were there in the tawny afternoon light:

Mythic Aschenbach on the Lido watching Tadzio. Tonio watching Hans Hansen. Joseph the interpreter of dreams, his treacherous brethren. All the doomed Buddenbrookses, of course, especially the last one, the frail and sickly scion, symbolic antithesis between life and art, the one imbued with creative longings, Hanno, the boy beloved for his beautiful flights of fancy and musical imagination. Unforgettable Hanno, of whom I never would be, never wished to be freed. Hanno on the steep slope above the steel blue lake, plunging down head over heels in the furious dust to test how life loves risk. Hanno in the blue Ford, my memory ecstatic, all the sunlit joy and fear in the presence of his eyes, *that* Hanno, yes, and the letter from the illustrious arbiter of cultural values trembling in my hand, please try to understand.

How anomalous it seemed, almost contrary to the principles of natural causality, to find under my door when I returned that afternoon to the hotel a note from Captain Jones.

Hôtel de la Cloche, Dijon
20 April 1945

Dear Sergeant Lord,

I've been away making sure General Giraud had a seat up front at the memorial service for the President in the American Cathedral in Paris, because it was FDR who forced de Gaulle to shake old Giraud's hand at Casablanca. I saw Larry Aldrich and he said to tell you hello. How about dinner tomorrow night? I reserved a table at the Trois-Faisans for 8 o'clock. If you can't make it, ring me at HQ G2, extension 307. Hope to see you later.

Winfield Jones

In my bedside cupboard alongside the chamber pot I kept a bottle of whiskey. The captain's invitation deserved a preparatory swig. He took me totally for granted—didn't he?—naturally assumed an inept NCO would leap through a hoop at the chance to have dinner with a good-looking, sophisticated, sexy officer, a Jones, moreover, of the New York Joneses. Winfield, a name with a chime, probably called Win in college because he won every important game, invincible hero of the football field. But what about Philosophy 1? Familiar with *The Symposium*, do you think? Confident in the credo that highest good is the attainment of true lovers pursuing a path toward eternal beauty. And Thomas Mann, the magisterial creator of characters personifying the conflict between art and life? I touched the letter in my shirt pocket. Would Captain Jones have been spiritually grieved by the passing away of Hanno? Not that he would *know*. It never occurred to me for one minute I might not show up at the Trois-Faisans at eight o'clock, and for the sake of anticipation I had another swig.

The restaurant was on the second floor of a fine stone building facing the ducal palace. Already arrived before me, the captain, trim in his tight-fitting pinks, stood as I came forward between the tables, and I was slightly stupefied, having forgotten how handsome he was, my God, and you could imagine him carried on the shoulders of his victorious teammates. I didn't know what to say.

Jones said, "Baffin got all lonely while I was away. So I offered him an ice-cream cone—chocolate because he's so white, you know—and he said no, thank you, I prefer vanilla. What *is* one to do?"

"Baffin? The polar bear?"

"In person. But I've decided to discipline him for being so choosy. No more of that nasty seal blubber till he screams for chocolate ice cream. Still, I suppose we ought to have some champagne, drink to Baffin's health, don't you think, because he introduced us. How about it?"

"Sure," I said. I wasn't sure, but I was willing. The champagne came in an ice bucket, we clinked glasses and said, "To Baffin!" and I thought this is crazy, and the captain smiled into my eyes. I was a fool for a beautiful face.

Our table was beside a window so we could look across the square at the palace while eating veal cutlets in cream. He was talking about the fabulous hoard of art treasures looted by the Nazis found in an Austrian salt mine, Rembrandt and Titian, Raphael, the Ghent Altarpiece. "Wouldn't you have sold your soul to see all that stuff?" said Jones. "*You* would have, I think, you're the type, *n'est-ce pas?*"

"Maybe," I said.

Admiring what's truly great if you can, I thought, if you know what you're doing, then everything grows richer and richer. Maybe indeed. The ice bucket, empty champagne bottle had vanished, replaced by burgundy, I was drunk, dizzied, and I slyly put my hand to the letter in my pocket.

And what turn would world events take now that our commander in chief was a man whose view of geopolitical affairs had been formed while selling neckties in Independence, Missouri? The British had liberated the concentration camp of Bergen-Belsen, a charnel house of nauseating iniquity, heaps of corpses pell-mell, and the prime minister said, "No words can express our horror." Philip the Good reigned in the nearby palace over one of the most powerful states in all of medieval Europe, a committed Crusader, and founded the Order of the Golden Fleece, did you know that? The captain was suavely in command of our soirée, seemed to be cold sober, and ordered candied apples baked in calvados for dessert. I was quite willing to be the tourist of the occasion.

"You're my guest, Sergeant," he said when the waiter brought the bill. "I insist."

"Okay," I said, since in any event he was practiced at insistence.

The sharp chill of Burgundian night had fallen onto the city when we came out of the restaurant. Lenient springtime was not the friend of that year. I thought I could almost see my breath, but that was probably an effect of alcohol. The abrupt cold seemed to sober up my bones.

"Baffin must be happy," said the captain. "Another fifty degrees down, and he'd feel like mating. Nothing like fornication to get the bodily juices flowing, is there?"

"Well," I said, thoughtful.

"I'll walk you home," he said.

It was fifteen minutes between the taciturn facades, one impoverished mongrel nosing among dead newspapers in the gutter, and I put down my boots with stubborn vigilance on the medieval cobblestones, each pace a step away from the whirligig eyesight of too much wine.

At my doorstep Jones said, "Hey, you know it's chillier out here than you'd have thought. Baffin must be shivering. What do you say I come up to your room for a nightcap? You must have a bottle of rot-gut up there, haven't you?"

"Yes," I admitted. "Just the bottom of a bottle of whiskey."

"Exactly what the occasion calls for." We plodded upstairs as if this outcome had been understood from the beginning.

I poured an inch for each of us. He downed it in a single gulp, exclaiming, "Say, it's sort of stuffy in here," and flung open the window onto the black air shaft, took off his jacket and dropped it on the chair, undid his tie too and opened his shirt. "That feels more like it." He sat down on the bed, patting the spot beside him. "Come over here, and I'll show you my tattoo."

How had I not known?

"Do you really have a tattoo?" I said.

"No, not really. Where do you think I ought to have one?" he asked, opening his shirt down to his navel, baring a Praxiteles torso. "Come over here and show me where you'd put it."

I kept back and said, "I wouldn't know."

He laughed and touched his fingertips to his nipples. "Take your choice." And when I didn't respond, he came to me, took my hands, placed them where his fingertips had been, and kissed me on the mouth.

"Don't," I said, stepping away.

"Come on," he protested, following me, "I know you like it." He started fondling the front of my pants, and what he felt inside proved him to be right. "Let yourself go."

Turning aside, I said, "Please. I don't feel like it."

"Don't I turn you on?"

"Sure you do. Maybe that's what's wrong."

"Stop thinking—will you?—for one minute. Concentrate on this instead." He took my hand and pressed it to the front of his pants. "There. Not as big as your friend H. But . . ."

"H!" I exclaimed, withdrawing my hand. "You know H? He's not gay."

"No? Well, for a guy who's not gay he delivers a fabulous blow job. And as for Robespierre, it could make you fall in love with the guillotine."

"Robespierre?"

"Sure. Don't you know? He calls his cock Robespierre? When people see it, they lose their heads."

I didn't laugh.

"Let's drop the talk, okay," said Jones, taking off his shirt now, "and do what we want to do, have a good fuck and call it a day." He seized me by the waist to turn toward the bed.

"Don't!" I cried, and a flash of recall summoning that sordid room in San Francisco, the Mexican's mouth stinking of tequila, and I pushed him away.

Jones's hands dropped away, his eyes going to slits and the anger in his throat. "I'm not good enough for you? You stupid little fag. I don't get turned down by the likes of you. My polar bear would never stand for it." He snatched up his clothes and stalked out, leaving the door open after him.

I looked down the stairway till the light failed. After closing the door, I drank the rest of the whiskey straight from the bottle, took the letter from my pocket but didn't read it again. Thinking of the corrupting effect Mann had mentioned. Was it merely the war? Being queer in the war, making the war itself queer.

Captain Winfield Jones and his polar bear wasted no time on preliminary niceties. Thirty-six hours later the order came like a very effective click in the clockwork of military machinations. T/3 LORD, James H. 12183139 report with all equipment to HQ G2 CON AD Dijon 1100 hrs. Myron van Stock, Major, MIS ET.

The major was regular army, so many ribbons on his jacket it looked like a Spanish omelet, and his wattles were turkey red. He said, "You're one lucky kid, Sergeant, at ease."

"Yes, sir."

"Don't have to sit around this back area any longer doing zero till you get carbuncles on your rear end. Follow the war, move on into Germany. It says here you've got experience interrogating prisoners."

"DPs, sir."

"Right. Experience. So you can use it. Looks like we've got about a million kraut prisoners on our hands, have to sort 'em out, see what I mean, tickle their balls till they fess up to all the war crimes they've been into. You know the drill, don't you?"

My throat seized up.

"Well, don't you, Sergeant?" snorted the major.

"Yes, sir." I sighed, "I know the drill."

"Right. Sergeant O'Reilly on the way out has all your papers, self-transport from here to Mannheim, Germany. Prisoner of war camp someplace near there. Motor pool is overflowing with jeeps, so you get your own, drive all the way. Cross the Rhine. War could be over any day now. As for those POWs, interrogate the hell out of them, *Okay?*"

"Yes, sir."

"Have a good trip. Uncle Sam says don't go easy on those Nazi bastards. Hear me?"

"Yes, sir," I said, and the echo in my ear was like the death croak of a gopher in the Gobi Desert.

"Dismissed," barked the major.

O'Reilly handed me a packet of orders. My jeep stood outside the gates of the motor pool. A PFC gave me a map, and I was ready to leave.

Fifteen

APRIL–JUNE 1945

That April was the cruelest month.

Freezing rain fell on the ruined roads north, leaving ice in the potholes, and whipped sideways into my face. A spasmodic tic of the left cheek had troubled me ever since Épinal, and it throbbed as I drove.

Beyond Vesoul the road twisted through the Vosges Mountains. In the nearby fields the wrecks of burned-out tanks rusted in the downpour, and the passing villages lay in ashes.

I spent the first night in a place called Felon, thought the name all too appropriate. A family of peasants took me in.

After Colmar, I came to the Rhine, the river huge and oily, smooth, beyond which lay the hateful fief of Hitler, Himmler, Goebbels, and their swinish accomplices, rooting through the garbage of their pestilential regime. Could anyone—*anyone*—doubt that the struggle to do them in—and never mind the ferocity of firebombs falling on defenseless cities—was anything but a very good war? True, the women, children, and outpatients of hospitals perish in the conflagration, but that, alas, as they say, is life.

At all events, while I jolted along beside the embattled river, there came to me from the cumulous sky a song as if from another lifetime, surprising and emotional, the melody, haunting and sentimental, from *Three Comrades*. It had been the dream theme of another Germany, a mawkish movieland country mournfully unlike the nation across the river. Yet the song sang to me still. And Hanno, he had been the incarnation of another Germany too—had he not?—the land of Goethe and the Buddenbrookses, Thomas Mann? So that song sang also of him, to greet him in his homeland. If music be the food of love.

In front of Ludwigshafen the sky collapsed, angry gusts of rain slanting across the blasted network of factories and foundries. MPs sullenly waved their batons toward the makeshift bridge. There was a sign: YOU ARE CROSSING THE RHINE COURTESY OF THE 82ND CORPS OF ENGINEERS. On the other side lay the ruins of Mannheim. They stared down at you as you haltingly maneuvered above the quick black river, and they very clearly were saying, You are not wanted here. Enter at your own risk.

The risk, to tell the truth, was great and unforgiving. No apocalyptic nightmare of catastrophe could ever have prepared you for the sight of that disaster-flattened city. Entire blocks, avenues, city squares, and housing enclaves, edifices of every sort and materials, were shattered, some of these with wrecked flooring suspended like monster slices of concrete cake above the void. No life could thinkably have survived or survive still in such sickening surroundings, made more so by the knowledge that we had done this. Stupefied by the brunt of circumstance, I saw that old women and small children were nonetheless bent beneath the pelting rain, uselessly poking here and there into the muddy debris.

To Thomas Mann defeat and annihilation were of foremost importance. Both lay before you here in harrowing extremity, destruction of an extent to defy comprehension and ridicule compassion. And although I could not have known it, Thomas Mann was even then at work on a book called *Doktor Faustus*, a tale of demonic violence and degradation symbolically akin to National Socialism, evoking yet again the artist's isolation in the world, and as if he'd seen Mannheim, the author speaks of "A destruction that would cry to heaven if we who suffer were not ourselves laden with guilt. As it is the cry is smothered in our throats."

Among the litter of hand-painted, lopsided signs pointing every which way throughout the luckless alleyways of Mannheim there were some for POW Camp 3. It lay a few miles south of demolished suburbs in the direction of Brühl. I found a village of which I never knew the name, a score or more of all-alike stucco houses down the road from the camp, which stretched over acres of mud and barbed wire toward the Rhine.

The house doing duty as camp HQ was the one with the sodden

flag drooping from a pole that had very recently been a tree. The commandant was a major aged anywhere from seventeen to thirty, lamb's wool hair, glassy eyes behind the heavy lenses of steel-rimmed specs, a guarded tightness of mouth, HOMER G. MULDOON, MAJOR MIS lettered on a cardboard wedge. His desk was heaped with books.

He said, "At ease, Sergeant. What are you doing here?"

"T/three Lord reporting, sir."

"I know that. An uncouth officer from Dijon. Name of Sloan, I believe, or was that somebody else? Kindly sit down. Or take a lodestone off your feet." He snickered and stuck a forefinger briefly up his nose. "Tell me then, if you please, what brings you to this nether neck of the woods. I mean, what's your business?"

"I believe I'm intended to interrogate POWs, sir."

"Nonsense. Nothing like that takes place here, I'm happy to say. It's bad enough as is, the MPs and Lagerführers martyrizing whomever they please. For proper interrogations we send them to Heilbronn or to Bad Kreuznach. Shunt them about by truckload like livestock or I might say like half-alive stock. A couple died only yesterday, I'm told."

"Then what am I to do, sir?"

"I have no idea. Do you speak Latin?"

"Of course not."

"*Tanta stultitia mortalium est.* Seneca. He too lived in times when a human life, including his own, was a paltry proposition. Some elucidation, in any case, seems due. This camp comprises ten stockades, or lagers, as the POWs call them, holding in toto between twenty-five and thirty thousand prisoners. Each lager is commanded by a German Lagerführer chosen by the prisoners themselves. It's a most unfortunate appellation, führer, but there it is. They exercise almost as much authority as an MP and beat the bejesus out of unruly prisoners whenever they feel like it."

"You can't mean to tell me that you tolerate that kind of treatment."

"*Quis custodiet ipsos custodes?* Judge not, Sergeant. Pity you have no Latin. I would gladly have loaned you Seneca. I'm on to Epictetus for the moment."

"So what am I to do, sir?"

"Contemplate, sergeant, contemplate. Inquire of the corporal in the other room. He will tell you which one of the houses down the road will have space available for your lodging. You can make yourself quite comfortable. Selected prisoners from the camp do the house-keeping, and I'm told there's an excellent chef for the mess. Myself, I take my meals at my desk," he said, tapping it. "I've been given to understand that you have the use of your own vehicle. Heidelberg happens to be only a few miles from here. The university is one of the oldest and finest in Europe in case you have the appetite for a taste of Hegel." He smacked his lips as if savoring himself a delectable mouthful.

"It is my duty," he resumed, "as the officer here in charge, and this being your first posting in Germany proper, to advise you of the non-fraternization ruling. It stipulates that United States Army personnel are expressly forbidden to engage in any social—or most especially, I should add, sexual—relations with German civilians, men, women, or children, because the official position specifies that there are no 'good' Germans. Is this clear?"

"Yes, sir."

"Some finesse may be required to define what constitutes a 'social' relation, however. Consider yourself Petronius. Ha ha ha." He smoth-ered his hilarity with wiggly, ink-stained fingers. "Well now, I believe that terminates our business, Mr. Lord. But please feel free to consult me if need be. I don't stand on military etiquette. You may run along now. I imagine you'd enjoy a nice hot bath."

"Thank you, sir."

"Actually I'm Professor Muldoon, Christ Church, Oxford."

"Thank you."

A large black No. 9 marked the house in which I was to be billeted. It looked new but gloomy, a place that, as it were, had no use for itself, molded from the same matrix as its neighbors and clutched in an over-growth of knotted greenery. I'd hardly stopped my jeep before a bare-headed figure ran outside, raising his right arm in a simulacrum of salute, saying, "I Karl, I Karl," pointing to his chest with his other hand. I supposed this must be the POW housekeeper mentioned by Professor Muldoon. In appearance sturdy and healthy, with Nordic fair hair and vivid eyes, he was clean-shaven but ragged in torn field gray ersatz fabric stitched up with twine, "POW" stenciled in black across his shoulders, and his frown of effort as he hefted my duffel bag was quick with malaise. I followed him inside.

My bedroom was a model of mass production, clean but uncomfortable. A hirsute soldier in olive drab underwear sauntered in. He had a pug nose and altogether the look of a pugnacious canine, hair all over him, chest and shoulders.

I said, "Hello."

"You're new," he said. "Welcome to the rain. My name's Beem, Larry Beem. You?"

"Jim Lord."

"Hiya, Jim. You MP?"

"No. MIS."

"MP myself but don't get into the camp that often. The krauts beat up on each other plenty enough without any help from us. Their fucking Lagerführers. Wild animals. So how'd you pull this lousy posting?"

"I don't know. I don't have a thing to do here, really."

"Hush-hush, huh? Myself I don't got much to do either. Mostly I cruise around Mannheim, look around for GIs hanging out with girls, I pinch 'em, nonfraternization slipups, you know, I could turn 'em in for it, so we settle for a carton or two. Easy score, easy fuck, the girl gets three or four ciggies, a pack if Joe shoots the moon, and I'm putting away pig money. You into the market?"

"Not really."

"Rich already, huh? Well, anytime you want a fifth, a carton, a camera, a box of candy, I'm your man. You outrank me, I'm a corporal, but back in Kentucky I'm a colonel, okay? We'll get along fine. Our boy Karl, he'll do spit and polish for you, good kid, Karl, scared of his shadow, and if he doesn't do things right, you whack him. They expect it."

"I'm sure everything will be fine," I said. "Which reminds me. Where's the mess?"

"House Thirteen, right down the way, hog heaven if you like sauerkraut."

I didn't, but I ate it.

A sunless slackening of rain lifted the sky slightly the next morning, chill though it still was, and I went to visit the camp. The entrance gate lay half a mile up the road. There were guard towers along the high perimeters of coiled wire, though I could see no guards up there, only searchlights. Two MPs loitered at the gate with carbines in hand, pistols, batons, and handcuffs at their web belts. One of them, a lanky jackknife of a fellow, unshaven and unsmiling, said, "What do *you* want?"

"I want to go inside," I snapped. He was a private.

"Waste of time, Sarge. Every man in there's been picked clean. Not a single wristwatch, camera, Iron Cross, belt buckle, fountain pen, billfold, not even a single pfennig left on them. Except maybe for generals. A general, he can stare you down. And the place stinks to high heaven. Maybe another corpse since yesterday in that mud. Who knows? Who cares?"

"I care," I said. "I'm going inside. Open the gate."

"Okay, okay. Be my guest." Unchaining the steel uprights, he shoved the gate partway open, and I walked through.

It was a bureaucracy of mud: inhabited by men of mud, shifting in the smear of drab daylight from side to side beyond the barbed wire in the stinking suck of the mud made even muddier by the shift of imprisoned feet, while their shapeless clothes were the garments of mud, hands and faces glaucous smudges of animal disgrace. Épinal had been horrible. This was worse. Épinal was a happenstance of the war, displaced persons held in places and conditions determined by circumstantial expedience, and if they were grim, that was bad luck. POW Camp 3 was deliberately degrading, a prison improvised in the open air for prisoners mass produced by the war, and if they were miserable, all to the good, for they should have known better than to go to war in the first place.

From the gate a broad avenue of mud ran down a slight slope quite far—hundreds of yards anyway, distances difficult to determine in that mire—and on either side behind the high fences lay the lagers, each with its own gate, a wretched hut alongside it and the Lagerführer, a glowering gorilla swinging in his right hand—of all things—a golf club, while behind him cowered the thousands of prisoners, pitiful, filthy, hungry, defeated soldiers, deprived of dignity and robbed of valuables, with invalid eyes and bloodless skin. Those near the fence as I slogged along saw me but didn't see me, nor did they have to turn away in order to be absent if I paused to seek a glance in passing. Their mortal indifference seemed to demand my own as rightful consideration due to the hapless. But I couldn't disregard the feeling of sympathy. It came like the flux in the veins, as if life-preserving, the humanity of mankind—well, I can't say I was aware of it, only the force of feeling.

Slop-slopping through the mud, I trudged down the avenue. At the far end awaited the only MP inside the wire, a gangly fellow, his helmet a size too large for him, his face strained by anxiety. He said, "You going somewhere?"

"Looks like I'm there already," I said.

"Could be. What's your mission?"

"Call it a tour of inspection."

"Call you a tourist? Trip to the zoo?"

"Well, I'm not here for the fun of it. And by the way, what are the Lagerführers doing with golf clubs?"

"Some officer asshole turned up with a bagful, so they use them to beat up on the other prisoners. They yelp something fierce. Oh, these krauts. Look at them."

I did, and saw immediately a difference in the lager to his left. Less crowded, less afflicted, peopled by figures less gray and glum, standing in uniforms less tattered and colorless. And there was no baboon brandishing a golf club. Of course. All these men were officers. And as I stared at them through the barbed wire, they stared back without a blink of subservience, stepping gingerly in the mud. Oh, yes, at least they had the mud, and because their lager was at the bottom of a slope, they had more of it than the enlisted men, as if the soil of their homeland acknowledged the deference due their rank by providing deeper and stickier mud in which they could demonstrate superior endurance of warfare's inconveniences. To observe their humiliated hauteur was wonderfully satisfying.

"I'll have a look inside," I said to the MP.

He said, "They ain't real friendly."

"That's why they're officers," I said as he unchained the gate and let me pass through.

These prisoners did not bear on their backs the POW stigma but carried it in their eyes with hatred and contempt. *They* were proud and honorable warriors; we were vulgar gunslingers, who, like the despicable Russians, had clinched tawdry victory by overabundance of men and matériel, not by the time-honored tactics of classical warfare. The mere set of their lips as they stood aside to let me pass expressed their superiority. Yes, here were the supermen who had led their regiments to exterminate inferior beings called Jews, Slavs, Gypsies, homosexuals, and other "undesirables" as a useful sideline to the business of annihilating the enemy.

In the center of the lager a makeshift shelter had been set up: four poles forming a square of roughly a hundred feet supporting several sheets of corrugated tin cobbled together to form a flimsy roof, the sides open to the wind, wet, and cold. Beneath this miserable pretense of refuge from the elements flickered a wispy fire, and around it six or seven POWs squatted, holding frail hands toward its futile warmth. Why this little group deserved a pitiful protection from the rain was evident as soon as you came near. They were generals. The red and gold flashes on their collar tabs made it imperiously plain.

These, then, were men who had given the *orders* to do evil, obeyed the mad whims of Hitler, and known exactly what was meant by Auschwitz and Treblinka and Belsen and a thousand other places of unthinkable use. If they had not actually *given* the orders, they'd done nothing to interfere with their implementation. I stared down at them precisely as if this place *were* a zoo and they were the prisoners, denizens of the reptile house, their unblinking eyes fixed like those of murderous vipers. In their haughty venom they clearly saw me as an undistinguished bungler from a country without tradition or honor, come to meddle in the glorious game of European history.

The drama of imprisonment is the drama of guilt, indifferent to extenuating circumstances. These generals wore their liability with defiant competence, like the ancestral armor standing in the vestibules of their castles. I wore mine with uncomfortable compunction. The burlesque playlet has to be enacted on both sides of its context in order to provide a right and desirable catharsis. The drama of imprisonment applies to the captors as pertinently as to their captives. The dehumanizing factor inevitably prevails whenever captors not only administer with impunity but superintend with complacency the misery of their prisoners.

A sallow sun shone the next morning through a temporary cleft in the clouds, deciding me to go for a ride through the ruins of Mannheim. Who knew what lucky prize of war might turn up on a street corner? I took along a carton of Luckies just in case. What turned up was neither a prize nor lucky but something that history would never forget.

Driving through the rubble at 10 mph, followed by the murderous stares of arthritic old men and dusty children, I turned and returned aimlessly, then suddenly in the distance of a surprising straightaway I glimpsed a serendipitous flash of green. It was a small public garden surrounded by a chain-link fence. Jagged fragments of cement sundered from an adjoining building lay on the grass, but nonetheless a few clumps of tiny blue flowers bloomed in pretense of spring. Several women with small children sat here and there on metal benches. To the right of the entrance hung a white sign with bold black lettering: EINTRITT FÜR JUDEN IN DIESE GARTEN IST STRENG VERBOTEN.

No translation was needed in order to understand the vile message of those black words, simple and terrifying, words that plunged you deep into the abyss of unbearable inhumanity. I parked, astonished that such a memento of an evil regime had remained in place after the people responsible for it were no longer in any position to enforce its purpose. Peering through the fence at the children playing in the grass, I thought how heavily the guilt of that sign must weigh upon their games, upon games of their progeny and their progenies' progeny and how at the same time the infamy inherent in it harked backward and backward in human history to the pristine Garden of the first morning and to the guilt of that tragic day.

The sign was fixed to the fence at each corner by heavy wire looped through the links and very solidly set when I tugged at it. So I fetched the tool kit from my jeep and attacked the wire with pliers, screwdrivers, and hammer. It took some time and trouble to detach the fucking thing, my pounding very noisy. I was surprised that the women inside appeared not to notice: a soldier in enemy uniform removing from their garden fence the sign that had been placed there by the municipal authorities, as if its message had been Keep Off the Grass. Why one would want to tear down such a sign was self-evident. Why to preserve it, however, hints at something perhaps shadowy and troubling, a message intended to effect the future. At the moment I simply put it into the jeep and drove back to Camp 3, where the thousands of prisoners milled miserably in the mud.

I wondered what Karl, the POW housekeeper, must have thought when he saw the sign propped on a chair in my bedroom. I'd concluded he was a pensive, emotional boy, melancholy as anyone would be when confronted with national catastrophe, disgrace, and captivity. I felt sorry for him but kept the feeling to myself, for his fate, after all, was not nearly so wretched as the prisoners', even the generals', surviving and sleeping in the mud, fed twice a day on watery stew, while Karl slept downstairs in the kitchen and ate C rations.

Heidelberg, lying a dozen miles away on the Neckar River, was a lonely, beautiful old town, not a soul on the streets when I drove over there a couple of days after finding the sign expelling *Juden* from the garden. It was after curfew, all Germans *streng verboten* to appear out-of-doors after 6:00 p.m., leaving U.S. servicemen masters of the landscape. The town was undamaged except for the bridges, which had been blown up for no strategic good. It was not a large and jolly place. You could walk from one end of the *Haupstrasse* to the other in half an hour, passing ancient sandstone buildings both baroque and neoclassical, reverie-laden squares with statues on high pedestals, empty streets haunted by the good-looking ghosts of students carousing, dueling, strolling arm in arm under the linden trees, singing:

> *Oh glorious old fellowship*
> *Whereto have you vanished?*
> *This golden time,*
> *So free and unfettered,*
> *It will never return.*
> *I search here and I search there,*
> *I do not find it anywhere.*

Old Heidelberg offered as its climactic focus of grandeur its vast and towering castle, a mammoth edifice of rusty sandstone set atop a steep incline high above the town. A fourteenth-century fortress, it was repeatedly rebuilt, aggrandized, and redesigned, Gothic, Renaissance, and baroque in style, stormed, subdued and burned, left at last partially in ruins, a hulking behemoth of bastions and dungeons tyrannizing the tranquil town below. Not a monument of beauty, it nonetheless was beautified for me the first time I saw it by dappling shafts of sunset setting fire yet again to the sightless windows and shattered battlements.

Then, too, a tidbit of Hegel, yes or no, pace Professor Muldoon, there was Heidelberg University, old and venerable as any in the world. Here the great thinkers of the Western mind had found welcome for the weightiest of ratiocinations. Philosophy and physics went to bed together, and both woke up refreshed. During the Thirty Years' War, Heidelberg fostered flickers of intellect amid the furies of faith. So everything jollied along for centuries, students sang, dueled and drank, until one day National Socialism made crime the law of the land. Professors of logic surveyed their prospects and, surmising that probity was likely to trouble the credentials of tenure, saw intellectual disgrace in the pedagogy of Jewish colleagues and dutifully denounced them, adding hortatory condemnation of the corrupt and degenerate writings of authors like the brothers Mann, Sigmund Freud, Walter Benjamin, Bertolt Brecht, Hannah Arendt, and their like. Whereupon swastika-intoxicated students ran amok, building bonfires in a hundred university courtyards to burn alive the books of German enlightenment and conscience.

I once again walked up to the camp after chow in the morning. The MP said, "We told you. They've been picked clean. Nothing worth piss in there."

I said, "I'm not in the business."

But I was, if you could call it business to be so concerned by the prisoners' plight that you wanted almost to participate in the day of reckoning. Not in the very vicissitudes, no. I said "almost." It was, if ever there was one, a proving ground for fellow feeling, an assessment for all of empathy.

My methodical inspection of the lagers was unwelcome. The prisoners' animosity grew clearly more bitter and pronounced as my curiosity appeared to taunt their indignity and humiliation. Which was the very last thing in the world that I wanted. So my scrutiny abated. With one curious exception. This was the first lager to the right beyond the main gate. From it there emanated an aura quite unlike the mood of

all the other lagers. Its prisoners were cleaner, more adequately attired, and, perhaps, less hostile, if indeed hostile at all, than the sullen
occupants of the other lagers. The Lagerführer, moreover, was conspicuous for absence of the golf club. He held only a shabby riding
crop. On an impulse I asked in English, "You don't play golf?"

"No, sir, I don't," he rejoined in faultless Oxonian English. "I have
never thought it worthwhile to chase a little rubber ball across the
countryside." He must have been about forty, clean-shaven, gaunt but
subdued, his thin smile studied and vigilant.

I said, "You are German, I presume."

"Quite. English by professional circumstances, you might say,
third-floor butler at Claridge's Hotel in London for seventeen years.
Until recalled home by family obligations at the worst possible moment. Lorenz Locher at your service, sir."

"I see. Very interesting. Your circumstances are certainly different
today, and your lager is different from the others too. Not only because you don't play golf."

He laughed, though with his mouth tight shut. "It is so," he said,
"and I can tell you why. If your interest is keen, that is."

"Please do."

"This is a *Passierscheinlager*." He picked from his pocket an orange
slip of paper printed in German and flipped it up and down. "A safe-
conduct pass. American airplanes dropped clouds of them over our
front lines, promising good treatment by the Geneva Conventions for
all men ready to surrender bearing this paper. So. All the men you see
in this lager are Passierschein men."

"I see. And all of you are held apart, I suppose, because you would
be considered almost as deserters by POWs taken in the field."

"Quite. With attendant unpleasantness."

"And every man in this lager has one of these little papers,
has he?"

"Must have. There are some men, to tell the truth, who needed a
safe-conduct for reasons foreign to the Geneva Conventions—if you
follow my meaning—and how they came by the Passierschein may be
open to question. Is it not so in all armies in all times of war?"

"I follow your meaning," I said. "I'll come to see you again." I
held out my hand through the wire.

He touched it briefly and performed a stylish bow, as if we were in the corridor of the opulent hotel rather than ankle deep in Rhineland mud.

The next day was Tuesday, May Day, and I drove to the camp, having filled my musette with provisions for Locher and his safe-conduct lager. As I came up to the gate, I felt the weight of an almost mineral hush bearing into the camp. One of the MPs leered with the self-importance of sensational news, waiting it out as I came from the jeep, and said, "Hitler's dead. It was in the *Stars and Stripes* this morning."

"Do *they* know?" I asked, gesturing beyond the gate.

"Oh, yeah. Wouldn't want to keep the good news quiet, would you? The yellow bastard blew his brains out. His whore snuffed it with him. The Ivans would have put them in an iron cage, and they knew it."

Or, I thought, strung up their corpses for the malevolent scorn of the mob, as the Italian partisans had done with the abject remains of their hateful duce, hanged by his heels in front of a Milanese gas station.

It had been my idea to have a chat with Lorenz Locher. Inside the wire. Man to man, so to speak. But not now. I didn't expect he'd be mourning the führer. Many of the POWs would, however, now feel doubly humiliated by the cowardly quietus of the man who had demanded, and received, the honor and loyalty unto death of his followers and led them not only to ruin but also to complicity in crimes surpassing in barbarity the statistics of history, leaving them at last leaderless and lost to cope with a legacy of bewilderment and guilt.

I was personally concerned by none of this, was I? My responsibility dwelt in a realm beyond barbed wire, though it acknowledged at the same time the categorical imperative of the wire itself. I stood on the outside looking in at these POWs whether they—or I—liked it or not, because *they* had hastened to obey the summons of a loudmouthed charlatan whose sole incentive was for murder and plunder. And yet what was it? The baffling lure I felt for the far side of the wire, where no raison d'être involved my future. I climbed back into my jeep and drove down to house No. 9, where a very different, rather ludicrous enactment of guilt was even then forthcoming.

Two MP jeeps were drawn up in front. I parked opposite. A minute later four MPs came from the rear of the house, dragging Larry Beem handcuffed between them. When he saw me, he shouted, "It's all a big mistake, you'll see, I didn't do a thing wrong; it's just a big mistake."

One of the MPs yanked up his wrists, while another hit him in the belly with a baton and shouted, "Shut your kisser, boy, black market asshole, big mistake getting caught, you'll live to love the stockade seein' as if you live," and shoved him into the rear of the first jeep, Beem groaning, and they drove away, tires strident on the gravel.

Locher greeted me as if we were on the sidewalk of Bond Street. When I suggested coming through into the lager itself, he opened his gate with courtesy suited to the welcome of a duke to his suite. I unpacked my musette. Cigarettes, soap, chocolate, coffee, and—I had hesitated, but why not?—a few packs of Wrigley's spearmint. I was surprised but shouldn't have been when Locher's thanks were no more effusive, though no less courteous, than in receiving a duke's gratuity. He added that his men would be ever so grateful.

At Claridge's he had commanded a platoon of underbutlers, valets, and waiters. Servants with such polish would become extinct in the postwar ebb of elegance. Not to mention the clients. Oh, the incomparable refinement, the breeding, the decorum, the exquisite sophistication and absolutely superlative chic of those clients. No one could equal the delicacy with which the marquess of Cholmondeley could slip you a banknote.

Locher clearly yearned to be back in the Claridge's of yore but was too lucid to imagine that that antinomian world of bright young people had a hope in hell of surviving the worst war of all time. It was the man's lucidity, his refusal to fool himself despite the plentitude of his loss, that made him likable, even estimable, and it was clear that the men in his lager respected him for what he was, not for what he could do. Besides, the fact that this was the Passierscheinlager imparted to its occupants a nimbus of moral decency that almost restored their atavistic esprit de corps as gallant men-at-arms.

I noticed, however, one fellow who kept apart, standing alone with a certain hauteur that made him seem taller than the others, wearing a strange cap set at a rakish angle, as if he were purposefully calling attention to himself. It was this, I suppose, that drew my attention. I can't say. What is true, in any case, is that I felt the urge to make some sort of move in relation to him.

"Who is that one," I said to Locher, pointing, "the one standing by himself?"

"Oh, that one," Locher said, "you would notice him. Everyone does. He's our enigma."

"So?"

"We know nothing about him. Except that he's Romanian. Must be middle class, had an education—he speaks French—because no one speaks Romanian. His name is Vasile Larrianu, lance corporal of the North Bukovina Fusiliers. He gave me his serial number, blood type O, and that's all we know. Strict Geneva Conventions. He won't answer questions."

"You believe he has something to hide."

"Well, sir, a man who has nothing to hide hides nothing. If you refuse to answer *any* questions, there must be at least one to which the answer might be compromising. Otherwise where would be the luxury of candor?"

I shrugged. "At least you know that he has a safe-conduct pass. Otherwise he wouldn't be here with the rest of you, would he?"

"He has the pass, yes, I've seen it. But how did he come by it? Not in Romania, sir. Those passes were dropped by your aircraft only above our lines."

"Well, the war has displaced millions of persons without good reason."

"It has. It has. The war has done the devil's own work. Who knows what, or where, or when? Millions of mouths have been silenced that might have told the story."

"I'd like to talk to him."

"Do as you wish, sir, certainly."

Corporal Larrianu turned as I approached so that we would be face-to-face, and he saluted very smartly. Neither good-looking nor handsome, yet he had well-made features that might have been comely had he not been so severe, taut, dour, a face of iron. His was not an attractive or a convivial presence.

I said in French, "At ease," and he let his hand fall but remained stiffly at attention. "You speak French."

"Larrianu, Vasile," he said, voice harsh and strained.

"Where do you come from?" I asked. He didn't reply, his eyes offering no sign of having heard, and I repeated the question . . . to the same effect. This reaction was not insolent, not even indifferent but simply deliberate silence. In the face of my superiority this was exasperating, foolish, and haughty. I strode away to the lager gate, where Locher waited. I said, "You're right. He's difficult, *your* enigma, and you're welcome to him."

After the detention of the heinous Beem, I was alone in house No. 9, alone, that is, with Karl, the POW man of all work, who saw to it with conscientious industry. We went about our separate occupations in silence. Now and then nonetheless our eyes met across the gulf riven by the war, and a speechless glance could say that we were much alike save for the artifice of the uniform. Naturally I saw him as a man, who was in fact physically appealing, fair, sturdy, virile, though circumstances set aside the suggestiveness of that view. I swear I never gave cause for the least assumption. Maybe it was the sun.

That afternoon the chilly drizzle of deceitful springtime suddenly ceased, and a flood of sunshine drenched the soggy fields. I went outside behind the house and sat down on a hummock of cement, lifting my face, eyes shut, to the unprecedented warmth. It was the rustle of grass that first hinted, then the scent of his sweat, before I opened my eyes. He was seated next to me, grinning; steel blue eyes fixed me full in the face. This had never happened before, and I wondered. Very quickly but softly he spoke to me in German.

I said, "I don't speak German. *Nicht sprechen deutsch.*"

He laughed quietly, and he must have known how winningly, because he put his hand on my knee and ever so gently began patting it as if, I thought, my leg were the rump of a pet dog. And he had to have known that he could allow himself this liberty, that I would not rebuff him, that indeed, I would agree to his touch. And I did. It had been so long. How long had it been since a man's smile and his touch had stirred such feeling? And it would have been so easy. We were alone.

He laughed. His teeth were brilliant and glistened. I hardly had time to be surprised when he put his hand on my thigh and pressed hard, cocking his head to one side in a quick movement, a question, a challenge, and the pressure hardened. So that my body understood what he wanted. And of course my own desire was quickened. I could see the thrust in his pants, and I knew how certain he was that he could have me.

But I couldn't accept him. My muscles pulsed with willingness, but I couldn't. There was too much pity, too much need, too much disparity. Our eyes told a story too foreign to us both to accept the longing of our bodies. I lifted his hand, holding it long enough to say "enough," then set it aside and stood up and went around to the front of the house to my jeep and drove away. I drove up and down the Rhine till dusk, had something to eat at the USO in Wiesbaden, and that was that.

My luck, so to speak, with Karl came the very next morning, because Frank arrived while I was eating toast. The house was never again empty. Nor did Karl and I exchange glances. Anyway, we moved out of there, Frank and I, five days later.

Frank Fasolo, a man of Italian extraction though no relation to the painter, aged thirty-one, a sensitive, intelligent graduate of Yale Law School, methodical in the dynamics of personal relations, was a gift of the gods to me. We were good friends by the time we'd finished lunch together that first day. Frank was a staff sergeant, spoke Italian, and had seen action as an MIS agent attached to an infantry division during the campaign northward after Cassino. His division had been relieved after crossing the Po, and like me, he had been posted from place to place for a reassignment that had no agenda and led to a bootless interview with Major Muldoon.

It was his experience as a young attorney, I think, as a counselor prepared to hear anything from anyone, that made our friendship firm and immediate. He was ready to listen, and I was eager to talk. The intricacies of intimacy were his business, and they were my good. Frank had the face of a beast of burden, which he was if you counted the weight of confidences he patiently carried. His features were wan and fleshy; he wore gold-rimmed glasses, was untidy in attire, and spoke with a silvery baritone. In short, you never met anyone more pleasing.

I ran into Major Muldoon in front of his mildewed HQ. He returned my salute and said, "Home sweet home," sniggered, flinging his left hand toward camp, adding, "if there's anything left of home besides a handful of filth, that's where they'll all be going. *Vae victis.* This camp will be the first to close when the surrender unconditional is signed. And they'll have to walk home, be it to the banks of the Black Sea."

It was a Tuesday. By midmorning the cloud cover had lifted and already everyone knew that the instrument of unconditional surrender had been signed by the German chief of staff. We even knew that Ike had refused to be present in order to manifest his contempt for an officer who had cringed before a criminal. The camp was quiet. Now that the war was over no one in point of fact could very well be a prisoner of it. The prospect of freedom, however, must have seemed subject to misgiving, in a homeland itself subject to armed occupation by the very forces that had wreaked unparalleled devastation upon its cities.

So we strolled off toward the Rhine as we talked with lulling confidence of having been on the right side and believing that *our* war had been a good one. It had, in any case, been necessary, but not pure, never beyond the call of compassion. For, after all, no government, no social system are ever so wholly bad that every one of their people may be considered without any virtue whatsoever.

Still . . . how deeply did the work of evil penetrate the body politic. U.S. authorities had already published a detailed account of the mass murder of Jews at Auschwitz. Thereafter accounts had continually proliferated of other death camps throughout occupied Europe, and in fact by the war's end the Nazis were administering some five thousand so-called labor camps and prisons, in which it was policy that maximum inmates die.

Conditions in these places of detention had been so monstrous as to beggar the most nauseating fantasy. How was it that the citizens of a state with an advanced economy and complex educational system could have entrusted their fate to a mob of uncouth and nefarious thugs capable of organizing such vast crimes? Was it possible that they didn't know, was it thinkable that they failed to catch a glimpse of what was going on in their backyards, or was it, after all, that they simply preferred to ignore the horrors being perpetrated in their name?

Just in case, however, that it was possible, thinkable, and preferable, the American war information agency (Amerikanischen Kriegsinformationsamt) published a sixteen-page pamphlet, entitled *KZ*, of text with detailed photographs of five concentration camps (Bildbericht aus fünf Konzentrationslagern), leaving absolutely nothing to the imagination and defying any imagination to ignore the human capacity to make garbage of mankind. The camps are Buchenwald, Belsen, Gardelegen, Nordhausen, and Ohrdruf. The photographs show mounds and troughs and stretches of naked, skeletal, emaciated human corpses, flung helter-skelter to the elements, staring death's-heads, heaps of bones like driftwood, and infant cadavers bloated and rotting. A vision of hell. Gardelegen, incidentally, lies ninety miles west of Berlin in the lovely Saxon hill country.

In case the meaning of *KZ* had been lost on recipients it also contained photographs of German civilians brought at gunpoint by Allied personnel to view the unspeakable evidence of the camps. It has been said that the downfall of a regime reveals its true character more clearly than all the hopes and promises of its ascent. What, then, could these granite-faced burghers conceivably have thought when faced with the proof of their leader's crimes? How did the fool's gold glory of Wagnerian torchlight pageants stand up to the spectacle of a hundred thousand stinking and leprous corpses?

Some of those summoned to learn what *KZ* meant were compelled to assist in burying the murdered prisoners, and their preparedness to do that was watched with diligent attention by British and American officers. It amazed—and disgusted—them to see no display of emotion on the faces of these men and women, no sense of responsibility or guilt, as they went about their macabre tasks under the vigilant scrutiny of armed guards, as if *they*—honest and dutiful citizens—were criminals.

I said, "But who are *we* to pass judgment?"

"Well," said Frank, "somebody must."

Orders came for Fasolo and Lord from Continental Advance Section HQ. A house had been requisitioned for our use in the Vangerowstrasse in Bergheim on the outskirts of Heidelberg. When we got there, we found that the occupants, an elderly couple, both white-haired and rather rickety, had been given one hour to vacate the premises and were surveyed in the process by an MP master sergeant wearing a Luftwaffe aviator's leather helmet and an MP private brandishing a machine pistol.

The woman was weeping and screeching in German, while her husband loaded bundles of clothing, a sack of turnips, and a battered barometer into an antiquated baby carriage, and the sergeant snarled, *"Macht schnell!"* A young couple in ragged pajamas stood to one side, doubled up with laughter. It was over soon enough. The destitute old folks plodded away in search of relatives or friends to take them in. The hilarious spectators were Poles, forced workers dragooned from the East to labor in Nazi factories. They were now to occupy the requisitioned house along with Frank and me, prepare our meals—goulash galore—shine our shoes, launder clothes, make beds, and tend to the meager vegetable garden in back, all of which added up to seventh heaven for them and commendable comfort for us.

Frank Mariano Fasolo was born in Brooklyn, brought up in a large, old-fashioned brownstone house, almost a mansion, in Park Slope, spacious enough to lodge Frank's parents, grandparents, and one great-aunt, all of whom to their everlasting honor dwelt together in judicious compatibility. Such a serene exception to the contentiousness of human nature was surely due to the atavistic affinity of the Fasolo men for civil harmony. This disposition was already theirs in the airy city of Urbino, from which they had immigrated in 1868, mindful perhaps of a famous remark made by the first duke of Urbino, who when asked what is most necessary in ruling a kingdom had said, *"Essere umano"*—to be human. Frank's grandfather Giovanni Fasolo had been a justice of the peace, known and respected for the generous informality of his decisions, especially liberal toward youthful offenders. His son, Enrico, Frank's father, began his legal career in the minor tribunals, police court, traffic court, and county court, graduating slowly to state district court, becoming a close friend of Fiorello La Guardia, and eventually a judge of the appellate court, whose charges to juries were more than once compared with Socratic dialogues by *The New York Times*. Was it any wonder, then, that Frank, having listened to the language of justice as a child, should make the law the rule of his adolescent aspirations and adult achievements? The family said, "Why not?"

MIS HQ, heedful as ever to the desideratum of a cushy venue, had settled into the Hotel Europa, Heidelberg's best, on the Bahnhofstrasse. We went there to sign in. The hall porter, a GI in a shiny blue suit, asked what was our business. When informed of our desire to find out, in fact, what this was, he said we'd have to wait. We waited for an hour and three-quarters.

A warrant officer received us in a large bedroom and told us in five minutes that we would be advised when our qualifications made it necessary, not before. Frank asked whether he might apply to the office of the adjutant general for possible service as a lawyer and was told to take the bus to Frankfurt-am-Main and apply to the military government HQ. In short, we were on our own with Mr. and Mrs. Poland.

Frank, needless to say, went to Frankfurt and found that his jurisprudential versatility proved serviceable, with the result that he commuted up and back seventy-five miles every day. That was Frank.

Bored and superfluous, I drove my jeep here and there at random around the storied countryside, a prosaic tourist in search of a sight for very sore eyes. I found it, of course, by chance, or it, rather, found me because inherent necessity had to. I like to believe that: a climactic coincidence in my queer war.

I was driving along the left bank of the Neckar due east of Heidelberg eight or ten miles, no more, a road I'd taken already more than once, taken, to be sure, without troubling to study the diminutive particularities of the landscape. A couple of miles before reaching the humdrum town of Rheinbach, slowing to take a curve in the river, I raised my eyes, and there in the miniature distance of the crest of a green hilltop saw the red-roofed silhouette of a far-off village, beguiling and beckoning below the blue sky above the blue river. It said, "Come up, come up." And who could but hearken to such an elysian summons?

There was a turning to the right. A sign: DILSBERG. Narrowing as it rose, the roadway wound around and around the hillside beside fields alive with billowing cherry blossoms, leading up steeply at last to a towered portal, in which, perhaps, the medieval portcullis had threatened wayfarers. And indeed, there was something strangely minatory about this portal, as if I'd seen it before, had had cause to beware of it. I couldn't say why or what. Anyway, there I was, and I drove through over the rough cobblestones up to a wide space, hardly a square, between ancient, half-timbered houses. There were no other vehicles, no people. Dilsberg stood solitary and silent in the midst of the sky as if held there forever by enchantment, a home to the romantic imagination, where the adversities and lamentations of the wide world were mere surmise in the valley below. No iniquity need seek atonement here.

The handsomest house rose to my right, three stories tall, a double staircase of russet stone in front with a wrought-iron balustrade of floral tracery and across the facade the word "Gasthaus." This was in mid-May, and the nonfraternization rule was still very much in force. *Stars and Stripes* said, "In heart, body, and spirit every German is a Hitler." That was nonsense, of course, and horny GIs everywhere were welcomed by and large by fräuleins glad to do them a favor in exchange for three cigarettes, the going rate; a pack was opulence. Though not eager to pick up a girl, or, for that matter, even a boy, I hesitated to go into the gasthaus. But Dilsberg was a place apart, an otherworldly, spellbound refuge from workaday worries. I went in.

To the left a stout wooden bar, several vacant tables and battered chairs, derelict upright piano to one side, and a dozen pairs of antlers nailed to the wall. Behind the bar a gray woman, hair pulled back above a heavy brow and black button eyes, a knife-thin mouth, not an inviting countenance, I, to be sure, an enemy soldier in uniform, one of those come to devastate her homeland and deflower her daughters. What could I expect? She said something in German, which I imagined must mean to ask what I wanted, and then smiled, a gleam of warmth wholly transfiguring her presence. So I said, *"Bitte, ein Bier,"* about the limit of my German. A stein was forthcoming.

I sat down at a facing table, from which I could look out the door across the rooftops at the sky above the Neckar Valley. Surely handsome young students had sat here too and sung their fervent songs in bygone centuries, and—who knows?—maybe this room had heard *my* song as well, the selfsame melody of *Three Comrades* that had for years accompanied my dreams and disappointments. I glanced about as if in anticipation of a dulcet echo, and my fancy fell upon the piano. It was an instrument no less dishonored than the one that had caused me so much trouble long ago, the wretched Mason & Hamlin that had betrayed me in the Hotel Chelsea. But here it stood, nor was I a feckless rookie now, nor was Dilsberg Atlantic City.

Turning, I beckoned to the elderly barmaid, pointed to the piano, then to myself, holding out both hands and wiggling my ten fingers. She smiled again, and with what affable goodwill, nodding, gesturing cheerful consent. So I drew up a chair, sat down, and opened the dusty cover. The keys were yellowed but all there, more or less in tune, tinny and twanging but not inharmonious, plangent as a piano of a hundred years ago might have sounded. Which may have been all to the good.

Anyway, might as well begin with Beethoven's Rondo, propitiating the despairs and demons of another time. My fingering fell easily into the unforgettable music, and it sounded all right, jingly and slightly asthmatic but blameless, alive at last with the innocence of the twelve-year-old composer. Behind me a gentle clapping of hands, I turned, bowed my head in a mock acknowledgment of applause. An understanding between performer and public, a blink of complicity. Well, I thought, why in the world not?

So I turned again to the keyboard, thinking again that it had surely accompanied such moving songs from the emotional past long ago when the three inseparable soldiers marched away into the gloaming, and my usual fingers on the warped and discolored keys automatically brought forth the soulful Germanic melody I knew by heart. This time, however, there was no semblance of applause. The momentary quiet broken by her voice: "'Übers Meer grüss ich dich, Heimatland.'" I didn't understand, didn't have to in order to realize that some emotive sentiment had been touched, and that that was enough.

Leaving some scrip on the bar, I nodded, she nodded, and I went out. Driving away over the cobblestones out beneath the fortresslike portal, I knew that I would come back. This immemorial village perched on its hilltop like the aerie of a baronial eaglet cast such a spell of safe and unimpeachable rightness. You'd have to be a fool to let its opportunity go.

Sex seldom bothered me during those weeks, and even when I thought of sexy boys in their underwear in shadowy rooms, I backed away from the too-simple solicitation. Besides, there were no boys or rooms. Sometimes in the street you'd come across a kid in an ill-fitting suit tricked together from an old uniform, a fortuitous student, but then you'd find he limped or lacked an arm or had St. Vitus's dance.

Frank said the absence of sexual élan might be caused by the psychic stress of warfare.

I said, "Queer war."

He smiled and said, "Oh, Lord, Lord Jim."

Dilsberg waited. It insisted. Reluctant to submit too soon to its enchantment, I also waited. Some days, a week.

The lady behind the bar produced a stein before I asked, then disappeared. Five minutes later she came back, followed by a stooped, aged man with a wattled face and a too-plump but bright-eyed little girl.

" 'Heimatland,' " said the old man, " 'Heimatland.' "

The lady made her fairest smile, held out her hands, wiggling the fingers, and nodded toward the piano. I should have expected it. In fact, faced with the appeal, I had. It was not Beethoven they wanted. So I played *Three Comrades*. I played it twice. And my select public applauded.

"Good, good, good," said the old man, his voice cracking for emphasis. "Fine good, my boy. You play singing music, you do. 'Übers Meer grüss ich dich, Heimatland.' From over the sea, I greet you to my homeland." My surprise evident, he added, "Yes, your language I know. *Englische* friend useful to it."

"Thank you," I said sincerely.

It was the greeting to his homeland that touched the moment. The singing music had sung a hymn to his homeland, not to camaraderie or to glorious old fellowship. But my emotion had long been fixed upon the blood promise of everlasting friendship always, always. And now devotion to one's homeland too; the faith of patriotism had become vital to the romance. To my amazement. My homeland. The dedicatee of the pseudopoem composed in a transcontinental train in a transport of juvenile verbosity. Certainly my doubts about high principle were widening and widening. Was I prepared to traverse the great divide?

Closing the lid of the piano, I again said thank you and went outside. A narrow street to the left led upward to the crest of the hilltop. There, windowless and sheer, arose the beetling walls of an enormous fortress, its topmost merlons menacing the steep slope below. So Dilsberg had dominated that entire curve of the Neckar Valley, and the minatory impression of its stern portal had by no means been for nothing and indeed seemed intended to say so.

I received a memo to report to the Hotel Europa at nine. The warrant officer was still in his pajamas, bed unmade, a tray of disheveled breakfast on a side table. He said, "Room service stinks. You're going to Heilbronn. Interrogation team at the POW camp. After lunch. Report to Colonel Bragg. He hasn't seen *Gone With the Wind* yet. On your way out tell the hall porter more coffee for Room Twelve."

"How long is this posting for?" I asked.

"Till Sherman burns Atlanta. Get a move on."

Heilbronn had been a prosperous industrial center of over sixty thousand, lying on the upper reaches of the Neckar about fifty miles southeast of Heidelberg. It was a prototype of disaster now. The fire-bombing had been merciless, killing seven thousand Germans in one night. Gutted houses, stumps of walls, heaps of rubble, a shattered cathedral, the scorched facade of a Historisches Museum, puddles of putrid slime, and whirlwinds of cloying dust were pretty much all that remained of the onetime palatial and imperial city. Our HQ was a resurrected building probably whacked together from debris by a detail of prisoners, a U.S. flag trailing from a high pole in front. I was admitted to the office of the CO, an oak leaf colonel, cigar-smoking lout named—according to the celluloid sign on his plywood desk—Braxton Bragg III. I saluted with an incongruous snap, a courtesy acknowledged by the colonel with a flourish of cigar.

"Who the fuck are you?" he inquired, enunciating each consonant with a Dixieland drawl.

"On orders from Heidelberg for interrogation team at the POW camp."

"Well, kiss my ass," said Bragg. "Those boys up there too busy sucking cock to know POW camp's no more, it's DEP camp now, disarmed enemy persons. No more Geneva Conventions hoopla. Heidelberg ain't learned nothing 'cepting two plus two makes twenty-two since the battle of Chickamauga. My granddaddy licked the nigger-loving Yankees there in '63. Yes, sir, War Between the States, that was the real thing, bayonets fixed.

"Now, I never asked nobody for reinforcements round here. Plenty manpower to work over the kraut convicts. Seeing as you're here, you want to hang around we got the village requisitioned up the Lauffen road a ways past the camp you can find a spot to house your ass. Dismissed."

The housing spot was not as comfortable as the house in Bergheim, my roommate a ginger-haired runt who warned me not to piss in the kitchen sink. The DEP camp was larger than Mannheim's Camp 3, must have held far more than a hundred thousand, not one of them comparable to clean and calm Passierschein POWs, and none was a general. There was no mud. The lagers stood on dirt packed down as hard as cement, ranged along roads that formed a cross, the barbed wire higher here, watchtowers more businesslike, and MPs stamping sullenly up and down, submachine guns slung underarm. This was a prison camp that was not fooling, and I thought that some of its inmates who may have had too much to do with Nazi camps must have felt that the Yankee model was beginning to get the idea.

At the main gate there were three MPs whose guns grew nervous as I approached. The principal gorilla bellowed, "Stop it right there, buster, state your business."

"Military intelligence recco," I retorted. "Open up."

"Authorized by?"

"Privileged," I said.

They snarled, jiggled their weapons, languidly unlocked several padlocks, drew back chains, and opened a wing of the gate wide enough for me to squeeze through, slamming it shut afterward with a clang. What, I wondered, needed to be so aggressively guarded on *both* sides of the wire? I saw something soon enough.

The central road sloped slightly to the intersection of the cross-road, then rose beyond it toward a large pyramidal tent at the end. The lagers on either side must have been packed in deliberate excess of capacity. Disarmed enemy persons were pressed against the wire, staring outward with glazed hatred. There appeared to be no Lagerführers here, but the MPs patrolling the roads clubbed the wire with their batons as they passed so that the DEPs had to watch out for their fingers.

The cage stood at the crossroads. Constructed entirely of doubled barbed wire stretched tight around and above four uprights, it was sized so that the prisoner inside could neither stand straight nor sit down but was compelled to crouch with the head bent and knees buckled, arms bound behind him, stripped to the waist, trickles of blood where the barbs had scratched, a hand-lettered sign hanging over his chest: DIESERN KERL HAT BROT VON EINEM JUNGEN GEKHOUT.

I yelled for an MP. "What the hell is this?"

"Punishment," said the MP, a flush-faced giant wearing a college ring with a large red stone on his right hand.

"For what? What does the sign say? I can't believe this."

"He stole some bread."

"He stole bread? Are you crazy? Why would he?"

"Must have been hungry. Ask him, don't ask me. I didn't put him in the cage."

"Well, who did?"

"The tent men. They take care of stuff like this."

"Nobody ever heard of Jean Valjean? I must be going out of my mind."

The prisoner, though he couldn't raise his head to look at us, must have understood we were talking about him, because he began murmuring, *"Wasser, Wasser, hitte, Wasser."*

"Can't you let him out?" I demanded. "He's begging for water. You just stand there and watch him die of thirst?"

"Come on, Sergeant," said the MP. "He's not my lookout. You want to do something, talk to the IPs."

"What's that?"

"Interrogation police. The men in the tent. They're professionals. But watch yourself. I wouldn't want to tangle with them."

And just then, as if to emphasize that the IPs were not men to tangle with, a wild howling came from the tent.

The giant MP squinted and nodded and said, "See what I mean?"

I said, "I'm going straight to Colonel Bragg about this."

"Take a tip from me, pal. Don't! Those guys are the colonel's personal recruits. You unhappy, get plastered."

I went back to the house and pissed in the kitchen sink. The next day I returned to the camp to see whether I had in fact seen what I had seen. I hadn't. That is, to my astonishment—or was I actually out of my mind?—without passing beyond the front gate I saw that the punishment cage and the prisoner inside it as well as the tent of the IPs had all disappeared. Yet I *had* seen what I'd seen. I said to one of the MPs, "What's going on here? Yesterday there was a cage down there, a big tent at the end. Today they're gone. How come?"

"Easy come, easy go. Inspection this afternoon. Three o'clock. International Red Cross. Come to see if the prisoners get treated right, cornflakes for breakfast, plenty of toilet paper, all the comforts of home."

"Yes," I said, "thanks a lot."

And so I was loitering along the road from HQ to the camp well before three. Pointedly on the hour a black Mercedes-Benz stopped about a hundred yards short of the gate. A chauffeur hopped out and opened the rear door. Bragg came out first, followed by a short, stout, elderly gentleman sporting a dove-colored homburg hat, then a captain in riding breeches and black jackboots.

I gave this trio a salute, irritably returned by Bragg as they strode on. Waiting only a moment, I followed behind and whispered to the inspector in French. "Monsieur, monsieur, I know why you are here, and I must speak to you in private. There are terrible things going on in this camp that will be hidden from you. It is your business to know about them."

The inspector turned, indignant, incredulous saliva seeping at the corner of his mouth. "Shtt!" he expostulated, adding in French, "Don't dare speak to me. You have no authority. I refuse to hear you. What I know is what I know. Scat!"

The colonel and captain also turned. Bragg roared, "Who the fuck are you? What's the meaning of this? You report to my office on the double. I'll see you shortly."

My good intention a fiasco, I sidled away and was waiting in the HQ anteroom an hour later when Bragg returned, his face the head of a puff adder. However, he settled into his corpulence and lit a pugnacious cigar.

"You a stoolie, are you?" he hissed. "In Tennessee we'd lynch your ass, roast your gonads on a spit, and I could have your stripes for conduct unbecoming, believe me, boy, put you in the stockade till hell freezes over."

"Yes, sir," I said, "but you won't."

"Won't I just?" he snorted. "Let me tell you, you piece of scum.

You rub my rear end the wrong way, I've got boys out there won't leave a mark on you but you wish you were dead when they go to work. But I'm not going all the way with you. You're not worth it. So you haul ass back to Heidelberg, and remember Braxton Bragg in your prayers. Beat it!"

I did.

En route a low-lying fog and damp mist eddied up from dusk along the Neckar, beading on the windshield, forcing me to lean forward, peering at the uncertain roadway ahead. The lights of rare vehicles loomed abruptly like the fiery eyes of wolves at the edge of the forest. Remembrance of Braxton Bragg, the inspector of the International Red Cross, the prisoner in the cage punished for stealing a crust of bread, the IPs in the tent who wouldn't leave a mark on you but make you wish you were dead, and the hatred in the famished faces of the disarmed enemy persons: none of them would require prayers in order to secure remembrance and indeed would stay with me as stubbornly as wolves in pursuit of straying wayfarers across the snowbound steppe.

What, then, was I meant to do? Battle Colonel Bragg and his interrogation police single-handed? Take the place of the prisoner in his barbed-wire cage? Seek atonement, after all, for trying to right wrongdoing? Had I fled college for fear of being found out to be queer, the gnawing guilt thereof, only to find myself faced with an inference more grave? Maybe. But what about a feeling for the feelings of others? Men imprisoned when prison deprives a man of the world. Men tortured when torture deprives a man forever of his faith in the basic decency of humankind.

I told Frank everything. He said, "The court considers you innocent until proven otherwise."

"Were it so fair," I said.

He told me he knew of worse. Not far from Frankfurt in the Palatinate hills on a bend of the Nahe River was a DEP camp called Bad Kreuznach. By its inmates it was called *Galgenberg*, or Gallows Hills, because so many men, probably a couple of thousand, most from hunger, had died there. John Dos Passos, who had been taken on a tour of the Rhineland camps, thought that deliberate starvation of prisoners was official policy.

Anyway, Frank maintained quite sensibly that war is not waged
with kid gloves, and it is consequently foolishness to suppose that
goodness must prevail amid conditions of meaningless chaos.

I said, "Well then."

All I wanted was to go back to Dilsberg. There dwelt quietude and
romance, songs high above the river valley quivering in the limpid air.
I drove up the serpentine road beside the billowing cherry blossoms,
the green grass now awash with fallen petals like the last act of *Madama
Butterfly*, though it was not Japan's but Germany's homeland that
made music of the rosy afternoon. And I drove again through that
stern portal, my jeep's tires grumbling over the medieval cobbles.

The lid of the piano, I noticed, was open, and the entire instrument
almost gleamed, obviously having been polished and readied to be
played. The familiar barmaid stood behind the bar, grinning. She was
not alone; the plump little girl waited with her but hurried out the
back door as soon as I came in the front. *"Ein Bier,"* said the lady, placing the stein before me. They must have heard the jeep. I took a sip of
foam, waiting. It wasn't long.

Of course I was a curiosity, if not something of a sensation: a soldier in the uniform of their homeland's enemy who nevertheless played
for them the emotional music of homeland. Nor did I appear to expect subservient deference.

The little girl returned in less than ten minutes, followed by the old
man with the Englische friend, another elderly and shriveled gent, a
younger fellow on crutches, his chin in a shiny steel saucer, and a lady
with rouged cheeks and voluminous bosoms wearing several strands
of pearls. My audience. The barmaid wiggled her fingers, whispering,
"'Heimatland,' 'Heimatland.'"

So it was as if I had come solely for this. And I had. The will had
been mine without a forethought, making me its agent, and I was
nothing if not eager to comply.

The piano itself seemed prepared to improve upon its previous
potential, so I tried to play with that additional feeling. And this was
enhanced by audience participation, a muted humming in time with
the song and the hushed murmur of words. I played it three times.
Afterward the patter of applause sounded all right, a music of its own.
I hesitated at the keyboard, wondering what I could offer that might

further such excitement. I knew perfectly well, but the dilemma was also obvious: how to decipher the dimension of the zeitgeist . . .

Standing up, with modest dignity, I hoped, facing my little audience, I offered a slight bow, smiling, and went out the door. I had barely tasted the beer and made no pretense of paying for it, because—was this the truth?—payment enough, and more, had been expected, exacted, and executed via the piano itself.

As I drove back down the cherry-blossomed hillside, I was accompanied by the troubling question, the inevitable one. The applause of the villagers had sounded sincere, an homage, after all, to their own national fervor. And yet the enemy uniform of the performer may have represented more than the national disaster so recently ended.

How could my audience have failed to know that only fifty miles away in one direction and seventy in another lay places where hundreds of thousands of German men—formerly zealous defenders of the homeland—were held in baleful detention. To be sure, certain POWs, the Passierschein, the very young and very old, were already being released, but none of the DEPs of Heilbronn and Bad Kreuznach. And if the Dilsbergers knew that, then what was the dimension of their moral status?

And then . . . then what *else* did they know? What did they think? Of the unthinkable crimes committed in their name? KZ. That flimsy pamphlet that weighed a ton of guilt. Had it made its atrocious way to their tranquil hilltop by the inevitable itinerary of the zeitgeist, and insidiously intruded upon the lovely premise of innocence, blemishing the optimistic geography, not to mention the melody, of the "Heimatland"? No wonder my little audience loved to hear that friendly tune, interpreted for them by their erstwhile enemy, come voluntarily to the lofty fortress to play with the vagaries of enchantment.

Frank had not yet returned from complimentary consultations at Frankfurt-am-Main when I got back from Dilsberg. Besides, I thought I was probably overdoing it as a client. This day, in any case, I had not been forgotten. Courtesy of the APO and Mr. Poland a letter from my home lay on my bed. My mother, as always, had been lovably attentive in providing epistolary proof of parental solicitude. So I sat down with a comfortable sense of durable well-being. It was not to survive.

*I am sorry, Jim dear, to have very bad news to write you. Teddy has
been killed.*

Teddy, my brother just three years younger than I, the white-
toothed, cowlicked, laughing boy, the glory of our household, the
one admired and run after by everyone, beloved by schoolmates, by
chums both rich and poor and especially by girlfriends who would lov-
ingly remember him till they too died, Teddy, audacious and chivalrous,
ready to equally befriend the forgotten man or the fellow Princeto-
nian, impatient to do his duty, shot dead by a Japanese sniper on the
island of Luzon.

Bearing the bad news and the unbelievable weight of it, I went
downstairs, letter in hand, and out into the decrepit garden in back.
Mrs. Poland followed me, but I gestured her away, unable to show my
contorted face, fearful of swelling tears. To grieve, to mourn, to lament, who was I? Tormented already by the unanswerable questions
of Dilsberg. There was a dead rosebush in the garden, incongruous,
and my eyesight settled upon its black, threatening thorns. Teddy was
dead, but it was I who had been awarded a decoration for heroic or
meritorious achievement. Teddy had heroically sought out danger and
achieved the merit of dying whereas I had miserably run away from
the inconvenience of being queer. The driblets of wet dripping down
my cheeks were almost for shame as sadly as for my brother, the tremor
of his face fading even as I clasped the meager proof of his loss and the
sun going down.

Frank came back later, and I found that I couldn't as yet talk about
my mother's letter or the loss of a brother. Instead I listened to stories
of the plight of the prisoners held in cynical disregard of the right of
habeas corpus. Then Mr. and Mrs. Poland served us overflowing por-
tions of goulash washed down with wine from the hillside vineyards of
Bad Kreuznach.

On the other side of the earth the heavily fortified island of Oki-
nawa finally fell to U.S. troops after three months of brutal combat,
some of it hand to hand, costing twelve thousand American lives and
more than a hundred thousand Japs, including two generals, who
committed hara-kiri. Japan had hardly been endeared to me by Teddy's fate, and in fact even before Pearl Harbor I'd felt neither sympa-

thy nor curiosity toward a remote and occult country, which the feudal dictatorships had reluctantly revealed to Western eyes less than a century before. Adding to my distaste was the Japanese liking for sadism and cruelty confirmed by shameless atrocities.

May 8 now more than a month in the past, European GIs began yearning to go home, put their feet under the table, tell tales of winning the war, and feast on apple pie. So the luckiest ones were presently packing the decks of the SS *Queen Elizabeth.*

Nazi POWs behind barbed wire were also yearning to go home, though none knew whether the walls of home, let alone its occupants, were still to be found either in situ or anywhere else or, indeed, among the living. Nevertheless the first of these vanquished survivors were soon to be seen trudging sadly and sullenly along Germany's roadsides. It was difficult not to feel a certain compassion for them, a quickening of empathy. They had fought bravely and much, much too well, defiant to the end even when the end threatened to be theirs.

Then the Satanic question inevitably popped up: Did they *know?* Had they, perhaps, to tell the truth, known from personal experience? The SS, the Waffen SS: their knowledge was settlement in full for services rendered in hell. The Wehrmacht? Were they induced—allowed?, privileged?—to lend a helping hand when necessity came along? Probably. But this probability had not entailed the Teutonic passion for documentary evidence. Thus the everyday infantryman slouched glumly homeward with the companionable presumption of guiltless allegiance to the homeland.

The summons to report to Room 212 at the Hotel Europa did not come as a complete surprise. Colonel Bragg catching up with me, I thought. But I was amused to learn the name of the warrant officer: Andover W. Fleete. New England, no doubt, via Plymouth Rock. I tapped on the door precisely at four.

He was wearing steel gray corduroy slacks and a tan cashmere sweater, "Sit down, Lord," he said, waving a rather languid hand. "It's almost drink time. Tell me, have you seen Larry Beem lately?"

Startled, I had to pull my memory together. I said, "Well, the last time I saw him he was wearing handcuffs."

"Ought to have been wearing ankle fetters too. Tricky son of a bitch, he escaped in transit to Rheims, fooled an idiot MP into thinking he was in charge of himself. You wouldn't have any idea where he'd go, would you?"

"No, I wouldn't. Not at all. What made you think I would?"

"You lived in the same house. Maybe he got friendly and gave himself away, telling you a few secrets. You're something of a smart ass, aren't you?"

"Am I?"

"Have to be. Talking back to Colonel Braggart. Blowing the whistle on him."

"It should have been a siren," I said.

Fleete smiled. "Okay. Let's get back to Beem. How much do you know about the black market?"

"I know about cigarettes, all the PX stuff. Everybody knows about it."

"And everybody does it. I've been known to negotiate a few packs, a carton or two myself. Peanuts. I'm talking about ten tons of coal, a thousand jerricans of gas, that's five thousand gallons, submachine guns by the dozen, field telephones, ten-ton trucks, you name it, you have no idea."

"Gosh," I said.

"Yes," he said. "And it's organized almost entirely by deserters, practically an industry, profits enormous."

"Enormous what? The money here isn't worth anything."

"Oh, they know that. Think gold, diamonds, postage stamps, Rembrandt etchings, anything valuable and small. And if you think big, Switzerland."

"Jesus. All of this goes on in broad daylight?"

"So I'm told. Seems you can bid for a Sherman tank on place de l'Opéra and sell it again right around the corner to a middleman from Indochina. If you get posted back to Paris, you'll see. You might even run into Beem."

"I hope not."

"Well, if you do, watch out. By this time he's likely to be dangerous. Anyway, drink time. What will you have?"

"Very kind. Scotch then."

He picked up the phone, asked for room service, and ordered two double scotches with ice and soda. "The room service, incidentally," he said, "has picked up quite a lot recently."

Fifteen minutes later, when a middle-aged waiter in a well-worn mess jacket brought in the drinks, I saw why. It was Lorenz Locher.

I gulped.

Locher nodded with stylish courtesy as if our meeting, far from being unexpected, had been prearranged. Setting down our glasses, Seltzer water, and a bowl of salted nuts, he said, "Sergeant, what an agreeable surprise."

"To say the least," I said.

"You two know each other?" said Fleete.

"Yes, sir," said Locher. "It was my good fortune to meet Sergeant Lord while still in Mannheim Camp Three. And if I may say so, he showed exceptional fellow feeling for the unhappy plight of prisoners."

"Oh, I'm not surprised to hear it," Fleete said. "It seems that that's his way. Could get him into bad trouble if he's not careful."

"But I am," I said, "very careful. Well, Locher, it looks as though things have turned out nicely for you. Everybody released from the camp?"

"Yes, very nicely, thank you. Our lager was first to leave. Except for the generals. They were taken away before anyone else in civilian cars, arrogant Prussians, as if they'd won the war."

"By the way, what became of the Romanian, the one who refused to answer questions? I forget his name."

"Larrianu, Vasile Larrianu, lance corporal of the North Bukovina Fusiliers. I do know what became of him, I'm sorry to say." He shook his head, holding off the service tray at an awkward angle.

"Well, what is it?" I exclaimed.

"He's dead. We were on foot leaving the camp, a group of us, eighteen or twenty, keeping south of the Neckar, and the first place we came to was Schwetzingen. There was a public toilet by the town hall not far from the palace. He went in. We waited. And he didn't come out. So we forced the door, and there he was. He'd hanged himself. Never could have done that in the camp."

"That's terrible. He was in perfectly good health. Why would he do that?"

"We'll never know."

"He must have had his reason."

"Oh, yes. To do a thing like that, you'd have to have your reasons.

Maybe his reasons were what kept him from answering questions. Maybe that is what killed him."

"How terrible."

"Yes, Sergeant. If I were you—forgive me for saying so—I wouldn't let the drama seem *too* terrible in times like these."

"No?" I said. "Perhaps not. All the same . . . Well, Locher, I'm glad things have turned out so well for you."

"Thank you kindly, Sergeant." He bowed, balancing the tray with practiced flexibility, and left the room.

Fleete steepled his fingers, saying, "Prisoners who commit suicide are escapees, aren't they? What's terrible must be what makes death so compelling."

"I suppose," I said. "I suppose you could say that."

We talked about the Big Three without Roosevelt and Churchill, justice, if possible, to be meted out to major war criminals. I learned next to nothing about Andover Fleete personally. After an hour I went back to Bergheim to have supper with Frank.

The cherry trees had long since ceased blooming. Now the hillside orchard looked like all the rest of the world, and the drive upward to Dilsberg no longer seemed to bathe in the rosy expectations of antinomian enchantment. So be it. This was not my doing. Still, it was my life, and I had idealized that place as a stronghold of the imagination. As I drove up to the familiar portal, however, I saw a different sort of stronghold, the entrance to a question. Nor was that my doing either. It was my decision.

A difference also awaited inside the gasthaus. For the first time I was not the only client. At the center table sat a young couple in front of a single stein. He was very young, and she looked even younger, both of them handsome, a demobilized soldier attired in the ragamuffin remnants of his uniform, tangle of blond hair shadowing pensive brows, laborer's hands awkward in front of him, she slim and pretty, mothlike lashes fluttering shyly above the sky blue eyes, her face untouched by makeup, demure tilt to her shoulders. They did not respond to my inquisitive look, indifference feigned as they glanced to one side, he taking a sip from the stein.

Behind the bar the changeless lady promptly set forward a stein while the plump little girl scurried hurriedly from the back door. Gone, of course, to round up my audience. They, at least, would know what was coming, whereas the soldier and his girl probably had no idea. I had time for a few sips of beer. The spectators were all the same, plus two more dewlapped old men and a small boy with a large brown dog on a leash, making eleven listeners, twelve if you count the dog. A very considerable audience for that faraway, almost fairy-tale town. I felt an authentic shiver of stage fright as the barmaid whispered, " 'Heimatland,' 'Heimatland.' "

Going to the piano, unsure of what I should expect of it, let alone of myself, I thought, What the hell, he's the greatest man of all their history. So I sat down and did my best by the Beethoven Rondo at the decrepit keyboard. It earned a modest patter of hands, having disappointed the expectant gathering. Beethoven indeed!

They longed for something else, something simpler and closer to home, swathed in sentiment, mnemonic, consoling, the ode to the homeland, and they knew that that was what I had to offer and what, indeed, I most desired to give, I the erstwhile victorious enemy sealed at their discretion for their good pleasure.

I played for them. Soulfully. To the dulcet accompaniment of their humming, murmurous words. I played it twice. Then again, a pianissimo reprise with a dying fall. That brought applause. Turning to face the audience, I saw that the young couple too had been moved to wide-eyed appreciation. And I had to wonder what the soldier thought, hearing the sentimental music of his homeland played by this stranger wearing the uniform of the armies that had brought his homeland to ruin and subjection. Well . . . It seemed plain that the audience was not entirely satisfied. They expected more, much more at the last. Unconsciously perhaps. But the deep desire was there.

I felt it. I understood what was wanted. What was wanted was not the mere emotional evocation of the homeland, no. What was wanted was the legendary, heroic apotheosis of it. Wotan in Valhalla. I realized that I could provide it. If I wished. Or dared.

Now, Brahms was not the only composer whose tunes had been pilfered for use as catchy songs in praise of the detestable prep school. Haydn too had been exploited, though in his case there was a certain precedent because the song bellowed by my schoolmates, and myself, happened also to be the national anthem of Germany, "Deutschland über Alles," not to mention a hymn of the Episcopal Church, "Zion City of Our Lord." A rousing melody, more spirited than the Brahms, and I had easily learned to play it by ear.

That was all very well in Massachusetts. In the barroom of the Dilsberg Gasthaus, however, things were otherwise. In my being confronted by an expectant and exacting audience, compliance was unknowingly taken for granted, as it had been, in fact, from the beginning, from the first glimpse of the wonderland village, the ascent through the cascades of cherry blossoms, and the blandishment of the runic piano. "Deutschland über Alles," the atavistic anthem of Saxon pride, "Germany above everything," a belligerent ambition that had almost been fulfilled but now brought low by my compatriots. And here I was, having come to Dilsberg, after all, to dissemble by song the judgment of that reality and by music defy the twilight of the gods. So I fell to the keyboard.

The dissonant twanging that had sounded sweetly melodious for "Heimatland" grew more resonant, forceful, and vocal for "Deutschland über Alles," and indeed, the words I heard behind me as I played were no longer murmurous but openly audible. A reprise became inevitable, and I gave it, not knowing at the same time what feelings would, or should, be forthcoming.

They were inscrutable. The concert terminated, I turned to face the audience. Not a sound, not a gesture of applause, came from them; not a single eye looked back at mine, and even the young soldier sat like a stone. I saw no good cause to try to fathom their sentiment. Oh, I knew perfectly well what it was anyway. Standing up without a gesture or a blink, I walked through the front door, got into my jeep, and drove back down through that minatory portal out of Dilsberg for the last time.

And on my way past the blossomless cherry trees I had occasion to ask the afternoon what had happened. I had played their anthem for them, and played into their hands. I knew now the nuance of their psyche; it faced me with the faces of the men staring through the barbed wire at Heilbronn, the "innocent" victims of their own crimes. Crimes either of intent or, so to speak, of misadventure. In any case, a crime of living everyday life in the knowledge that evil has become daily bread without diminishing one's appetite, the Dilsberg barroom becoming the psychic analogue of a concentration camp from the pages of *KZ*. And they *knew*! The barmaid knew, the man on crutches knew, the bosomy lady, the young soldier, the dewlapped old men, the little girl and small boy—and why not also his dog?—they all *knew*. And this was as normal, as ordinary, and as banal as a drop of water in mid ocean. And that was the tragedy of tomorrow.

But what of *my* misdeeds? How easy it was to compute the guilt of others without one's own reckoning. Yes. Still, there would be time, time to do better and to do far worse, time to sleep on it, and time when time itself is running out to confront the fundamental question.

To tell Frank what had happened that final afternoon in Dilsberg turned out to be impossible. Not that I was unwilling. I was unsure.

We discussed the imminent reassignment of intelligence personnel instead. The danger of being posted to the Pacific Theater had passed, though it was estimated that invasion of the Japanese mainland might cost a million casualties. With luck we would probably end up in Paris. The Vésinet venue having been terminated as being too cushy, almost scandalous, MIS men were said to be relocated in some of Paris's many requisitioned hotels.

Gertrude Stein had offered to read some of my writing and give me her opinion of it. I'd sent her the play. On the next to last day of June I mailed a postcard saying, "I'll be coming to see you soon." I also expected to see Picasso. And who could tell how many good-looking young men?

We packed our gear and loaded up the jeep, said auf Wiedersehen to Mr. and Mrs. Poland, who kissed us goodbye, gave them some money, and joined a convoy of three other vehicles for the drive to Paris. It was eight o'clock on the Wednesday morning, the Fourth of July, Independence Day 1945, when without regret we bade goodbye to Germany.

Sixteen

JULY–NOVEMBER 1945

It took us four days. Or, rather, we took four days to make the five-hundred-mile drive. The other men in our convoy were willing accomplices in leisurely travel but kept to themselves, we suspected, in order to keep watch over their loot. Frank and I reverted to the status of tourists.

In Paris on the place de la Concorde I drove straight into the rear end of a prewar Citroën, enraging the driver, a lady past middle age wearing a wide-brimmed hat festooned with a salad of celluloid fruit. "You Americans exaggerate," she shrieked, "think you can come to a civilized country and ride roughshod over us all; it's an outrage." The dent in her rear end was the size of a fifty-cent piece, and I said I was sorry. "You boor!" she sputtered. Her husband, a gentleman in spats and pigskin gloves, attempted to calm her, but she hissed, "Shut up, Pierre, you're worse than useless," got back into the Citroën, and drove up the rue Royale.

Frank said, "The French honeymoon is over."

We went to report at the HQ located on the place St. Augustin where the boulevard Haussmann and the boulevard Malesherbes intersected, a forbidding behemoth of a building called the Cercle National des Armées de Terre, de Mer et de l'Air facing the massive architectural mess of St. Augustine's church, a pile of bulbous ugliness that would have driven the bishop of Hippo back to his confessions.

Since it was Saturday, a straw contingent was on duty to receive us. A bored corporal said we could bunk at the Hotel Ambassador, 16 Boulevard Haussmann, one of the better of the 167 hotels requisitioned to house U.S. personnel in Paris. However, we would have to turn in our jeep at the Porte Maillot motor pool, compelling us to get about by metro or on foot. The Hôtel Ambassador, a two-and-a-half-star, two-hundred-room outfit, had been at its plenipotentiary best in the twenties, constrained subsequently by the war to be polite to Nazis and thereafter cordial to GI Joe, which diminished its diplomatic sheen. Frank and I had a large double room on the third floor with Second Empire twin beds and a bathroom of pockmarked tiling, both windows opening onto a meager air shaft. The hot water was tepid, the telephone didn't work, and a notice stipulated that cooking was not permitted in the room. We were overjoyed.

Frank had already arranged before leaving Frankfurt to continue in Paris the lawyerly duties in which he had proved his competence, leaving me alone to apply for a serviceable assignment.

Returning on Monday to the Cercle des Armées, I was directed to an office on the second floor, where I found myself face-to-face with Peter Fahnestock, now a staff sergeant. The full bloom of boyish beauty, I thought, had faded slightly, dimples notwithstanding, or maybe that was my caustic mind's eye. He said, "Hello there. Everybody turns up sooner or later. You can go right in. Colonel Aldrich happens to be free."

He too, I thought, seated at the very same desk, seemed slightly timeworn despite the shiny silver eagles. He said, "At ease, Sergeant Please sit. A pleasure to see you again. Cigarette?" The gold case lay beside him. When I said no, thanks, he said, "All right. Tell me what you've been up to, and we'll see what we can get you up to." He smirked though neither of us thought it was funny.

I told him about the POW and DEP camps, albeit carefully censoring the atrocities of Heilbronn, denouncing Braxton Bragg, and, of course, the inscrutable contretemps of Dilsberg.

"Right," said Aldrich, lighting his cigarette. "I recall that you had had experience interrogating prisoners."

"Displaced persons," I said. "In Épinal."

"Oh, yes. Then I sent you along to Captain Jones. How did that work out?"

I swallowed my reply and said, "He was very friendly."

"That's nice. Well, I think I see a possibility. What do you know about the black market?"

"I've heard it's big business."

"Very. The BM in Paris is run by two thousand American deserters. We try to catch them red-handed. It's not easy. They operate mostly out of hotels requisitioned by the army. Now, how familiar are you with clandestine work?"

"Slightly. At Ritchie we touched on it."

"Someone here can brief you on surveillance. It's like the movies really. Come back in forty-eight hours, and Fahnestock will put you in touch, give you credentials. That's all for now."

Frank said it sounded as if they were preparing to make a gumshoe of me. I said, " 'Tis elementary."

Fahnestock had a sheaf of papers for me. A credential signed by the general, granting the bearer authority to conduct at his discretion any and all investigations into unlawful or unbecoming conduct by members of United States forces in the Paris zone of command. There was a roster of the best-known sites of clandestine business and storage of illegal matériel. Urgent attention advised concerning cash flow, amounts received, where banked, with a list of shady exchange offices, a few fences, and so-called banks. Findings worth reporting for further inquiry and/or prosecution to be referred to Major Caskey in the adjoining office. For surveillance briefing and practice, see Sergeant Mulligan around the corner at 121 rue St. Lazare opposite the station.

"That should keep you busy," Fahnestock observed, adding, "but not sure to keep you out of trouble."

On my way down to the street, almost at the front door, someone caught me from behind, pressing both hands over my eyes and laughing in my ear. Struggling free, I turned. It was H.

"You devil," I cried.

"Jim baby," he said, "tell your daddy you've not been naughty while I wasn't watching."

"I've been so good it hurts. Let's get out of here."

We went up the Champs Élysées, laughing at the lucky avenue, and took an outside table at the café on the corner of the Georges V. "So," I said, "how is Robespierre?"

H chuckled and said, "Oh, he's a terror," took a beaded sip of gin fizz, and inquired, "How did you hear about him?"

"How did I hear about *you* is the question. The answer is Captain Jones."

"Jonesy, oh, yes, the boy with the crazy tits. Tweak 'em and he loses his mind."

"But you're straight, H, you're not gay."

He giggled. "I should deprive the pretty pretty boys of pleasure? They like it, ladies like it, everybody likes it, it's so good." He sighed and closed his eyes.

"Well, well, well. Does Aaron know you swing both ways?"

"Course he does. Knows about me. Knows about you. Himself, he's restricted to females. Saw him two days ago, he's getting big in the hush hush racket, your boy from Boston, just off to Lyon to pick through the clues of Gestapo shenanigans down there. And you, my lad, what skulduggery have you been up to?"

"If only I knew." I sighed. "I can hardly say. But I was assigned to a couple of prisoner of war camps."

"You don't say. So was I. Where did you do it?"

"Mannheim, Heilbronn. You?"

"Bad Kreuznach, Oberstein. What an assignment! All those boys. They'd lost everything, and they were ready for anything. And I was ready to give it to them. All those sex-starved kids. Course you had to clean 'em up a bit first, feed 'em a little, but then . . . Whew! Blond and blue eyes fighting form all over again. So I gave 'em what they wanted, what they *needed*. What a wonderful war! So how did you make out?"

"Are you actually telling me you had sex with the prisoners?"

"Naturally. Didn't you?"

"Of course not."

"Why the hell not, you silly goose?"

"It wouldn't have been right. Taking wrong advantage. They hated us anyway, and that would have only made it worse."

"Don't be an ass. You'd have been doing them a favor. Oh, yes, at first some of them were a bit Wagnerian, wanted to be the great warriors all over again, but they got over that soon enough when their pants came down. They didn't really hate us. They were just hungry. You could say they were war-starved, and fucking with the enemy, well, it was like they were fighting again, and, you know, every orgasm is a kind of victory when you're swimming in the other guy's come and there's nothing else. It's all just sex, is what it's all about. If you know what I mean."

"But how did you do it? In the camp in front of everybody?"

"Naw, course not. You could take a prisoner in and out as easy as pie. The MPs had their own rackets anyway, didn't give a shit. You don't know what you missed. Some of those boys, the ones who could speak a little English, begged me to take them back to California, and natch I said I would. It *was* war, and all's fair, and it was even love too. What can I tell you?"

"I wish I knew," I said sincerely. "I wish I knew."

"Well, listen," said H. "I've got to run. Some freak put my name down for liaison with the HQ of a frog called Colonel Rol. He's a Commie, I think. But who cares? Why don't we get together at that gay club in the rue du Colisée, the Cow on the Roof."

"What?"

"Le Boeuf sur le Toit. You can't miss it. Just off the Champs Élysées. It's one of the smartest spots in Paris. Cocteau and Picasso and everybody used to go there before the war. I'm in and out. See you there." He clapped me on the back, leaving me at the table with the bill.

Sergeant Mulligan's venue was a large windowless room at the rear of a dreary courtyard. It contained one metal table, two metal chairs, and one high-powered standing lamp, a room made for interrogations. The sergeant was an albino, translucent, off-white but with bright pink eyes and a formidable physique, somewhat sinister of mien. Yet his greeting was courteous and cordial. The clandestine world, he said, was actually as simple as ABC. Hunt or be hunted. Surveillance is disappearance. You become invisible, a figure in a field jacket, no insignia. Change one item and you're somebody else. Stick to hotels and restaurants, bars, nightclubs with more than one way out. Railway stations, the metro coming and going, entrances and exits, always use the stairs, in an elevator you're a trapped rabbit, public toilets only in extremis, chronology and itinerary are all, no slinking around, walk, never run. Strict attention to the time of day, minutes, not hours. The quarry you're stalking is only a presence, not a person, remember, you turn him in, you're not doing anybody any harm.

I said, "I'm a detective."

"No," said Mulligan, "you're a sleuth. No handcuffs, no weapon. It's a game."

Frank said, "Maybe. Supposing the guy you're following has a blackjack, he spots you, does a double turn, and bang."

"It's a game," I said. "The brass isn't expecting gang busters. I lurk outside the Hôtel California, follow Joe Blow around the corner, go inside and ask to see what they've got put away in the cellar. Sergeant Mulligan isn't waiting for me to bring in Larry Beem, and Major Caskey doesn't know my name. I spend the afternoon sitting on the pont des Arts and becoming artistic."

In furtherance of this proceeding I went along to the nearby rue Christine, No. 5, to call on Gertrude Stein and Alice Toklas. The two women had recently been escorted in an army plane around Germany, Miss Stein making speeches to the troops and posing on the blasted terrace of Hitler's hideaway in Berchtesgaden. The GIs apparently enjoyed Gertrude's no-nonsense, didactic but natural talk, and we were encouraged to consider her a folksy mother of us all.

Fresh from experiences that cried out for expression and understanding, quantities of GI writers and intellectuals were on the lookout for someone of consecrated achievement and authority around whom to crystallize personal longings and who would offer them in return a vicarious intimation of attainment. Gertrude Stein had given proof of her aptitude to a previous generation with celebrated results. So her rue Christine salon was regularly crowded with eager listeners to the cello voice of that imposing lady. And the presence of all those soldiers, like all the Picassos on the walls, seemed to everyone concerned a delightful and self-evident demonstration of cultural inevitability.

Miss Stein took me by the arm into the entry hall. She had read the play and had clearly read it with care. "Your writing reads well," she said, "and maybe someday writing will be a reality for you, and I have one piece of advice to give you that every writer who is going to be a real writer must be given sometime by somebody, and it is to consider your emotions more carefully. A real writer must be very sure of his emotions before putting a pen to paper, so that is what I advise you to do, to consider your emotions more carefully."

She had been gracious and kindly. I thanked her. It was excellent advice. I took it to heart as especially relevant to recent experience and events. And I thought that if writing is to become a reality someday for a writer, then what he must to do in consideration—precisely—of his emotions is to write, to write at length, interminably, to write his heart out, so to speak, in order to make readable writings out of his emotions.

Oh, yes. And yet . . . fidelity to the facts of experience presupposes unquestioning faith in one's power to define reality, which lies beyond the reach of reason, because the real world is not the one we know. Our relation to both experience and existence is consequently an inexplicable one of which no responsible account can realistically be expected. Emotions, however, conscientiously considered though they may be, cry out for expression, and the writer is serving a life sentence without parole in the prison of himself, condemned to hard labor in the sweatshop of his vocabulary. Interminably talking, interminably writing, Miss Stein herself seemed to personify such a sober rationale of the creative life. Of course it is something of a truism to say that an artist does his best by dying. But nobody worried about that beneath the fiery sapphire air of Paris that July.

The Cow on the Roof was in fact an ox, and it bellowed aloud, calling gay men to carouse at the long bar and beyond in the latitudinous rooms, where room was rampant for almost anything. I was startled. *Gay Paree*, indeed, but so gay as to make the Statler seem staid I'd hardly foreseen. There was a lieutenant waving a shawl of indigo chiffon, and could it have been a chaplain wearing the bonnet, pompom ablaze, of the French sailor seated on his lap?, a medic singing "Lili Marlene" in German, a couple of Anzac pioneers with their hands inside each other's pants, gentlemen in three-piece blue suits, one of them with an orchid in his buttonhole, to whom his American companion said, "Get you, Miss Proust," and a numberless jostling of soldiers of all the Allied armies plus some probably of none, there to make, as it were, the scene.

I had gin and Dubonnet, shouldered into the crush, eyeing the eyes but not deliberate about it, though aware of how aware I was after the months of sexlessness. Maybe it's true that things genital are mostly mental.

A French trooper bumped into me, splashing half my drink down the backside of a British ensign who didn't notice it. The trooper said he was sorry, and I told him not to be. He asked to buy me another drink. I said no, thanks, it's okay. He wasn't bad-looking, no beauty but sweet, a mane of curly hair, complexion flushed with summer and half calf eyes of likable clarity. He insisted, put his hand on my arm, said please and his name was Roger. Purpose explicit and understood, I said all right. We talked.

He was in Paris on leave from an engineer battalion in the Jura but expected to be mustered out soon, lived with his mother in the rue Clavel near the Buttes Chaumont in the Nineteenth Arrondissement. And are you garrisoned in Paris? Well . . . billeted for the time being at the Hôtel Ambassador, 16 Boulevard Haussman. American, yes, and pretty much at loose ends here in Paris, for that matter. Roger drank brandy and soda, was taller than I, looked into my face through those eyes, and said why not go out for a stroll, the night's so mild?

We walked back to the Champs Élysées, crossed over, Roger took my hand, and we wandered, as if aimlessly, into the gardens behind the Petit Palais. These were a miniwilderness of blighted underbrush, shrubbery, and bracken. The Nazis hadn't bothered to tend Parisian pleasure grounds. Irony overtook their negligence. A sigh, a gasp of voluptuous sensations became audible before we could see into the leafy shadows, and we almost stepped on a copulating couple. A boy and girl, and he waved us cheerfully away, missing not a throb or a pant.

Roger whispered, "It's perfectly safe in here. Nobody cares who does what." And then he kissed me.

Under the remnants of a withered azalea we found a patch of pliable weeds into which we subsided, yielding and clasping and fooling with our clothes in mutual forgetfulness, swallowing the communicable substance of each other, our bodies arching, while every motion made us both cleave together in the unique spasm of surrender. We lay there in the weeds, washed in sweat and semen. And when we had kissed, said hello, and made a rally of our clothes, on our way out of the garden, we once again nearly stepped on a copulating couple, two boys this time, and they also made nothing of our inadvertent intrusion.

When we came out from our own darkness and the lecherous underbrush into the lights of the city, Roger said, "We'll meet again,
won't we? You say when."

I said, "I don't know."

"Today's Tuesday; let's say Saturday. Do you have a place where
we can go?"

"No. But I can take a room in one of these little hotels."

He threw himself to my chest, kissed me, and whispered, "Oh,
yes, yes."

It was up to me to do the disentangling. We said till Saturday, and
he ran off to take the last metro at the Clemenceau Station.

Walking back toward the Egyptian obelisk in the square, I realized
that my sexual life had been revived after a very long hiatus. Long and
strange. The vital, powerful flux of virility had lain dormant ever since
I'd first set foot in Europe a year before. Since then I'd certainly come
within fucking distance of the war, but to no effect. And I'd come
within waging distance of the war to no effect either. To what degree,
then, may the one wartime have interacted with the other? To what
purpose? If it was true that the passion of fighting men for fighting
made lust ever more fierce, the war had passed me by even as I was
pledged to its wherewithal. I had never engaged in killing other men—
only men, incidentally, made war—I'd never participated in that fatal
act that compounded sexuality by making the power of taking life
concomitant with the power of creating it. That was the queerness
within the queerness of war itself and of my empathy for the men who
waged it. I lusted for their bodies, yes, but all I wanted was their physical surrender to a climactic instant of sterility. I did not yearn to change
places with Timmy Morreton. Anyway, I learned that he'd been killed.
The terrible joy of combat was the secret of sexual mythology, and for
me its battlefield had been the *waging* of guilt, the view halloo of
men's eyes when the war had made them vulnerable to my compassion. In the *Heimatland* of mythic transfiguration I had been Ulysses,
young Werther, the lance corporal of the North Bukovina Fusiliers,
Otto, Erich, Gottfried, and the great lover of military mystique in the
orgiastic underbrush of the Champs Élysées.

Picasso of course was a killer, a wily warlord who reinvented the
tactics of the battlefield every morning to suit his objective and but

half awake could stupefy, outmaneuver, and trounce that day's opponent (probably of his own creation anyway). He was the soldier and
general, of both his allies and his enemies; he reveled in the luxuriance
of fighting, of killing, and of fucking. His sexuality was as stupendous
and omnipotent as the master seducer of the female form, and he happily peopled the world with his progeny. About terror and compassion, cruelty, tenderness, tyranny, and love there was little he hadn't
known, and he held up before the world the prodigious pictures of his
omniscience. To watch him, study him, strive to know him, however
slightly, this was a war within the war, and he knew it, he fought it,
and he was its victor as well as its victim. I stood by the ragged edge
of the action in fear and fascination, and I dreamed that maybe my
mere proximity might make the story of my queer war the history of
an epic. And indeed I possessed already circumstantial evidence of
Picasso's good offices in the form of two effigies of myself signed
by him.

The artist came downstairs in his underwear, kissed me on both
cheeks, and said that he had bought an automobile. The chauffeur, a
burly fellow named Marcel, came in presently and announced that the
car was ready down in the street. Picasso went back upstairs to get
dressed. He returned in five minutes attired as if for an elegant recep-
tion in a dark suit, white shirt, necktie, gold chain in his lapel buttonhole but asserted nonetheless as a bohemian artist by incongruous
openwork sandals. He was accompanied by Dora Maar, wearing an
ostentatious cloche and smoking a cigarette. She said Picasso had been
singing my praises, a hymn clearly not attuned to her taste. The artist
went to the stairs down to the street, followed by Marcel, Dora, and
me, Sabartés remaining behind to lock up.

At the opposite corner waited a shiny black automobile. I said it
was a beauty, and I'd like a snapshot of Picasso standing in front of it.
I had a small camera in my hip pocket. He snatched it from my hand
and pressed it upon Dora, declaring that if a photograph were to be
taken, better have a professional do the job, and Dora, being a pho-
tographer of genius, might not be happy to let a stranger usurp her
place. He neighed with laughter at that, adding that I must stand beside him in front of the car, because it's not every day that a photog-
rapher gets a good-looking soldier for a model. Dora cast away her

cigarette and snapped the shutter the minute I had taken my place beside Picasso.

Afterward without a word the artist stepped onto the sidewalk, flung open a door of the car, and leaped inside, impressively agile for a man of sixty-three, the motor detonated, and the car pulled speedily away, its phenomenal passenger glancing neither to the right nor to the left.

Dora handed back the camera. "My professional pride," she said, "is not so great I worry about anyone usurping my place. Good afternoon."

I went to the Hôtel California and asked to see the officer in charge. A harelipped captain named Melvin Schoop haughtily inquired my business. When I presented my credentials, his hauteur shrank to sheepish embarrassment. Requested to produce an up-to-date and comprehensive inventory of all the supplies on hand on the premises, he at first maintained it had been mislaid, but when advised that its loss could constitute gross negligence, he managed to find it in the bottom drawer of his desk under a jumble of empty cigarette packs and canceled PX ration cards. Though his deformity had been mended, the scar was very unsightly, and I felt rather sorry for a man made ugly for life by an accident. On our way to the storerooms in the cellar he asked me whether I cared for scotch. Sure, I said, when so inclined, why not? Well, he had some to spare, as it happened, and would be glad to send a case of Black Label to my billet. What he had to spare turned out to be a couple of dozen extra cases of whiskey, a mound of five-gallon buckets of paint, bales of waterproofed battle dress, heaps of K rations, cartons of wireless field telephones, jerricans of gas, and heaven only knows what else.

I said, "Well, Captain, I suppose you realize what this means."

"I know. Don't think I don't know. But what am I going to do? Have a heart, won't you? Take anything you want. The last inspector took ten cases and a ton of coal."

"I don't want anything. What would I do with a ton of coal?"

"How about some cash? Dollars. Swiss francs. A pack of blank ration cards."

"Stop it—will you?—for God's sake. I'm not going to turn you in. But I'm not about to let you make me as guilty as you are. All right? Take me out of here."

Captain Schoop went with me to the front door and said, "You've got to understand. I came up the hard way. Four kids and the missus sits by the radio all day drinking Cuba Libres and doing her nails."

I said, "I understand," but I didn't, and I went outside into the rue de Berri.

In the street a pimply PFC trotted along beside me, saying, "Hey, Sergeant, wait a sec, will ya?"

Startled, as I wore no insignia and was of mediocre appearance, I couldn't think why he might have recognized me. "Do I know you?" I asked.

"Did once. When ya was stockin' up for Sergeant Jars down in Kwimper. Least ya claimed ya was, signed for him, and the chits come back okay."

"Morlaix!" I exclaimed. "And you're still taking ten percent, are you? From Murfreesboro, what's more."

"You remember. Yeah. You hanging round the California must be in the black business yasself."

"Yes and no. Truth is I was getting ready to arrest Captain Schoop. I'm an inspector."

"Jeez, Sarge. Forget you ever saw me. Okay?"

"Oh, I forgot you," I said, "before I saw you. But tell me something. You ever hear of a guy named Beem, Larry Beem."

"Hear of him?" cried the PFC, his pimples suddenly suffused with blood. "Christ! Who hasn't heard of Beem, the big man of the big men, boss of the pig money?"

"You know where he hangs out? Take me there."

"Ya gotta be kiddin'. *They* ain't. Break your balls as soon as you say bonjour. Naw, people fool with Beem, they better off in a stockade than a hospital, believe ya me."

I did believe him as he scuttled apprehensively back inside the Hôtel California, and strolling toward the faubourg St. Honoré, I saw that I'd had done with the surveillance business in a single day, pace Major Caskey, from whom I never heard, and I thankfully said farewell also to Sergeant Mulligan and the clandestine world, for which I would never be suited.

Maybe one of these days Colonel Aldrich, while toying with his gold cigarette case, would think to find me a more exotic assignment, but I wasn't alarmed by him. I wished for nothing more than freedom to do as I pleased day and night in this captivating city, call on Picasso, Gertrude Stein, visit art galleries, and linger on the boulevards, bridges, esplanades, gazing at palaces, places of worship, and seats of state. Oh, and occasionally making love with Roger.

When, as I expected, he said he was in love with me, I felt assailed as by the enigma of time and didn't possess an answer to it, so I held him secure and said, "Together we're just right."

Picasso had recently provided me with an ideal friend. One morning in the studio, as was often the case, I was not the only caller. Among the others, chatting with Sabartés, stood a handsome young fellow, tall and lean, an unruly mop of black hair, lofty brow, severe eyes, bright white teeth. Separating him from the secretary, Picasso led him to me and introduced us. And said since we were both young foreigners in Paris interested in art, we ought to be acquainted. I think we both immediately saw we'd see eye to eye, and we did.

The name was Youla Chapoval. He was Russian, born in Kiev but brought as a child to Paris, where just before the war, aged nineteen, he met Picasso and started to paint.

We left the studio together, Youla and I, that morning, and in the rue des Grands Augustins he asked me to join him and his wife for lunch. They occupied a modest and cheerful apartment-cum-studio above a small restaurant on the Boulevard St. Germain overlooking the gardens of the Cluny Museum. Youla's wife, Jeanne, gracious, blond, handsome, and high-spirited, had something to do with the restaurant. An inner staircase led down to it from one corner of the apartment, and food and wine came up from below, an arrangement of rare convenience at a time of strict rationing. Youla's paintings were scattered pell-mell, and the apartment was fragrant with the scent of turpentine. Why Picasso considered the work promising was clear, because the pictures, mostly still lifes, were reminiscent of cubism, albeit a cubism more sparkling and fancy-free in composition and color than the well-disciplined inventions of 1911. It was evident too that the young Russian worked with a restless dash of self-assurance that allowed him, like his Spanish admirer, to produce a highly finished work of art in an afternoon.

During those summery and autumnal months of 1945 I was with Chapoval almost every day. All those amethyst afternoons together,

Youla painting, Jeanne preparing tea, and I addressing notes to the future while on the ancient gramophone the *Gymnopédies* of Erik Satie made a plaintive refrain. As I faced that young fellow of twenty-five, it was a wonder to see how masterfully his talent made mature use of aesthetic originality and energy. As if the terrible brevity of life had already overwhelmed his years.

It had. For a Russian Jew, indeed, the hellish threat of Nazi savagery challenged the creative vocation with particularly fiendish cruelty. The cruelty and the challenge had been all too true. The young artist's mother and sister had perished in the gas chambers of Auschwitz, their ashes scattered to the elements. And in intolerable memoriam Youla possessed a snapshot smuggled out by a survivor showing the main rail entrance of Auschwitz-Birkenau just after the liberation of the camp, the railway lines converging to a single track leading to a tower beneath which passed the cattle cars bearing to inhuman annihilation millions of human beings.

But wait! That tower! I had seen it before. I had sensed its menace. Did its mere aspect betoken the far-flung imperium of the Germanic zeitgeist? I had already guessed at the guilt that lay beyond. It *was* the entrance to a region from which no man returns with his humanity unimpaired. Could ever sweet surcease redeem from infamy such multitudinous wrongdoing? 'Twas a matter to bewilder meditation. I might have done well to think of that while playing "Deutschland über Alles" on the piano in Dilsberg. Dilsberg! The dreamland town of cherry blossom slopes, of the minatory portal open to jejune romanticism, the Dilsberg of "Ubers Meer grüss ich dich, Heimatland." Homeland native to song and soldiery, philosophy and atrocity, the language of love and hatred, worship of wrong and of forgiveness. Homeland of Hanno. What had become of him, where was he now, the beloved I'd never again look in the eye?

There was a place called Luigi's Bar just a few steps off the Champs Élysées, and I had fallen into the habit of stopping there for a drink now and then in midafternoon. Nothing too strong, thanks, a sweet sherry or glass of sauterne. At three-thirty or four I was usually the only client. The bartender, a companionable fellow past middle age bursting out of his trousers, made me welcome as a fighter for the Nazi defeat, so I didn't bother to tell him the truth. The wall behind the bar held a huge mirror, into which I sometimes stared, wondering who I was, where I was, why I was there, and to what port traveling. Like the figure in the painting by Gauguin? Not really, no.

That afternoon, in any case, as I sat eye to eye with myself, I noticed that the bartender was slicing a lemon, a fact noticeable inasmuch as lemons were rare, and I thought it might have come from the Hôtel California. Anyway, I asked the bartender to loan me his knife. Surprised, he nonetheless handed it over. Having it in hand, I went downstairs to the men's room, found there another mirror, and took my place before it. Raising the knife level to my forehead, I pressed it hard till it hurt and drew it back and forth slowly, slowly, forcing the pain until blood, which wasn't very much because there's little flesh to bleed beneath the forehead's skin, seeped through. But it was enough. I went upstairs, put down the knife, and the bartender gasped. "What is it? What have you done? There's something wrong?"

My throat had seized up. I could barely speak, put some scrip on the bar, and turned to leave. "No," I croaked, "nothing wrong. It's nothing."

Out in the street I pushed my cap down to cover the wound, knowing I'd never again set foot in Luigi's Bar. Yes, however, there *was* something wrong. What it was I couldn't say. The wound mark of transgression. Oh, but this was not the first time a weapon had been taken to my flesh by myself.

Frank, when I came into our room in the Hôtel Ambassador, cried, "Lord Jim, *what* have you done?"

I couldn't pretend to Frank that it was nothing. I couldn't face denial, flung myself onto my bed, grunting, "It's terrible," and wept.

Frank sat by my side and touched my shoulder blades, murmuring, "Lord Jim, Lord Jim."

I heard him as if from the distance of the story written half a century before. Yes. *Lord Jim*. By Joseph Conrad. Could Frank have known? Maybe. But not entirely. I knew without the benefit of understanding.

Lord Jim is the story of a man's lifelong search for atonement following an act of impulsive cowardice. One of the officers of a vessel carrying hundreds of Muslim pilgrims, he frantically abandons ship with the other officers when it appears the vessel is about to sink, leaving behind to certain death the pilgrims. But the ship, after all, does not sink. The pilgrims are saved, and those who abandoned their posts become outcasts. Harrowed by guilt, Jim wanders about the South Seas and eventually finds a measure of self-respect from a useful life among friendly natives, who gratefully accord him the title of Lord. A second crisis arises when he is wrongly accused of complicity in the murder of the chieftain's son. Nonetheless he willingly gives himself up to native justice and is executed, winning back his lost honor, and triumphs in death.

A profound and moving tale, it is one of the finest by Conrad, who wrote with such passion of man's moral dilemmas, his psychic solitude and inner mystery. *Lord Jim*, when I was a schoolboy, was naturally a book that cast a spell for me, the inversion of names seeming strangely apropos, and there had been plenty of people before Frank who called me Lord Jim, knowing as little as Frank did, and caring far less, about the phenomenal relevance.

That Tuesday began like any other weekday in our goof-off agenda. After breakfast I sauntered down the avenue de l'Opéra, crossed the Louvre courtyard, the pont du Carrousel, and followed the Seine up-river to the rue des Grands Augustins. It was in Picasso's studio I learned that that day was one to become forever memorable in the history of human doings, and I felt immediately how fitting it was to have heard about it in a place which also bade fair to be forever memorable. A Japanese city we'd never heard of called Hiroshima had been totally obliterated by a U.S. bomb we'd never heard of, the *atomic* bomb, a device so stupendously devastating that in an instant it had killed eighty thousand human beings. Such carnage inflicted by a single explosion seemed superhuman, although three times that many deaths had been caused by a single storm of bombs, for example, over the city of Hamburg. The cost was cruel, to be sure, but it would hardly seem unreasonable should it lead the Japanese to surrender. Besides, they had been formally warned well before Hiroshima that they now must choose between capitulation and annihilation, an ultimatum they chose to ignore. As for cruelty, the Japanese had proved themselves sadistic connoisseurs, having raped, maimed, tortured, starved, burned alive, buried alive, beheaded, disemboweled, and done to death by unimaginable means countless humans.

The wait for surrender proved fruitless. Three days later a second atomic bomb fell on the city of Nagasaki. And now some people began protesting that it was intolerably inhuman to resort to such satanic weapons, criticizing the United States for having thrown open the Pandora's box of indiscriminate death. If so, then the criticism questioned the morale of man's insatiable quest to fathom the secrets of God's machinery. At a high price in Japanese lives, indeed. But the war, after all, was their doing, and if it is a platitude to observe that those who sow the wild wind must be prepared to reap the cyclone, so be it. Anyway, bomb No. 2 provoked sober fact-facing, and presently the emperor informed his council that the time had come to "bear the unbearable." And ten days after Hiroshima the rising sun cast upon the Japanese Empire the unbearable shadow of unconditional surrender. In Paris people jumped for joy. So the world would put away its weapons for a few minutes and consider coming to terms with the bequest of its tragedy.

The Louvre had been closed throughout the war, its treasures spirited to secret hideaways in remote châteaux. To celebrate the renascent culture of free France, a small exhibition of selected masterpieces had recently been inaugurated in the Grande Galerie. I went to see it with Frank. It was a dazzling display. Among the French paintings was one by Cézanne, the greatest artist, in my willful opinion, since Rembrandt. It was a still life of flowers in a blue vase, entitled *The Blue Vase*. I was thrilled to see it and endeavored to persuade a lukewarm Frank of its subtle finesse, emphasizing with an outstretched forefinger the dense and poetic handling of flowers, vase, a small bottle, and several apples on a table, all placed in near-symmetrical relation to one another, creating a sense of simultaneous dynamism and repose. But in the midst of my ardent disquisition a guard came bustling across the gallery, stridently bellowing, "It is forbidden to touch the works of art. Keep your hands down."

But my finger had never been within an inch of the painting. "I did not touch that painting," I irritably retorted.

The guard, however, a puffed-up runt with waxed mustaches, pomaded hair, and the eyes of a stoat, was not a man to be fleeced of righteous indignation. "I saw you touch it," he shouted, "your dirty fingers on it. You Yankees think you own the universe, do as you please, no respect for the culture of the country, come here and trifle with things of beauty, great works of art, no reverence, no awe, no understanding, cigarette bigwigs is all you are, supermen of the chewing gum world, that's all you are," whereupon he paused to breathe, face claret red, ready to reinflate his tirade.

Leaving me mute and distraught. Cézanne I loved more than any other painter. Maybe not the greatest of all time, but for me the most moving, most spiritual, most humane, timeless, and monumental. To be accused and bullied before a crowd of unsympathetic onlookers was hateful and heartbreaking. Though I was innocent of wrongdoing, the guard's vociferous denunciation aimed at the solitude of art made me by definition guilty before Cézanne and before spectators who would never love him as I did. Without the wretched pretense of an apology I took to my heels and fled from the museum.

Frank found me in tears in the sad scrap of garden in the forecourt of the palace. He said, "Jim," and put his hand gently onto my head. I noted the elision of my surname, which was something, and I thought he might never again call me Lord Jim, and he never did, and it would be enough to be a lord of the chewing gum world.

"Jim," Frank said again, "don't take on so. Not for a miserable bureaucrat, a boor, a lout, a Pharisee in the temple of disestablishmentarianism. There! The big word versus the little bugbear. *Basta così!*"

I smeared the wet from my face, wryly smiling at the clever usage, and said, "Anyway, Cézanne is worth it, and he always will be."

"I believe you," said Frank.

Among the many who thronged Picasso's studio that exhilarating summer of worldwide peace, there was none—excepting Chapoval, of course—whom I found particularly compatible. Only one of them went slightly out of his way to be cordial, a poet named Eluard, a tall, stooped, gray-faced man about fifty, who talked to me about C. Day-Lewis, of whom I'd never heard, remarking how odd it was that such a perspicacious intellectual should have quit the Communist Party just before the war. I had no idea and didn't give a damn, and Eluard clearly didn't give a damn about my opinion. I gathered he was himself a committed Communist, like Picasso, and he always came to the studio accompanied by another poet, also a Communist, called Aragon, whom I immediately disliked, feeling he was sneaky, alert to the main chance, and eager to take advantage of Picasso's goodwill to further the causes of the party.

It came about by chance—if chance, that is, ever had anything to do with what came about in Picasso's studio—that these two men, and Sabartés, were the ones present that morning when Picasso delivered his extraordinary and unforgettable prediction anent my future.

The artist—some people call him the minotaur—seized me by the shoulders and turned me to face the others. "Here is my young friend Lord," he said. "Look at him closely. Someday he will surprise us. There will be great things in his future. He will do something to astonish us all someday."

Confounded, embarrassed, I stood dumb and stock-still, which was the best thing I could do, because the moment didn't last long. The others were taking their leave, and I willingly followed, neglecting in my confusion to thank the artist for the flattering prophecy. But fate is not eligible for gratitude, and thanks would have spoiled the miraculous effect.

When I thought about what Picasso had said, I didn't know what to think. It goes without saying that an acknowledged genius may be supposed to possess greater perspicacity than common mortals. It is likewise self-evident that young men who dream of great accomplishments believe by definition that they have it in them to astonish the world, and if they can believe that, to be sure, they can believe anything, which gives them their chance. So I was satisfied to think that I might someday fulfill Picasso's prophecy by writing and publishing something astonishing.

Chapoval had a friend of Flemish extraction named Roger van Gindertael whom he had met while both were in hiding from the Germans during the war. Gindertael was an older man, worn by anxiety and poverty, gaunt and pinched, yet of exquisite politesse and sage reflection. He had been a painter but given it up in favor of writing about painters. I met him several times at Youla's apartment-studio and would have liked to know him more, but he and Youla preferred tête-à-tête meetings. One day, however, Youla took me aside to make a request.

Gindertael was so severely impoverished that his clothes were falling to pieces. Could I not acquire an outfit for him at the PX? Plenty of French civilians during those years were comfortably fitted out with GI attire. Thanks perhaps to the merchandising versatility of L. Beem. For me to procure what was needed would be easy (without having to apply at the Hôtel California). We took Gindertael's measurements, and he was presently arrayed in olive drab shirts and trousers and an officer's short coat. He was delighted, did a little dance, and we all drank a lot of wine brought upstairs by Jeanne from the restaurant.

The recipient of this military apparel insisted that I must have a gauge of his gratitude and proposed drawing my portrait. He had kept his hand in as a draftsman, and it would benefit from exercise. I said okay. The drawing could almost have been the likeness of a person quite different from the one portrayed by Picasso. It was in any case not a work of masterful virtuosity, but it did provide a penetrating semblance of the model, particularly as I was just then: somber, grave, brooding. Not a very ingratiating image, but there it was, and my thanks to the artist were sincere.

Chapoval, like everyone else in Paris, had heard of Gertrude Stein's extraordinary collection of Picassos, and he longed to see them. I had fairly regularly attended the afternoon gatherings at 5 rue Christine, believed myself on cordial terms with Gertrude, and told Youla that I'd take him with me to see the pictures.

When we went to make our visit, it was a rainbow day of later summer, and any youth in Paris then could feel that he held the wide world in both hands simply by being alive. Not bothering to telephone in advance to Dan 65-06, we went along at about four o'clock, and I was surprised when Gertrude in person opened the door, which was not at all her custom. Still, she greeted me amiably enough. I introduced Chapoval to her, then said I hoped our visit was not inopportune and explained that we did not mean to intrude but only wanted to have a look at the pictures.

The grossness of my blunder became clear immediately. Miss Stein bristled and said, "This ain't no museum. You can't come round here to gawk anytime you feel like it. Besides, it's not convenient."

"But Chapoval is a friend of Picasso," I ludicrously protested.

"Well then, let him go and ask Picasso to see some Picassos," Gertrude retorted. "Picasso has a lot more Picassos than I have. Go ask him to show them to you, then maybe you'll see the sort of man Picasso is, if you don't know already, then you'll see something about Picasso. But you can't come bursting in here."

Embarrassed, mortified, I stood back on the landing in clumsy, flushed silence.

"Well," said Gertrude after a pause, "I'm going out to do an errand in a minute, and you can both walk with me if you want to. Just wait here, then we'll go down and you can walk with me while I do my errand."

She closed the door. Turning to Chapoval, I said not to worry, she'd calm down if we listened to her talk.

After a few minutes' wait Miss Stein returned with Basket on a leash, and we went down to the street. I walked alongside her, Chapoval following a few paces behind. Turning into the rue St. André-des-Arts in the topaz sunshine, she spoke of the GIs who were already being shipped from home for discharge. Their visits had begun to weary her, but she was sorry to see them go. And sorry for them as well, she added, because never again in their lives would they be so happy.

At that moment there was hardly an American in uniform who didn't long to shed it as quickly as possible. We were sick of the army, sick of the war and its stresses and qualms. I disagreed with Miss Stein and said so.

She stopped abruptly and faced me on the sidewalk in the sun. Repeating what she'd already said, she dogmatically added that war possesses an irresistible appeal for young soldiers caused by the thrill of a superhuman power to kill with impunity, and because of it, because of the naive confidence that no harm can come to them, they have at their fingertips a greater power than ever in their lives they will wield again, and they are like bloodthirsty gods united in the climactic comradeship of killing, and that is why they will never again be so happy.

I was indignant at the pontifical self-assurance of the lady, solid as cement in her tweed suit, and I once more said that I disagreed with her.

She said it didn't matter because I was too young, too inexperienced, and too obtuse in my emotions to realize she was right.

I stood there. I was transfixed. And then I said she was not right, she was wrong, she was a stupid old woman and didn't understand anything.

I turned away. Without waiting for her to answer, I turned away abruptly and left her standing there in the street with her white dog on the leash, walked to the rue des Grands Augustins without once glancing back, went around the corner, and I never saw Gertrude Stein again.

Chapoval understood that things had gone wrong, apologized for having asked in the first place to visit the famous collection, invited me to come soon for dinner, and hurriedly left me by myself.

I was shaken with anger at having been talked down to by an elderly woman. But I realized she'd been amazingly prescient and had understood the true facts of life of fighting men as well as I did, though she had never heard artillery fire or faced a Nazi tank. My irritation wanted to be vindicated even at the cost of making Miss Stein appear to have been in the wrong. So I climbed the staircase to Picasso's studio and rang the bell. He opened a crack and asked what I wanted at that inconvenient hour. When I replied that his friend Gertrude was talking nonsense, the door swung wide, and he beckoned me inside, saying to tell all, tell all. I may have fiddled with the truth, but this suited Picasso, who muttered, That slut! That pig! He said she'd always been a Fascist, had a weakness for Franco. For Pétain too. Imagine. An American. A Jew. Fat as a pig; once sent him a photo of herself standing in front of an auto, and you couldn't see the auto she was so fat. As for Toklas, that little witch, why does she wear her hair in bangs? Picasso laughed out loud. She had had a horn in the middle of her forehead. A growth like a rhinoceros. So they made the ideal couple, the hippopotamus and the rhinoceros. But then Alice had the horn cut off and her bangs are supposed to cover up the hole. And Gertrude Stein talks about my pictures as if she'd painted them herself.

His laughter suddenly ceased. He shook himself like a bather who has just emerged from ice-cold water, turned away from me, saying he had important things to do upstairs, I would have to leave.

Surprised, perplexed, and rather awed, I walked back toward the Hôtel Ambassador, and when at length I arrived there I was able to wonder what foolish youth had had the temerity to defy a wise old lady who knew only too well what she was talking about. At least I had the good sense to tell Frank I'd wandered all afternoon up and down the city without seeing a single person I felt like speaking to.

Rendezvous with Roger growing more and more occasional, I indulged in the desultory visit to the Cow, where I picked up no one but did catch a glimpse of Colonel Aldrich and young Fahnestock in civilian clothes seated at a table in the back room. Then of course I ran into H.

"Months since I've seen you," I said. "Assumed you'd gone home to the tangerines."

"Not likely," he said. "I shrink from those groves. Far prefer lounging on the Riviera. My new ladylove owns Juan-les-Pins, head over heels with Robespierre, calls him Bobby, daughter-in-law of a robber baron made his pile swindling the railroad tycoons. And you, sweetheart, and you, making out, are you, in the trousers department?"

"Not so's you'd notice it," I said. "Sometimes I feel improper stirrings down there, but I master them, you know how it is."

"Not so's you'd notice it," said H. "The Reign of Terror bonks along, can't say no to Bobby. But listen, sweetie, what do you say to a little wine tasting in the cellars of Burgundy? Beaune. Meursault. Mercurey. You name it. Ladylove has been teaching my taste buds to live it up. Besides, Aaron's making mischief down there, longs for a little company, says he can make arrangements. Our buddy Aaron, he's fallen into something a little more underground than wine cellars I'd wager, but we'll never find out. And who cares? Are you on for a long weekend?"

"Sure," I said. "Aaron a spook? What would they say in Boston?"

"They'd say the tea tastes of salt water. I'll pick you up Friday morning, and we can drink to Shirley Temple's marriage now that she's sweet seventeen."

We left from the Porte d'Italie, driving due southeast on Route N7 in the forest green Bugatti cabriolet on loan to Bobby from ladylove. The sun yawned through low-lying mists, and blue spots shone out here and there. Already the treetops had given up their summery hue for muted russet, autumnal veils spreading surrender across the pacified landscape. This was sweet October, Indian summer. The world moved on. Clocks ticked. But today the barometer of pleasures pointed to "Fine," and together H and I sang the refrain of our freedom, luminous and invulnerable, our personal cosmology, Copernican revolution, fragile and dense.

We stopped en route at a town called Avallon, where we had a remarkable dinner of frog legs wriggling in a puddle of garlic soup. Aaron was waiting, lounging against the well in the courtyard of the Hôtel Dieu, wearing an olive drab short coat with a black velvet collar. He said we'd have lunch at his place a few miles away in a hamlet very suitably named Bouzy.

The wine cellars were vast catacombs, fading into subterranean subfusc, huge casks in place of sarcophagi, our guides sickly gentlemen who led us from spigot to spigot. At each one we were given a copious taste, thus onward from cask to cask, inhaling the vintage bouquet and emerging from the fumes of each cellar into the drunken daylight only to plunge yet again into the vinous reaches of rare Burgundian appellations secreted far underground. And so at last to blunder toward the blinding sunset, three comrades united forever for an hour or two by the intoxicating delusion of universal brotherhood. Aaron said merely that each of us might sometime be offered an opportunity to pursue more responsible missions, or maybe not, but if we were, it would be well to go for it. H and I drove back in the Bugatti toward Paris, stopping overnight in Avallon, where the only other guest in the chilly hotel was an enraged police dog that writhed at its chain and barked like a three-headed Cerberus all night long.

Frank said I might have thought to bring back a bottle or two of something, and I said there's nobody more selfish than a drunkard, and he said, "Thirty days in the county lockup."

You couldn't believe how many art galleries there were, Left Bank and Right, with wonderful things for sale. Picasso etchings by the score, Cézanne watercolors, seascapes by Courbet, Delacroix sketches, charcoals by Degas, drawings by Matisse, Miró, and Léger. It was incredible, and I haunted these places, unable to afford much but managing a Blue Period etching of a sad little boy, a nude athlete by Delacroix, and several fine books illustrated by my friend Picasso.

In a Left Bank street one windy morning I came upon a gallery I'd not yet visited, the Galerie Marcel Lenoir. The painting in the window was an academic still life of fruit and flowers, rather labored in execution, with heavy impasto and insipid color, signed Marcel Lenoir. To my supercilious eye it held out little promise of enthusiasm for the paintings visible on the walls inside. I went in anyway, more for shelter from the elements than for a feast of visual delights. And there were none. In ornate gilt frames of Louis Philippe style, diverse in subject matter but tediously similar in heavy-handed workmanship and pedestrian style, stodgy, prosaic, and utterly lacking in inventiveness, the two dozen or more pictures on exhibit were all signed Marcel Lenoir. In short, the gallery bearing his name was a showcase devoted solely to the work of this painter, whose name I had never heard. This display of creative ineptitude was presided over by a husky lady well on in years, attired in tatty velveteen, heavy of jaw but sharp of countenance. I saw no reason to keep from this person the poor opinion I had formed of Monsieur Lenoir's paintings and said something condescending.

She took it amiss and replied with asperity that Marcel Lenoir, deceased these fifteen sad years aged but fifty-nine, was an artist of undeniable greatness, extolled in his lifetime by the foremost critics and collectors. Besides, how could I, a commonplace American soldier, have an opinion worth anything?

I loftily replied that the great artists of the time were well known to all, even to sundry.

"Name them," she snapped.

"Matisse, Braque, Léger, Rouault," I tartly retorted, "and the greatest of all, Picasso."

That was the name she must have been waiting for, because it catapulted her into a fury. She fulminated against Picasso and concluded by stating that as she happened to be none other than Madame Marcel Lenoir, she knew all about creative greatness for having witnessed at first hand how it came into being.

I said that I had also had that privilege.

She sniffed, looking at me scornfully up and down.

"It may surprise you to hear this," I said, "but Picasso happens to be my father."

That statement gave her pause. A moment of crazy gratification for me. But then she said, "If that's so, I feel very sorry for you," and turned her back.

Madame Lenoir had had the last word, doubly final because wounding ambiguity prevailed on whether her pity and contempt were directed more toward the pernicious effect of Picasso as a parent or the woeful folly of my fabrication. I got out of there in a hurry, but the bizarre issue of my lie followed immediately behind. To be sure, the search for paternity is never-ending, but I knew nothing about Picasso's potential as a real-life parent. The transcendence of genius notwithstanding, it might have proved perilous to have to answer to the minotaur as the father of one's fate.

The chestnut trees were the first to give up their foliage. The violet hazes of October had dwindled away. A few, but not many, of the cafés were heated, and clients sat for hours in front of a single cup of adulterated coffee. Black market coal cost a fortune. Parisians shivered and said it was the chilliest November they could recall. President de Gaulle declared that the furnaces of the Élysée Palace would stay unlit; a few fireplaces would do. Chapoval's apartment was warmed by updrafts from the cooking stoves downstairs. Picasso wore a coat of shabby fur, a sleeping cap of double cashmere, and his dog drowsed beside a ceramic incinerator that burned sawdust. The Hôtel Ambassador was so comfortable Frank and I left a window open at night. The California must have been piping hot.

H made up his mind to take his discharge in Paris, where Bobby apparently promised a provident future. As for Aaron, he passed through Paris like a breeze from the reaches of terra incognita, invited us to dinner at the Ritz—mediocre food, wonderful wine—and said we'd hear from him the next morning, which of course we didn't. I could barely contain my haste to get home, shed my uniform, and go to the opera. But I had to wait, and maybe I did hear from Aaron after all.

It was a Monday, and that day we learned that the Butcher of Belsen had been condemned to death and that the vilest of the Nazi war criminals were finally in the dock in Nuremberg to be judged for their crimes against humanity.

An order came to the hotel instructing me to report at 3:00 p.m. to a lieutenant colonel Halstadt at the Cercle National des Armées. The colonel's office was on the third floor, facing the square. In the afternoon a secretary in civilian clothes told me to please be patient for a few minutes. The wait was brief.

Colonel Halstadt sat behind a severe steel desk, a neat packet of papers and two telephones in front of him, his back to the window.

The daylight fell full in my face, my sight half failed, and I blinked against nothing, supposing it must be deliberate, the disadvantage. The colonel appeared a handsome man, a fine figure in a well-styled uniform, tapping the papers on his desk with slender fingers, a signet ring on the left little finger. He didn't speak, tell me to stand at ease as I waited uncomfortably at attention before him, disadvantage cumulative, and I slowly sensed something strange, perhaps a little creepy, in our confrontation, yes, definitely. The brass nameplate at the front of the desk: LT. COL. MARTIN L. HALSTADT. And it struck me suddenly, rushed over me like a wave obliterating time. I was standing face-to-face with Hanno's Martin, the Martin coming toward me through the crowd at the Statler bar, afterward outside on Arlington Street in the accursed storm, the quiet, invidious snow falling like the final ax as he flung his arm across Hanno's shoulders, and their silhouettes together were as cruel as their climb into the taxi, its bloodstained taillights fading into the baleful flurries as it carried both of them out of my life forever. Till this minute. Hopeless: I struggled to swallow the recognition, clenching jaws, my mouth gone parched, eyes tight shut.

At least he spoke. "Sit down, will you, for Christ's sake. Yes, yes, I know. But how could I have known? There must be thousands of Jims in the army."

"Must be," I murmured. My tongue felt like lead.

"Martins too, naturally. He never mentioned your surname."

"Never mentioned me much at all probably. Oh, my God, what is this anyway?"

"It's the war; it's the army. Don't fight it."

"Oh, no, I won't. I never have. Anyway, it's too late."

"Maybe, but I—"

One of the telephones rang, imperious and brassy, Martin answered, then immediately, quickly spoke in impeccable German, throaty, rough cut as that language requires through occasional falls of cadence, and he talked on for several minutes before hanging up with a sigh.

"Surprised?" he asked.

I sighed too. "Well, what *could* surprise me now?"

"The language was one of the things," he said, "that brought us— well, it kept us together. We always spoke German when we were alone. It meant a lot to him. Too much maybe. We'll never know. You see, Jim. Do you mind if I call you Jim?"

"Of course not."

"I'm not going to pull emotional rank on you. My family was as German as his was. Oh, you could probably guess my middle name in a minute. Even if I don't go around posting my preferences on the front doors of churches."

"Luther," I said.

"What else? Hanno liked the hint of defiance in that name. Part of his passion for the great myth of *Deutschland über Alles.*"

"Oh, yes. I remember that." I had to laugh—almost—to myself. "Why, even the Lone Ranger was sort of Siegfried on the Rhine journey."

"Certainly he was. Which might partially account for the lost year. He never spoke to you about it, did he?"

"What lost year? No. I've never heard of it."

"No, I imagine not. He took off a year from high school, went alone to Germany. That would have been '38. Where, why, nobody knows. We only found out when the FBI did the background clearance checkup after he left Ritchie."

"I thought he must have gone through there. Being in training, he said, in Maryland, near Washington. But why would the FBI check up on him?"

"He was assigned to secret work. And by that time we were at war with Germany, no way to find out what he was doing there as a kid, had to take his word for it. Even his parents didn't know for sure. He said he'd been studying at Herrlingen."

"What's that? Some school?"

"Never mind. A place in Germany. Not many people would know. It doesn't matter now."

"No," I said. "Oh, by the way . . . you two met in Washington, he said. In the National Gallery. In front of a painting by El Greco of the Good Samaritan."

"That's what he sometimes said, yes."

"But it isn't true. I went to the National Gallery and looked. There's no such painting by El Greco in there."

"No, there isn't, you're right."

"Then why would he lie about it?"

"Who knows? The story appealed to him. Maybe he saw something there. Part of his legend. I can't tell you."

"Well," I said, "it's a funny story, and that's a fact. This man gets beaten up, stripped naked, and left by the roadside, then along comes Mr. Samaritan, has pity on the guy or something and takes him to an inn, and they spend the night there, and in the morning he leaves some money for him. So . . . you think Hanno . . ."

"I see what you mean. About the story. But about Hanno? What can I say?"

"Then did you meet in the National Gallery?"

"Oh, yes."

"But not in front of the picture by El Greco."

"No. As a matter of fact, if you want to know, we met in the men's room."

"Well, that's rather more worldly, isn't it? Still, while we're in the museum, there *is* a painting by El Greco that may have caught your attention."

"Of course there is. *St. Martin and the Beggar.* Naturally, considering my name, the picture has something. It's a very appealing picture."

I laughed, but I meant it gently. "Yes, it has an appeal all right. Here you have this fine-looking soldier all in armor on a white horse befriending a naked man, pretty attractive himself, who doesn't look much in need of handouts. Is this a pickup? Do they spend the night at a nearby inn? Or is it just kindness without the loving part?"

"Are you talking about the painting? Or is that a personal question?"

"Excuse me, sir. I didn't mean to overstep."

"Sure you did. Come on, Jim, loosen up, will you? The saint's namesake is no saint, nor was the soldier in the painting, because his calling as a monk came along much later, and he wasn't into abstinence and celibacy, and in that department, anyway, neither was Hanno very saintly."

"Lucky you."

"Don't take it that way. He loved you, you know, I'm sure he did, the way he spoke about you, but you were both too young, too afraid of each other and of the army to make much out of your little opportunity."

"I know that. And you? How did it turn out for you two?"

"The way it had to. The war took us in different directions."

"To your lasting regret."

"Mine, oh, yes. I can't speak for him. Nobody ever could, as a matter of fact."

"The man of mystery?"

"You have no idea. Always on the way to becoming, if you know what I mean, never quite being. As if he had something to prove but didn't know what. Why he was so reckless, couldn't resist another dangerous leap into the dark."

"I know what you mean."

"And apparently he couldn't resist the last one, that is, the final one . . . in the end."

"What? What do you mean *final*?"

"I don't really know. Probably no one ever will know. And that's so like him. You see, he was on a mission. Alone. Verbal orders only. Right from the top. Secret secret. Last days of the war. Eight months ago now. And never came back. So . . ."

"My God. Poor Hanno. It's too sad."

"Not necessarily. Someday you walk into the bar of the Hotel Mayflower in Washington, D.C., and there he is saying, 'Sit down and have something on me.'"

"Ghosts," I said.

"Too bad. And we have nothing to remember him by. Christ, he was *that* handsome! Do you realize there's no extant photograph of him?"

"Yes. I know that. I know it. But I don't know why."

"He had something to hide, Hanno had. Maybe it was only himself hiding from himself. We'll never know. Even his parents. The only photo they have was taken when he was eleven."

"Why is that?" I asked. "Why is it like this?"

"It's because we're queer, my dear."

That solution to the insoluble silenced me. The colonel and I looked each other in the face, and the daylight still fell through the room, and the grumbling of ten-ton trucks in the square outside was audible.

Eventually I said, "That isn't why I'm here, is it?"

"No, it's not. Indeed not. It has to do with the intelligence service. The strictly military aspect ended when the war did, but the espionage game never goes out of business. The Office of Strategic Services has

been disbanded. Some of the agents have gone home. They'll never be decorated for their achievements, but you already have been. By the way, was the general's name really and truly Twaddle? It's too Evelyn Waugh for words."

"That was it, and his chief of staff was Golightly."

Martin chuckled but promptly resumed. "Now we're on the look-out for fresh personnel, and someone recommended you. Don't feel you have to commit yourself in a hurry. You volunteered for the army, why not volunteer again to do something important for your country? And don't worry about being queer. We've found that gay boys are often more inventive and adaptable than straights. Could be because they've had to be inventive to get along in straight society. The army, though, doesn't care who you fuck as long as they don't know about it."

"So you have to lead a secret life in order to work in the secret world?"

"In a word, yes."

"Not for me, thank you. Besides, I'm in a hurry to get back on civvy street. There are things I want to do. I know the offer is something like an honor, and I can guess who recommends me. I don't deserve it. Deserved the decoration even less. Not at all, in fact. A mistake. But thanks all the same. Don't hold it against me for saying no."

"We wouldn't want you if you didn't want to do anything for your country."

I pursed my entire face. "Do you mind if I call you Martin?"

"Certainly not."

"Well, then, it has nothing to do with that. Listen, Martin. About Hanno. You know what? I can't help thinking. If he's really and truly gone for good. Maybe in the end, the leap into the dark, if it *was* the final one, then maybe it was something very extraordinary, almost superhuman, and maybe, after all, in his own queer way he was a sort of saint himself."

"Who knows?" said Martin.

"That's just it!" I exclaimed. "We don't. And if it's so, we never will, which is what makes it great. Like a work of art. Do you see?"

"No, I don't," he said, "and of course I'm not meant to. I'm the man in the street. Art is your department. He told me you had creative ambitions."

"Jeez. I wasn't aware I'd ever been such a fool as to mention it."

"You wouldn't have had to. He could see beyond the biological brain. And you're no fool. Sometimes when we were lying in bed half awake before the sun came up in the morning, I could tell he was dreaming about you. Now, my friend, you must go about your business because I still have a couple of prospects to egg on for Uncle Sam so they'll go spying on our friends and neighbors. It's been a pleasure." He held out his hand.

I was tempted to take it. But that would have been the facile, frivolous way. I snapped to attention, performed a parade ground salute, held it a moment, turned on my heel, and walked out of that life.

In the street, across the square, Joan of Arc sat astride a warhorse, brandishing her weapon. There was someone truly saintly. She had taken the definitive leap, and 'twas nothing to her that five centuries had had to elapse before sanctity was bestowed by mere earthlings.

My goodbye to Roger came as a surprise to neither of us. In fact it was what we had both been waiting for. With companionable eyes, not impatience. We drank flat champagne together at Le Boeuf sur le Toit, and that was that.

Picasso—despite his astonishing prediction as to my future surely had not been concerned by the imminence of my goodbye. He had more inspiring matters on his mind and beautifully at hand in the person of Françoise Gilot, a maiden forty years younger than the aging minotaur, voluptuously replacing the cast-off Dora Maar. Sabartés told me the traumatic details of her repudiation with a certain glee, as he had detested the haughty Dora. Another skeleton, as it were, littering the perilous labyrinth.

Having received orders to report to the staging area at Le Havre on November 22 and from there take ship for home, I made my way the preceding Tuesday for the last time to the rue des Grands Augustins. I came bearing gifts, keepsakes, things to remember me by should the artist chance to forget the youngster of whom he'd said momentous things were to be expected. The army relinquished its human matériel with little care for equipment originally intended to produce and protect expendable soldiers. So I arrived bringing not only a musette replete with cigarettes, coffee, soap, and toilet paper but also the steel helmet I'd worn at the front, my trench knife, ammunition pouches, and studded web belt.

I piled my gear onto the long table below the dusty windows. Picasso fingered it studiously but said nothing. What he'd ever do, or did, with it I never would know, nor did it matter. I left on those legendary premises the remains of a self now nearly done with, the equipment that had been supposed to protect him from harm during the conflict. Was this the surrender of a disarmed soldier to the omnipotent artist? Albeit the war with circumstances lasts as long as life does.

So I made my emotional farewells to Inès, Marcel, and Sabartés, all of them, even the austere secretary, vivid and warm, and then Picasso went with me to the door and at the top of the stair kissed me goodbye on both cheeks. And this time I did not need to limp away from the building.

The staging area in the slums of Le Havre from which we were to go to sea was itself a sea of mud. Flapdoodle tents trailed their flimsy sidings in this sticky, malodorous slop. If you let your hand dangle at night from the tilt of the cot, it came up in the morning looking like the suppurating paw of some Mesozoic crawler. You might have been a displaced person encaged in one of those nauseating camps. Well, not quite.

After the cosseted conveniences of the Hôtel Ambassador this comedown was more than mortifying. It was punishment. The elite status of an MIS agent was physically as well as psychically oppressed. Gratuitously, deliberately, insolently. Yet one had done nothing wrong. Or had one? 'Twas all the same to the daily diet of mud and guilty spaghetti. I refused to cut my hair, even to comb it, slept with my boots on, and almost envied the garbage. However, the sentence was waived after a lifetime lasting five days.

To confront the horizon of the urgent west, our ship was by no means sufficiently splendid. Still, it throbbed, heaved, and sloughed down the channel, no music swelling to its progress. There again lay the Norman coast, a seashore now unlike any other, beachhead of the imaginary life, opening upon the battlefields of my queer war. Nor had the Roman legions in all their spectacular trappings fought one more strange. A revelation of conflated contingencies. Liberation of diverse supernumeraries within a single uniform. Cryptic opportunities. A broadening of remote perspectives and tentative grasp of absolutes. And so much more, never to forget the irony, resignation, defiance, the stirrings of the creative mind or the savagery of mankind's daily bread. And always to remember that everything in an individual's experience has a meaning, nothing is truly accidental, what may appear to be a happening is in reality an act.

After eight noisome days afloat we docked at the provisional port of Perth Amboy, New Jersey. Trucks conveyed us to the banal barracks and impending freedom of Fort Monmouth. And there, three years, one month, and seven days after the inexplicable morning on Lexington Avenue, I was granted an honorable discharge from the United States Army on December 11, 1945, a drab Tuesday of nonevents in the ambient chaos.

My parents drove down from Englewood to fetch me home. One of the first things my mother asked concerned the tiny scar on my forehead. I said that it was nothing, an accident not in the line of duty, nothing at all. And when we came to Hillside Avenue, I went straight upstairs to my room, closed the door, and locked it, lay down on my bed, and stared at the ceiling.

EPILOGUE

The return to civilian life for soldiers from overseas was widely held to be difficult, not to say traumatic. Hiding in my bedroom, listening to Beethoven's last quartet and rereading *Tonio Kröger*, I made fun of this notion. I slept late, appeared downstairs only for meals, did talk of this and that, returned to my room, lay on my bed, and made friends with stress. Thus passed unbeknownst to me a winter and a spring.

My parents grew concerned, asked what I wanted to do. I replied that I wanted to write a book. I didn't set about doing this immediately, but I did eventually go back into the world of bumblebees, automobiles, and boys, though what I did there other than to think about writing doesn't signify.

By the mercy of its means the book at last began to grow on me. As for its growth, its purpose, theme, meaning, and elaboration and, above all, its egregious pretentiousness, it may seem that some *apologia pro opera sua* would be appropriate, but I have none to offer because the scenario speaks for itself.

To give conceptual substance, as it were, to my book, I planned from the beginning to base it structurally, thematically, and symbolically upon *The Divine Comedy* by Dante, referring metaphorically, indeed, to certain specific passages and even using whenever it seemed figuratively cogent Dante's own phraseology. If this be preposterous, it may be provocative to recall that Joyce's *Ulysses* as well as *The Magic Mountain* played crucial roles in the evolution of my dreams and aspirations.

·

Most of the action of this novel, which never received a title, takes place in a prison camp for captured German soldiers during the last weeks of the European war and for an unspecified period of time thereafter. The protagonist is a young American sergeant named Peter, a military intelligence agent, speaking impeccable German, assigned to work in this camp, his duties unspecified, though with considerable authority. Peter's background, troubled formative years, and troubling wartime experiences are related in order to prefigure a disposition for transcendental experience.

In the lager over which this young man chooses to exercise a certain authority he forms semifriendly relations with the Lagerführer. He then encounters a young prisoner, filthy and disheveled, sullen and withdrawn, but physically sturdy and, beneath the dirt, handsome, with whom he becomes friendly, providing him with cigarettes, soap, and extra food from the PX. This attachment is emotional but never sexual, because in Peter's constitution the sexual element is strangely suspended, allowing, perhaps, for a superior claim on other senses. The prisoner's name is Hans. His background is described in detail, for he lived through the tragic and corrupting experiences pitting his young unworldliness against the Nazi machinery of evil.

A bond is joined between the two young men. They grow aware that they are united—without realizing quite how or why—by an affinity beyond the sphere of ordinary experience. A joint identity, so to speak, of spirit turns out to be well reflected in the physical. When Hans is cleaned up, better fed, and decently clothed, he stands revealed in the flesh as a viable portrait of Peter. The two youths are stunningly, almost supernaturally similar in personal appearance—stature, facial features, color of eyes and hair, the very shape of fingernails—and even in expressive mannerisms to such a degree, for example, that when they laugh, the right eyelids of both flutter slightly so that they appear to be winking at the world. In short, they are much more alike than the most identical of identical twins, a fact recognized with astonishment by the other prisoners but not by Allied personnel, who have no occasion to see them together.

When the European war comes to a conclusion and POWs begin to be released, Hans is further detained. There is something amiss in his record, a period or posting unaccounted for, blank and puzzling,

which Hans himself has been, and continues to be, unable or unprepared to clarify. Inasmuch as the German Army has surrendered without condition and in principle no longer exists, the German prisoners
kept in detention have no recourse to outside protection and become
disarmed enemy persons. Hans, being a DP with the question mark
of his past hindering his future, finds himself assigned early in June for
transfer to Bad Kreuznach. The parting of the two friends presents
itself as unacceptable.

Postings for intelligence agents have become lax. Peter promptly
transfers himself to Bad Kreuznach, where he finds Hans in painful
condition, mental as well as physical, once more disheveled and filthy,
crestfallen, given to periodic seizures of uncontrollable weeping. When
pressed to explain, he finally blurts in a whisper the ghastly story of the
gap in his past. Inducted at age seventeen into the Waffen SS, he was
trained and served for a time as a carter in an artillery maintenance
battalion, whereupon an abrupt error of registration allotments transferred him overnight for duty as a guard at a concentration camp in
the Thuringian hill country near a town called Ohrdruf.

If absolute evil can be collated, conditions in the camp at Ohrdruf
were of the worst. Guards as well as kapos flogged the inmates with
metal-studded whips, pissed in their faces, and set maddened dogs to
tear off the genitals of naked boys. Hans was stricken down to his entrails again and again by the spectacle of suffering, its clamor and
stench, the puling screams, excrement, gasps and grunts, the laughter
of the guards, emptied eye sockets of dying children, and agony of the
Jewish virtuoso playing *An die Musik* on a battered violin while mutilated girls made love to the boots of an Albanian.

Still, between splayed fingers pressed to his face Hans ogled in spite
of himself the orgy of cruelty. Here were the kapos splattered with
mucus and blood, grinning as they tortured Russian officers, beckoning with sadistic forefingers to Hans, to incite him, to excite him, to
tempt him to participate in the satanic debauch. Beside himself with
terror and agitation, even as his bowels heaved, yet tempted by quivering nerve ends in his belly, Hans moved closer and closer to default of
the senses, touching the handle of a whip and abruptly swooning into
the blackness of overpowering excitement, and he did as the demon in
us all decreed he must do: submitted entirely to the deafening aban-

don and power, unable to hear the screams of a victim above his very own gasps of exertion—again and again—until the climactic instant, whereupon he stumbled away into the mists of eternity. And in a twinkling he had become as one possessed, the demiurge of cruelty, while at the same time each night at its darkest seduced him with remorse and he sobbed at the remoteness of redemption, though the exhaustion of dawn restored the beast to its bloodstained frenzy. So Hans became known as the Ogre of Ohrdruf.

When American forces advanced across the Neisse River and captured Schloss Wartburg, threatening Thuringia, the Ogre of Ohrdruf managed to slip away, tramp north to Erfurt, and there insinuate himself into a straggle of ordinary POWs marching under light guard southwest through the woods toward the Rhineland detention camps, and it was in Mannheim Camp No. 3 that Hans and Peter met.

That was the story told to the ear of darkness in Bad Kreuznach. Atonement is all Hans lives for, the bliss of expiation. Yet he fears other DPs might recognize the erstwhile ogre and do unto him as he has done to so many others. He grasps Peter in his arms, praying for deliverance though he knows he has no right to it. Peter says that it need not be so, something could be, something *should* be, done to make things right. Peter swears that this could come about.

Shortly thereafter one evening Hans asks Peter not to come to the camp the following day. During the night, however, Peter has a troubling premonition as of impending crisis. He hurries to the camp.

In a corner of the lager set apart from the rest he comes upon the naked, bloody corpse of his twin. The body is lacerated with cuts, wrists, ankles, and groin brutally mangled. The jagged end of a broken Coca-Cola bottle lies at hand. But the brow is clear. Peter touches the dead cheek, cold as a stone. His fingertip leaves a dimple. An inexplicable transport, exquisite and dreadful, seizes him. Is this murder by vengeful compatriots? Is this suicide? Death does not engage in repartee.

The dead boy's clothing lies carefully folded beside him, his identification disk on top. Peter does not have to be hurried by the unnatural to undress in an instant, scatter his own uniform round about, hang his dog tags about Hans's throat, take the dead man's disk on its greasy string for his own neck, and pull on the abandoned clothing of the deceased, sidling away in the obscurity of the mutilated remains of an American soldier.

So begins Peter's mystical ascent toward the culmination of his purpose. In the person of Hans he is held for questioning about the apparent murder of the American. His answers are studied, tending to be convoluted and lengthy, punctuated by laborious teleological asides. The interrogators weary, patience oftentimes tried beyond forbearance. They have no alternative, however, but to abide and heed. The proceedings eventually lead to a formal charge of murder in the first degree with critical malice aforethought. Hence a court is convened in Frankfurt-am-Main to consider the charge, hear the accused, render a verdict, and deliver a sentence.

The hearing of the accused by the court is prolonged. This proves inevitable because it presently becomes evident that the accused who stands before his judges is none other than the man once known as the Ogre of Ohrdruf. He proves prepared to speak at almost interminable length, determined, moreover, that the court should hearken with tireless discernment, virtually with reverence, to the intricate, sometimes lyrical, but always metaphysical ratiocinations with which he endeavors to calibrate, as it were, the confession of his unspeakable crimes.

Witnesses, to be sure, are not needed, but they cry out to be heard, and are heard by the score, shrieking, weeping, gesticulating at the monster, and demanding divine retribution. Thus the trial endures and endures, an ordeal of endurance for all. For all save the accused, who perseveres with equanimity, surveying the spectacle of his guilt as if the chorus of condemnation and the courtroom itself were but providential elements of his imagination.

When at long last it comes time to hear verdict and sentence, the breath of the chamber is itself almost exhausted. Guilty as charged. Consequently to be hanged by the neck until dead.

It is a day of heavenly radiance that morning when Peter is led to the scaffold. As the noose is fixed about his throat, it may have appeared to the few spectators present that his mouth is touched by something rather like a saintly smile.

Be that as it may, when the trap is sprung, Peter glimpses as he falls a flash of brilliance in which seems to be subsumed the love that moves the sun and the other stars.

•

The foregoing synopsis conveys an approximate notion of my novel. It was extremely long. In finished form the typescript filled three separately bound volumes, each of roughly four to five hundred typed pages. Like every beginning writer, I longed for publication. In my thoughtless audacity I turned once again to Thomas Mann, with whom I had maintained a sporadic correspondence, asking him to recommend my book to his publisher. He did so. It was rejected. The great man, who had never set eyes on me, winner of the Nobel Prize, author of masterworks like *Death in Venice* and *The Magic Mountain*, sent me a kindly letter.

> *Dear Mr. Lord:*
>
>   *With you I am disappointed about the failure at Knopf's. He had written me that your person made a very favorable impression on him. But even if his office's verdict of your novel was negative, I feel you should not give up the matter without a struggle. After all, Knopf is not the only publisher to be considered. You should try to offer your work to one or the other house. If in the end your book should be judged too unaccomplished for publication, you will find consolation in renewed creative efforts which will benefit by your growing years and inner maturing.*
>
>

With kindest wishes.
Very sincerely yours,
Thomas Mann
>

I did not seek another publisher. My manuscript made its way to the wastebasket, and I entrusted my future literary aspirations to the problematic effect of inner maturing. In the fullness of decades this has had to do what it could for the story of my queer war.